Subseries on the History of
Japanese Business and Industry

Fueling Growth
The Energy Revolution
and Economic Policy in Postwar Japan

Harvard East Asian Monographs
147

Subseries on the History of
Japanese Business and Industry

Japan's rise from the destruction and bitter defeat of World War II to its present eminence in world business and industry is perhaps the most striking development in recent world history. This did not occur in a vacuum. It was linked organically to at least a century of prior growth and transformation. To illuminate this growth a new kind of scholarship on Japan is needed: historical study *in the context of a company or industry* of the interrelations among entrepreneurs, managers, engineers, workers, stockholders, bankers, and bureaucrats, and of the institutions and policies they created. Only in such a context can the contribution of particular factors be weighed and understood. It is to promote and encourage such scholarship that this subseries is established, supported by the Reischauer Institute of Japanese Studies and published by the Council on East Asian Studies at Harvard.

Albert M. Craig
Cambridge, Massachusetts

FUELING GROWTH

The Energy Revolution and Economic Policy in Postwar Japan

LAURA E. HEIN

Published by COUNCIL ON EAST ASIAN STUDIES, HARVARD UNIVERSITY, and distributed by HARVARD UNIVERSITY PRESS, Cambridge (Massachusetts) and London   1990

Printed in the United States of America

Index by Olive Holmes, Edindex

The Council on East Asian Studies at Harvard University publishes a monograph series and, through the Fairbank Center for East Asian Research and the Reischauer Institute of Japanese Studies, administers research projects designed to further scholarly understanding of China, Japan, Korea, Vietnam, Inner Asia, and adjacent areas. Publication of this volume has been assisted by a grant from The Shell Companies Foundation.

Library of Congress Cataloging-in-Publication Data

Hein, Laura Elizabeth.
Fueling growth : the energy revolution and economic policy in
postwar Japan / Laura E. Hein.
p.   cm. — (Harvard East Asian monographs ; 147)
Includes bibliographical references.
ISBN 0-674-32680-6
1. Energy policy—Japan—History—20th century.   2. Japan—
Economic policy—1945–   I. Title.   II. Series.
HD9502.J32H45   1989
338.2'0951—dc20
89-38541
CIP

To My Family

Contents

Tables

Abbreviations

CLRB	Central Labor Relations Board
DRB	Deconcentration Review Board
EPDC	Electric-Power Development Company
EROA	Economic Recovery for Occupied Areas
ESB	Economic Stabilization Board
ESS	Economic and Scientific Section (SCAP)
FRUS	Foreign Relations of the United States
FTC	Foreign Trade Commission
GARIOA	Government and Relief in Occupied Areas
GATT	General Agreement on Tariffs and Trade
HCLC	Holding Company Liquidation Committee
IMF	International Monetary Fund
JDB	Japan Development Bank
MCI	Ministry of Commerce and Industry
MERI	Mitsubishi Economic Research Institute
MITI	Ministry of International Trade and Industry
NA	National Archives
NRS	Natural Resources Section (SCAP)
NSC	National Security Council
OCI	Overseas Consultants, Inc.
PAG	Petroleum Advisory Group (SCAP)
PUC	Public Utilities Commission
RFB	Reconstruction Finance Bank
SCAP	Supreme Command for Allied Powers
Stanvac	Standard Vacuum Corporation
SWNCC	State-War-Navy Coordinating Council

Acknowledgments

The wisdom and generosity of many people have enriched this study—and the life of its author. In its earlier incarnation as a dissertation, my teachers at the University of Wisconsin, John W. Dower and Solomon B. Levine, urged me to be both precise and bold. Each has continued to encourage me in the most satisfying way possible—by finding my ideas stimulating and plausible. They have my gratitude and respect. In Japan, the members of the Japanese Association for the Study of the History of the Occupation, whose high standards of scholarship are matched only by their kindness, provided steady guidance and support. Professors Sodei Rinjirō and Koseki Shōichi, in particular, helped me at many points. The professors at the Economics Department of Hosei University, Professor Funahashi Naomichi of the Ōhara Institute for Social Research, Professor Sumiya Mikio, then of Japan Women's College, Professor Miyoshi Shuichi of Sophia University, and Professor Yada Toshifumi of Kyushu University gave generously of their thoughtful comments and tremendous expertise. Librarians at Hosei University, Hitotsubashi University, Tokyo University's Economics Department Library, Tokyo Keizai University, the Ōhara Institute for Social Research, and Harvard's Yenching Library all assisted me through their collections. Masaaki Chiyo and Hoshi Kenichi at the National Diet Library and Katsumura Toshiko of the Institute of Energy Economics library were particularly helpful. Mori Kazu single-handedly turned Tokyo into a warm and friendly place. My research there was financed by the Japan-United States Educational Commission (Fulbright Program) and the Japan Foundation.

Special thanks to several people who helped me move from dissertation to book. Andrew Gordon's subtle analysis has enriched this work, while Ezra Vogel showed me how to build my argument with style and vigor. Professor Albert M. Craig, Thomas R.H. Havens, and Daniel Yergin each gave sage advice. Colleagues at Northwestern University have contributed in many ways. Harold Perkin and Arthur McEvoy read and commented thoughtfully on entire drafts of this manuscript. Each of them clarified my thinking just when I was sure nothing could. Meanwhile, Michael Sherry provided friendship and an unfailing wry wit. The audiences at the East Asian Institute at Columbia University and the Department of History at Northwestern University provided valuable insights when I presented some of these ideas in 1987. I did most of the revisions at the Edwin O. Reischauer Institute of Japanese Studies, where I very much enjoyed a fellowship in 1986–1987. Mark Peattie, Corky White, Robin Yates, and Barry Smail were some of the many people who helped make it fun and intellectually stimulating. Since then, Florence Trefethen has more than lived up to her reputation as a fine editor.

This book is dedicated with warm thanks to my family. George Hein and Emily Romney not only encouraged me but also fed me dinner for most of my year in Cambridge. Jenny, Stephen, and Hilde Hein remain some of the smartest, most interesting people I know. David Merriman, whose partnership in my life has already taken him as far as Asia, has greeted every fresh challenge with enthusiasm and grace.

Fueling Growth

ONE

Introduction

As the memories of World War II fade on both sides of the Pacific, so does the recollection that Japan entered the postwar era as a desperately poor country. Photographs of Tokyo in 1945 reveal a barren landscape, punctuated by random buildings freakishly left standing. The people in this desolate landscape are puffy-faced from poor nutrition, and their ragged clothing is dirty, while rare autos spew black smoke from their charcoal-burning engines. It is hard to reconcile these images with the sleek and prosperous Tokyo of today. Within one generation, the Japanese have rebuilt their nation into an economic world leader. This dramatic transformation in only forty years is an impressive accomplishment that still has not been fully explained.

This study examines economic policy and economic development in postwar Japan through the prism of the three main energy industries—coal, electric power, and petroleum. At the end of World War II, the dearth of energy supplies posed one of the biggest problems of economic reconstruction; the first postwar decade can be characterized accurately as one long energy crisis. Energy was thus at the heart of economic planning, often central to the development of grand economic policy. Japanese debates over energy in the postwar years very quickly became debates over the viability and direction of their entire economic strategy. Nor has time diminished this problem. Energy supplies are a major element of Japan's dependence on world trade to this day. Although the Japanese have devised a number of approaches to minimize the dilemma of securing energy, it is ultimately unresolvable. Despite recurring hopes, Japan has not had adequate domestic energy resources since well before World War II and has no prospects of developing energy self-sufficiency within the next century. Thus, a study of coal, electric power, and petroleum provides an opportunity to explore the interrelated aspects of postwar development and planning of the whole economy, focusing on an issue of abiding significance.

In retrospect, it seems obvious that, if the Japanese hoped to have a strong postwar economy, they had to accept reliance on imported energy. We know now that Japanese coal reserves were a wholly inadequate foundation for economic recovery, and that the country was endowed with neither significant oil nor uranium deposits. More recently, all the major industrial countries have faced energy shortages and have had to develop policies in response to this problem. Energy as an economic-policy problem has penetrated planning everywhere. However, none of this was clear at the end of the war; Japanese and Americans alike were optimistic about possible coal and oil discoveries in Japanese territory. They hoped that new exploration techniques would yield results in Japan, as they did in many other parts of the globe.

Not only were expectations about energy *supply* optimistic; few people expected the great postwar surge in *demand* for energy. It only gradually became clear that the fastest-growing sector of Japanese economy, heavy industry, would also be the most energy-intensive. Nor did the Japanese foresee their growing dependence on petroleum. The fifteen years after World War II were precisely the period when Japan moved from primary reliance on domestic coal and hydroelectricity to imported oil. This was part of a global trend toward greater use of petroleum in industry, encouraged by both oil discoveries in the Mideast and the surge of new oil-based technology invented during and after the war. This structural shift meant that Japanese coal was competing more with petroleum and less and less with imported coal, for which it could easily substitute whenever prices fluctuated (as they did throughout the 1950s). As the Japanese gradually discovered, this introduced new barriers to a resurgence of coal as a dominant energy source. Each time a firm built an oil-storage tank or a pipeline, or bought a new piece of power equipment, chances grew slimmer that the coal industry would ever again supply it. By 1960, the Japanese had invested in a future fueled by oil. This had a cumulatively disruptive effect, one profound enough to be dubbed the "energy revolution" in Japan.

The Japanese only gradually realized that an "energy revolution" had taken place and recognized its implications. This process largely meant coming to terms with the decline of coal, one of Japan's most important industries. The failure of King Coal to continue to power the economy—or to abdicate his throne gracefully—posed difficulties for the entire postwar Japanese economic strategy. Accepting coal's growing marginality was a lengthy and complex process. Although most of the coal industry's problems were evident by 1949, it was at least another decade before the Japanese abandoned economic plans based on its centrality. They reiterated the same arguments endlessly, searching for a clear solution when none existed. In their debates over coal, the Japanese wrestled with problems of conflict between managers and the unionized labor force, inadequate financial resources, and sectoral decline. These problems spanned the postwar economy, and the coal industry appeared to be only the most acute sufferer of general economic ills. Before the late 1950s, few Japanese rejected the idea that coal was not just typical, but archetypal of a crisis in the whole economy.

As the Japanese struggled with these dilemmas, they moved from policies directed at coal or oil toward a true, integrated energy policy, in itself one of the major conceptual breakthroughs of postwar economic thinking. More generally, as the Japanese grappled with developing and, later, replacing, coal supplies, they gradually worked out increasingly sophisticated economic strategies. Their persistent energy problems crystallized Japanese thinking about infrastructural development, inter-industry linkages, and ties to the international economy. Frequently, massive debates about fundamentals of economic organization began as deceptively small questions, such as how to finance the coal mines, whether to change the number of electric-power companies, or whether or not to deregulate oil prices.

It is not surprising that the Japanese struggled and argued over how to reconstruct their economy, although the myth of Japanese harmony and consensus has often obscured the intensity of these disagreements. Defeat, occupation, and popular unrest had cut away the foundations of pre-surrender economic institutions. While many pre-surrender elements remained important, such as the pattern of business-government relations, they survived in a radically altered domestic and international context. The Japanese could not rebuild on the basis of low wages at home and the empire abroad, as they had up to 1945. Reconstruction in Japan did not simply mean rebuilding past structures. Because of this, economic and social goals were widely debated in postwar Japan, and much can be learned from that debate. There was no early, grand blueprint. Energy policy—and grand economic strategy—developed gradually as issues of power were renegotiated within Japan and with the United States. Discussions were heated and consensus impossible, reflecting the fact that these decisions would determine the paths to power and prestige in Japan for decades to come.

These debates involved a wide variety of people in government and business, as well as two groups rarely included in analyses of national policymaking—labor unions and American policymakers. The actions of these two very different groups and their interactions with Japanese business and bureaucratic leaders are integral to an understanding of postwar Japanese economic strategy. The involvement of both groups required that the organization of energy production and of the entire economy be reconstructed along lines other than those of pre-surrender Japan. This was a traumatic shift, one instantly recognizable to citizens of other war-devastated countries, but alien to United States experience.

Throughout postwar Japan, newly empowered Japanese presented a sharp, persistent challenge to the traditional policies of elites. The focus in this study is on labor unions, but representatives of small businesses, local political-interest groups, and leftist political parties also agitated for change. Organized coal miners and electric-power workers forced adjustments in their industries and in the whole economy. Their influence was strongest during the first postwar years, when they were actively involved in making national energy policy. Their contributions at that time, along with those of other unions, ensured that postwar Japanese economic reconstruction would be founded on different principles than the presurrender economy—principles that accommodated a more powerful labor movement. Although this direct role in national policymaking subsided later, when management groups, aided by the Japanese government and Occupation forces, were able to blunt the force of independent labor unions, this did not mean a return to pre-surrender status. The presence of organized labor continued to shape the range of possible choices for policymakers, even when workers did not participate directly in the planning process.

The pre-surrender energy industries also had been essential pillars of the empire, through colonial labor, the development of natural resources outside the home islands, and as key components of military planning. Defeat and occupation precluded reconstruction along these lines. The Japanese had to rebuild without the empire in a new and hostile international climate. Primarily, this meant responding to United States foreign policy. This was, of course, most intimately true during the seven-year Allied Occupation of Japan, but was not limited to that era. The twenty years after World War II were the apex of U.S. power, and Japan, like most other countries, had to adjust to American interpretations of global problems. A study of Japan's efforts to thrive under these conditions illuminates the nature of the American world order as much as Japan's place within it. American policies established a set of parameters of constraints—and opportunities—within which the Japanese had to operate. As with the labor unions, the Americans did most to reshape Japanese economic institutions in the first postwar years, but still wielded significant influence later. These two forces both necessitated changes in economic development, although they moved from very different directions.

The simultaneous emergence of these two new actors on the policy scene was not coincidental. American policy in Japan initially encouraged a broad spectrum of dissent and debate in Japan, and Occupation-imposed economic reforms laid the legal groundwork on which the unions built. More generally, defeat in World War II weakened Japanese elite power at home while destroying it internationally. Both domestic and foreign pressures were a response to the failure—on a grand scale—of earlier elite policy and economic strategies. The triple disruptions of war, defeat, and occupation meant that traditional Japanese leaders could not retain a monopoly on decision making.

In the first postwar months, the traditional business and bureaucratic elites barely participated in economic policy decisions. The economy got scant official attention in the early chaotic months. At that point, political goals, particularly the personal and institutional safety of the Emperor, took precedence. Nor did businessmen initiate economic recovery. Taken aback by the Occupation's demilitarization and democratization reforms and the buoyant labor movement, they did not act decisively to reconstruct the economy for over a year after Japan's surrender. Part of the problem was that the Occupation forces rejected ideas that would have recreated the prewar economic order. Zaibatsu leaders and bureaucrats, the two elite groups that had contributed most to economic planning in the presurrender years, did develop some plans but, since these ideas did not take U.S. policy or their own loss of power into consideration, they were not approved.[1] Astonishing as it may seem in retrospect, until late 1946 no real consensus existed among the traditional elites even on the need to concentrate on economic reconstruction.

When important economic policy initiatives did emerge in 1945 and 1946 that were acceptable to Occupation forces, they came from a new source, organized labor. Rather than looking to traditional but politically discredited elites, union members began to search for alternative ways to build Japan. Labor unions in both coal and electric power suggested completely new forms of management for their industries, and in both cases these were thoughtfully developed proposals. Although the labor unions were most concerned with immediate issues of wages and job security, they also addressed larger and more overtly political problems of reconstruction. They recognized that national policies on such matters as choosing which industries to redevelop, guidelines for food and materials allocations, and production goals would have tremendous repercussions on workers' lives. In the unsettled conditions of postwar Japan, it was unusually clear that problems of political and social power were intertwined with economic recovery. Their vision centered on labor-union participation in management and eventual nationalization of important industries in a socialist state. This long-term agenda was not realized, but the unions, nevertheless, significantly influenced economic policy in a number of ways.

Most dramatically, the unions shouldered responsibility for production, earning respect throughout Japan and creating an unflattering contrast to the managers of industry. They also successfully pushed for higher wages. As early as October 1946, the electric-power workers' union, Densan, pioneered a new wage *system,* which created a standard framework that firms across Japan could use to calculate wages. Densan also tied wages to the cost of living, a significant victory in highly inflationary postwar Japan. Furthermore, the unions worked for more comprehensive planning and a larger role for labor in the planning process. These efforts gave them unprecedented legitimacy and authority at this crucial moment when Japanese institutions were changing. They also pointed the way toward a more managed, planned economy, containing a more comfortable niche for labor.

The first viable postwar economic plan adopted by the government developed in good part in response to labor's challenge. This "priority-production" policy was not begun until late 1946, although the theoretical basis for it had been set out by a study group at the Ministry of Foreign Affairs nine months earlier. This plan successfully revived production, and thereafter the government was able to seize the initiative in economic recovery. The lesson was well learned: After that moment, economic growth became a primary goal of government policy in Japan. Nevertheless, the early hiatus is revealing. It shows the dissension and struggle for political legitimacy by both elites and non-elites that underlay the later common concern with rebuilding the postwar economy. The strong fo-

cus on economic growth from late 1946 was itself created to reconcile, or at least defuse, deep political conflicts in post-surrender
Japan.

The priority-production plan, which concentrated on the pivotal
coal and steel industries, embodied several economic principles that
were to endure in postwar Japan. The simplest of these principles
was stress on industrial production, that is, getting the economy
moving again. Second, like all later government plans, the priority-
production policy was based on the assumption that Japan would
embark on the path toward becoming a high-wage, high-value-
added economy, with sophisticated export goods. This early decision set the scene for all subsequent visions of postwar economic
development. The priority-production policy also promoted long-
term planning as against a straight market approach to the economy. This is probably the most enduring legacy of that early postwar policy and was a conscious, careful act. From that time, heavy
industrial production, a sophisticated high-wage economy, and
planning that incorporated both unions and management all became key elements of the postwar Japanese economic strategy. This
was a marked departure from pre-surrender Japan, especially organized labor's stronger presence. Adoption of this policy marked the
beginning of a new stage in Japanese economic strategy and economic development.

The priority-production plan integrated business, bureaucratic,
and labor concerns within a private-enterprise economy. It defused
a variety of tensions within Japan while evading demands to change
existing forms of economic organization. A shrewd compromise
among all the competing economic ideologies, it gave labor high
wages, but also channeled funds to existing managers. The priority-
production policy revived production without changing the management form of firms. Although the new policies institutionalized
the concerns of labor, they also strengthened aspects of the existing
economic structure, notably private enterprise, that the Socialist
and Communist-led unions had hoped to eliminate eventually.

Japanese acceptance of economic planning remained central through
the postwar era. Opinions on this subject varied, but, by American

standards, the majority of Japanese—and their European contemporaries—were committed to well-developed, extensive state involvement in the economy. Opposition to this view came from a few powerful individuals, like the electric-power mogul Matsunaga Yasuzaemon and Kyushu coal operators, but even most businessmen were willing to accept some government involvement in the management of their industries in return for financial assistance. Rebuilding after the war was too large a task to leave to the free market. The general opinion in the business community, as elsewhere in Japan, was that the nation had to allocate its scanty resources wisely and well. This required planning.

Japanese acceptance of planning derived from a variety of congruent sources. Buttressing the main argument that scarcity dictated planning, their reasoning ranged from the fascist theory and practice developed in Japan during the war years to a socialist vision of a new Japan. These two theoretical sources merged in a corporatist concept of a "fair," planned, state-controlled economy. They shared a deep distrust of capitalism's ability to improve life for Japan's poorer citizens. They also intersected with the developing creed of professional management. Many young, technically trained personnel (notably the economists in the Economic Stabilization Board) saw economic management as a job for specialists. They did not necessarily want state control, but they did believe in planning and scientific management by experts. Aspects of their technocratic attitude were encouraged by U.S. Occupation officials, who were themselves examples of the international rise in influence of professional planners and managers. In general, although the Occupation officials were hostile to the idea of central planning, they tolerated it as necessary, especially in important industries like coal. Nor did the Japanese abandon this approach when the hardships of the immediate postwar years abated. The 1947 Katayama Cabinet did the most to institutionalize national economic planning, but later developments, such as the outbreak of the Korean War, further strengthened Japanese commitment to planning as a strategy for development. The fluctuations in the Japanese economy caused by the war demand represented yet another argument for planning.

Uncertainty, even in the absence of scarcity, threatened economic growth.

Given their disastrous war experience, the Japanese were certainly aware of the dangers of authoritarian state rule. One general problem they faced was that much of the wartime bureaucracy was still in place. Most Japanese believed that specific individuals, institutions, and policies of the wartime state were dangerously autocratic and should be eliminated. Many wartime state-controlled companies, like the national electric-power generating company, were notoriously inefficient. Under the existing militarized system, it was very difficult to force such companies to be more effective. This meant a constant friction between immediate plans—designed to protect Japan from abusive state power—and long-range goals to enhance that power. The Japanese also remembered however, the tensions that had preceded the establishment of controls. The twin dangers of an undemocratic state and of unplanned, unfair development marked the boundaries of policymaking in most postwar minds. They seemed to many to be, respectively, the evil legacies of the 1930s and of the 1920s. These twin dangers served as political touchstones for all the proposed solutions to the Japanese economy, and the tension between them delineated the Japanese debate.

A number of key problems were still unresolved after adoption of the priority-production policy. One was the question of nationalization and state control of industry. These options were both widely discussed in the first postwar years, even after the adoption of priority production, particularly in energy production. In the electric-power industry, for example, Densan began a discussion of nationalization with management and relevant government bureaucrats, both of whom endorsed Densan's right to initiate and participate in a plan for "socialization of the electric-power industry," and hailed its "future government operation under a government that was established on a popular basis."[2] The issue of state control of industry, already made less central by the success of the priority-production policy, was definitively thrashed out in a major struggle over the coal mines. State control was ostensibly achieved there in December 1947, but in truth the advocates of control by private man-

agement won the battle. This was an important defeat for the nascent efforts of the labor unions to shape broad economic policy
along independent lines. It was also a great blow to the Japan Socialist Party, which had defined state control of the mines as a referendum on its own effectiveness. Thereafter, postwar policy moved
in new directions.

The American "economic-recovery" policy prodded Japan's economic development into a new direction in 1949. Washington began reevaluating its policy to "demilitarize and democratize" Japan
in 1947 in response to two problems that originated outside Japan:
the Cold War and the need to reconstruct the international capitalist economy. This meant rebuilding Japan both as a bulwark of
stability against communism and as the economic workshop of Asia.
Washington's primary strategy was to revive Japan's foreign trade.
At first, the American officials planned to achieve this through foreign aid, but, by December 1948, they had decided that method
was too expensive. Instead, they insisted on an austere program of
domestic belt-tightening as a prerequisite to resuming foreign trade.
The Americans hoped that this would halt inflation and end reliance
of Japanese industry on the two legs of the artificial "stilts holding
up the economy," that is, government subsidies and American aid.
Beginning in 1949, the Americans took over and balanced the Japanese budget. This forced an end to the free-spending priority-production policy. Once again, the parameters of the Japanese debate
were redrawn by the United States.
The theoretical response to this new state of affairs emerged out
of the newly established Ministry of International Trade and Industry (MITI) in 1949 as an industrial "rationalization policy." The
Japanese hoped to use foreign technology to stimulate productivity
in key industries, without massive government investment. Such a
strategy was possible because Japanese technical development had
fallen behind the West during the war years. These productivity
gains would, it was hoped, create enough profits to allow *both* modest consumption increases and capital investment. Capital investment, in turn, would facilitate future rationalization, productivity

increases, and thus higher consumption. The first two industries targeted were, as before, coal and steel. The rationalization planners enjoyed notable success in steel, and later in both electric power and petroleum refining, but the coal industry proved to be a major disappointment.

The bureaucrats were particularly concerned about improving the quality of Japanese goods, because the rationalization policy was aimed at promoting exports as well as domestic consumption. Given the prevailing "technological sloth" of Japanese industry at the time, they knew that foreigners—that is, anyone with a choice—would not buy Japanese goods until quality improved, which was impossible without technology imports. These imports included machinery, such as energy-efficient power plants, and new techniques, for example, quality-control methods. The rationalization policy (which would later evolve into industrial-structure policy) centered on Japan's development within the world economy. It aimed to encourage the quality of industrial exports so that Japan could become self-sufficient in global trade, the most serious problem left unaddressed by the earlier priority-production policy. It was clear to all Japanese that Japan's economic problems were intrinsically international, since Japan could not grow enough food to feed its population, let alone clothe and house them. Unlike the United States, which, until recently, depended far more on internal than export markets, nearly all aspects of the Japanese economy were tied to the international economy. This focus on high-quality exports had profound domestic implications, committing the Japanese to an economy marked by extensive government planning within a capitalist framework, a highly educated and well-paid work force, and close ties to the United States.

Like the priority-production policy, the rationalization plan had important socially integrative functions among bureaucratic, business, and, to a lesser extent, labor concerns. It firmly linked economic efficiency to a private-enterprise economy and the use of market competition to improve efficiency, as business wanted. This argument had been pioneered by the coal-mine owners during the debate over state control of the mines. At the same time, it left room for government involvement, especially in energy improvements, coordination, and planning—thus creating a new general basis for consensus on economic policy among business and bureaucratic leaders. The policy also discarded some of the least workable aspects of the wartime system, such as industrial subsidies. In other words, rationalization provided a strategy of economic recovery within which business and government could iron out future differences.

Rationalization policy had a more mixed effect on labor. Although it incorporated some of labor's goals (high wages, incentives for education, growth of higher-status jobs), the unions at the same time faced a direct attack on their political, economic, and legal power. Rationalization itself had two faces—positive and negative—for workers. While introducing new machinery and processes made workers more productive, so did enforcement of longer hours and lower wages. This second method did not in itself improve product quality, however, and so was an inferior strategy, even from a management point of view. Nevertheless, it was widely practiced in 1949–1950 along with the more positive form of rationalization, because of changes in the political climate at that time. The new U.S. foreign policy included a more critical attitude toward social disorder. By late 1948, the conservative Liberal Party had returned to power. Along with management organizations, it welcomed the opportunity created by U.S. policy shifts to weaken its political opposition, and passed a number of regulations in 1948 and 1949 to curb the unions. The rationalization policy provided a convenient justification for these conservative attacks on the labor movement.

Densan and many other unions were unable to prevent this attack because they were crippled by quarrels within their ranks in 1949 and 1950. Conservative elements within Densan cooperated with management to oust the activist leadership. They did not fully appreciate—until later—how much this weakened the union as an organization. The union movement then regrouped in a new federation, Sōhyō, and, in 1952, tried and failed to gain control over the relationship between rationalization and wages. Densan and the coal miners spearheaded a major drive to tie wages permanently to the cost of living, while employers insisted on using productivity (that is, the fruits of rationalization) as the basis for any wage increases. Intervention by the government tipped the scales in favor of the managers and also dealt a fatal blow to Densan.

Yet it would be a mistake to dismiss rationalization as essentially an attack on labor unions. The need to accommodate the aspirations of organized labor was explicit in the rationalization plans. MITI argued in 1949 that "the rise in influence of the working classes" meant that a new policy, one aimed at enlarging the domestic consumer market, had to be adopted. Although the relative share of profits going to workers would decrease, this was only feasible if their absolute standard of living improved. The key problem was the need to satisfy both these agendas. When managers tied wages to productivity, this diminished labor's control over wages but not labor's share. This strategy could only work in an expanding economy. Unionized workers also won considerable guarantees of job security, although at the expense of non-unionized workers.

Technology acted as the bridge for rapprochement between management and labor. Industrial rationalization offered a rising standard of living and improvement of status to workers through the potentially democratic avenue of technology. Thus, it addressed the central goals of the labor movement. Technology, it was imagined, would relatively painlessly do away with workers' main grievances—without changing economic forms. It promised to incorporate workers into the existing system at a higher level. At the same time, however, the rationalization policy directly cut away at the basis of union arguments that nationalization and greater worker input in planning were requirements for economic democracy. It offered a sophisticated alternative to fledgling union visions of economic and social change. The arguments for rationalization, like earlier *labor* concepts, stressed (1) higher productivity without lowering per-hour wages, and (2) the equal importance of blue-collar and white-collar workers in production. However, they retained earlier *management* concepts of subordination of the separate interests of workers and managers toward a common goal and the primacy of economic efficiency. Thus, rationalization acted to contain labor's objectives within a larger and management-controlled economic framework. These efforts were successful in many industries: Japanese unions are well known for their acceptance of industrial rationalization. In declining industries such as coal, however, where new technology did not drastically improve productivity, the rationalization policy had no such unifying effect.

This faith in the ability of technical solutions to defuse broad social tensions was certainly shared by many of the Americans in Japan, and was globally an integral part of postwar U.S. foreign policy. Higher production through greater efficiency was touted by Americans as the means to avoid class struggle both at home and abroad in the postwar decades. In this American vision, planning became, not a tool of socialism, but a way to avoid inefficiencies. Redistribution of wealth would come from the elimination of waste rather than from the rich.[3]

The central role of technology in Japan's economic strategy brought energy into the foreground. As it turned out, the global shift from coal to oil and gas was the most far-reaching technological development of the 1950s. This was not evident to the Japanese until 1960 but, by choosing rationalization as their industrial policy in 1949, they committed themselves to acceptance of the "energy revolution" a full decade before they understood what they had done. Through those years, the Japanese still expected that domestic coal would remain Japan's main energy resource, despite mounting evidence to the contrary. Over the course of that decade, they struggled with the contradiction between their commitments to coal and to rationalization of industry.

Energy laid bare one of the fundamental implications of Japan's development strategy. Although they called it "self-sufficiency," the logic of Japanese rationalization policy required greater integration into the international economy. The Japanese were quick to recognize this problem but unsure of how to resolve it. For a decade after the Korean War boom, they argued at length over the appropriateness of various development models. In a long-running debate on energy and infrastructure, Arisawa Hiromi spoke for one camp in his insistence that import-minimization measures, particularly development of coal resources, should be paramount. Nakayama

Ichirō argued against him that the route to "self-sufficiency" could be shortened by increasing the volume and value of foreign trade and so maximizing net exports. Nakayama eventually carried the day, although elements of the import-minimizers' argument lingered for decades. Japan simply did not have the energy supply base to support a true import-substitution policy, as the Japanese slowly came to accept.

Both camps rejected the United States and its historical development as a model, although most Americans working in Japan assumed that this was the only appropriate development path. The Japanese assumed that the United States, with its vast territory and natural resources, could never be a template for Japanese economic growth. They had already moved away from American practice simply by systematically *addressing* the problem of economic development; and they also had more specific criticisms of laissez-faire capitalism. The Japanese rejected the idea that the economic market alone was an adequate indicator for development, regarding that as a wasteful luxury that Japan could not afford. Some Japanese also criticized it as an inherently unfair system. Now that the "Japanese model" is being assiduously studied in American universities, it is easy to forget the intensity of this debate a mere thirty-five years ago.

While they rejected America as a model, the Japanese relied extensively on U.S. patronage for their economic recovery and reintegration into the world economy. American assistance was most important in three areas: securing markets, providing technology, and supplying capital. The single most important example of this was the U.S. military procurement program, which provided Japan's first "export" market following the outbreak of the Korean War. Between 1951 and 1956, U.S. military purchases in Japan paid for over a quarter of Japanese imports and, equally important, provided a steady dollar income. In effect, this constituted an unorthodox (at the time) form of financial aid to Japan. While the outbreak of the war itself can be attributed to chance, the Americans decided to use it as an opportunity to pump capital and new processes into Japan. Overseas U.S. military installations were even more significant as a market for Japanese goods and services through the 1950s and again during the Vietnam War. They gave the Japanese opportunities to earn dollars without the need to sell abroad.

America was the primary source of the technology and training crucial to Japanese reconstruction. The Japanese were fortunate indeed that, in the 1950s, the United States viewed technology dissemination as a major weapon against communism.[4] Within Japan, Occupation officials worked at every level to improve Japanese technical efficiency. In 1948, the Natural Resources Section of SCAP chartered a train, the Black Diamond Car, in which they toured Japanese coal mines with technical information, mine-safety manuals, and mapmaking equipment.[5] From 1949, numerous American management-training experts, industrial statisticians, and other specialists crossed the Pacific to advise the Japanese. The most famous of these, W. Edwards Deming, introduced the concept of quality-control systems to Japan. Nor did these American efforts to improve Japanese technical performance end with the Occupation. The Japanese continued to engage foreign specialists and send trainees abroad. In 1952, for example, Overseas Consultants, Inc., which had been to Japan in 1948 to survey Japanese industry for reparations payments at the request of the Occupation, was brought back by the Japanese government to evaluate two potential hydroelectric dam sites. The contrast between their 1948 visit to evaluate war reparations policy and the 1952 trip to develop the Japanese economy is a telling comment on the changing U.S. vision for Japan. In another demonstration of the intimate links between Japanese industrial development and U.S. public and private technological assistance contracts, the U.S. Army helped provide training in the use of heavy equipment to the Japanese who built these dams. Meanwhile, the Japanese lobbied extensively for foreign capital from American firms. The electric-power companies were among the most successful in acquiring loans for equipment, while the postwar oil-refining industry relied overwhelmingly on direct foreign investment (to the envy of Japanese in other industries). In dozens of ways, American foreign policies enabled the Japanese to carve out their own niche in the international economy.

The Americans harnessed Japanese economic aspirations to their own military as well as economic strategy. Before signing a peace treaty, the Americans insisted on military arrangements that gave them "strategic trusteeship" over Okinawa (relinquished in 1972) and the right to station troops on Japanese soil. Political independence was also withheld until Japan accepted an economic embargo of the People's Republic of China and officially recognized the regime in Taiwan. Japanese government officials tried to extract the most from a distasteful situation and haggled for economic aid on top of political independence in return for these concessions. They understood that the Americans wanted a strong Japan but not a completely independent one. This desire was embodied in American treatment of Japan's petroleum (and later, atomic energy); in the last years of the Occupation, the Americans assured Japan a steady supply of this economic commodity but still discussed its control with other Allied nations to guard against Japanese remilitarization.

The energy industries themselves marked the apex and nadir of the rationalization policy. Soon after the Korean War, the Japanese realized that rationalization did not work equally well in all industries. The most distressing failure was coal, for which the policy had originally been designed. The decline of the coal industry was an unanticipated and unwanted effect of the transition to a more rationalized economy. Originally, the Japanese had assumed that all industries could be improved equally easily through industrial rationalization, and had chosen coal mining and steel as the first areas on which to concentrate. Since coal was a central industry, it was at the heart of all Japanese economic plans in 1950. Only gradually did the Japanese realize that natural-resource depletion and the international trend toward oil made rationalization of the coal mines very difficult. Coal became the "sick man" of Japanese industry. Throughout the 1950s, coal's plight posed serious economic, political, and social problems for Japan. The failure of the coal industry caused a long and divisive policy debate within Japan and eventually forced reappraisal of rationalization policy.

The consequences of this failure appeared first in industrial relations. After losing the struggle to tie wages to the cost of living rather than to productivity in 1952, the miners concentrated on the issue of job security. They were more successful there, winning the right to control layoffs at the Miike mine after a grueling 113-day strike. This event, popularly known as the anti-rationalization strike, indicated the miners' unyielding opposition to rationalization measures. With considerable justification, they saw rationalization in their industry as "nothing but a dagger constantly brandished" at them. For the miners, rationalization was a betrayal, delivering none of the government's promises of economic betterment.

In industrial policy, too, the gap between planning and reality in the mines meant increasingly acrimonious battles between coal operators and user industries over expensive coal. Within the government, similar battles raged between, for example, MITI's Steel and Coal Bureaus. The Japanese were stalemated, unable to decide how to resolve this conflict; coal's failure to rationalize threatened their entire strategy of economic reconstruction. It still seemed possible that the industry could prosper, and the Japanese clung to this forlorn hope as long as they could. Coal's decline raised dilemmas of unemployment, regional destitution, and foreign control of energy supplies, all problems that would have remained dormant if the mines had rationalized as originally hoped and planned.

The experience of coal was, however, no longer typical of the Japanese economy by the mid-1950s. In rapidly expanding industries, notably electric power and oil refining, rationalization did generate substantial increases in real wages. The relative quiescence of unions in those industries reflects this fact. Moreover, in 1955, the Sōhyō union federation invented a new tactic, the "spring wage offensive" (*shuntō*), to maintain labor's share of productivity increases. This tactic, which essentially consisted of better coordination of union efforts in an annual wage drive, proved to be extremely effective. It increased wage rates for all Japanese workers and helped standardize wage increases across industries and between large and small firms within an industry. Although the coal miners were among the original inventors of this tactic, it developed too late for them to benefit much from it. The "spring wage offensive" transferred to labor a larger share of the profits derived from rationalization. In coal, where these were nonexistent, such transfer was impossible.

In 1955, the Japanese chose a set of compromises that they hoped would solve these problems. Oil refining and petrochemicals were allowed to develop in order to provide cheap, abundant energy to key industries. The Japanese conception of oil at that time was more as a service to other industries than an industry in its own right. Plentiful oil, they reasoned, would aid rationalization in the processing industries. Both government and business leaders agreed that coal was still the basic energy industry of Japan. They hoped that, by both allowing expansion of oil and protecting coal, they had found a viable compromise. By 1960, these two goals were seen as contradictory, but recognition of that fact came very slowly.

The Japanese did have a new candidate which could theoretically fill the place of coal as a domestic fuel. This was atomic power, developed by the electric-power industry from 1955 with the enthusiastic support of the government and the main business organizations. The atomic-energy program however, never provided the energy independence dreamed of by the Japanese. The first disappointment came with the discovery that Japan has no significant uranium deposits. The Japanese, moreover, found that they were reliant on foreign companies for sophisticated atomic-plant technology, just as they were for conventional-power and oil-refining technology. Nuclear energy also was disappointingly slow to develop. It soon became obvious that atomic energy was, at best, a long-term solution to Japan's energy needs.

By 1960, there was an urgent need for a new synthesis. Once again, new international pressures, this time to liberalize the economy, clamored for attention. The unsatisfactory non-resolution of the energy problem adversely affected all Japanese industry. In December 1959, the influential Arisawa Commission Report argued that domestic coal was a victim of the international "energy revolution" and that Japan should change its energy policies and economic strategy to rely on imported oil. By this time, the electric-power industry, energetically led by Matsunaga, had already moved from a "hydro-main, thermal-secondary" policy to one that stressed not only thermal power, but also oil-fired thermal plants. The Arisawa Report reflected a conceptual shift into a true, integrated energy policy rather than discussions of coal or of oil imports alone. This insight was crucial to the evolution of rationalization policy into a more sophisticated concept.

Industrial-structure policy, as the new rationalization policy came to be known, took the postwar idea that Japan should upgrade the level of its imports one step farther. Industrial-structure policy conceived of this process as a permanent event; the industrial structure of Japan should continually evolve within the world economy. The Japanese had moved from a "catch-up" rationalization policy to a dynamic concept of industrial development. Most relevant to the coal industry (and in recent years to oil refining and petrochemicals), this allowed them to include strategies for declining, noncompetitive industries, something that rationalization policy had not incorporated. It created economic justification for a re-incorporation of the issues of social welfare and redistribution into discussions about the economy. This was demanded by the coal miners at Miike mine during a six-month strike in 1960. They lost the strike, but were able to shift national discussion from profitability of the mines to questions of welfare, fairness, and national security. The fortunes of the union members declined together with their industry, but they had won a "soft landing" for workers in future failing sectors.[6] This is the industrial policy that Japan uses today.[7]

General economic policy underwent an important shift along with the changes in energy and industrial policy. This is best signified by the 1960 "Income-Doubling Plan," given form by Prime Minister Ikeda Hayato. This plan reaffirmed the government's commitment to raising the standard of living of the Japanese people. Concurrent with the Miike coal strike, it meant a national return to the basic goal of the labor movement throughout the postwar period—improving living standards. It also reflected the new ability of the unions to attain this goal through their "spring-wage-offensive" tactic. The "consumer boom" of the early 1960s testifies to the rising consumption level in Japan, a boom that finally provided the domestic,

stable market Japanese industry had always lacked. Enlarging the
domestic market was the key missing ingredient in the postwar
economy to that date, although it had been a goal since 1946.[8] This
was the beginning of a period of great prosperity in Japan.

The importance of the Americans to Japanese economic development shows that luck and international developments outside
Japanese control assisted the Japanese in developing their economy.
The elements of luck included the fact that the international technology gap was especially large for Japan after the war's end. Moreover, it was an artificial gap in the sense that the Japanese had the
technical skills to adopt new techniques in the 1930s and 1940s
but were prevented by political schisms and war. Unlike a newly
developing country, Japan could absorb American and European
technology very quickly when it arrived after the war.[9] In another
stroke of luck, the Japanese sought to expand exports just at a moment when international trade was increasing and this goal was
comparatively easy to achieve. Yet another chance boost for Japan
was provided by the precipitous drop in global oil prices during the
1950s. While disastrous for the Japanese coal industry, this too
eased Japan's export drive. All these factors must be considered in
any explanation of Japan's economic growth.

Even within the confines of the domestic economy, policies did
not always develop as planned. Labor unions and other groups traditionally barred from power shaped the range of possible choices.
Government policies were an important factor in the growth of the
energy industries, but some, such as those toward coal, were spectacular failures. When successes did occur, the unintended legacies
of government and business plans were often as profound as the
intended ones. In electric power, for example, Japanese government
aid was important to the expansion of the industry, but additional
and unintended spurs to rationalization were provided by reorganization of the industry into nine private regional monopolies. This
1951 reorganization was decreed by the Americans, but neither they
nor Japanese government officials anticipated the fruitful competition it created among the new firms. The urban power companies

used their access to American technology and financial resources to better compete with rural regions that were rich in hydroelectricity.

Although any serious explanation of Japan's postwar economic growth must incorporate these factors of chance, international assistance, and the postwar struggle within Japan to define even the most fundamental aspects of economic strategy, they are underplayed in most existing theories of postwar economic growth, which tend to present explanations that confuse luck with planned success and award amazing vision and freedom of action to Japanese leaders. Rather, energy policy and grand economic strategy developed gradually and haltingly as issues of power were renegotiated within Japan and with the United States. Shifts in power reflected struggles, and, at each discrete stage, decisions were the result of some compromise and some bitter battles lost.

At present, the most common analysis of Japanese society among political scientists is that it is manipulated by a triumvirate of the Liberal Democratic Party, the government bureaucracy, and organized business, which has maintained its influence by various means throughout the postwar years.[10] Institutional methods of control by this power elite include political funding, movement of ex-bureaucrats into the Diet or into *amakudari* retirement slots in business, and government advisory committees. Personal ties among this tightly knit community are cemented through marriage and kinship, common schooling, and shared social clubs. The elite also share a common value structure and set of priorities, which, it is argued, ease decision making. In the economic sphere, the most important of these priorities has been a common commitment to revive the economy. In contrast to the United States and Western Europe, it is argued further that the Japanese political elite can make important decisions about Japan's future without open debate or compromises with "outsider" groups. This analysis stresses the exclusionary quality of the conservative triumvirate in Japanese society. Bluntly put, relatively few people are able to influence policy decisions, and so the decision-making and implementation processes are greatly simplified.[11] Since these arguments are put forward to explain Japan's

impressive postwar economic achievements, they contain the implicit argument that elite control of policy leads to economic success. The basic point is that power was limited to a small group
with relatively homogeneous interests, whose interests were articulated in relation to both those of the mass of Japanese people and
those of "foreigners." Therefore, it was fairly easy to reach consensus
within this small, united, and self-defined group.

The scholarly debate recently has moved inward, toward an exploration of the contours of the decision-making process within this
power-elite framework. This sub-debate, which downplays the role
of the Diet,[12] has concentrated on two linked questions: Does the
bureaucracy or the business community make policy? How much
dissent exists between business and bureaucratic groups? Political
scientist Chalmers Johnson heads up the "bureaucracy-rules" faction, arguing that, in the postwar years, "most of the ideas for
economic growth came from the bureaucracy, and the business
community reacted with an attitude of . . . 'responsive dependence.' "[13] His is the strongest voice arguing that economic decision making occurs mainly within the bureaucracy.

As pointed out by others, Johnson's thesis neglects a number of
battles within elite bureaucratic and business circles over funding,
economic philosophy, priorities, and timing. There were frequent
squabbles among bureaucracies, between government and business,
and within industries. Dissent was present and was loudly expressed. Moreover, at times the bureaucracy tried but failed to impose its ideas on determined business groups. These events suggest
a much more complex and bargained decision-making process than
Johnson's thesis permits. This focus on conflict within and among
business and bureaucratic groups rejects the notion of a consensual
society, stressing instead the conflict underlying important policy
decisions.[14] It also refutes the idea of a monolithic "Japan, Inc."
run by government bureaucrats—or by the sons of the zaibatsu.
However, since this research is limited to government and big business, it still retains the assumption that elite groups control Japan.
It fails to consider the extent to which labor unions (for example)
have participated in business or government plans. Moreover, it

ignores the extent to which the Japanese have been forced to operate in a world economy where the rules were established beyond their shores and without their consultation. As such, it is still too simple an explanation of the realities of Japanese life.

Some economists, while accepting the triumvirate-of-power model as valid for the *political* realm, have rejected it as explanatory of Japanese *economic* growth. Instead, they stress the free market, arguing that Japanese businesses were highly competitive at home and also benefited from the general increase in international trade after World War II. This domestic and international market performance explains Japanese success, they argue. Moreover, economic decisions are not made centrally by either the government or business federations, but are the incremental product of many separate decisions made at the level of individual firms. This model stresses competition within the Japanese economy and the limits of planning.[15] As such, it diverges considerably from the primarily political-science debate over economic policymaking, since it dismisses policy as minimally relevant to economic performance.

There are two points at which this model is less than convincing. One is a problem shared with the previous triumvirate-rule model. Like the political scientists, the economists have not fully recognized the importance of American policy to Japanese development. The special opportunities deliberately created for Japan by U.S. trade and technology assistance limit the value of the "free market" concept for postwar Japan. Both of the dominant explanations of Japan's postwar growth underestimate the importance of its specific international context.

Where the free-marketeers' arguments are least satisfying is at the point of their inception. These economists look to a broad consensus on the need for economic growth to explain Japan's postwar economic successes. This consensus, in the economists' model, extends throughout Japanese society rather than existing only within the business and bureaucratic elite. This seems to impart a democratic touch to the model. Yet, even very thoughtful analyses of economic development simply posit the existence of this general consensus about the goals of Japanese society. Thus, one of the most sophisticated students of the postwar economy, Yasusuke Mura-kami, has stated that, "in postwar Japan, the agreed goal was to catch up with advanced countries and the agreed strategy was to emulate the technology and industrial structure of advanced economies. Such consensus was the most important internal condition for the successful rapid economic growth."[16] Given the emphasis on this initial consensus, it is surprising how little attention has been paid to its origins, its participants, or its limits.

Consensuses on strategies for economic growth, or even the decision to concentrate on economic growth, did not spring, fully formed, from the wartime rubble. Rather, they were the slow product of much debate. Fifteen years elapsed before the Japanese began to enjoy high-speed growth. The policies they developed during that decade-and-a-half reflected the political struggles and diverse goals of that era. Discrete stages in this process emerged as successive compromises were achieved. Japanese government officials—like businessmen, labor-union members, and the Americans—were groping for solutions to Japan's economic problems. Rationalization policy and its daughter, industrial-structure policy, provided an eventual foundation for this postwar economic development by providing for consumption as well as production. It met the needs of non-elite as well as elite groups, all of whom were involved in setting postwar economic priorities. This wide base of policymaking paints the Japanese decision-making process in more diffuse and unfocused tones than is often posited. The key that holds this process together is not tight control by the Japanese elite or the government bureaucracy, but a common commitment to economic planning and economic recovery itself, a commitment that grew out of postwar labor-union efforts as much as bureaucratic or business ones. It is also essentially a compromise position. Development through rationalization was not the first choice for all Japanese but, after the marginalization of alternative paths of economic development such as state control and labor-union participation in broad economic planning, industrial-structure policy became an acceptable settlement. The Japanese consensus on this route to development was the result of compromises and defeats rather than any shared national vision.

It was also compatible with U.S. global foreign policy, which deeply affected Japanese choices. Japanese postwar policy could not have succeeded without extensive American assistance. At the same time, American aid was designed to pursue U.S. policy goals, which, while friendly to Japan, limited Japanese choices within the Pax Americana and laid the groundwork for persistent conflict within the alliance. Nor has Japanese economic success eliminated these tensions. Completely unanticipated on either side of the Pacific, the spectacular recent Japanese economic growth has not resolved the terms of the relationship. Issues of independence, trust, fairness, and respect continue to ignite conflict within the larger framework of bilateral cooperation.

Throughout this period, energy was a catalyst for grand economic policy. As the Japanese first tried unsuccessfully to rebuild domestic coal and then shifted to foreign oil as their key energy source, they had to reconceive many other aspects of economic policy. At home, these strategies implied very different approaches to labor unions, regional problems, tax and subsidy programs, and tactics to encourage technological innovation. Their search for stable energy supplies led the Japanese into an examination of state control of industry, exploration of various sources of capital (including foreign investment), and a theory of how the development of one industry affects others. Abroad, the shift to imported energy required a new stance toward the international economy, one which maximized trade and links to U.S. foreign policy. This shift proved decisive for Japanese postwar economic growth and prosperity. Over the span of fifteen years, the defeated, economically adrift Japan built a new oil-burning engine and anchored itself in the postwar American lake.

TWO

The Energy Industries in the Prewar Years

Although the postwar context rendered many aspects of prewar industrial experience useless, the Japanese could harness some of their prewar achievements—such as their excellent railroad system—to the task of postwar reconstruction. Perhaps the most important prewar legacies were intangible. One was simply the limits past experience placed on imagination. Few in 1945 could envision an economy in which coal did not power the economy as it had for decades. Equally important, the major postwar economic debates drew on prewar beginnings. These debates ranged over such issues as the implications of reliance on foreign capital, the value of competition, and the appropriate role of the state in the economy, notably in the energy industries. Throughout the reconstruction years, the Japanese regularly drew on explanations of economic problems established before 1940, even when prewar practice was rejected. Prewar (and wartime) developments in all three energy industries provided the mental jumping-off point from which the Japanese started in 1945, although the details of this legacy differed in each case. Often the postwar debate echoed prewar disagreements, such as that between private electric-power-company executives and government officials or between small and large coal operators over control of their industries.

The three energy industries started from very different beginnings. Coal was a central industry on which Japanese leaders from the early Meiji period pinned their hopes for a rich nation and strong military. Coal also financed the ascension of the great zaibatsu houses through their oligopolistic control of the best mines and very low wages. They used price agreements and production restraints to maintain their dominance over smaller firms in the industry. The zaibatsu coal-company executives reigned supreme, enjoying great power and prestige in both zaibatsu councils and the government bureaucracy. Coal epitomized the prewar Japanese development strategy in its reliance on oligopoly, cheap labor and colonial raw materials. Rather than technological innovation, this strategy powered Japan's economic growth in the prewar decades, masking the gradual depletion of the coal seams and precluding attention to that more fundamental problem.

There were innovative industrialists in prewar Japan, notably in electric power. The power industry itself was younger and was started up by maverick entrepreneurs rather than by the zaibatsu. Unlike the coal industry, the electric-power-company executives were very interested in adopting new technology. They paid for this with money borrowed overseas, itself an innovation in Japan. Politically, however, the electric-power entrepreneurs never could achieve the kind of influence on economic planning wielded by the powerful coal operators. Acceptance as a core industry eluded them until after World War II, despite electricity's real significance for industrialization. Instead, the electric-power industry, like petroleum before it, became incorporated into Japanese military plans.

These, and firewood, were the key energy forms in prewar Japan. Coal was the most important source; in 1936, it provided 51.4 percent of Japan's energy needs, serving both industry and households. Firewood and charcoal, the other important household energy sources, accounted for 18.6 percent of Japan's total energy consumption. Electric power provided most of the rest of Japan's energy, at 21.3 percent. (It was a slightly more important *industrial* energy source, at 25.0 percent, while coal powered 71.2 percent of Japanese industrial operations.) Petroleum accounted for only 7.9 percent of Japanese energy use, but, since this was largely for military use, it had disproportionate strategic importance. By 1940, coal had become even more important, supplying 66.1 percent of

Japan's energy needs, while electric power provided 16.2 percent, firewood and charcoal 10.7 percent, and petroleum only 7.0 percent.[1]

Depressed economic conditions after World War I affected the industries providing coal, electric power, and petroleum as they did all Japanese industries. During the long business slump of the 1920s, firms competed viciously for markets; in each area, a few survivors emerged victorious. The survivors were known as the Big Twenty in coal, the Big Five in electric power, and the Big Six in oil sales. These were uneasy alliances, and business leaders began to look for ways to moderate the ongoing competition. Their desire for stability (and a floor for profits) meant they were at first sympathetic to government calls for greater regulation. Such demands emerged out of the military and civilian bureaucracy more and more frequently through the 1930s. The Japanese military, concerned that Japan was economically unprepared for war, pushed for greater state control of the economy beginning with petroleum. The Japanese government took an unusually large interest in petroleum, and allowed the oil industry itself only a weak voice in business discussions throughout the prewar era. It was the first industry to come under state control, in 1934, although many others followed, including coal sales and electric-power production. The cumulative effect of these measures began to alarm business leaders, who had accepted the early market consolidations for their own reasons. By the second year of the Pacific War, war requirements had carried state power farther than business leaders wanted in all three industries, leaving a legacy of conflict as well as one of cooperation for the postwar years. The echoes of these prewar battles would reverberate through all postwar debates on reconstruction.

COAL

Coal was a crucial link in the development of Japanese industry throughout the prewar era. Originally, the Meiji government had initiated development of the coal- and metal-mining industries, and coal exports were a key source of foreign exchange for the new government. The Japanese were fortunate to have coal resources in their own territory. There were significant reserves in Kyushu and in Hokkaido and smaller reserves in the Ube and Jōban areas of Honshu, all intensively developed from the Meiji period. The Jōban fields, although small, were important because they are the site of Japan's only indigenous metallurgical coal. The Kyushu region had been exploited for the longest period and was characterized by smaller mines with lower quality coals than the less extensively mined Hokkaido fields, although a few of Japan's largest and best mines, such as Miike, are in Kyushu.[2]

During the 1880s, the government leaders sold off the mines to several big firms as a cost-cutting measure. These mines provided the resources for those companies to grow into diversified conglomerates with enormous economic power. This was particularly true of the industry leaders—Mitsui, Mitsubishi, and Sumitomo—which used the mines as seed capital for venturing into new lines of business. The mines, which were extremely profitable, acted as "money boxes" to finance the companies' ventures and their development into zaibatsu conglomerates. According to Shibagaki Kazuo, "The bulk of the profits of the Mitsubishi conglomerate came from the coal and mining division, at times as much as 80 percent, while, in Mitsui's case, in contrast to the stagnation of the firms in the Industry Division, the mining company was the second source of profits after Mitsui Bussan Trading Company."[3] In those days, the mines were a cornucopia of wealth for their owners.

The use of the mines as "money boxes" to extract capital for other uses had implications for how the industry was structured. Most important, it discouraged modernization of the mines in a number of ways. First, the mine owners sought to run these money boxes as inexpensively as possible. They were interested in the mines purely as an extractive industry; except in the few best mines, they did not use their profits from coal to develop better mining techniques. This meant that the mine owners kept miners' wages low and relied primarily on labor power to dig the coal. Japan's poor-quality mines could finance the new ventures of the zaibatsu firms only because they denied labor most of its share in the wealth generated. At first the mines used convict labor, but later they turned to an indirect hiring system known as the *naya* or crew-boss system.

The basic problem was that the mines paid so poorly that they could not recruit workers by ordinary methods and so had to resort to coercion. The crew-boss system merely removed the mine companies farther away from the sordid details and inserted one more person who took his livelihood from the miners' meager wages. The details were sordid indeed. The *naya* system was based on control of the dormitories where the miners were housed. The crew boss subcontracted with the mines to recruit new miners, to direct them, and to allocate the jobs among them. He collected the miners' pay and distributed it after taking a kickback. He also sold them food, clothing, and tools. The miners, sometimes kidnaped farmers, were viciously beaten and tortured by the crew bosses' goons if they tried to run away. Despite this, an investigation by a major mine company in the late 1920s found that 41 percent of its 8,366 workers had escaped or tried to flee the mine, dramatically testifying to the harshness of the work.[4]

A second implication of this status as "money box" was that there were very few incentives to mechanize the mines. Rather, the larger mine operators relied on cheap labor and a variety of market-restricting measures to maintain their profits. One was to gain control over all the mines that produced high-quality coal, or were especially low-cost producers. It is an oversimplification to equate large mines with zaibatsu ownership, but in fact the large coal companies tended to own the mines with the best natural conditions and highest-quality coal. This split was regional. The Jōban and Chikuhō fields used cheap labor in the form of part-time farmers in the destitute Tōhoku and Kyushu regions, and so were able to continue in the longstanding pattern of many small mines with many workers and little machinery. Other areas, such as Hokkaido or the mines that extended under the sea, Miike and Takashima, were more difficult to mine on a small scale and quickly became zaibatsu-dominated.[5] This distinction sharpened in the 1920s, a time of deep economic depression in Japan. Until the China War began in 1937, the coal mines struggled with years of poor sales. The big companies responded to this era of hardship by expanding their control over the mining industry. In 1921, unsold coal stockpiles had risen to over 4 million tons and over 200 mines had closed because of the depression. By 1926, the 10 largest companies controlled 62 percent of Japan's coal reserves. By 1937, Mitsui was estimated to control 31 percent and Mitsubishi 19 percent of the industry's total invested capital. Not only were the totals high; the two companies owned most of the best mines in Japan.[6]

This concentration of ownership, paralleled by increasing concentration of production in a few large mines, was achieved through mine closings and a short-lived mechanization and rationalization movement in the early 1930s. Mechanizing the mines encouraged large-scale production and allowed the mines with greater potential to expand output rapidly. Most of the new machinery was for surface operations, especially mechanical coal-sorting and washing machinery. Mines producing less than 100,000 tons annually accounted for 27 percent of production in 1922 but only 15 percent in 1931. Conversely, very large mines producing over 1 million tons accounted for only 6 percent of production in 1922 but for 27 percent in 1936. By 1935, although there were 450 active mines in Japan, three-fifths of the coal came from 30 mines, each with an annual output of 350,000 metric tons or more.[7] These figures indicate the great differences in quality between the zaibatsu mines and the myriad small ones.

Although the large mining companies did turn to mechanization measures for a short period in order to gain control of the market, they did not maintain this strategy after having achieved that goal. Once the big firms controlled the coal market, they abandoned their rationalization plans. Mechanization generally increases output, but the operators already faced a situation in which coal supply exceeded demand. Improving efficiency simply threatened to further swamp the market. Instead, the big coal companies worked to restrain production from the mid-1930s rather than increasing coal productivity with more machinery.

That moment, when the mines began to introduce some expensive machinery, was a point at which the reliance on forced labor might have been reduced. In fact, a few companies abolished the crew-boss system relatively early because it encouraged immediate production but discouraged rational development of the mines. In general, substitution of capital for labor in an enterprise requires fewer but more highly trained workers, and it is at this stage that employers cultivate loyal employees at higher salaries.[8] Takashima mine was the first to eliminate crew bosses in 1897, but, in 1923, 50 of the 81 mines in Fukuoka prefecture still employed the crew-boss system,[9] for two reasons. First, the main rationalization period of 1929 to 1932 was only a partial shift, and most employers still relied more on wage cuts than on capital inputs to reduce their production costs. They needed the coercive power of the crew bosses to enforce this. G. C. Allen calculated that "the average wage per man-shift in Kyushu (including the Ube district) fell from 1.66 yen in 1929 to 1.40 in 1932, rising again to 1.58 in 1934. In Hokkaido the wages were 2.22 yen, 1.43 yen, and 1.68 yen for the same years." Allen figured that wage reductions accounted for 24 percent of the 37-percent cost reduction between 1929 and 1932.[10] Not only was the shift to machinery unenthusiastic; it was also short-lived. In the mid-1930s, the rationalization movement was aborted, and the mine operators returned to labor-intensive techniques.

This was partly because a new source of low-cost labor was becoming available to the mine owners. These were the colonial peoples, especially Koreans, who were brought into the Japanese mines as forced workers. During the Pacific War, the number of Koreans conscripted into the mines multiplied. By 1944, there were 35,209 Korean miners in the Hokkaido mines, 74,736 in the Kyushu mines, and 18,245 in the mines of Honshu. They comprised 31.9 percent of all miners in Japan at that time.[11] The Koreans were nominally contract workers, but most of the 40,000 Chinese laborers were prisoners of war who had been sent to the mines instead of prison camp. From 1942, other Allied nationals were also interned in the Hokkaido mines. By 1945, the foreign miners had become an even more significant proportion of the total mine labor force, particularly of the underground workers, and, in some Hokkaido mines, foreign underground workers outnumbered Japanese 3 to 1. In April 1945, there were 150,000 foreign miners in Japan. This had declined to 140,000 by July but was still 37 percent of the mine labor force. These dry figures—10,000 workers dead in only three months—indicate the extremely harsh conditions under which they labored.[12]

This history of atrocious working conditions provides the background for the postwar labor movement and explains its particular strength and intensity in the coal mines. It also provides a significant explanation for the coal industry's chronic unprofitability in later years. The demands of the postwar coal miners that they receive a greater share of the proceeds in the form of higher wages and decent housing impaired the basic profitability of the coal companies, which had uniformly relied on enforced low wages to make money. The fact that Japanese coal was competitively priced in the prewar global market "was due entirely to cheap labor and tight labor control."[13] The rise of labor unions was unquestionably the single most important change from the prewar years within the mining industry.

Firms such as Mitsui and Mitsubishi Coal Companies had yet another reason to prefer production restraint to improving their mines in Japan. They were part-owners of strip mines in Manchuria as well as other high-quality mines in Sakhalin, Korea, and Formosa. The enormous Fushun mine in Manchuria alone produced nearly 10 million tons of coal in 1936. Other overseas mines, like Mitsui Mining Company's Kawakami Mine on Sakhalin, promised a higher return than the partially depleted Japanese mines, and so the companies used their development budgets there instead of at home.[14]

Development of these mines in Asia was the preferred strategy because it resolved the persistent problem of obtaining coking coal for steel production. The colonial mines were cheaper to operate, it is true, but this was not as important as the quality of their coal. The new mines solved the historic problem of obtaining coking coal without reducing zaibatsu control over coal supply. The quality of Japanese coal is fairly low, and quality rather than quantity has traditionally been the limiting factor in Japan's coal production. As one American Occupation official explained, "While the effort required for producing a given amount of coal is high, the cost for a given amount of heat is still higher."[15] The general consensus was that Japan's coal reserves "were ample for her prewar needs except in anthracite and coking varieties."[16] However, Japan never had enough of these special types of coal.

The big coal companies could afford to discontinue mechanization because they had a secure hold on the industry by the mid-1930s. They enjoyed oligopolistic profits on domestic and colonial high-quality and special coals, which were consistently priced higher per kilocalorie than poorer quality coals. They were also in a very strong market position for ordinary grades of coal because they owned the mines with the richest coal seams. Yada Toshifumi, a leading scholar on the Japanese coal industry, has called these better natural conditions (known to economists as "marginal rents"or "monopoly rents") "a wellspring of profit for the owners." Moreover, he points out, "the better that natural conditions at a given mine were above those at the worst mine, the higher were the marginal rents."[17] The owners of the best mines actually benefited from the continued existence of the smaller, less-efficient mines, which helped set the cost of coal at a relatively high level.

Thus, by the late 1930s, the coal industry was bifurcated into two groups. The first was composed of about 20 very large, powerful firms which enjoyed great profits from their mines with only limited investment. They introduced a minimum amount of machinery, mostly to improve the quality of their coal, but this was a minor factor in their profitability. They relied far more on control of high-quality coal, their lower production costs due to good mine conditions, their supplemental profits from colonial mines, and their tight control of labor. Thus, although the rationalization movement in the early 1930s did raise productivity in the major mines, the big companies derived their profits more from owning better mines than by improving mining methods.

The other mine operators suffered a perennial disadvantage. Their smaller mines often had poor natural conditions and so were far less profitable than the large ones. Lacking capital and access to banks, they were not able to raise money to buy machinery. These mines, which were extremely labor-intensive and maintained a precarious existence, were not able to strengthen their position in the industry. The major mine operators did not try to wipe them out because, as Yada has explained, the existence of the small firms pushed up the price of all grades of coal and allowed the large firms to make higher profits.

The two groups of producers clashed bitterly, but did agree to maintain coal prices through several price-fixing and production-restraint agreements. This strategy satisfied both groups of mine operators, although it did not eliminate the tensions between them. The first industry-wide organization dedicated to the goal of stabilizing prices was a production-restraint cartel, the Coal Owners' Union (Sekitan Kōgyō Rengōkai). The industry leaders established this cartel in 1922 and succeeded intermittently in controlling production. In 1932, the Japanese government strengthened the cartel arrangements by forming the Shōwa Sekitan Company. This new organization worked closely with the Coal Owners' Union to establish production restraints and negotiate import controls. Shōwa Sekitan, composed of coal-industry executives, also set official coal prices and regulated domestic supply.

The small Kyushu producers felt inadequately represented by these bodies, however, and organized their own self-help organization, the Mutual Aid Society (Gōjo Kai) in February 1933. They were particularly annoyed that the Shōwa Sekitan Company maintained artificially high prices for better grades of coal relative to lower grades. The Mutual Aid Society concentrated on lobbying the bureaucracy, the South Manchurian Railway, and the Diet to limit imports of Manchurian soft coal, a goal less attractive to the zaibatsu producers who owned the Manchurian mines.

This rift between the large and small coal producers and their split into separate trade groups foreshadowed postwar industry organization. It also reflected the growing bifurcation of the industry in both the 1930s and 1950s into two very distinct groups of coal-mine owners: about 20 huge mining companies that, in the prewar years, were part of large, integrated economic combines, and myriad smaller regional coal operators who were politically powerful in Kyushu but no economic match for the Owner's Union. Coal-industry policy, both before and after World War II, had to be thrashed out between these two sets of firms. Programs that appealed to both, like the price restraints of the 1930s, were always the easiest to implement.

From 1937, the biggest problem for the coal operators of the previous fifteen years—slack demand—disappeared as the expanding war in China revived the economy. It was at this point that government involvement in the industry further institutionalized its bifurcated structure. At the same time, as in the rest of the economy, the concept of state control of this important industry began to gain strength. State control was introduced to make the coal supply system both more efficient and more fair, the twin rationales for state control generally. Shōwa Sekitan lifted its ceiling on coal production in 1937, but coal consumers were still resentful of the high prices the cartel had established. Shōwa Sekitan came under harsh criticism when it hiked coal prices (in increments during 1934–1937 from 1.45 yen to 6.50 yen per ton). This time the government stepped in with decreed prices of its own. In September 1938, the government ordered the industry to lower prices by 1.50 yen for lump coal and by 50 sen for powdered coal on the legal basis of the Commodities Price Control Ordinance (Bukka Tōsei Rei).[18] Then, in March 1940, the Cabinet converted the private control organization, Shōwa Sekitan, into a state-sponsored "national-policy company" in the hopes that it would lead to smooth distribution of inexpensive, high-quality coal. All the coal operators had opposed this move, but their position was undermined by a scandal in 1939. In the midst of a severe drought, Shōwa Sekitan supplied such poor quality coal to the electric-power companies that they could not operate their plants. Public opinion, already roused by the price hikes, turned against the coal companies, and the government placed the coal market under full formal state control.

The new state company, Japan Coal Company, Ltd. (Nippon Sekitan), became the exclusive buyer and distributor of coal at prices

set by the Japanese government. The state provided an initial budget of 6.25 million yen to capitalize the new wholesale operation.[19]
The increasing need to mobilize the economy for military purposes,
combined with the belief that the coal companies were unscrupu-
lous, created elements of an adversarial relationship between the
industry and the bureaucracy during the Pacific War. This antagonism was carried on after the war in the struggle to nationalize the
industry.

There were also important elements of cooperation between the
Japanese government and the coal operators. Significantly, the government preserved the status quo between the Coal Owners' Union
and the Mutual Aid Society through import restrictions, sanction
of cartel agreements, and, later, fixed prices and subsidies. The
small companies continued to exist but never could win the right
to design industry policy along with the zaibatsu firms. This was
partly because the government had a dual and conflicting set of
goals for the coal industry. It wanted to maintain the small producers in order to raise coal production levels, but was committed to a
strategy of building Japan economically and militarily by channeling capital into the zaibatsu firms. The simultaneous pursuit of
these two goals institutionalized the bifurcated structure of the coal
industry.

This was especially clear during the Pacific War. General policy
was to maximize coal production, which meant supporting the small
as well as the large producers. However, the wartime Coal Control
Association enhanced the power of the largest firms. There is some
debate over whether these Industry Control Associations (there were
21) were dominated by the bureaucracy or the businessmen, but
that they ignored small producers' interests seems to be a point of
unanimous agreement.[20] This is corroborated in the case of the coal
industry by the various examples of mergers and takeovers by the
largest companies during this period.[21] The government's primary
concern was coal output. As long as the zaibatsu coal producers
maintained supplies, their absorption of small firms was congruent
with government policy. Labor policy was also an important area of
agreement between the government and the mine owners. It was

the Japanese Army, for example, that sent Chinese prisoners of war to work in the coal mines.

Coal remained a central industry throughout the prewar years in Japan. Its role as a basic industry meant that it was always important to the economy. Moreover, its great profitability made coal central to the zaibatsu empires. Thus, the coal industry, especially the major mine owners, enjoyed tremendous power and prestige throughout the period.

ELECTRIC POWER

An important new energy source, electric power, developed in Japan in the mid-Meiji period. The first electricity producer was the Tokyo Electric Light Company in 1883. It produced power for lamps only, using coal as fuel. Tokyo Electric Light was established by an independent engineer and a bureaucrat, after the engineer, Fujioka Ichisuke, failed to win business interest in the project. Thus, it differs from the coal industry from its inception in that the zaibatsu corporations ignored electric power and left its development to unaffiliated entrepreneurs and bureaucrats. This pattern was to extend well into the postwar years.

Thirty-three electric-power companies had been founded by 1896 and were operating in fierce competition with each other, causing electric-power prices to decline. Lower prices were further encouraged by the introduction of new technology from about 1907, which in turn encouraged greater consumption.[22] In fact, from the 1920s, the cost of electric power to consumers began to drop relative to that of coal, so that electricity became a significant competitor of the coal industry. This was due in part to faster technological progress in the electric-power industry, but was also a result of the rate structure. The comparatively high rate for electric lighting subsidized cheaper rates for motive power, which competed directly with coal. Thus, although electric lighting accounted for only 44 percent of demand in 1913, it provided 77 percent of the revenue for the industry. This subsidy to industry at the expense of electric-light users—offices and households—was sanctioned by the government.[23]

Electric power is different from other energy forms in that it is sometimes a primary energy source (hydroelectricity), and sometimes a secondary source (coal and oil). More recently, nuclear energy has created a special third category. This means that there is usually both a competitive and a cooperative element in the relationship between the electric-power and coal industries. From an early date, the Japanese case followed this pattern. The first electric-power installations were coal-fired, but hydroelectricity gradually gained in importance. The Japanese electric-power industry relied on water power for its main generating source from the 1920s, but always had to supplement this with coal-fired thermal plants. Because the Japanese hydroelectric plants typically lacked storage facilities, thermal plants were necessary in the low-water months. Thus, there was a seasonal cycle; the industry relied more on hydroelectricity in the summer and on coal-fired plants in the winter. In addition, regional variations in water supply meant that some areas, such as Kyushu, always required more coal-generated electricity than others.

The labor force and working conditions in the electric-power industry differed markedly from the coal mines. Because hydroelectric facilities were scattered all over the country, many of the employees lived in isolated rural regions. Maintaining these plants and transmission equipment, however, required skills, and the electric-power company employees were often relatively well-educated and respected members of their communities. Their work in a new and "modern" industry also carried prestige. Thus, they can be considered as part of the Japanese prewar "labor aristocracy." These characteristics were also true of the electric-power workers in the postwar years.

Cutthroat competition in the early twentieth century forced many smaller electricity suppliers out of business until, by 1928, the 5 most powerful generating companies had consolidated their control of the industry. These were the Tokyo Electric Light Company, the Tōhō Electricity Company, the Daidō Electricity Company, the

Ujigawa Electricity Company, and the Nippon Electricity Company. One reason these firms had prevailed was that they had more cash, which they had raised through the risky step of borrowing heavily abroad. In 1923, Tokyo Electric Light borrowed about 29 million yen in Britain, while Daidō Electricity looked to America for 30 million yen the following year. By December 1931, the Big Five owed 357 million yen abroad, or 16 percent of all foreign debt in Japan.[24]

Competition between the 5 firms remained so fierce that some weak-willed Tokyo homeowners accepted contracts with two companies—one for the first floor and one for the second—while big companies alternated daily between Tokyo Electric Light and Tōhō Electricity in order to maintain peace with both suppliers.[25] The price wars among the firms were so ruinous that the industry leader, Tokyo Electric Light, ceased paying dividends in 1932. At that point, the major banks, led by Mitsui, Yasuda, and the Industrial Bank of Japan, stepped in to mediate. As a result of these negotiations, the electric-power companies agreed to establish and abide by standard electric-power rates and also to share equipment under the auspices of a new industry organization, the Electric Power Federation (Denryoku Renmei). The Electric Power Federation was organized by the bankers to provide stability and served, in part, to subordinate the independent electric-power capitalists to the needs of the established zaibatsu groups.[26]

At the same time, the growing need to rationalize industrial production for military goals and to bring electric power to impoverished farm villages meant that reform bureaucrats began to place greater importance on stable and inexpensive electric power. The bureaucrats were pleased by the stability and centralization created by the bankers in the electric-power industry, but they wanted to use it to raise production and lower electric-power rates rather than to maintain profits. They increased pressure for state control toward those ends. A big step in the direction of state control came in 1931 when the Major Industries Control Law gave government authority to existing industry-wide agreements to limit and allocate production among the firms in an industry. This law officially recognized the Big Five's Electric Power Federation as a formal cartel in 1932,[27] the same year that the Shōwa Sekitan Company was established in the coal industry. In 1931, the 1911 Electric Power Industry Law was amended to give the government regulatory control over power rates. Primarily concerned with the needs of the munitions industries, the Transportation Ministry ruled that power rates could not increase faster than general prices. While the government favored the stability of an oligopoly in electric power, it was not willing to inflict oligopolistic prices on its carefully nurtured heavy industries.

The real question from 1931 was not whether the industry would centralize, but only whether it would do so under self-rule or under reorganization by the government. The most successful private firms were ready to restrict costly competition—if they could control the terms. They did not, however, want to lose managerial control of their industry. At first they were supported by the majority of business leaders, but, after full-scale war began in China, the government's argument that state control of electric power was necessary to Japan's defense undermined this opinion both in the business world and in the Diet. The desire of bankers and the top firms within the electric-power industry itself for stability dovetailed with the separate impetus of military and bureaucratic efforts for reforms to establish state control of the industry. This congruence of interests eventually led to the creation of a state-controlled industry—to the later dismay of the private electric-power company executives.

During the 1930s, support for greater state control of the economy in general, and the electric-power industry in particular, grew in response to war mobilization. The arguments for state control included efficiency and fairness. The advocates maintained that a single generating system would eliminate inefficient redundancies in equipment investment, transmission lines, and other expenses. Eliminating these redundancies and the need for profits would bring down rates, which would aid the military buildup. Furthermore, the highly centralized structure of the electric-power industry made it a prime candidate for state control, in contrast to the fragmented coal industry. The high cost of generation and transmission equipment, driven even higher by the expensive and often imported technology needed to generate electricity, made state control of this industry seem even more appropriate.

This extreme capital intensity of the industry led to its designation as a "natural monopoly" and regulation in the United States. In Japan, the same problem was treated as an argument for nationalization. Since the electric-power industry served all other important industries, its control would be a powerful tool in broad economic planning, the military planners hoped. The electric utilities were also criticized for underserving farm villages; advocates of nationalization believed that the state could be expected to be more attentive than for-profit firms to this problem.[28] Typically, most Japanese homes in the 1930s had electric power—in the form of a single, low-watt electric light bulb.

Government officials tried twice to bring the industry under state control in the late 1930s, succeeding the second time. The first plan was introduced to the Diet by Communications Minister Tanomogi Keikichi of the Hirota Cabinet in January 1937. This proposed to create a privately owned and state-managed power-generating company out of all previously installed equipment of 50,000 kilowatts or more. By taking over managerial control without seizing ownership, the Japanese government avoided the expense of indemnities and maintained a facade of respect for private property. Tanomogi's plan was explicitly based on European fascist economic theories and was supported by the Army's Suzuki Teiichi as a first step: "If we can impose strong controls on the enormous electric-power industry, then, after that, it would be easy to enforce strong policies toward other important industries."[29] The electric-power-company owners and the majority of the business community protested this attack on private property. They fought the Tanomogi plan so hard that the Cabinet decided to withdraw its bill from the Diet.

In July 1937, however, Japan began full-scale war in China, and attitudes rapidly shifted. Bureaucrats in the first Konoe Cabinet dusted off the Tanomogi plan but, before resubmitting it to the Diet, they established a joint business-bureaucrat study committee, the Kokusaku Kenkyūkai, to analyze the question of state control of the electric-power industry in the interests of national defense.

This time, when they sent a bill to the Diet, it already had the support of many influential business leaders and passed the Diet in March 1938.[30] This law led to the establishment of Nippon Hassōden Kabushiki Gaisha (Hassōden), a state-controlled but privately owned "special corporation" (*tokushu gaisha*) which generated power and sold it to transmission and distribution companies. It was created by forcibly consolidating 33 generation companies across the country. (All generation plants of over 10,000 kilowatts, 7,000 kilometers of distribution network, and 94 transformer stations, valued at 653 million yen were transferred to Hassōden.)[31] The company began operations on 1 April 1939. Later, more hydroelectric facilities were incorporated into Hassōden, and, in September 1941, electric-power transmission and distribution were similarly centralized into 9 regional privately owned and state-operated firms, known as Haiden.

As in coal, the government set low official power rates and paid a subsidy to Hassōden when costs exceeded revenues. Again as in coal, the size of these subsidies rose gradually through the war years. The government was able to achieve a relatively large degree of control over the electric-power industry—unlike steel or coal, where tension remained high between the private control association and the state well into the 1940s.[32] This was achieved by working through Hassōden, the only electric power firm with independent access to funds. The industry depended on government subsidies, since rates had been set low but, while 28 percent of Hassōden's receipts came from subsidies in 1944, the Haiden did not receive any directly. Thus, they had to subordinate their accounts to those of Hassōden in order to enjoy the state largesse.[33] After Pearl Harbor, the industry was further integrated into the war effort through restrictions on power use by ordinary civilians, and, in November 1943, jurisdiction over electric power was transferred to the Ministry of Munitions.

PETROLEUM

The Japanese began importing petroleum products from the United States immediately after the Meiji Restoration. They also hired

American experts to prospect for oil in Niigata, and found some small oil fields. Thus, both imported and domestic petroleum arrived very early in Japan, but only on a small scale. Like electric power, the Japanese began using petroleum almost as soon as Westerners, although, for fifty years, it remained more a badge of modernity than a significant part of the economy.

This changed after World War I, when the oil industry went through the same process that had prevailed in the electric-power industry—vicious price wars, leading to consolidation of the market by several big companies, more price wars, and state intervention. State controls in the petroleum industry, too, developed out of the same combination as had prevailed in electric power: business pressure for stability and government actions to integrate strategic industries into the defense effort. There were some differences in the case of petroleum, however. For both strategic and commercial reasons, the Japanese turned to state control in order to limit the influence of foreign oil importers. Moreover, the petroleum industry was, from the start, far more closely tied than the other energy industries to Japan's expansionist ambitions. Only 10 to 15 percent of Japan's petroleum requirements were supplied domestically, so controls of imports were always of much greater importance than those of Japan's meager home production.

Military officers were among the leading voices calling for economic planning and controls in the prewar years, and, of course, their economic plans began with industries that were closely tied to military requirements. The military, particularly the Navy, was the most important petroleum consumer in the 1930s. Total demand—Army, Navy, and civilian—for petroleum products rose from about 2.5 million kiloliters in the early 1930s to 5.4 million kiloliters in 1937. After the Sino-Japanese War began, the government instituted consumption controls on civilian uses, including shipping. By 1941, total consumption had dropped to 3.8 million kiloliters, and the military consumed over half of this. Civilian gasoline use was most severely rationed, dropping from 1.3 million kiloliters in 1937 to 438,000 kiloliters in 1941.[34] The Army encapsulated its attitude in the slogan "One drop of gasoline is one drop of blood!"[35] The Navy was even more dependent on oil; in 1941, when it was fully mobilized, its ships burned 15,000 kiloliters of fuel oil each day. It controlled about 75 percent of Japan's oil stockpiles at that time. Capturing the oil of the Netherlands East Indies was a primary goal of both branches of the military by 1940. Once the Pacific War began, the two services controlled the Southeast Asian oil, refusing even to tell the civilian government how much they imported to Japan.[36]

The oil industry was an obvious launching point for greater economic control because it was dominated by two foreign companies—Rising Sun Petroleum Company, a Royal Dutch-Shell subsidiary, and Standard Vacuum Corporation (Stanvac). These two firms, which imported refined oil products and sold them directly to Japanese consumers, established marketing operations in Japan in 1899 and 1900.[37] Most of this oil came from the United States, although some was imported from the Netherlands East Indies, where both companies owned extensive oil fields. At the turn of the century, 30 Japanese oil companies shared the Japanese oil-sales market with the 2 international giants. These companies bought oil products abroad and sold them in Japan, and also refined and sold domestic crude. The international oil companies had originally prospected for crude in Japan but abandoned this relatively high-cost venture before World War I. This unusually large dependence on foreign sources and foreign firms for raw materials in the petroleum industry made the Japanese military planners very uncomfortable and fed their interest in state controls. In particular, they hoped to encourage more refining in Japan by Japanese companies.

The second wave of support for tighter controls on petroleum came from the domestic oil companies. In the 1920s, the 2 international oil majors began importing very cheap refined products from California, just after several Japanese companies built refineries in Japan, sparking a price war. This caused great problems for Japanese companies, particularly those that had ventured into refining, but also affecting those that just sold oil products. By the mid-1920s, most of the oil-sales business had been narrowed down to 6 companies, only some of which refined in Japan: Stanvac, Rising Sun, Mitsubishi Shōji, Mitsui Bussan, Nihon Oil, and Ogura Oil

Companies. The price war among them was ended temporarily in 1928 when the Big Six petroleum marketers in Japan signed a market-division and price-maintenance agreement on gasoline in 1928. This agreement awarded Stanvac and Rising Sun 60 percent of Japanese sales. The Japanese companies were somewhat resentful of the two foreign firms for demanding the lion's share of the market, but they preferred this arrangement to a continuation of the ruinous price war. This delicate balance was upset, however, in 1933 by an independent Japanese trader who imported oil from the Soviet Union, causing gasoline to drop from 130 to less than 70 yen per kiloliter in early 1934 and the price wars to resume.[38] This spurred the Japanese oil-industry leaders to lobby for the Petroleum Industry Law.

This business impetus merged with the military one to speed the Petroleum Industry Law through the Diet on 28 March 1934.[39] This law, the first of many to regulate specific industries for the war effort, empowered the government to license oil producers, importers, refiners, and marketers; to set prices; and to award the Japanese companies 50 rather than 40 percent of the home market. The law required all importers to maintain at their own expense oil stocks equal to six months' sales within Japan. It also mandated the merger of the many small Japanese oil refiners into fewer and stronger firms.

In a special case, three Mitsubishi-affiliated companies and Associated Oil Company of the United States (later renamed Tidewater) entered into a joint venture in 1931, which they titled Mitsubishi Oil Company. They were equal owners in a refinery in Japan, for which Associated supplied the crude oil and technology. Associated Oil did not experience the criticism by either the military or businessmen that was directed against Stanvac and Rising Sun because it worked together with a Japanese firm and because it had different interests in Japan. Unlike the other two foreign firms, Associated supported the Japanese effort to move toward imports of crude oil and refining within Japan rather than simply marketing finished products. This was Mitsubishi's first step into the oil-refining business, although its trading company had imported refined products from Associated for a number of years. (Mitsui declined to enter oil refining, preferring the simpler operation of importing and marketing petroleum products.)

Neither the military (which hoped to limit foreign entry to the industry for security reasons) nor the Japanese oilmen (who were more interested in enlarging their share of the market without completely antagonizing their international suppliers) were entirely successful. The Army continued to push for controls. It passed a more radical law in Manchukuo, which forced the international oil companies to leave the area by declaring a state monopoly on petroleum. Later, when the Ministry of Commerce and Industry established a Petroleum Industry Bureau in 1937, the military increased its intervention in the bureaucracy by sending active-duty officers to supervise a civilian agency for the first time. Nonetheless, they were unable to eliminate Japanese dependence on the two oil giants.

The international companies were able to maintain a presence— and a profit—in Japan despite the Petroleum Industry Law. As a protest against the Petroleum Industry Law, Stanvac and Rising Sun tried to convince independent American oil producers and exporters not to sell crude oil to Japan and Manchukuo but were unable to secure an agreement. The two companies also enlisted the aid of their governments. The U.S. Ambassador to Japan formally requested that Stanvac's interests be protected, although the State Department refused to threaten to embargo sales of crude oil to Japan and Manchukuo, as Stanvac had requested, if it was forced to abide by the rules of the Petroleum Industry Law. Nevertheless, this intercession by the government on behalf of the oil company added to Japanese uneasiness about oil dependence. Stanvac's ready access to the U.S. government further underscored the strategic importance of petroleum—and the power of the international oil companies. Although the foreign companies could not mobilize a boycott or an embargo, they were able to win concessions on both the expensive stockpile requirement and the quota adjustments. The international oil companies also continued to undersell their domestic competitors. Japanese imports of their refined oil actually rose during the following six years.[40]

The law did, however, act to consolidate the domestic refining industry, which by 1940 consisted of only 8 firms, most of which constitute Japan's important oil companies today—Shōwa Oil, Maruzen Oil, Daikyō Oil, Nihon Oil, Kōa Oil, Mitsubishi Oil, Tōa Nenryō Kōgyō, and Nihon Kōgyō Companies. The last two firms supplied the military forces exclusively. In 1940, the government tried to merge these firms further but was rebuffed by the industry.[41]

The Japanese government also took a number of measures to stimulate domestic exploration and production of petroleum. The most important of these were the 1937 Imperial Fuel Industry Company Law, which gave "special attention to consolidating, controlling, and subsidizing the development of the nation's petroleum . . . resources" and the 1941 Teikoku Petroleum Company Law, which created a new company (50 percent government-owned) to manage 95 percent of domestic production.[42] The government also tried to stimulate synthetic oil production. The Navy had pioneered research in this area at the Fushun mine in Manchuria.[43] However, these measures had disappointing results in that domestic output increased only slightly. They were most significant in that they wasted scarce resources and heightened the Japanese sense that a dearth of petroleum was a threat to national security. Their failure meant that the Japanese military turned its attention ever more persistently to a search for petroleum abroad.

Japanese concerns over oil vulnerability were well-founded. British and American officials discussed imposing an oil embargo on Japan as early as 1934. The two foreign oil companies, Shell and Stanvac, also participated in these discussions. However, the American government moved cautiously through 1941, fearing that a total petroleum embargo would drive the Japanese into a decision to seize the Netherlands East Indies. The first limits on oil to Japan, effective 26 July 1940, simply required export licenses for aviation fuel and scrap metals. This action, which did not name Japan, seemed to the Americans to be the pinnacle of restraint, but in Tokyo the message was received quite differently. The Japanese leaders saw the move as a sinister intimation of American plans to block Japanese economic and military strength. They still hoped to buy oil

legally from the East Indies, and, in fact, the United States government allowed Stanvac and Shell to renegotiate an oil-supply agreement there in the fall of 1940. This eased tensions temporarily. At
that point, few people on either side of the Pacific felt ready for a
war between Japan and the United States. Trouble flared up again
the following year, however, as the Americans became increasingly
convinced that Japan intended to attack the East Indies. Even so,
they never came to a clear decision to embargo petroleum. Rather,
they froze funds and invented bureaucratic hurdles, resulting in a
de facto embargo from August 1941. The Japanese, who considered
oil the issue, not whether the embargo was legally mandated, responded exactly as feared. Deciding that war was their only option,
they advanced on the East Indies simultaneously with the attack on
Pearl Harbor.[44] The Pacific War had begun.

There was a clear hierarchy of influence among industries in the
prewar period, with implications for the power and autonomy of
business leaders. Different economic debates emerged out of each of
these industries, debates which extended beyond 1945. Coal, as the
central energy source, enjoyed both considerable freedom from state
supervision plus state largesse. Indeed, the coal-mine owners benefited from most of the government activity in their industry. Although, by the late 1930s, a few hints of decline were already dis-
cernable, King Coal's reign was still secure. His throne would topple
only after the Japanese rejected their prewar economic strategy for
a more democratic and peaceable one.

The electric-power, and to a lesser extent the oil-refinery, industry executives were much farther from the center of political power
in prewar Japan. They could not prevent state takeover of their
firms in the name of efficiency and national security. Rather, they
impotently sat out the war, hoping that peace would bring new
opportunities for their entrepreneurial talents. Their patience was
rewarded in 1949 when opportunities appeared for businessmen
willing to use technology rather than low-wage labor to rebuild
Japan's economy.

THREE

War, Defeat, Occupation, and

the Energy Industries

By August 1945, the Japanese had been at war in China for eight years and in the Pacific for nearly four. The long conflict took its toll; World War II was as much an economic as a military defeat for Japan. Food production had declined steadily during the war years, while destruction in firebombings alone caused approximately 500,000 civilian deaths and left millions of city dwellers homeless.[1] During that time, routine maintenance and repair went undone in every sector of the economy, from mulberry trees to electric-power lines. Skilled workers left for the battlefront, leaving only novices to operate increasingly temperamental machinery. Widespread shortages of even the most commonplace items—like metal wire—exacerbated the economic disruption. These problems actually deepened at the end of the war, when the munitions plants abruptly shut down, leaving many Japanese without jobs. Food disappeared from the stores at official prices, to reappear in the expensive black market. Over the next few years, 6 million demobilized soldiers and repatriated settlers from Asia returned to Japan, further straining already-too-scarce resources. Industrial production remained well below needed levels. After food, the most serious commodity shortage was energy.

Wartime destruction was especially acute in the coal and domestic oil fields because Japan was gradually running out of these resources. Hydroelectric installations were not affected, but the severe deforestation of the war years washed eroding soil into the nation's rivers. Reckless denuding of the hills and mountains of Japan caused the abnormal level of floods and landslides in the first postwar years. It also contributed to the general energy shortage, since charcoal and firewood remained scarce throughout the Occupation period. The special problems for reconstruction in the energy industries reveal themselves more clearly in hindsight, however. Although wartime destruction made the problem of resource depletion more acute, it also masked it, since the larger problems of neglect and disrepair were common to all Japanese industries in 1945.

It is clear now that World War II left Japan not only a legacy of destruction but also one of transformation. Total war, as the Americans also discovered, required that the national economy be restructured to serve military needs. By August 1945, the Japanese economy could no longer provide consumer goods or even feed the Japanese population. Instead, it had been transformed, as best the Japanese knew how, into a huge military supply unit. These changes were structural and could not easily be reversed. They had significant implications for postwar development, including economic centralization through bureaucratic controls, the introduction of economic planning, and increased reliance on industrial policy—all changes dictated by the need to mobilize for total war. Often these policies and controls were inadequate, but they did serve to legitimate the process of economic planning. In another important shift, the war encouraged a bias toward those goods used by the military, that is, heavy industrial products. This bias heightened the appetite of Japanese industry for energy. This wartime economic transformation was not in itself a negative thing; indeed, some aspects of it have clearly hastened later economic growth.[2] The war encouraged new developments in in-firm production techniques, product standardization, and technical training, all of which became key factors in Japan's postwar economic success. However, neither these structural economic changes nor their positive implications were obvious in 1945. They were completely overshadowed by the immediate problem of how to realign the war-distorted economy to meet peacetime needs.

Although the experience of mobilizing for and fighting total war caused similar changes in other national economies, the Japanese experience also involved losing the war.[3] Surrender marked the failure of a national economic strategy that had relied on imperial expansion and tight control of the domestic population. It necessarily meant a new relationship with the other strong nations, particularly the United States of America, the preeminent postwar power. Defeat implied a discrediting of the Japanese military establishment and, more generally, a shift of social and political power within Japan. Equally important, pre-surrender solutions to economic problems—indeed, much of the shape and direction of the pre-surrender economy—suddenly had become inappropriate to postwar conditions. For example, Japan's main prewar trading partner had been its colonies and sphere of influence in Asia. Even if these areas were to become again economically available to Japan, which was by no means certain in 1945, it would be on very different terms. The carefully constructed yen-bloc trade system was shattered, and neither the Chinese nor the Koreans were likely to accede to its revival.

Domestically, the Japanese elite could no longer enforce very low wages on the urban population nor very high rents and taxes on the rural one. These political power shifts triggered by defeat had enormous economic repercussions. They forced the Japanese to undertake a qualitative reordering of the political economy as much as a simple quantitative rebuilding. Postwar reconstruction required a new vision of the economy. This was the real challenge facing the Japanese in 1945. Somehow, they had to create a social, political, and economic strategy appropriate to the new context of the postwar world.

DEMILITARIZATION AND DEMOCRATIZATION OF JAPAN

A key element of this new context for Japan was military occupation, particularly since Occupation policy demanded major changes in Japanese institutions. The Occupation of Japan was carried out almost exclusively by the American armed forces under General Douglas MacArthur; other Allies never played a decisive role in governing Occupied Japan. Thus, from the first, the Supreme Command for the Allied Powers (SCAP) was primarily an extension of U.S. foreign policy, although there was significant tension between Washington and the Tokyo-based American officials.[4] American policy toward Japan was to have a profound influence on all aspects of Japanese society, including the energy industries.

The main purpose of original U.S. policy toward Occupied Japan can be summarized in the contemporary pledge to "demilitarize and democratize" the nation. Demilitarization both meant the immediate disarming of the imperial forces and a permanent renunciation of war. This principle was institutionalized in the new Constitution of 1947, which stated in Article 9 that "the Japanese people forever renounce war as a sovereign right of the nation and the threat or use of force as means of settling international disputes."[5] During the first postwar years, the Americans retained the wartime vision of a neutral, permanently disarmed Japan.

The demilitarization policy originally included an economic as well as a military component, as is clear from a perusal of the policy recommendations on war reparations. This report, written by a team led by Edwin Pauley, was one of the most sweeping original Occupation critiques of Japan. Pauley worked from the principle that Japan should relinquish its role as the most industrialized country in Asia, arguing that it had achieved that status by military and economic exploitation abroad. In late 1945 and early 1946, he set up a reparations program that would have brought Japan's level of industrial development down to the average Asian and the 1930–1934 average Japanese standard of living. While he recognized Japan's need to export some goods, he expected the Japanese to expand raw material exports of silk, tea, and lumber, and of simple manufactured items, such as porcelain and toys made from indigenous materials. Pauley also emphasized the need to limit imports drastically by increasing food production in Japan.

The reparations program entailed removing Japan's excess plant capacity and physically transporting it abroad. Pauley based his plan on a clause in the Potsdam Declaration which called for "the exaction of just reparations in kind," such as industrial plants, in order to avoid the type of currency inflation engineered by the German government in the early 1920s.[6] In Pauley's mind the choice was clear. He concluded his preliminary findings, in a press release timed to coincide with the fourth anniversary of the Pearl Harbor attack, with the comment that "we must always remember. . . . that in comparison with the peoples she has overrun, Japan has the last priority."[7] The Americans hoped to ensure that Japan would never dominate its Asian neighbors by either military or economic means. They planned for a modest Japanese economy based on light industry and minimal exports, in direct conflict with the wartime evolution toward a large heavy-industrial base. They banned altogether militarily important industries, such as petroleum refining, to slash Japanese war potential.

This American policy blocked a return to Japan's earlier energy policy. The prewar Japanese had looked to Asia for a supplement to their own energy resources, especially for coking coal and petroleum. The richest coal reserves were in North China, and the Army's strategy there was intimately tied to the problem of securing coking coal for the Yawata steelworks. Historically, Japan also had imported coal from Korea, Manchuria, and Sakhalin; the loss of these trade partners at the end of the war was another serious blow to Japanese coal consumers. Empire had been the prewar Japanese solution to a variety of problems, including overpopulation, but one of the key reasons Japan sought dominance in Asia was to secure coking coal and oil supplies. This *was* a solution of sorts, but one totally inappropriate to postwar conditions.

The Americans also saw "democratization" in both political and economic terms. The new Constitution protected basic civil rights and relegated the Emperor to a lesser status as "symbol" of the state, as well as renouncing war. Even before the new Constitution was promulgated, the Americans had initiated a series of reforms aimed at fundamentally altering the Japanese political, social, and economic order. This intrinsically radical policy had ramifications for a wide range of fields. These included the release of political prisoners, legalization of the Japan Communist Party, new legal rights including the vote for women, bureaucratic reforms, a restructured

educational system, a purge of militarists, and curbs on the power
of the police. The Americans reasoned that the tensions caused by
repression at home had impelled Japan into aggressive acts abroad.
Establishing a more democratic Japan, in this analysis, was the best
insurance against renewed militarism.[8]

Many of these reforms, although they were imposed by a foreign
military power, had strong support within Japan, ensuring their
survival past the end of the Occupation. The continued resistance
to a strong Japanese military, despite American pressure since 1950
to rearm, most clearly illustrates this indigenous support. Even when
the Americans repudiated this original reform, it has remained in
place in principle and, to a lesser but still significant degree, in
practice. There is a certain abiding tension in Japan about the fact
that the reforms were imposed by an outside power, however. Sodei
Rinjirō caricaturizes this Occupation-era relationship as an illicit
but pleasurable love affair. Instead of the traditional "obstinate and
barbarous" Japanese elite, the "handsome and rich" SCAP reformers
appealed to "the masses of people," who, "delighted, jumped into
bed with their conquerors, cooperated, and gave birth . . . to the
reforms." His racy imagery captures both the fact that the reforms
were—and are—widely supported in Japan and a certain embar-
rassment over this embracing of changes that were forced on Japan
by an occupying power.[9]

The Americans were far more concerned with democratizing the
Japanese economy than with its economic vitality. They saw Japan's
economic recovery as a distinctly secondary—and Japanese—concern. As Edwin Pauley, writing in regard to reparations, put it:
"Lowered standards in Japan are primarily a question of political
and administrative disorganization naturally resulting from a thor-
oughly deserved military defeat. It is up to the Japanese to elect
themselves a government which will clean up that part of the mess."
Pauley was echoing Washington's basic instructions to MacArthur,
to "assume no obligations to maintain, or to have maintained, any
particular standard of living in Japan."[10]

Democratization policy extended to the economic sphere through
an extensive land reform, the establishment of rights for organized

labor, economic deconcentration of industry, and a purge of businessmen who had cooperated with the military. The two reforms
that had a particularly strong impact on the energy industries—and
all Japanese industry—were labor reform and economic deconcentration. Together with concurrent land reform in the countryside,
these two reforms embodied the Occupation policy of defining democratization as an economic as well as a political goal. They were
designed to make the Japanese economy fundamentally a more
democratic, open system. At the same time, they were supposed to
reconstruct Japan in the American ideal model. The Occupationaires hoped that the labor reform, land reform, and economic deconcentration programs would act to defuse political tensions in
Japan by easing access to wealth. Their concept of economic democracy was intimately linked to the goal of creating an American-
style political system in Japan. These programs, it was hoped, would
give urban workers, farmers, and small businessmen a strong stake
in a liberal, capitalist society and prevent the rise of revolutionary
movements from either the right or the left. They also granted new
legal protection to those Japanese already dissatisfied with existing
economic structures.[11]

THE RIGHTS AND PRIVILEGES OF WORKERS. There is no question that
the Occupation reforms gave previously weak groups greater bargaining power, not least coal miners and electric-power workers. In
an early step, the Occupation established fundamental civil rights
of assembly and free speech. This was reinforced by the December
1945 Labor Union Law which granted workers the explicit rights
to organize, to bargain collectively, and to strike. These measures
stemmed from the assumption that democracy was not possible unless ordinary Japanese people enjoyed some basic economic safeguards against exploitation. Not coincidentally, this reform also
addressed a longstanding international complaint, in that it was
expected to end "unfair" competition and "social dumping" by Japanese firms.[12]

The Labor Union Law was followed by the SCAP-sponsored Labor Relations Adjustment Law of September 1946, which specifi-

cally outlawed such practices as refusing to recognize a certified union or dismissing a worker for union activities. Like their model, the U.S. Wagner Act of 1935, these laws were designed to even the balance of power between employer and employees and to create a stable and predictable framework in which to resolve labor disputes. SCAP then addressed the problem of working conditions by ordering the passage of the 1947 Labor Standards Law, which established new safety, overtime, and health regulations. SCAP also encouraged the formation of a Ministry of Labor in 1947 to oversee labor issues. The Occupationaires wanted to create a non-political union movement that would concentrate on workplace issues like wages and job safety.

These early measures sparked a flare of enthusiastic labor-union organizing in Japan, notably in the coal and electric-power industries. In June 1946—less than a year after Japan's surrender—there were 12,006 labor unions with 3,679,971 members, or 40 percent of the work force. A year later, these totals had risen to 23,323 unions with 5,692,179 members, or 46.8 percent of all workers. Certain industries unionized especially rapidly. In December 1947, 89 percent of all transport and communication workers, 82 percent of all miners, 72 percent of all finance workers, and 67 percent of employees of electric, gas, and waterworks, belonged to unions. [13] By far the most important SCAP economic reform from the perspective of the coal mines was the new labor legislation. The coal miners were the first to form unions and joined them at unrivaled rates. Their new power fundamentally changed the economics of mining, since labor was no longer a nearly free commodity.

Not only did the number of unions grow, but their concepts and tactics began to threaten the establishment of the stable, capitalist state the United States was trying to create in Japan. Most alarming to the Americans was the fact that one of the two large union federations, Sanbetsu, was dominated by Communist Party members, while the other, Sōdōmei, was close to the Japan Socialist Party. The Japanese unions regularly clashed with Occupation officials over the latters' efforts to limit them to strictly defined economic issues. The unions, like the conservative Japanese who opposed them, saw economic and political issues as intrinsically related. Unlike the conservatives, however, they never accepted the American definition of the proper sphere for labor.

At first, SCAP's emphasis was on reducing the disproportionate power of employers, but it soon shifted to the problem of stability within a capitalist solution. In the name of stability, the Labor Relations Law established some restricted categories of workers. In addition to firemen, police, and prison guards, who could not form unions or strike, civil servants lost the right to strike, and workers in public utilities, such as electric-power plants, were required to wait for 30 days before any strike.

SCAP dissatisfaction with union activity came to a head in January 1947, when Sanbetsu and Sōdōmei scheduled a general strike for 1 February. The strikers' goals were political as well as economic, in that the unions hoped to topple the openly anti-labor Yoshida Cabinet. This was going too far for SCAP, which construed the strike as an attack on its own authority; on the eve of the strike, the unions were ordered to desist. The SCAP authorities thereafter became much more wary of the labor movement. Increasingly, SCAP officials in the labor field dedicated themselves not to preserving rights of working people but to wresting the labor movement away from left-wing leaders.[14] Despite this retreat, the Occupation set the legal framework that allowed labor unions to develop.

ECONOMIC DECONCENTRATION. The economic-deconcentration plan attempted to democratize the internal Japanese economy, just as the reparations program strove to balance relations between Japan and other Asian nations. Although it was one of the most controversial of the early democratic reform programs, the economic-deconcentration policy has left a powerful legacy, especially in the destruction of the tightly controlled holding companies.

Marlene Mayo has shown that wartime U.S. government planners in Washington decided that the concentrated economic power of the zaibatsu was an obstacle to a peaceful, democratic Japan. In a structural critique of Japan's economy, the American planners had determined that the great power of the zaibatsu necessarily hampered both the development of political freedom within Japan and friendly commerce with other countries. These planners based their recommendations, sent to Tokyo as part of "The United States Initial Post-Surrender Policy for Japan," on the assumption that huge oligopolies and cartels were both economically inefficient and politically undemocratic.[15] On the basis of this document, SCAP officials ordered 4 zaibatsu holding companies to "voluntarily dissolve" in October 1945. This policy was widened after a March 1946 report by a special mission headed by Corwin Edwards recommended that the power of big business in Japan be further decentralized.[16]

Edwards recommended five major changes: breaking the power of the zaibatsu holding companies; destroying the influence of zaibatsu family members; eliminating centers of economic power that, while not zaibatsu, were still excessive; establishing an Anti-Monopoly Law; and introducing fair-trade legislation.[17] The sections of this policy that dealt with the zaibatsu holding companies and control by the zaibatsu family members were the most rapidly and effectively carried out. Both holding companies and zaibatsu family power have faded from importance in Japanese economic life. The fourth and fifth recommendations resulted in an Anti-Monopoly Law, passed by the Diet on 12 April 1947, which established regulations on business activity and provided for a Fair Trade Commission as an enforcement body.[18]

The history of the non-zaibatsu economic deconcentration program, which deeply affected the electric-power industry, was the most complicated of the five. Edwards's recommendations formed the basis of a State-War-Navy-Coordinating Committee (SWNCC) policy paper, which, in turn, was the blueprint for the Japanese Law to Eliminate Excessive Concentration of Economic Power of 9 December 1947. The designers of economic-deconcentration policy wanted to break up private, but not public, concentrations of economic power. The Economic Deconcentration Law specified that a firm had to be "any private enterprise conducted for profit, or combination of such enterprises" in order to be an excessive concentration of economic power.[19]

At the time the original definition of economic concentration was established, SWNCC was more concerned about *inadequate* government power than the reverse. In 1946–1947, the Washington and Tokyo planners saw government control as preferable to private concentration, although less desirable than free competition. The cautions against allowing the Japanese government control largely stemmed from the assumption that the zaibatsu had too strong a hold on the bureaucracy, not from a criticism of excessive government control of private industry. That analysis did not emerge until later.

The SWNCC report called for:

> support for varied and diffused types of private ownership of elements of these dissolved concentrations, as well as support for government ownership of such of these concentrations as cannot be dissolved and of such elements of the dissolved concentrations as do not lend themselves to competitive operation.[20]

The concern here was not for excess government control per se, but for the government's susceptibility to manipulation by the traditionally powerful private businesses of Japan. When faced with the murky semi-public, semi-private economic forms of which the Japanese were so fond, the Americans opted in the first years for bodies that were clearly governmental.

As the electric-power industry discovered, however, this was neither a firm policy nor a consistent one throughout the Occupation. The law was used to break up 18 firms, in addition to the electric-power companies, of which 4 were at least partly government owned.[21] By the time the deconcentration program ended in mid-1949, it had become a tool to limit the role of government in business as much as one to reduce the power and size of private holdings.

THE ENERGY INDUSTRIES

The energy industries suffered with the rest of the economy through the disruptions created by war, defeat, and occupation. While their experience was not unusual, the consequences were especially harsh.

Persistent energy crises widened and deepened the general economic collapse. Fuel supplies were simply insufficient: Coal production dropped to 36 percent, electric power to 66 percent, and oil imports to a scant .004 percent of their prewar peaks. Economic recovery was unthinkable without early attention to rebuilding energy supplies.

The energy industries' woes did not disappear in 1945 during the first wave of recovery. Demilitarization and democratization policy posed profound, although varied, problems for energy production. The original Occupation emphasis on peaceful, domestic reconstruction translated into an aggressive SCAP coal policy, with SCAP often more enthusiastic than the Japanese government about raising coal output. Coal was the center of Japanese economic planning in 1945–1948 partly because it figured so large in Occupation thinking. At the same time, Occupation labor reforms meant that the coal industry could no longer rely on poorly paid workers. This exploitative labor system, which had been institutionalized by state action as well as by the mine owners, could not survive in the new postwar context.

SCAP's attitude toward the electric-power industry was less clear-cut and is, in many ways, quite surprising. SCAP approved of development of hydroelectricity because it relied on Japan's most abundant natural resource, water. However, the reparations and economic-deconcentration policies severely disrupted the industry. SCAP actions toward the electric-power industry consistently ran counter to larger American policy in Japan, first when the electric-power companies were inappropriately designated as excessive concentrations of economic power, and then when the policy was retained exclusively in that industry. Electric power thus gives some insight into the complex maneuvering for control of economic power that was taking place behind the postwar drive for reconstruction.

SCAP balanced its support of coal and reorganization of the electric-power industry by prohibiting petroleum refining in the early Occupation years. SCAP ordered all Pacific Coast refineries closed to prevent future Japanese remilitarization. This demilitarization policy was changed in July 1949, when the refineries were not only reopened but greatly expanded to allow the Japanese oil companies, in conjunction with the international majors, to establish a Japanese petroleum market. By then, however, grand U.S. policy toward Japan had changed.

COAL UNDER WAR AND OCCUPATION. Wartime destruction was particularly acute in the mines, since it occurred on top of the already-developing problem of resource depletion. Rallying behind the slogan "Coal is the source for planes, warships, and bullets," the Japanese increased domestic coal production during the Pacific War, but at the price of lowering ultimate recovery rates from the mines. (The drop in coal quality also caused poorer-quality metals production.) Domestic coal production peaked in 1940–1943, but, since very little effort was expended in those years on exploration or development of new seams, the high rate of production could not be sustained for long. The consequences of this policy were already visible before the end of the war as production dropped in 1944 and 1945. A 1953 MITI study found that, in 16 large mines, coal faces had become significantly deeper, farther from the mine mouth, and more likely to contain water or gas than in 1934. The mining companies achieved production rises by increasing the number of workers in the mines and the hours they worked rather than by more efficient mining methods. Near the end of the war, the government conscripted more miners for military service, and production levels immediately dropped.[22]

Compared to coal production rates of over 4 million tons monthly through most of the war, in early 1945 coal production began to fall as tools and spare parts grew scarce. In August 1945, production dropped to 1,673,000 tons, then down to 890,000 tons in September, until it reached the postwar low of 554,000 tons in November (see Table 1). This was not even enough to supply the needs of the Japan National Railroads. The shortfall was most severe in the manufacturing sector, which received its quota only after transport, heating, internal mine use, and the Occupation forces were supplied. As a result, coal allotments to manufacturing in 1946 were only 35 percent of 1935 consumption. Moreover, few

Table 1   Monthly Japanese Coal Production, April 1945 to
March 1947 (1,000 tons)

Month	Planned Production	Actual Production	Percent Achieved
April 1945	4,122	3,598	87.3
May	4,301	3,677	85.5
June	4,078	3,514	86.2
July	3,612	2,788	77.2
August	3,619	1,673	46.2
September	3,769	890	23.6
October	1,500	594	39.6
November	1,600	554	34.6
December	750	856	114.2
January 1946	1,050	1,198	114.1
February	1,100	1,349	122.7
March	1,400	1,643	117.4
April	1,650	1,638	99.3
May	1,750	1,710	97.7
June	1,700	1,604	94.4
July	1,720	1,632	94.9
August	1,650	1,795	108.8
September	1,730	1,755	101.4
October	1,873	1,791	95.6
November	2,025	2,024	99.9
December	2,193	2,196	100.2
January 1947	2,178	2,033	93.4
February	2,140	2,056	96.1
March	2,487	2,290	92.1

Source: Nezu Tomoyoshi, Sekitan Kokkai Tōsei Shi, p. 617. His source, Sekitan Rōdō Nenkan, original data from Nihon Sekitan Kōgyōkai.

consumers actually obtained their full allotments, so the bottle-necks were more serious than the statistics suggest.[23] The coal shortage hampered industrial recovery in every field.

All the problems outlined above—inadequate supplies, dearth of metallurgical coals, wartime deterioration in the mines, and technological backwardness—threatened Japan's postwar economic reconstruction. Furthermore, the wartime structural changes toward a more rationalized, planned economy using heavy industry put

Table 2 Coal Production in Japan,
1930–1960 (1,000 metric tons)

1930	31,376	1946	20,382
1931	27,987	1947	27,234
1932	28,053	1948	33,726
1933	32,524	1949	37,973
1934	35,925	1950	38,459
1935	37,762	1951	43,312
1936	41,803	1952	43,359
1937	45,258	1953	46,531
1938	48,684	1954	42,718
1939	51,111	1955	42,423
1940	56,313	1956	46,555
1941	56,472	1957	51,732
1942	53,540	1958	49,674
1943	55,500	1959	47,258
1944	52,945	1960	51,067
1945	29,879		

Source: Japan Statistical Yearbook, Prime Minister's Office, 1954, p. 214; 1961, p. 142.

greater strains on the coal mines. Heavy industry needed plentiful, high-quality, and stable energy supplies, something the coal industry was never able to provide after 1945 (see Table 2).

The Occupationaires made coal production a central peg of their economic program in Japan from the first days of the Occupation. In a general directive on 15 September and in one specifically devoted to coal on 17 September 1945, SCAP emphasized the need to increase coal production. SCAP stated that "authorization is given for production of the maximum quantity of coal that can be mined and for its use in all essential requirements, including the operation of trains."[24] These SCAP directives resulted in Cabinet orders to raise wages and commodity rations to miners in order to attract new workers and special allocations of transport trucks for hauling coal, but they were only halfheartedly enforced. SCAP sent a blistering note to the Japanese Government on 6 December 1945, ordering the Japanese to "take immediate steps to increase the production of coal in Japan," and followed it up with a scolding on 11 December chiding the Japanese for a response that was "inadequate and unsatisfactory."[25] Six months later, on 23 May 1946, the Natural Resources Section of SCAP issued a report which criticized the workers, mine owners, and government for the sluggish performance of the coal industry.[26] These efforts had some effect, as is clear from the rising monthly production levels, but they were not Japanese initiatives so much as compliance with direct SCAP orders. The Japanese government also continued its wartime distribution, allocation, and subsidy programs in the coal industry.

The economic-deconcentration policy did force several changes in the coal industry. It led to the division of Mitsui, Mitsubishi, and Sumitomo Mining Companies into separate coal- and metal-mining firms. This impaired the profitability of the three industry giants, which had used their control of the two commodities as mutual hedges against price drops in either one. It also broke the ties of stock ownership that allowed large mines to control many smaller ones. This gave the small mines more independence from the large ones than they had enjoyed for decades. During the war, many small, less-efficient mines had reopened in response to production-expansion drives; these mines continued to do well under SCAP's coal-production-maximizing policy. Perhaps the most disruptive aspect of the economic-deconcentration policy, however, was the dissolution of Mitsui Bussan and Mitsubishi Shōji. The two trading companies had not only bought coal from their zaibatsu cousins, but they had also acted as wholesalers for many small and mid-sized coal companies and had monopolized the prewar coal-import business. Their loss made it difficult to return to private coal sales after the public sales body was dismantled in 1949.[27]

At first, the American emphasis on coal mining seems inconsistent with SCAP's initial policy to minimize its involvement in the economy, but coal was one of the few industries that did not imply an imperialist relationship with the rest of Asia (if one ignores the colonial contract workers). It thus seemed like the ideal basis for a reconstructed, peaceful Japanese economy. Even within the strict limits suggested for Japan by the Pauley report on reparations or the Edwards report on economic deconcentration, it was clear that the coal industry would remain relatively unscathed. Reliance on domestic coal was consistent with American plans for a small, light-industry-oriented economy.

In the early years, aside from the question of economic deconcentration, the Americans saw coal as a domestic natural resource and so approached the problem of increasing coal output as a natural-resource policy problem rather than as one of industrial recovery. This is particularly clear in the documents of the Natural Resources Section, which administered coal together with the Economic and Scientific Section. These SCAP officials believed that, if Japan could develop adequate natural resources at home, it would remove one of the major incentives behind such aggressive acts as the conquest of Manchuria. A Natural Resources Section official wrote in 1951 that "Japan's Home Island paucity of mineral resources, due to lack of adequate known reserves, poses a threat to future peace unless through development of additional reserves she can become self-sustaining at least to the extent of her normal civilian requirements."[28] The Americans were reasonably confident of that goal. In a 1953 publication, Edward Ackerman of the Natural Resources Section estimated that Japanese mines could supply 95 percent of domestic coal consumption "for as long a period as fuel needs reasonably can be anticipated." He added, "For nearly all purposes the Japanese islands may be considered sufficiently, although not abundantly, supplied with coal reserves."[29] SCAP officials also worked hard to develop advanced techniques of processing Japanese coal as an alternative to importing coking coal, albeit with limited success. Instead, the Japanese came to rely on coking coal imports from the eastern United States.

Based on this reasoning, SCAP began exploring and developing Japan's natural resources from the very first days of the Occupation. According to internal SCAP records, the Americans even considered enlisting the Emperor as a mine recruiter. "Col. Ballard reported the statements of Kyushu coal miners to the effect that plenty of experienced coal miners are available in the coal mining districts but only a request from the Emperor himself would persuade them

to return voluntarily to the mines under present circumstances. It
was indicated that such a proposal was before the Chief of Staff
now."[30] This was before the economic-recovery policy gained strength
within SCAP, but the emphasis on coal production adapted well to
the new priority; developing Japan's natural resources for commercial exploitation was compatible with both the early democratization and later economic-recovery policies.

When American policymakers decided to pursue Japanese economic recovery rather than further demilitarization and democratization, it created policy battles within SCAP over many different
questions. Coal production, however, was one area where the "reverse course" did not cause conflict, since all parties within SCAP
agreed that domestic coal (and hydroelectric) resources should be
developed as much as possible. This intra-SCAP unity eventually
became an important reason for the Japanese to put coal at the
center of their reconstruction plan, but, in late 1945, they were
still not ready to take decisive steps that might make them vulnerable to deconcentration, reparations, or purge measures.

ELECTRIC POWER. The long war wrought its usual destruction on
the electric-power industry, particularly on thermal power plants.
In general, wartime neglect of transmission and mechanical equipment was severe because, curiously, Hassōden was not designated
as a munitions supply company until April 1944 nor the Haiden
until April 1945, despite their recognized importance to the war
effort. The power companies thus did not have priority for spare
parts or basic repair materials until very late in the war. There were
even incidents in which transmission lines were pulled down to
recycle their copper wire for munitions production. Most of Japan's
urban thermal power plants and many transformer stations were
severely damaged in bombing raids in 1945. The hydroelectric power
plants, generally in remote mountain valleys, had escaped intensive
bombing, however. Their relative good repair meant that the industry was able to supply all its customers by late 1945.

Electric power enjoyed immediate but illusory economic recovery. In the first postwar weeks, demand for electric power had so

precipitously dropped that Japan's remaining hydroelectric plants could easily meet it. But, in just a few months, power use far outstripped supply and rationing of power consumption was reimposed on 24 August 1946. In fact, electric-power shortage was one of the most serious barriers to economic development in Japan until the early 1960s. As such, it was a chronic problem for economic planners, one unresolved until well into the high-speed growth period.

The enduring postwar problem was not so much a drop in electric-power supply as it was a steady increase in demand. At first, this was largely attributable to greater household use of electricity, since industrial production plummeted when the war ended. This was partly a natural readjustment from the war years when household consumption of electricity had been curtailed by law. It was also a reflection of the terrible coal, charcoal, and firewood shortages. Households that had previously used solid fuel for heating and cooking were turning toward electric hot plates instead (often by illegally splicing into power lines). In fact, the coal shortage strained the electric-power supply in two ways. Former coal consumers were now using electricity as an energy alternative, and the remaining coal-fired thermal plants were not able to obtain coal.

The Japanese Government was gloomily aware of the dimensions of the problem:

> Demand for electric power increased because of tremendous increase of demand for heating use in households and factories as a substitute for coal after the war, increase of loss caused by the deteriorated conditions of equipment, and increase of illegal consumption as a result of meter shortages. Restriction of power consumption was also not so successful as expected. Consequently, the balance of demand and supply of electric power was entirely broken, causing frequent emergency power stoppages and serious power shortage for both household and factory use. . . . When we consider the expected further increase in power requirements following the advancement of industrial production in general, the prospects in the supply and demand situation of electric power are not bright.[31]

The electric-power industry was unable to meet demand until 1962, but the problem became industrial rather than household demand from the time of the 1950 Korean War boom. The Korean

War period itself was one of the moments when the lack of electric power severely hampered economic recovery. In early 1951, at the height of the boom, industrial plants had to do without electricity for two days each week. Demand for electric power steadily outpaced supply, as electric-power consumption skyrocketed over the first fifteen postwar years: from 21,900 million kilowatt hours in 1945 to 46,269 million in 1950, and more than doubling again to 115,497 million in 1960.[32] Restrictions on power use had to be applied periodically throughout the 1950s. From the point of view of the power industry, this meant a constant assured market (see Table 3). The industry leaders knew that the faster they built new plants, the more electricity they could sell.

SCAP policy toward electric power contained a number of contradictory impulses. In general, SCAP approved development of hydroelectricity for the same reasons it favored development of domestic coal, although electric power received far less attention at first. As one SCAP expert wrote, "In fact, the evidence is overwhelming that one of Japan's chief hopes for establishment of a self-supporting economy is in further development of its hydroelectric energy."[33] Americans were much less enthusiastic about Japan's thermal power plants, as revealed in the first reparations plan. Pauley recommended that half Japan's thermal power capacity be shipped to other countries, since a smaller Japanese economy would not need as much power. The Japanese vigorously resisted this: "The Japanese managers of the industry were determined to prove that installations designated for removal were essential to the power system, and much effort and money were expended in rehabilitating these plants . . . this diversion of attention to plants designated for reparations retarded the overall rehabilitation of the industry."[34] The tone of this official report indicates SCAP skepticism toward such pleas.

At first, SCAP officials saw their distinction between development of hydroelectricity and limits on thermal power as compatible, but gradually, as coal output failed to meet minimum requirements, they accepted the Japanese argument that a major *expansion* of the electric-power system—including thermal plants—was nec-

Table 3 Electric Power Generation by Source,
1940–1960 (million kw)

Year	Hydro	Thermal	Total
1940	23,646	6,957	30,603
1941	28,545	5,228	33,773
1942	23,629	5,826	29,455
1943	26,314	4,931	31,245
1944	26,842	2,980	29,822
1945	18,945	555	19,500
1946	26,373	929	27,302
1947	27,119	1,956	29,075
1948	30,474	2,713	33,187
1949	33,071	3,030	36,101
1950	34,125	5,789	39,914
1951	33,794	7,293	41,087
1952	35,306	8,811	44,117
1953	38,249	10,227	48,476
1954	40,474	9,667	50,141
1955	42,953	11,638	54,591
1956	47,057	15,442	62,499
1957	51,042	19,133	70,175
1958	55,194	19,409	74,603
1959	55,945	30,807	86,752
1960	53,104	48,604	101,708

Source: Tsūshō Sangyō Shō. Kanbō Chōsaka, *Enerugī Tōkeishu*, p. 140.
Note: These figures are for public utilities only.

essary. In June 1949, SCAP approved an ambitious electricity-development plan and allocated counterpart funds for it.[35] By that time, they had also abandoned the reparations policy.

It was the economic-deconcentration program, however, that most disrupted the industry. In February 1948, all 10 power companies were designated as excessive concentrations of economic power. The debate over their reorganization completely absorbed the industry for three years until 9 private companies began operations on 1 May 1951. Not only did the turmoil over this issue prevent reconstruction within the electric-power sector; it significantly hampered general industrial recovery. Despite the fact that, by this time, the Americans had redefined the top priority in Japan as economic recovery, they allowed this debate to drag on surprisingly long. In part, this was because American attitudes toward state control of important industries became more hostile as the Occupation wore on. The electric-power-reorganization case also reveals the Occupation officials as at times disorganized and unable to define their goals. It suggests as well that some Japanese, in this case the former private electric-power-company owners, were able to decisively influence Occupation policy.

It is not quite fair to attribute this lengthy stalemate to economic-deconcentration policy, since the debate over reorganization of the electric-power industry took on a life of its own. Not only was it based on a dubious reinterpretation of the original economic-deconcentration policy, but it lasted much longer than the basic policy itself. One curious aspect of SCAP electric-power plans is the anachronistic flavor imparted by the legal framework and rhetoric of the economic-deconcentration policy long after it had been discarded nearly everywhere else. In the electric-power industry, the true debate shifted to a referendum on state control of important industries, although it still maintained the formal legal shell of economic-deconcentration policy.

PETROLEUM. In 1945, petroleum was the least important energy source of the three under review. Japan did have a small number of oil wells, mainly near Niigata on the Japan Sea, but domestic production had fallen after most of Japan's petroleum engineers and oil-field workers were transferred to the potentially more lucrative Southeast Asian fields. The domestic oil fields also were removed from the "essential-industries" list for several years during the war. From December 1943, after transport problems had become acute, the Japanese shifted to a desperate attempt to develop the domestic petroleum wells, but had only marginal success. Likewise, heroic attempts to develop oil in Manchuria, Sakhalin, Formosa, and other occupied territory suffered from the same problems of transport and never became important. Japan also had a pitiful synthetic-fuel industry, which, by 1945, had been reduced to such efforts as extracting the flammable pitch from pine-tree roots. This was a Navy project, launched under the slogan, "Two hundred pine roots will keep a plane in the air for an hour."[36]

Lack of oil had crippled both military services by the end of the war. Training for airplane pilots and ship navigators had been nearly eliminated by 1944 to conserve fuel. As the months went by, more and more strategic decisions were made on the basis of fuel. The nightmare of the prewar Japanese military planners had come true: Japanese power was only as great as its supply of petroleum—and that could be withheld by the United States (see Table 4).

Oil had never been an important part of the domestic Japanese economy and, during the Pacific War, strict rationing had cut civilian use drastically. For example, civilian gasoline consumption dropped from 1 million kiloliters in 1940 to 240,000 in 1941, to 40,000 in 1944.[37] Taxi drivers and other ingenious motorists experimented with charcoal and wood-burning vehicles. Oil supplies, especially of gasoline and kerosene, were inadequate at the end of the war, but the civilian shortage was not nearly as severe as for coal and electricity.

Initial U.S. policy toward the oil-refining industry was very harsh. In October 1945, SCAP ordered all Pacific Coast refineries closed and an end to crude-oil imports as a way of slashing Japanese war potential.[38] This was because, like the Japanese, they considered oil to be a strategic rather than an economic commodity. Their actions implied that Japan should be denied free access to oil to prevent future aggressive acts. The Japanese, who were allowed to finish refining crude oil already in stock in 1945, dragged out the last refining to prevent closure, but, in Autumn 1946, SCAP reissued orders for their shutdown, due to "strategic considerations." Theoretically, this policy meant that Japan's entire oil-refining industry was considered a primary war facility, and so top priority for reparations; but most of these plants had been bombed so heavily that Pauley found no oil refineries fit for reparations. The demilitariza-

Table 4 Domestic Oil Production and Imports, 1930–1960
(1,000 kl)

Year	Domestic Production	Imported Crude	Imported Products	Total Imports
1930	317	570	1,515	2,085
1935	351	1,332	2,911	4,243
1940	331	2,292	1,922	4,214
1941	289	694	197	891
1942	263	560	6	566
1943	271	980	4	984
1944	267	209	—	209
1945	243	—	15	15
1946	213	—	151	151
1947	203	—	1,178	1,178
1948	179	—	*	*
1949	218	24	2,010	2,034
1950	328	1,541	844	2,385
1951	372	2,844	1,172	4,016
1952	339	4,432	1,022	5,454
1953	334	5,748	2,967	8,715
1954	338	7,440	2,959	10,399
1955	354	8,553	2,386	10,939
1956	350	11,438	1,900	13,338
1957	361	14,833	3,427	18,260
1958	410	16,311	1,986	18,297
1959	454	21,621	1,848	23,469
1960	593	31,116	3,238	34,354

Source: Japan Statistical Yearbook, Prime Minister's Office, 1953, pp. 202–203; 1961, p. 203.
Notes: * = not available.
1941–1946 imported products includes only gasoline, kerosene, and lubricating oil.

tion and democratization policy in oil thus affected future plans more than current oil production, by preventing reconstruction in the petroleum-refining industry.[39]

As in the case of the coal industry, SCAP emphasized exploration and development of domestic crude. Natural Resource Section's petroleum engineers, working with the semi-governmental Teikoku Petroleum Company (privatized but not deconcentrated in 1950 under the deconcentration law) and the Ministry of Commerce and Industry determined that earlier exploration had been substandard and anticipated major new finds along the coast of the Japan Sea. The Japanese were also very hopeful on this score, but were eventually disappointed. Japanese domestic reserves at their postwar peak totaled only 4.2 million kiloliters.[40]

In a unique arrangement, SCAP oil policy was made by a special civilian body attached to G-4, rather than to the Economic and Scientific Section. This Petroleum Advisory Group (PAG), established in October 1945, was composed of employees of the major oil companies on loan to the Army. These men, many of whom had prewar experience in East Asia, were to advise "the Commander in Chief on the supply to the armed forces of petroleum products and on the development of civil petroleum supply projects and agencies in this theater."[41] British representatives of Shell were allowed to join the PAG staff "as an exception to policy" limiting SCAP jobs to Americans. From 1949 on, some of the senior members of PAG left SCAP and reestablished the Tokyo offices of their own companies, which had paid their salaries while they were on loan to the military.[42]

Official U.S. policy seems to have followed the wishes of the major oil companies fairly closely in Occupied Japan. In fact, one could make a solid argument that, in the case of oil, precisely the kind of relationship existed that the economic-deconcentration policy was trying to eradicate in the *Japanese* political economy. In 1945 and 1946, it suited the major oil companies to close down their Japanese competitors. Advocating a kind of private reparations, the Chairman of the Board of Stanvac made his wishes very clear to the State Department:

Socony, with a pre-war six million dollar investment in Japan in storage and distribution equipment, fears for its investment and future operations if the Japanese are permitted to retain their post-1930 built refining capacity which provided for a *civilian* consumption of 21 million barrels in 1938 as against 12 million in 1931. Socony, therefore, calculates that the reported permitted capacity will be sufficient to care for consumption for at least five or ten years, leaving foreign distributors of refined products (imports) completely out in the cold with a useless investment and a loss of business. . . . Socony feels that unless reparations reduce Japan's capacity to the use of indigenous oil (two million barrels per year), they must request that they be allowed to acquire an interest in Japan's most modern refineries, else their fifty years' built-up trade and heavy investment will be lost.[43]

SCAP policy followed these recommendations to close most of the Japanese refining industry. In 1948, this policy was reassessed and dramatically reversed, but, until that time, Japanese refiners were limited to Japan's own crude, while the international oil companies imported refined products for the Japanese market.[44]

The Japanese thus faced formidable problems in reconstructing their economy. The tragic war itself had created tremendous burdens, but the consequences of defeat were even more severe. Constrained by Occupation policy and global mistrust, the Japanese had to invent a brand new economic strategy simply to feed and house themselves. Defeat and occupation changed the nature of domestic politics and power radically. This too called for a new approach.

FOUR

Economic Policy and the Labor Unions

Japanese texts almost uniformly refer to the first postwar years as a "period of confusion" (konranki). This term conveys the disarray of Japanese leaders in the face of defeat, Occupation reforms, and the entry of organized labor and leftist parties into the political arena. Most of all, it suggests their uncertainty about Japan's future. The Japanese policymakers in the first postwar years faced a formidable task. Not only did they have to stimulate production in scores of industries, fight inflation, and rebuild the country's battered infrastructure, but they also confronted profound questions about the desired nature of the new economy. Moreover, prewar imperialist strategies of development were closed to the Japanese after their military defeat. Many people had already rejected those strategies because of their spectacular failure.

One of the most striking aspects of immediate postwar Japan is that the initiative for economic planning passed temporarily from traditionally elite groups to historically weak ones. Labor unions, in particular, took on new importance in shaping Japan's economic future. The infant unions, notably in the coal and electric-power industries, were among the first to take on the problem of rebuilding the Japanese economy in a way that correctly analyzed the new postwar context. They moved toward a vision of a significantly altered Japanese economy, characterized by socialist control of industry and labor participation in company management. Their solution to the problem of reconstruction centered on raising the economic standard of living and political power of the Japanese working class.

This autonomous, socialist vision of the economy went unrealized, but many of its elements were incorporated into the developing postwar structure and have become distinctive characteristics of Japanese capitalism. These features included a strong focus on production as well as redistribution by the labor unions, a concept of the firm that centers more on managers and employees than on stockholders, and economic planning within the firm. The unions directed their efforts toward increasing the stability of employment and worker (and union) participation in the enterprise. At the industry and national level, the unions sought greater economic planning, partly as a way to institutionalize their own role in economic policymaking. The primary reason for planning, however, was to rebuild Japan as a high-wage economy with a greatly expanded domestic market. This was the vehicle by which the unions hoped politically and economically to transform their society.

The labor movement was able to participate in shaping the postwar economy because it grew very rapidly; 40 percent of the labor force was unionized by June 1946. This is one of the key differences between postwar Japan and earlier eras. Together with the rural land reform, it was the source of an expanded domestic consumer market (conspicuously lacking in prewar Japan) and of a mass culture based on consumption of the same goods and information. The need to rebuild Japan as a high-wage, high-value-added manufacturing nation derived in part from labor-union pressure. Their successful struggle to be accepted as legitimate actors in the economy sets the postwar years apart from earlier Japanese history.[1]

The strength and creativity of the unions were spurred by desperation. In 1945, the issue for many Japanese was one of survival. Food, shelter, heat, and a job to pay for them were the problems powering this search for new economic approaches. Shortages of all the daily necessities meant that life continued to be very hard for most Japanese after the war ended. By 1945, the economy produced airplanes rather than consumer goods; thousands lost their jobs when war plants abruptly shut down. Approximately 7.9 million people needed work in early 1946. Paychecks bought less every day as inflation whittled away their value.[2] Early Occupation policies also provided the unions unprecedented opportunity to exercise power, providing a context in which unions could, for the first time, become a potent force in Japan.

Union activity contrasted with the hesitation of the traditional elite. Military defeat and occupation had discredited business and bureaucratic communities and left them temporarily bereft of viable economic plans. Given the trend toward more planning up to 1945, the lack of an appropriate and organized plan by either the government or big business for postwar economic recovery is unexpected. The sudden end of the war caught people both in government and private business by surprise. Although some business leaders began meeting immediately after the war's end, the Occupation economic-democratization policies deflected their attention from reconstruction. These policies came as an unwelcome surprise to Japanese leaders. The Japanese elite were happy at first that Japan would be occupied by Americans rather than Russians and assumed that the United States would allow Japanese business to continue as usual. Despite the content of the Potsdam Declaration, they were totally unprepared for SCAP economic-democratization measures. Edo Hideo of the Mitsui Holding Company recalled that he and his colleagues had no idea what the Americans meant when they promised "the dissolution of the large industrial and banking combinations." When they understood that Mitsui was the target of zaibatsu dissolution, they shelved a three-year reconstruction plan they had sketched out in late August. Similarly, the head executive of Mitsubishi maintained until his death in December 1945 that his company had done nothing for which it should be punished. This difficulty in adjusting to new conditions was not limited to Mitsubishi and the other great zaibatsu, but represented the attitude of the business community in general.[3]

Without any "vision" for Japan's economy, the dominant policy response in the first year among the Japanese elite was to wait and see. This passive response incorporated some very destructive elements, however. Because the economy had been so skewed toward military production, most firms had lost their main supplier and main buyer when the war ended. Business spent much of its time in the first postwar months requesting government indemnities, participating in the disbursement of military stocks to industry as gifts, and agitating for abolition of economic controls. Inflation also totally disrupted financing and insurance for all goods. The result was that almost every major firm in postwar Japan faced bankruptcy. Moreover, business actions contributed significantly to the two biggest postwar economic problems—inflation and production decline. Given inflation and fixed prices, industrialists found it more profitable to hoard their raw materials for sale on the black market than to run their factories. This response, although rational, was a very serious obstacle to production recovery. It also contributed to the popular distrust of traditional leaders, especially after a 1948 Diet subcommittee inquiry into hoarding revealed huge caches of goods.[4]

When business leaders did provide a proposal for reconstruction in these first months, it failed to incorporate postwar political conditions. In early September 1945, the Minister of Commerce and Industry contacted the four major business federations of the time and asked them to develop a joint economic program. The businessmen responded with a set of negotiation demands for the Allied powers. They advised that the government "negotiate with the Allies with a firm determination not to concede anything vital to the survival of the Japanese nation," an attitude that was wildly inappropriate to the government's actual power. Their report went on to lay out their assumptions about the postwar Japanese economy. These included continued trade with the former colonies and revival of Manchuria, Taiwan, and Southeast Asia as raw materials suppliers to Japan. This was essentially a return to Japan's prewar industrial structure, both international and domestic, in that it relied on a low-wage export sector to pay for the expansion of capital goods. This proposal had to be totally reexamined after the Pauley Interim Report on reparations was released on 6 December 1945, shocking the business community with its punitive content.[5]

Business groups were similarly unprepared for the rapid growth of the labor movement, and were prevented by SCAP from fully mobilizing against the fledgling unions. SCAP did not allow a national employers' association until 1948, for example. Regional and industry-wide groups did organize earlier than that, especially in the coal mines, but they were still very tentative in their actions. These anemic groups as yet gave little indication of the powerful force they would become. The labor policies of the business groups thus tended to be responses to the unions in the first year. They did indicate some of the directions in which Japanese employers would later move, notably a rejection of government control within the firm and a preference for single-enterprise labor-management bargaining.[6]

The bureaucrats at the MCI, which had solicited the September proposal, and other government officials shared in the erroneous assumption that SCAP was planning to leave the economic structure much as it had always been. They had expected American policy toward the economy to be one of benign neglect and were unpleasantly surprised by the economic reforms and the upsurge of labor unions. During the Shidehara Administration, Foreign Minister Yoshida Shigeru spent long hours in an unsuccessful attempt to protect Mitsui from the dissolution program, while the Finance Ministry was immobilized by American economic reforms. The unexpectedness of the labor organizing drive meant that, for example, the Ministry of Education lost all opportunities to control the early postwar teachers' organizations, although it had successfully done so before the war.[7] An influential Japanese report dated September 1946 stated that "the government, which has lost the capability of comprehensive planning and leadership, remained an idle onlooker of the collapse of wartime control system and of the resultant confusion of the economic community." Similarly, "the industrial circles . . . not knowing what to do with the uncertain outlook and restraints in various fields . . . are marking time in vain. Definite ideas are lacking both in the government and private circles as to the direction in which and the means by which the postwar economy should be reconstructed." This response of marking time in confusion contributed to the ongoing economic stagnation.[8]

It is in this context of widespread confusion in both business and government circles that the labor and other popular movements developed. The sudden end to the war and the lack of ongoing political movements, due to their wartime repression, meant that few people had any clear sense of direction. The feeling that a change was necessary was strong, but coordinated plans were rare. Nevertheless, although ordinary Japanese shared the confusion of the elites in the face of these new conditions, they were the first to overcome them by devising methods for economic recovery.

The rapid growth of unions in the first year was not centrally directed. Rather, unions of all types sprang up independently throughout the country in response to the new political freedoms and the terrible economic hardships. Unions most commonly organized in the enterprise, or plant, rather than a whole firm or industry.[9] This striking institutional feature of Japanese work place organization has endured to this day. The much-studied enterprise-union system has both strengths and weaknesses from the union point of view. It allowed Japanese workers to mobilize very rapidly and effectively. However, its limitations emerge at a larger level, notably lack of communication across firms in an industry and vulnerability to cooption by management. Officials of the electric-power workers' union, Densan, and the coal miners' union were aware of these weaknesses but were not able to resolve them. Both unions shared the goal of industry-wide unity and the power that came with unity, although this proved elusive in the coal miners' case; the terrible factional divisions within the union were a barrier, while Densan ultimately perished over this issue in 1952.[10]

SŌDŌMEI AND SANBETSU

The unions represented only one of several strands of popular movements in postwar Japan.[11] Tenants' rights groups sprang up in the countryside as soon as the war was over, as did an array of political movements. In the political sphere, the Socialist and Communist parties both participated in union organizing, partly as a way to develop a political constituency. Thus, in early 1946, when

the new unions began to organize into national industrial federations, two separate inter-industry coalitions emerged, associated with
the two parties. These were Sōdōmei, the Japanese Federation of
Labor, and Sanbetsu, the Congress of Industrial Unions, each with
approximately 1 million members. In August 1946, the two federations began operating as competing organizations. Their rivalry
weakened the new labor movement, and much energy in the next
few years was consumed by political infighting.

Their platforms did not differ significantly at first. Sōdōmei, the
Socialist Party affiliate, pledged to work for improved laboring conditions and benefits, full employment and revived production, collective bargaining and labor-management committees, and recognition of the negotiation tactic of worker takeovers of production.
They also called for immediate socialization of banking, production, and distribution, and declared that labor unions must take
responsibility for economic reconstruction. Sanbetsu, which was more
loosely associated with the Communist Party, three weeks later
adopted a similar platform. Sanbetsu, especially its radical left wing,
was to retain this platform much longer, however, as Sōdōmei drifted
toward a policy of greater accommodation with employers.[12]

In the early years, Sanbetsu was the more active of the federations, and more impatient about compromise with the Japanese
government. Its members believed that the union movement should
be as broad-based and coordinated as possible. This implied that
real power would ideally reside in the national industry-wide and
inter-industry federations rather than in the enterprise unions. With
this end in mind, the "October offensive" of autumn 1946 was
organized as a series of strikes in different fields which could reinforce each other and help Sanbetsu affiliates win 3 demands. These
were industry-wide contracts, cost-of-living mechanisms, and guarantees to unions against mass firings in the prevailing shaky economic conditions.[13] Sanbetsu and its member unions moved toward
a solution to the problem of economic reconstruction based on the
assumption that labor had to take primary responsibility for the task
of reviving production and that a socialist state should play a major
role in economic planning and operations. Management was to play

only a minor role in this scenario. Sōdōmei did not press for this autonomous vision of labor unions for very long. Instead it stressed labor-management cooperation through joint councils. Like Sanbetsu, however, its focus was on increasing production as well as on redistribution. Sōdōmei supported nationalization of the coal mines, but in general became less enthusiastic than Sanbetsu about state control.

Sanbetsu was originally the more effective wing of the labor movement because of its more coherent vision and creative tactics. It was also the leading force in the general strike movement of early 1947. It lost much of its prestige, however, when MacArthur canceled the general strike, due to Sanbetsu's miscalculation of SCAP's reaction. At that point, the labor movement as a whole moved toward electoral tactics to effect political change and voted in a Socialist-led coalition Cabinet in April 1947. This tactical shift also meant a stronger position for the Socialist-affiliated Sōdōmei federation and Sōdōmei's more conciliatory stance toward managers.

From 1947, it was increasingly obvious that the Sanbetsu vision of a socialist economy led by autonomous unions was unlikely to develop in Japan. Sanbetsu simply did not have the power to impose its independent and alternative economic program on the whole nation. Yet it would be a mistake to dismiss the union federation as of no historical significance. Although unable to create a socialist economic structure, the Sanbetsu unions did affect the reconstruction of the capitalist structure. Their priorities helped shape the basic orientation of postwar economic policy in Japan, particularly through the efforts of the coal and electric-power workers.

The scope and speed of labor-union organizing were particularly dramatic in coal and electric power. Planning in those industries could not proceed without active cooperation from the unions in the first postwar years. This was established early by strikes and work stoppages, especially in the coal industry where working conditions had been particularly vicious. Both the coal and electric-power workers were important Sanbetsu affiliates, and their actions set the tone for unions in many other industries. Both unions are famous for their innovative tactics and militancy, with the coal miners more oriented toward direct action and the electric-power workers more skillful at winning mediated disputes. These two unions were tactical and strategic trailblazers for the postwar labor movement.

ENERGY INDUSTRY UNIONS: ZENTAN AND DENSAN

COAL MINERS. Japanese surrender freed the foreign conscript miners. These workers were the first in Japan to organize and the first to develop the direct-action tactics for which the miners became famous. The Chinese, as nationals of a victor nation, immediately asserted their new civil rights. The Chinese workers at Mitsubishi Bibai mine left work on 15 August, one hour after the Emperor announced that Japan would "endure the unendurable and suffer what is insufferable."[14] They seized control of their barracks in the mine compounds, but still received only starvation rations and could not leave the mine area. On 18 September, they demanded better food, a distribution of clothing, and their personal liberty, and, on 19 September, fought their way past mine guards and the police to visit the Chinese at Mitsui Bibai, where they joined forces. From there, the two groups went out to "inspect conditions of treatment" of Chinese workers at other Hokkaido mines.

This escalated into a major clash with mine, police, and Occupation authorities. The incident began on the 23rd, when 150 Chinese miners from Bibai were stopped by 60 police officers and mine officials outside Mitsubishi Yūbari. They submitted their demands for more food, clothing, and personal liberty for the Yūbari miners locked inside. They were orderly and law-abiding, but the following day they slipped in a back way. The Chinese at Yūbari, where conditions had been especially bad, rebelled and rioted. They beat up two mine officials and killed a Chinese miner who had avowed that "we are not treated cruelly by the company." They took the mine manager and the police chief hostage and demanded food, clothing, and 100 yen for each Chinese miner.

At that time, a telegram arrived from the U.S. officials in Hokkaido, ordering the Chinese to return to the mines. Four hundred police and 350 militiamen, who had been waiting for this signal, arrived and arrested all the Chinese. Six people were killed or wounded in the battle between the augmented police force and the Chinese at Yūbari. A proclamation of the Colonel of the U.S. Eighth Army empowered the Japanese police to arrest and shoot to death the Chinese.[15]

American actions during this episode, although not in keeping with the reform policy, were an accurate reflection of the military attitude toward civilian disorder. The Eighth Army was involved in several mine skirmishes on the side of the owners in the first months of the Occupation, mainly against the foreign miners. On 1 November, SCAP issued a proclamation specifically addressed to the foreign miners, ordering them to dig coal for the Occupation forces. This was insensitive, since the Americans had been made aware of the nightmarish conditions inside the mines by the Western prisoners of war there.[16] It was also unenforceable when the miners vigorously resisted this order, demanding to be sent home. This was an awkward situation, and the Americans began to reconsider their posture.

Korean laborers soon followed the Chinese example. On 2 October, the nearly 7,000 Korean miners at the Hokutan Yūbari mine in Hokkaido formed a workers' union and went out on strike for two days. They demanded transportation back to Korea, better food and the right to distribute it among themselves, and a raise of a total of 3 million yen to equalize wages between Korean and Japanese workers, including an immediate distribution of 50,000 yen. At about the same time, Korean miners in the Jōban fields in northern Honshu independently formed a union with similar demands. They also joined with the Chinese miners to insist that an investigation be made into the hoarded stocks of goods at the mines and that these be distributed equally to themselves and to the Japanese workers. From this time, the Chinese and Koreans worked together to form unions throughout the Hokkaido and Jōban regions.[17] However, although the Korean and Chinese formed unions, their primary goal was to return home, not permanently to change their workplace.

From early November, SCAP decided that acceding to the for-

eign miners' demand for repatriation was the wisest course and col-
laborated with the Japanese government in a speedy repatriation
program. The activities of the foreign miners had caused a huge
drop in coal production. SCAP ordered "a special priority . . . for
the repatriation of Chinese and Korean coal miners residing in
Northern Honshu. They will be evacuated at a rate of 1,000 per
day beginning not later than 14 November 1945."[18] By the end of
December, most of them had been sent home.[19]

Japanese miners in Hokkaido, who did have a stake in the future
of the coal industry, were already well organized by the end of
1945.[20] Beginning in October, the foreign miners had encouraged
the Japanese miners, whose working conditions compared favorably
only to their own, to organize. The Japanese miners in Hokkaido
soon created a regional body, the Hokkaido Federation of Mine
Workers' Unions (Hokkaidō Kōzan Rōdō Kumiai Rengōkai). Established on 10 November 1945, it was renamed the Hokkaido
Federation of Coal Miners Unions (Hokkaidō Tankō Rōdō Kumiai)
in February 1946. Preparations began in February 1946 for Zentan,
a national coal-miners' union, founded on April 22.[21]

The coal miners suffered, however, from the same factional disputes as the labor movement in general. While Zentan was strong
in Hokkaido, two competing unions in Kyushu weakened the labor
movement there. In general, workers in the small Kyushu mines
affiliated with the Sōdōmei union, and those in the big mines with
the Kyushu arm of Zentan. Then, some of the biggest mines formed
unaffiliated enterprise unions rather than joining regional federations. Even in Hokkaido, one union activist described his local as
constantly disbanding and re-forming over political and strategic
disagreements. The differences among the various unions and federations posed a major problem for labor unity in the mines.[22]

The coal miners were among the most aggressive unions. They
did not hesitate to engage in direct actions, including violence.
This was partly because their working conditions, wages, and status
were especially low. What is perhaps more surprising is that they
were also quite disciplined and turned their energy in constructive
directions. This is probably due to the presence of politically expe-

rienced leaders among both the Chinese and Japanese miners. Moreover, since mining takes place in isolated areas, the miners could
organize their entire local communities behind them. The importance of the coal industry to the national economy and the high
level of controls on it also made industry-wide settlements easier to
achieve, explaining much of the coal miners' militancy and their
success.[23]

One of the first of these direct actions was the "public negotiations" initiated by the Mitsubishi Yūbari miners in October 1945,
when the company refused to recognize their fledgling union. This
was the first use of mass negotiating techniques, or simple intimi-
dation by numbers, by the labor movement. Yūbari was the mine
where the Chinese had fought the police, and the environment there
was already very tense. The "direct negotiations" at Yūbari were
actually a *de-escalation* to nonviolence, although the implied threat
that the orderly union meeting could become an angry mob undoubtedly was crucial. In the face of these "public negotiations,"
the manager immediately accepted the union demands.

The mass-negotiation tactic was repeated at Mitsubishi Bibai in
February 1946, when the mine manager and two assistant managers
were forced to undergo a "people's court." After three months of
fruitless negotiations, about 1,000 miners decided at a mass meeting on 17 February to make the mine managers respond in person
to their demands for higher wages and participation in management. The miners captured the three men at their executive retreat
and forced them to defend themselves against the charges of mal-
treating the miners. As Joe Moore has recounted, this was an emotional event for all concerned. The "people's court," lasting for 32
hours, consisted of testimony by miners and their families about the
hardship of their lives. Moore quotes a participant's account of an
elderly woman who broke down in the crowded room after telling
the managers, "We worry about something to eat every day, every
day, and it feels like we will go crazy over getting something to
eat. While I'm standing here right now I'm thinking about what
we will eat this evening."[24] The involvement of the families in this

event presaged the importance of whole-community organizing to the coal miners in later disputes.

This court, similar to the later "self-criticism sessions" of revolutionary China, was a terrifying experience for the managers but a deeply satisfying exercise for the miners. Until the end of the war, miners had no rights to protest their slave-like working conditions or to bargain collectively. The "people's courts," which were a negotiating technique rather than a trial, represented a demand for political power by a group that had been at the bottom of Japanese society and were the first exercise by a union of the right to bargain collectively in postwar Japan. The most important issue for the coal-mine unions, according to one miner, was human rights. He meant both an end to the beatings and incarceration and the extension of common courtesy to miners by employers. The "people's court" was a way of demanding that respect.[25] Moreover, the tactic worked. The cowed managers at Mitsubishi Bibai agreed to large wage increases, paid vacations, health coverage, democratic reforms of the company, and formation of a labor-management council. This was a tremendously potent model for other Japanese workers. The message was simple: If the wretched coal miners could demand rights, so could everyone.

The coal miners underscored this message by accepting responsibility for revival of the economy. In fact, their attitude contrasted favorably with the foot-dragging of the coal operators. The miners were able to combine disputes over wages and work conditions with their pledge to dig coal through the important tactic of "production control." Production control consisted of running a business without the supervision of the managers. MacArthur had specifically disallowed strikes in the coal mines as "inimical to the objectives of the Occupation."[26] Since this left the miners bereft of their most powerful weapon, they were very interested in the tactics of the *Yomiuri* newspaper union, which took over control of that paper in late October 1945 and ran it without management. This imaginative tactic had the beauty of maintaining—and often increasing—production while still retaining the power of a strike.

One of the first production-control incidents was a Mitsui Bibai mine in December 1945, after the company failed to respond to demands for a wage raise, an end to the crew-boss system, guarantees of food, and discharge of corrupt mine officials. One of the regional union leaders knew about the *Yomiuri* production-control incident and suggested that the same tactic be used in the mines. He explained later that he had favored production control because "the workers themselves must shoulder the burden of industrial reconstruction for a new Japan."[27] Production control lasted at Mitsui Bibai for 12 days. During that time, coal output doubled over the preceding 12-day period, despite a cut in daily work hours from 12 to 8. Neither side in the dispute budged until the Hokkaido government mediated, but then, in late December, the union won most of its demands.

This impressed the other Hokkaido miners' unions. In February 1946, miners at neighboring Mitsubishi Bibai instituted production control after the company cut back on previously negotiated wage raises.[28] It was while this mine was under production control that the workers staged the "people's court." The miners delivered a statement to the managers that took full responsibility for raising production. "Due to the fact that our legitimate demands have been denied, we will all begin production control on 8 February, in order to exercise our rights and responsibilities. This is so that we can complete the valuable work that we have been assigned as our legal duty."[29] Production control allowed the union to paint itself as patriotic and constructive.

The Shidehara Cabinet had been unsure of what to do about production control, but the Yoshida Cabinet officials saw production control as a direct attack on private property and denounced it vigorously. Their unease grew when the unions, blockaded by government organs and firms that would not buy their production, began selling directly to consumers. This tactic would have meant the creation of an alternative and independent avenue of economic recovery and, therefore, loss of economic power for both the bureaucracy and established business management. The Yoshida Government's first response was to treat production control as an illegal act, but SCAP ordered the administration to submit the question of legality to the courts and prevented any repressive action until the court had ruled.[30]

Employers also denounced production control. In June or July 1946, the industry trade group, the Japan Coal Mining Association, issued a 4-point statement denouncing production control as an obstacle to production, as an attack by the union on the firm, as the result of excessive behavior on the part of the union (like people's courts), and, finally, as disruptive to general economic planning and rationing in Japan. They were also embarrassed by the unions' tactics. When coal output rose during a production-control campaign, it lent credence to the union arguments that employers were shirking their responsibility to provide coal to Japan.[31]

Both the Socialist and Communist Parties were divided over production control. The Communist Party did not lead the unions into use of this tactic, although individual Zentan officials were Communist Party members. Many Party organizers in both groups saw it as a challenge to their leadership, since it shifted momentum away from the Party and, in the case of Sōdōmei, from national union headquarters to the workplace.[32] This meant that the workers who engaged in production control not only were not led by the directives of the political parties; they did not even have consistent support for their actions. Although the leftist parties supported production control ideologically, they opposed it in practice as a threat to their own political power.

SCAP's attitude that production control was an acceptable labor tactic shifted as SCAP officials gradually became uneasy about the consequences. In June 1946, MacArthur issued a warning against direct action that was widely interpreted as a criticism of production-control tactics. In response to this and to continued government pressure, the number of production-control incidents decreased from that time.[33]

The movement away from direct-action tactics such as production control focused attention on another important vehicle for worker-centered economic policy, the labor-management councils. These councils provided for labor participation in management within an existing firm. They were originally proposed by unions, beginning in 1945. In August 1946, both Sōdōmei and Sanbetsu adopted a plank supporting these councils as part of their founding platforms. The Sōdōmei unions put particular stress on labor-management councils, and they became a central part of that federation's organizing strategy. They appealed to Sōdōmei's more evolutionary vision of change, its desire to maintain central control over its member unions, and the federation's sense of rivalry with Sanbetsu. The Sanbetsu affiliates saw the councils more as a transitional—but important—step toward socialist control of industry. They also thought of the councils as *part* of an organizing strategy that also included more autonomous actions. There was a certain theoretical inconsistency to this, since the labor-management councils provided a forum for workers and executives to cooperate, while production control rendered the managers redundant. However, unions like Zentan adopted both types of demands.

When production control was popular, Japanese business and government leaders encouraged labor-management councils as an alternative. A new business organization, Keizai Dōyūkai, warmly endorsed the concept of labor-management councils as an explicit alternative to production control, at its first meeting on 30 April 1946. Keizai Dōyūkai was composed of younger Japanese businessmen, who were alarmed by the continuing inability of senior industrialists to respond to either the economic collapse or to labor-union demands. They proposed a new approach of "modified capitalism," which would involve greater economic planning and the separation of management and capital. In a major departure from other business groups, Keizai Dōyūkai's ideas involved a more stable, cooperative relationship between managers and workers within a firm. Keizai Dōyūkai, which describes its most fundamental characteristic as "progressiveness" and its mission as "preservation of democracy," presented a two-edged response to the labor unions. The business organization both attempted to control the labor movement and to meet its legitimate concerns for a functioning economy and a more stable position within it. Labor-management councils seemed to Keizai Dōyūkai the best means to reach this dual end.[34]

Keizai Dōyūkai members realized that, when Japanese industrialists had allowed workers to take the initiative on production recovery, they had lost much of their power to shape the nature of that recovery. These businessmen fervently believed they could only regain the respect of the Japanese people by actively working toward rebuilding the economy. The labor-management councils provided a way to do so and, at the same time, harness the energy of labor-union members to mutually acceptable goals. In contrast, production control not only moved the labor unions farther away from cooperation; it also made the managers marginal to reconstruction. Thus, Keizai Dōyūkai worked together with Sōdōmei for recognition of these councils.

Participation in the labor-management councils signaled commitment to economic reconstruction in postwar Japan. By agreeing to work with labor unions, managers hoped to recoup legitimacy. This was also true of the Economic Reconstruction Committees which were established at the whole-economy and industry levels. Like the labor-management councils on which they were based, these committees were originally proposed by the unions. Both Sōdōmei and Sanbetsu set up Reconstruction Committees in the coal industry first and other industries later as a way to increase production. In May 1946, the Sōdōmei unions founded a Coal Reconstruction Committee, arguing that the way to "conquer the production crisis" in coal was through "industrial democratization and economic planning." Similarly, Sanbetsu pledged to raise coal production in August 1946 through local, regional, and national Coal Reconstruction Committees, which would serve as "the battlefront of industrial democratization" and of economic planning. In October, Keizai Dōyūkai and Sōdōmei began negotiating a joint national Economic Reconstruction Committee, which Sanbetsu, the major business groups, and several government agencies later joined. As with the labor-management councils, Keizai Dōyūkai believed that managers had to demonstrate their willingness to revive production, especially of coal. Thus, they were ready to join this union-sponsored program.[35] The labor-management councils and Economic Reconstruction Committees were the product of compromise accepted by an elite, which hoped to avoid giving more by giving something. They stressed the goal of raising production—something that conferred legitimacy on all the parties who participated. In the coal industry in particular, they were important vehicles for restoring production levels.

Once the labor-management councils had been adopted, the next point was to determine the range of their powers. Typically, the unions wanted them to be active decision-making bodies with full responsibility for management, while the executives hoped to limit them to a more passive role. This meant constant, small battles between the unions and managers within each firm over the scope and influence of their council. In practice, each council was as strong as its union. Over time, they grew less powerful as the labor movement as a whole lost power. Koji Taira found in a 1970 study that, while in 1949 72 percent of the unions that had joint councils were actively involved in production decisions, by 1957 only 45 percent were.[36]

A major production-control incident in April 1946 occurred at the Hokkaido Colliery and Steamship Company (Hokutan).[37] This dispute was notable in part because the demands were for economic and political democratization as well as for wages. Specifically, the union wanted: (1) the right to bargain collectively, (2) dismissal of several company officials, (3) an end to distinctions between blue-collar and white-collar workers, (4) a management council with 2 worker representatives for each management representative, (5) democratic revamping of the local neighborhood association, and (6) several other points, such as reinstatement of workers who had been fired for union activity. The company gave in on all but what it considered the main issue, the management council. Instead, it agreed to a consultative council, with little union power. In this case, the council became not a vehicle for labor participation in managing the company but a glorified suggestion box. Hokutan was unusual in that the management took such a firm stand on the actual power of these councils from the beginning. This was probably the influence of one man, Maeda Hajime, who later founded a national employers' organization, Nikkeiren, to fight for management prerogatives.[38] In most firms, the scope of the councils was very broad at first, but, as management reorganized, it fought to limit the range of discussion within them.

The government and business leaders who had advocated labor-management councils in 1946 withdrew their support later. When the menace of autonomous labor power through production control subsided, the active councils lost much of their appeal for employers. From 1948, the newly formed Nikkeiren aggressively campaigned against strong joint labor-management councils. The government shifted its position as well. In 1948, the Vice-Director of the Economic Stabilization Board told a Diet committee that labor unrest and specifically labor-management councils were among the obstacles to foreign investment.[39]

The history of the labor-management councils demonstrates both the achievements and the limits of labor organizing in postwar Japan. The unions were able to establish the principle that workers had a legitimate interest in management. This was far from the official wartime ideal of workers under military discipline. Yet, the unions had not fully worked out the implications of their demands for economic democracy or their strategies for achieving it. They were inconsistent and at times accepted the role of obedient and loyal subordinate that was assigned to them by their employers and the government. Their vision of Japan's economic future remained vague and incomplete. The demand for "democratization of management" tended to get pushed behind the urgent concerns of wages and job security, especially after the most galling daily inequities had been met, such as switching to more respectful forms of verbal address.

Yet, the importance of the union demands for greater power lies in the fact that Japan was at a crossroads in its social and economic organization. Defeat and occupation had created both the opportunity and the necessity for profound reevaluation of Japan's future. Simply by exploring alternatives to conservative rule and capitalist economic organization, the Sanbetsu unions had broken some of the barriers to change. They were often lost and confused in the new territory in which they found themselves, but the act of cutting their own road weakened the authority of the traditional guides.

ELECTRIC-POWER WORKERS. The electric-power workers' union was one of the first to recognize the importance of this process and is widely recognized as a trailblazer in postwar Japanese industrial relations. The electric-power workers pushed as far as designing a new organizational structure for their industry, one that featured a greatly enhanced role for labor. Their ability to institutionalize labor concerns and unions is reflected in the Japanese economy today.

The electric-power workers labored in a highly centralized industry, which aided their organizing drive. Their union, Densan, like most Japanese unions, was enterprise-based, but, since there were only 10 major power companies, this still meant large and powerful units. Densan did not have to contend with a strong rival union in its early years. The first area to unionize was the Tokyo local, the Kantō Haiden Rōdō Kumiai, established on 8 December 1945, with 16,000 members. By 7 April 1946, all the locals except Hokkaido were organized and affiliated in the Densan Rōkyō (Zen Nihon Denki Sangyō Rōdō Kumiai Kyōgikai) federation, later reorganized as a single national union, and renamed Densan (Nihon Denki Sangyō Rōdō Kumiai).[40] By October 1946, the union boasted over 120,000 workers.

Electric workers were on the average more skilled, had been on the job longer, and had a higher education than the typical Japanese worker (certainly than the average coal miner). In an August 1947 survey of Densan officers, 29 of the 92 people questioned had achieved a high-school or college degree (31.6 percent). Densan also favored non-antagonistic forms of pressure rather than the direct confrontations of the miners. Densan workers initiated several new struggle techniques, such as coordinated power blackouts, carefully designed to avoid areas declared "essential" by the Occupation. They generally stayed within the framework of law, creatively inventing legal ways to pressure for change. For these reasons, Densan was called "the intellectual union."[41] Densan workers represented a very different segment of the labor force from the Zentan miners, but they worked well together, perhaps because both were imaginative and daring in their own ways.

The first major union action was by the young Kantō Haiden union in January 1946, which used a "business-strike" tactic to win its demands. This involved providing power, but refraining from any office work, such as billing customers.[42] They demanded a contract guaranteeing a 50-percent increase in wages, an 8-hour workday, the establishment of a monthly wage system, more democratic work organization, union participation in management, and payment of the workers' electric-light bills by the company. (They won all but this last point.) This combination of demands and the principles behind them were representative of Densan's platform for the next several years. By October 1946, when Densan participated in the Sanbetsu "October labor offensive," these principles had been boiled down to 3 demands: (1) establishment of a minimum-wage system based on the cost of living, (2) improvement in the retirement-pay system, and (3) democratization of the electric-power industry. These 3 demands were the core of the Densan platform through 1949.[43]

The electric-power workers, like the coal miners, fought for industry-wide collective bargaining agreements. They formed Densan Rōkyō as a tightly organized federation in order to more effectively pressure the managers toward that end. Although the member unions continued to bargain separately with their companies, they all followed an 8-point set of guidelines, set up when Densan Rōkyō was created.[44] The new federation also had an activities policy, which specified that actions of member unions should be in the interests of the entire industry, rather than one enterprise and its union. Later, Densan members agreed that their activities should be directed toward the 3 goals of wages, industry-wide contracts, and democratization of the industry.[45] By these efforts, the electric-power workers were able to establish an industry-wide union through the Occupation years.

The high inflation of the first postwar years meant that wage increases were a continual focus. Although the Kantō Haiden union and the larger Hassōden union won, respectively, 50- and 30-percent wage increases in January 1946, inflation soon whittled away the size of their raises. In both coal and electric power, the combination of inflation and labor strength meant that the companies had to put out a much higher percentage of their holdings for wages than in previous eras.[46] This involved not only firms but also the government and national treasury, because the government aided both industries with subsidies and low cost loans (which were de facto subsidies since they rarely were repaid). Densan's solution to this conflict was to have ramifications for all Japanese labor.

Densan's major contribution of a new wage *system* was the single most important step both in regularizing the wage bill and in altering the tone of management-labor relations in immediate postwar Japan. First, union successes meant that companies, and ultimately the government, had to find more money to pay wages. Second, the Densan wage system established wages as a fixed cost to firms that could not be cut without reneging on the union contract. This is often cited as a key difference between Japanese and American firms. Treatment of labor as a fixed cost also affected national policy by strengthening the trend toward a more planned economy. The Densan wage system created a formula for wage payments that a firm or the Economic Stabilization Board could use to project future costs. Third, it eliminated routine wage discrimination within a firm on the basis of education, status, or whim of the employer. Fourth, it established the principle that wages should be linked to a minimum standard of living and provided a mechanism to do this. Finally, the sophistication of the plan itself—from a union established less than a year earlier—forced respect from employers, the government, and the Central Labor Relations Board. These effects went far beyond Densan workers in that, for the first time, the new agreement provided a general standard for wage levels in all Japanese industry.[47]

The system included a standard base wage for all union members, which was calculated to provide for the minimum needs of the worker and family. This was the bulk of the average wage, 68.2 percent when it was first established. Supplementary allowances were added on the basis of seniority (3.7 percent), skill level (19.4 percent), and regional and seasonal allowances (8.7 percent).[48] The minimum standard of living was pegged to *current* real prices and the union suggested that wages be recalculated when these prices changed. This "slide" mechanism allowed the unions to adjust their wages for inflation within a set framework. Because of its rationality and flexibility, the Densan wage system quickly became the model for wage decisions in many other industries "and it marks an epochal point in the history of salary systems of Japan," as even an official corporate chronicle recognized.[49]

The union's new wage structure had important implications for national macroeconomic policy. In the words of Ōkōchi Kazuo, "This Densan type of wage structure threatened the capitalist plan to reconstruct the Japanese economy through capital accumulation by the means of pegging wages while allowing prices to rise."[50] Its adoption by firms across the country meant that workers' real earnings increased as well as their nominal inflation-swollen wages. This prevented the use of inflation to return to the kind of low-wage economy first envisioned by business and government leaders at the end of the war. On a more general plane, the unions were trying to institutionalize themselves within the Japanese economy. By encouraging a wage system and a more planned economy, they could also include a secure place within it for organized labor.

Densan's wage system was part of an attempt by the unions to increase economic planning at the national level. The Economic Reconstruction Conferences were another manifestation of this. They focused on planning in order to raise the important question of whom the postwar economy was supposed to serve. Japan had few resources in these years, and had to pick and choose which of the many important areas could be aided and which had to be neglected for a while longer. The unions wanted some input into these basic decisions, which they correctly understood would affect Japanese society for decades to come. Planning was to be the vehicle for democratic participation in the economy.

Economic planning and all political action by the Japanese unions was a very controversial issue, and SCAP vetoed many union moves on the grounds that they were excessively political in nature. Even so, the Chief of the Labor Division of ESS, Theodore Cohen, explained the political involvement of the unions as follows: "Politicizing could not be avoided. The circumstances of the years 1945 to 1947, where so much of what counted for the worker—food rations, price controls, wage restrictions—was determined by government action and not by employers, as well as the political history of the Japanese labor movement, predisposed workers to thinking in political terms."[51] The Americans stood alone in their assumption that this was unnatural. At that time, Japanese from across the political spectrum understood that economic decisions were inherently political.

In the electric-power industry, industrial democratization continued to be one of the electric-power workers' 3 main demands from 1946 to 1952. This was not simply rhetoric. Densan submitted a report on industry democratization at each major meeting, and the union's central committee maintained a standing subcommittee on democratization, revealing the importance that its members placed on the issue.[52] Democratization meant two general categories of reform. The first was internal to the firm. This included things like firing "anti-democratic" or militarist managers, and removing status distinctions and petty regulations. Hassōden agreed to both these points "in principle" when it settled with its union in February 1946.[53] The second type of democratization involved a widening of the control of industry to include labor. The demand for labor-management councils in existing firms (also agreed to by Hassōden in 1946) was the most common manifestation of this desire. Densan pushed its attack on bureaucratic and capitalist control of its industry farther than any other union, to the point of proposing a new form of management for the entire industry.[54]

Densan was disenchanted with the inefficient and repressive bureaucratic control of the industry that had been instituted during the China and Pacific Wars. The union leaders warned that continuing this system would enhance the political power of the bureaucracy and politicize their industry. However, the power workers did not want to return to the prewar system of privately owned and operated electric-power companies. Instead, on 7 October 1946, Densan Rōkyō proposed to the electric-power companies that their industry be governed by a commission, composed of general members of the public rather than by the MCI. Later, the union suggested a tripartite committee of capitalists, workers, and consumers. Densan called for new laws to socialize the electric-power industry along these lines. The union wanted to run the industry as a non-profit public utility, characterized by "separation of capital and management" and "denial of the search for profits." Finally, Densan argued for one unified generating, transmission, and distribution company. The union argued that this was technically a superior form of organization, and also that it was socially more adapted to Japan's needs.[55]

The council was to be a transitional system. Densan argued that, "in the future when a democratic government has been achieved, then we can have state control of the industry."[56] The electric-power workers were critical of the reactionary bureaucracy with which they had dealt, but this was a criticism based on distrust of the specific government in power rather than of state control itself.

The employers accepted Densan's proposals for reorganization of Hassōden and the Haiden and a new commission to establish "socialization of the electric power industry" on 7 October, pledging further that "complete agreement has been reached on these points and we will cooperate fully to bring them into existence."[57] Not only was this set of goals accepted by the employers; it was also endorsed by the Yoshida Administration. On 24 December 1946, Hoshijima Nirō, the Minister of Commerce and Industry, released a statement that "the Japanese government concurs that the electric-power industry should be privatized, and endorses the plan already drawn up by the employers and employees to establish a committee to study this problem." The government statement went on to detail the composition of the proposed committee and methods of selecting members so that they would represent labor, management, and the general public in the form of outside experts.[58] This report was also sanctioned by the Central Labor Relations Committee in its first important case.

The Densan proposal led to a committee established within the industry-wide labor-management liaison group, (Denki Jigyō Min-shuka Kyōgikai). It held its first meeting on 21 January 1947 and deliberated for nine months, but could not resolve a stalemate between the labor and management representatives. Finally, on 15 September 1947, Densan filed a grievance with the Central Labor Relations Board for breach of contract and submitted an independent bill to the Diet for centralization and socialization of the power industry. (This was during the Katayama Cabinet's attempts to establish state control of the coal industry, which hurt Densan's chances.) The bill, like the earlier Densan proposal, called for a single, integrated electric-power company, privately owned but operated by a committee of labor, management, consumers, and outside experts under state guidance. It retained the strict division between ownership and management that had characterized Hassō-den. Densan still pledged to "abolish autocratic bureaucratic control" of the industry. However, the state had assumed a larger oversight role in the union's program, reflecting Densan's disillusionment with the joint labor-management committee. In August, the Japan Socialist Party submitted a similar proposal, except that it was for a state-owned *and* operated firm. Neither bill passed the fall session of the Diet, and both were still stalled in committee when the 10 power companies were ordered to reorganize by the Holding Company Liquidation Commission in February 1948, on the basis of the Economic Deconcentration Law. From that time, the reorganization question moved into a different realm.

Densan drew from a variety of sources in its exploration of planning and state control. The most obvious was socialist theory, but the union also drew on Japanese fascist theory, which shared important points of congruence with socialism. This gave Densan's radical ideas continuity with official wartime thinking and traditional values, and so made them more generally acceptable. For example, the idea that workers had a duty to produce and to work hard was carried over from the war years *by the unions* in their use of the production-control tactic rather than the strike. This residue of fascist thinking gave their dispute actions legitimacy because the workers accepted the obligations they had been assigned under war-time ideology.

Similarly, the union advocated state control of the electric-power industry out of a sense that basic commodities, by natural right, should be available for the good of all citizens. This notion, that people have a right to basic commodities and that private companies, whose first responsibility is to their stockholders, are less reliable providers, is one that the unions shared with the fascist military reformers of the 1930s, who had originally centralized the industries. This was an assumption held by a large cross-section of the population, and represents the intersection of socialist and corporatist thinking. "Socialization" was not a great leap from the structure of organization in existence in many industries in Japan in 1945. A large number of industries (and other services, such as news gathering) had been centralized under state direction during the war. These industries were seen as crucial to the people's livelihood, giving the state a greater responsibility and right to intervene. In fact, Densan's wage system drew directly on unsuccessful wartime bureaucratic proposals for a wage system based on livelihood needs. Harking back to a much older tradition, the demand for a "right to a livelihood" also echoed Tokugawa-era petitions for tax relief based on what Stephen Vlastos called the "right to continue as peasants."[59] This "right to a livelihood" concept was the basis for Densan's wage system.

The idea that the individual needs of firms or workers should be sacrificed to the national good was not new in postwar Japan. This fascist formulation of the problem had been transmitted to the labor movement through the wartime national labor front, Sanpō, which stressed the need to think in terms of the national good rather than of a single firm's profit.[60] What was new was that the unions demanded the right to help determine what constituted the good of the whole nation instead of leaving the interpretation of this question to the managers and bureaucrats. The ideology of the traditional elite that the nation should act in concert lingered on beyond that elite's capacity to determine the content of such actions. This theoretical continuity with traditional formulations of economic problems made Densan and the other unions seem much less radical than they might otherwise have appeared. Their "socialist" vision sparked a positive response from Japanese across the political spectrum.

The labor unions provided a new and key element in postwar Japan, which the Japanese elite had to accommodate to a greater degree than ever before. Union efforts ensured a higher standard of living for workers, a larger and institutionalized role for unions, and more careful planning of the economy. The unions were unable to transform the economy as they had hoped, but this fundamental reshaping of the postwar economy and the minds of postwar policymakers survived. Moreover, union emphasis on production and on planning provided the eventual bases for compromise with bureaucratic and business elites. Unlike state control or socialization of industry, these were ideas that enjoyed broad support. These two points of congruence were to become the foundation of economic policy in postwar Japan.

FIVE

Government Economic Planning and the Debate over State Control of the Coal Mines, 1946–1948

All Japanese over a certain age remember where they stood between noon and one o'clock on 15 August 1945. As one novelist has recalled, "The entire Japanese nation held back its hushed voices as an enormous page of history was turned without a sound."[1] But this moment of inaction did not last long. Within hours, the political landscape of Japan was already beginning to change—despite the physical devastation of the country. In Manila, General Douglas MacArthur prepared for his new command by reading the "Initial Post-surrender Policy for Japan," which called for the demilitarization and democratization of Japan. In Hokkaido, the Chinese prisoners of war marched from mine to mine, liberating their compatriots and organizing Japan's first postwar labor unions. Over the next few days in Tokyo, prewar political figures hammered out the details for the Japan Socialist Party, while the gray haze over the government ministry buildings testified to the haste with which bureaucrats were burning evidence of the past. A few miles away, as yet oblivious to the implications of these events, the Mitsui presidents' group met to plan the future of the Mitsui holding company and branch firms. They congratulated each other on the fact that the Occupation was to be American rather than Soviet, and speculated that the Americans would favor them over firms more closely tied to the military. Meanwhile, a small group of academics, bureaucrats, and businessmen met in an obscure corner of the Ministry of Foreign Affairs to plan for the postwar economy. Their plan would eventually become the basis for government economic policy and would underpin the entire postwar political-economic structure of Japan. It represented a striking break with the past, both in its reorientation of the domestic economy and its new formula for Japan's place in the world economy. Their views were not immediately influential, however, and they worked on their own initiative, while the Japanese government gradually lost control of the economy.

The most important economic debates of the first postwar years centered on the coal mines. Because of the coal industry's key position in the economy, and because the government was incurring huge expenses through subsidies to the coal operators, the mines became the single most important focus for discussions about industrial reconstruction. When the government finally did reassert control over economic planning, it was by concentrating on reviving the coal and steel industries. This was through the "priority-production policy," modeled on the Ministry of Foreign Affairs group's recommendations. The priority-production policy provided a crucial step in postwar reconstruction and reconsolidation of Japan's political economy. It not only stimulated production, but also set the tone for subsequent economic development based on high wages and high value-added. It institutionalized economic planning and addressed the demands of government officials, labor unions, and private firms.

Coal also served as the testing ground for the other major economic debate of 1947—whether to nationalize key industries. The priority-production policy had neatly evaded this controversy, which came to the fore when the Katayama government pressed for state control over the nation's coal mines. This debate stood proxy for a struggle over the right to determine the nature of the postwar Japanese economy and the economic role of the state. The supporters of the plan to nationalize industry wanted both to improve industrial efficiency and to give workers greater power over their lives. The Japanese were not alone in pursuing this solution. They knew about contemporary British and French debates over nationalizing coal. Many people around the world in 1947 believed that enlarging the state's role in the economy was a prudent and equitable response to the global problems of the previous twenty years. Nevertheless, the proponents of private enterprise won the controversy, although a spineless bill for temporary state control of the mines did pass the Diet on 20 December 1947. The mine owners had forged an alliance with Yoshida's politicians which both vitiated the coal bill and established a pattern for postwar business funding of the Liberal Party. In an important shift, they redefined economic goals more narrowly, focusing on technical production levels rather than the broader questions of economic organization. These two developments—the success of the priority-production policy and the failure of state control of industry—marked a new stage in postwar reconstruction.

GOVERNMENT ECONOMIC ACTIVITY

The first two postwar Cabinets made little headway in solving Japan's economic crisis. The Higashikuni Cabinet, which presided over Japan for only seven weeks from 17 August, concentrated its attention on political rather than economic matters. Nevertheless, it did leave its mark on the Japanese economy, by several actions that removed the restraints on inflation. Both prices and money supply rose fast during the Higashikuni Cabinet's tenure—the number of Bank of Japan notes in circulation increased by 40 percent between 15 August and 31 August alone. The Cabinet contributed directly to inflationary pressure by relaxing wartime controls on prices and materials. It also paid outstanding contracts to munitions producers (some in advance), bankrupting the Treasury by November.[2]

The Shidehara Cabinet, which took office on 9 October, tried but failed to control inflation. In February 1946, all bank accounts were frozen and banknotes with a value of 10 yen or more replaced by "new yen" of a lower denomination. At the same time, the Cabinet reimposed some price controls and attempted to choke off supplies

to the black market, although these programs were not strictly enforced. The Japanese government also levied a 100-percent tax on
the indemnities it had offered munitions firms during the war. This
was a very controversial move, since nearly all the major manufacturing firms of the nation relied on the indemnities to stave off
bankruptcy. Finance Minister Shibusawa Keizō bitterly opposed this
tax, but other Japanese supported it, including Professor Ōuchi
Hyōe, who publicly derided Shibusawa as "reckless" in a radio
broadcast. More important, Ōuchi's opinion coincided with that of
SCAP, which eventually forced the reluctant government to levy
the tax.

These measures only temporarily slowed the inflation rate. Moreover, since none of them addressed the equally serious problem of
increasing production, shortages became more acute every day.[3] Worst
of all, the 1945 rice harvest was the lowest in over twenty years,
raising the specter of mass starvation. By April 1946, the Shidehara
Cabinet could no longer withstand charges that its passivity and
poor leadership had caused the ongoing economic crisis. Economic
conditions became still worse that spring, as food supplies dwindled
and inflation grew more severe. The political situation was extremely tense, particularly after several huge rallies against the government occurred in Tokyo. The Shidehara Cabinet fell in April,
and Yoshida Shigeru was able to form a conservative coalition cabinet only after a hard month of negotiation in late May. If Yoshida
hoped to retain control of the government, he had to come up with
a plan to revive the economy. This problem was made more urgent
because the labor unions were perceived by many Japanese as contributing to production recovery, in contrast to the low popularity
of the government and major industrialists.[4]

Yoshida Shigeru, who was about to emerge as a formidable political leader, did not himself favor economic planning, but he realized that, without a strong economic program, he would lose control of the government. By improving economic performance, the
new Yoshida Cabinet hoped to build a solid political base and win
future elections. Moreover, Yoshida realized that it was necessary
to face the challenges created by socialist and labor-led redevelop-

ment. He was personally very anti-labor[5] but understood that the unions were strong enough that they could not simply be ignored. Nor, given Occupation policy, could they be crushed. It was necessary to meet their concerns to some extent, but also to frame them within a larger, explicitly capitalist structure.

Yoshida met the challenge by bringing in a group of younger bureaucrats and academics to formulate a new approach to the problem of economic recovery. This group, which had been meeting at Yoshida's own Foreign Affairs Ministry since the last day of the war, included men who had criticized the military during the war, some of whom were Marxist thinkers. Members of this group included Ōuchi Hyōe, Arisawa Hiromi, Inaba Hidezō, Nakayama Ichirō, Tsuru Shigeto, Ōkita Saburō, and Gotō Yonosuke.[6] They were fairly marginal until Yoshida brought them forward. The fact that Yoshida chose them is interesting, since they were far more committed to economic reform and state control of important sectors of the economy than was he. Yoshida realized, however, that, not only was reviving the economy the most important task facing his administration, but reconstruction plans had to contain some new elements, especially in regard to agriculture.[7] These men had worked out a strategy for economic reconstruction, culminating in a March 1946 report, *Basic Problems for Postwar Reconstruction of Japanese Economy,* which analyzed the present state of the Japanese and world economy and recommended future actions for Japanese planners.[8]

THE MINISTRY OF FOREIGN AFFAIRS REPORT. The Ministry of Foreign Affairs report provided the guidelines for economic policy under the first Yoshida Cabinet and set the pattern for Japan's postwar economic development to this day. It represented a major break from the past. The key insight was that Japan had to maintain its position halfway between the Western countries and the rest of Asia in terms both of wage and technological levels. Japan also had to be ready to redirect its economy to meet changing international conditions. The Ministry of Foreign Affairs group shared some basic concerns with the labor unions, and there are striking points of congruence in their suggestions, especially in their rejection of a return to a traditional Japanese economy. The first economic policy to be influenced by this new strategy was developed under Yoshida's Minister of Finance, Ishibashi Tanzan. This was supplemented a few months later by the production-oriented "priority-production policy," first suggested by members of the Ministry of Foreign Affairs group.

The 1946 report contained two important conclusions. The first was that a constricted domestic market had led to militarism abroad and that postwar strategies must center on expanding the purchasing power of the average Japanese. The group was particularly critical of the rural landlord system which allowed landlords to extract high rents from their tenants and discouraged any improvements in agricultural technology. The tenants, who were left with only bare subsistence levels after rents were paid, provided a constant supply of cheap labor to the cities, which also kept industrial wages low. Paralleling contemporary Occupation thinkers, the planners in the Ministry of Foreign Affairs argued that this system had to be reformed to build a healthy and democratic economy. They advocated further measures to raise the purchasing power of industrial workers, such as support for labor unions.

Their other main conclusion was that, since Japan could not ever become self-sufficient in basic commodities including food, it needed to develop viable export industries. In the prewar years, most of Japan's foreign exchange was earned by textile exports. However, the group's report argued, international conditions had changed since then. The silk market in Western countries was threatened by new synthetic fibers, and many other Asian countries were developing their own cotton-thread and fabric industries, which both eliminated them as markets and introduced them as competitors for third markets. Furthermore, if the Japanese were to cultivate the domestic market, they could not return to an export strategy based mainly on low wages. Instead, they had to use technology to develop new, more sophisticated industries for export. The crucial point was that the Japanese had to maintain their position halfway between the Western countries and the rest of Asia in terms of both wage and technological levels. "Japan must maintain a superiority in know-how over other Asian countries by a constant advancement of its own technology so that it may be able to export industrial manu-factures to these countries." At the same time, Japanese wages had to stay lower than Western ones in order to attract customers among Asian countries that wanted technologically sophisticated goods but could not pay high prices for them.[9] Some industries that the report specifically mentioned as appropriate for this strategy were electrical equipment, communications apparatus, precision instruments, tools, gauges, scientific equipment, vehicles, chemicals, medical supplies, and dyestuffs, all of which have become important Japanese ex-ports.[10] The first step to solving both these problems, stated the report, was to raise production levels, particularly of heavy-indus-trial goods, and bring more products into the economy.

The Ministry of Foreign Affairs group stressed the importance of economic planning. They argued that economic planning at a na-tional level was crucial to Japan's survival in the international econ-omy, and that these plans would have to extend into the manage-ment practices and use of technology by individual firms in order to be effective. It was not enough for the state to draw up general economic goals.[11] They pointed out that one of the positive legacies of the war was the experience of economic planning and called for greater efforts in this direction.[12]

In one of the many points of congruence with the labor unions, the report's authors saw an international trend away from laissez-faire capitalism toward societies that made the welfare of the whole population their main concern. As the report noted, "There is, in general, a worldwide tendency that the individualistic economic systems are changing gradually to cooperative economic systems."[13] In the case of Japan, the report recognized that the United States would set the conditions for Japan's participation in the global economy but explicitly warned against using America as a model for the postwar Japanese economy. One of the main ways in which Japan needed to chart its own course was that the government should play a larger role than the U.S. government in developing the economy. In capital-poor Japan, only the state could generate the resources to develop large-capacity industries. The 1946 report argued:

> Fair and free competition alone cannot be a sole solution. Are not, after all, the socialization of financial institutions and major basic industries, and the planned and fairly strict State control of economy required in the process of Japan's economic democratization? In such case[s], however, the government that should play a principal role in economic controls needs to be a democratic government for the people, and must not be a resurgence of the past bureaucracy.

They recognized both a need for democratic reform and strong central guidance of the economy.

The report's authors looked toward a future in which the state would control basic industry and banking, but they were obviously searching for a solution that would guard against two different dangers. One was the problem of the war years, when an autocratic state wrested control of economic decisions for military ends. The other was, in their view, the evil of the 1920s—that private firms would make decisions affecting the entire nation solely on the basis of their own profits. The problem of which was the greater evil, bureaucratic absolutism or selfish capitalism, was the key question in this analysis. The report argued that, ideally, this should be resolved by a two-phased reform, first to democratize the bureaucracy and then to assume control over private industry. "The first stage in the desirable process for Japan's economic democratization will be to relieve the economy from the control by the feudalistic bureaucracy and to make it operate freely and unrestrictedly." This will enable the economy "to proceed in capitalistic free competition. New accumulation and concentration will be started during such process as the second stage for the nation's economic democratization; and the foundation will be formed for gradual transition to a socialization of the economy." This was their ideal plan.

Yet, Japan did not face ideal conditions in 1946. The need to resume production to feed and house the population overshadowed the threat of excess state control. Since only the state could marshal the resources to restart economic activity, it had to be used. "The

Japanese people are on the verge of starvation. . . . Every possible measure will have to be contrived toward solving this problem of economic subsistence. In order to assure the people equally of their right to live, a forceful and thoroughgoing public control of the economy will be necessary. . . . In other words, if the transition from feudalistic, bureaucratic controls to democratic public controls is made completely during the emergency period, its reversion to free economy will become unnecessary. In case such transition is imperfect, however, a more or less relapse into free economy may be required in order to eradicate feudalistic characteristics."[14] The goal was a strong state-controlled economy, but the danger was that this would be accomplished before the wartime bureaucratic apparatus was forced to democratize.

The report advocated several specific reforms of the civil-service system and bureaucratic training to remove "the feudalistic character of the past civil-service system." It warned that this transition had to be made quickly because Japan could not afford to wait very long before the state took greater control over "economic and social life in general" to "ensure survival to its nationals." The vulnerability of Japan's economic position in the international economy—specifically, the problems of economic backwardness, a constricted domestic market, insufficient raw materials, and a capital shortage—meant that the Japanese state had to coordinate activity in the domestic economy.[15]

The Ministry of Foreign Affairs group hoped to create a new economic system, based on a strong and democratic state.[16] These concerns—and the solution—were very close to the electric-power workers' suggestions for reform of their industry. Like the power workers, they struggled with the dual problem of how to protect Japan against either excessive control by the bureaucracy or by businessmen. Both groups urged speedy establishment of democratic public controls on the economy as the only assurance against these twin dangers. Without new institutions, they feared, Japan was doomed to repeat either the mistakes of the 1920s or those of the 1930s.

In a grand sense, their analysis resembled Occupation criticism of the failure of democracy in the prewar political economy. This kind of economic reform, however, moved in precisely the opposite direction from the concurrent Occupation economic-deconcentration program. The deconcentration program was designed to promote competition among private firms, not to enhance the economic power of the state. At first, the Americans were willing to consider nationalization of industry in Japan, because the problems of spiraling inflation and commodity shortages meant that some kind of economic controls were necessary. However, this was only an interim measure for the Americans, who believed that a free-market economy was the best alternative for Japan.[17] Thus, they were never enthusiastic about Japanese proposals for state control of industry. Conversely, the U.S. ideal of laissez-faire economic democracy was rejected by most Japanese as an inappropriate model for a country that depended on international trade.[18]

The Ministry of Foreign Affairs report was an early blueprint for Japan's economic development in many ways, but its recommendations were ignored in this significant area. The report called for a much more important role for the state in direct control of the economy than has actually occurred. The authors of the report represented an opinion popular in 1946—that the state should control important industries—but this option was to disappear over the course of the Occupation years. One reason was that the lack of SCAP support weakened the effectiveness of state-control measures, certainly in both the coal and electric-power industries.[19] The political shambles that developed over state control of coal in itself became a separate deterrent.

FINANCE MINISTER ISHIBASHI TANZAN. The first government policy to be influenced by this new strategy developed under Yoshida's Minister of Finance, Ishibashi Tanzan. This was the first active postwar Japanese macroeconomic policy. Ishibashi shared one aspect of the Ministry of Foreign Affairs group's vision of the new economy, the emphasis on developing heavy industry. Ishibashi concentrated on the financial side of the problem of stimulating the economy. His predecessors at the Finance Ministry had concerned themselves with the problem of stemming inflation, but Ishibashi took a wholly new approach to this issue. He contended that the price increases Japan was experiencing were not the symptoms of classic "inflation" but were "famine prices," or the result of commodity shortages. Since they were not caused by classic inflation, they called for policy measures that stimulated economic growth rather than deflationary measures.[20]

Ishibashi concurred with the Ministry of Foreign Affairs group that raising production was the key to economic recovery. He also agreed on the importance of technology, expanding heavy industries beyond what had existed in the past, and providing jobs.[21] Since Ishibashi believed that production recovery rather than monetary stability was the first step to a healthy economy, he supported policies that encouraged production, such as low taxes and easy access to loans for businesses. He also opposed zaibatsu dissolution, on the grounds that it would fragment the economy and slow production recovery. In his memoirs, he described a meeting with a group of major coal operators in which he offered them unlimited money if they would promise to bring coal production up to 30 million tons in 1947.[22]

Like the Ministry of Foreign Affairs planners, the goal of his plan was reintegration into the world economy. Ishibashi's policies "represent preparations on our part for the day when the Japanese people will be permitted to take part in international economic activities. Thus, we have to readjust our country internally so that we may be well prepared to take part in all phases of [the] international economy whenever permitted. Such preparedness is likely to accelerate the admission to [the] international economy." From the first postwar plans, the Japanese were refashioning their domestic economy with one eye on the international context.[23]

Ishibashi, however, diverged from the Ministry of Foreign Affairs analysis on the second key point—that Japan must move quickly toward a high-wage, high-consumption economy. His policy was aimed at business and investment recovery rather than at consumption recovery; while it included subsidies to industry, it did not include protection against inflation for consumers or workers. Indeed, Ishibashi saw protection of ordinary workers and consumers as an obstacle to recovery. In a discussion of economic rationalization, he explained, "Regrettably, the production efficiency today has become increasingly lower. Under these circumstances, therefore, the standard of living in Japan should be necessarily lowered."[24] This lopsided approach contrasted with the program proposed in the Ministry of Foreign Affairs report.

Ishibashi's contemporaries sharply criticized his program for two other reasons. Its contribution to inflation was most controversial, but the plan also failed to stimulate production of basic materials.[25] In several significant cases, stockpiles were still declining. For example, steel production in mid-1946 depended on hoarded ex-military stockpiles. The steel mills had no new sources to replenish their existing stores of materials.[26] This could not continue indefinitely; by mid-1946, the steel industry had stopped increasing production levels; by August, only two blast furnaces were operating; and, by September, one of these had closed due to lack of supplies. The Japanese economy moved toward a complete collapse of production. Government economists calculated in Autumn 1946 that supplies of several major industrial ingredients, including coal, were nearly exhausted and this would halt the gradual reconstruction process. This fear was expressed formally by Inaba Hidezō and other bureaucrats, now at the Economic Stabilization Board (ESB), as the "Theory of a March Crisis." They predicted that, by March 1947, all existing sources of industrial materials would be exhausted, causing a vicious circle of production drops and consequent unbridled inflation.

THE PRIORITY-PRODUCTION POLICY. It was out of this fear of impending materials shortage that the "priority-production" policy, based on the Ministry of Foreign Affairs report, was born in late 1946.[27] It was the brainchild of Arisawa Hiromi, a Tokyo University professor who worked closely with the ESB in this period.[28] He suggested that all available resources be concentrated in the coal and steel industries before trying to rehabilitate any other industries. This plan did not contain radically new elements, but it concentrated resources, integrated existing programs, and enforced previously enacted laws far more than had earlier directives. It was the first government or business program to organize many disparate elements into a coordinated plan, and to emphasize planning itself. The most important aspect of this was the integration of financial policy and materials policy to increase production. The primary focus of the policy was heavy industry, especially the coal, steel, fertilizer, and electric-power industries.

This plan was first adopted by the Yoshida Administration in late 1946 and remained the dominant government economic policy until the Japanese were forced to abandon it by Occupation orders in early 1949.[29] One reason it lasted past the Yoshida Cabinet's fall in May 1947 was that priority production was really more representative of the thinking of the Socialist and Minshu (Ashida's party) Parties than of Yoshida's party, which was liberal only in the sense of classical economic laissez-faire ideology. The commitment to national economic planning implicit in the priority-production policy was not shared by Yoshida himself, and the fact that he initiated it is the anomaly, rather than Socialist retention of the plan. Yoshida's economic advisors initiated planning under the argument that it was an emergency measure, but these men, unlike Yoshida, believed that long-term planning in itself was beneficial. The short, socialist-led Katayama Administration greatly strengthened and institutionalized this tendency toward planning in 1947. The Katayama and subsequent Ashida Cabinets also shared Ishibashi's assumption that production increases would control inflation, and so continued the policies of subsidizing basic industries with loans and grants. Coal was the single most favored industry throughout, with the result that it became a model for other basic industries.

Arisawa explained why he placed such great importance on coal in a radio broadcast on 20 December 1946:

> The fundamental cause of inflation today is the absolute shortage of material goods themselves. Thus, a precondition for overcoming inflation is first to effect an increase in production levels. However, since it is not possible to raise the production level of all goods evenly . . . we are handling the problem by concentrating our priorities on raising production of the unique

> basic raw material, coal, as our total economic policy. . . . Our pressing
> need is to raise production rapidly in this basic sector and use that as a
> lever to increase the general level of production.[30]

Arisawa's emphasis on raising production closely followed that of
Ishibashi. Steel and coal were chosen as the two basic starting points
for this "slanted" approach to raising production levels, but, in
early 1947, the fertilizer industry and then, in November 1947,
the electric-power industry were also designated as priority-production industries.[31] This designation was highly coveted in capital-
and resource-scarce Japan. The electric-power industry, for example, assiduously lobbied the Diet for inclusion in the program.

The 3 concrete sub-policies that made up the priority-production
policy consisted of preferential allocations, subsidies, and the Reconstruction Finance Bank (RFB). Designated industries received
first priority in all these areas. By the time the program ended in
1949, it was clear that the coal industry had received the lion's share
of assistance. The electric-power and steel industries were also heavily
favored.

The allocation program funneled badly needed supplies of labor,
steel, cement, electric power, timber, and other goods to the designated industries in a short-term effort to get the economy moving
again. It drew on the extensive allocative and rationing powers that
the state had acquired during the war, although it was based legally
on the Temporary Materials Supply and Demand Control Law *(Rinji
Busshi Jukyū Chōsei Hō)* of 30 September 1946. This law allowed
the ESB to allocate materials to all firms in the designated industries
and also to distribute coal to industry.[32]

Other industries besides coal benefited from this program, but
one analyst figured that requests for materials allotments by the coal
companies were honored twice as often as for any other industry.[33]
"During 1947, allocation of supplies to the coal mines comprised
about 80 percent of requirements, while other industries were restricted to less than 30 percent of requirements."[34] These allocations went to all firms, no matter how small, and are one of the
main factors contributing to the great postwar increase in output
from the smaller classes of mines in the coal industry.

A subsidy system was also in effect which, like allocations, was a partially transformed wartime legacy. Subsidies in the coal industry began in 1940 with the creation of the Japan Coal Company, Ltd. Before then, the price paid to the producers and that charged to the consumers had been identical (20.13 yen),[35] but, in 1940, the Japanese government instituted a policy of maintaining low prices for consumers even when production costs rose. The Japan Coal Co. paid producers a per-ton amount based on average mining costs. It then paid subsidies to high-cost producers, guaranteeing them profits in the interests of raising production. In 1940, it was expected that North Asian coal would become increasingly available, and these subsidies were introduced only as interim measures.[36] This assumption was incorrect, and the sum paid to coal producers gradually rose from 13.75 yen per ton in the second half of 1940 to 58.88 yen in the first half of 1945.[37] A very similar pattern developed in the other basic heavy industries. For example, subsidies were instituted in the electric power industry after Hassōden was formed and were continued throughout the war. Subsidies were also introduced in the iron and steel, fertilizer, and soda industries, all to encourage production and hold down prices of a wide range of products that used these basic industrial materials.

This policy carried on into the Occupation era. Again, the main function of the subsidies was to aid basic industry, which soon overwhelmingly meant the coal industry. The actual system of subsidies was extremely complicated. There were several types during the war (one, for example, designed to encourage the development of new mines), but most were ordered ended by SCAP in November 1945. Then, in mid-1946, Ishibashi instituted new subsidies for firms operating at a loss to encourage higher production. In the case of coal, Ishibashi would have preferred to raise the price of coal to consumers but agreed to raise the subsidy to coal operators instead, since a price hike would have meant politically unacceptable increases for consumers.[38] Other new subsidies were used to spur imports and exports by manipulating the foreign-exchange values. The subsidy and rationing systems consistently favored industrial over household consumers both during and after the war.[39]

The cost of the subsidies had been reasonably stable during the war, but postwar changes completely upset the wartime system. Inflation unbalanced the subsidy structure by pushing production costs far above the fixed prices for subsidized products, while the democratic reforms led to sharply increased labor costs.[40] Firms needed more and more money to operate, and the total cost to the government skyrocketed. In 1946, subsidies accounted for 16,055 million yen, or 13.4 percent of the general budget. In 1947, this rose to 52,514 million yen or 24.5 percent, in 1948 136,847 million yen or 28.9 percent, and the original draft of the 1949 budget allocated 309,248 million yen or 43.8 percent for subsidies before the Americans vetoed this expenditure.[41]

Not only did subsidies suddenly become a much larger share of the national budget, but the coal mines swallowed up nearly a third of them. The mines accounted for 54.9 billion yen or 32 percent of the subsidies to all industry between 1946 and 1949.[42] The sale price of coal to consumers rose steadily, but it was never enough to stabilize the coal industry. This price, which had been set at 20.13 yen per ton from 1942 to the first half of 1945, was revised to 85 yen from November 1945. At the same time, the subsidy rose to 170 yen. Both were raised again in March 1946, to 150 and 220 yen, respectively. In November 1946, as part of the priority-production policy, the government adopted a stratified pricing system, which favored industrial use. The new coal prices were 401.70 yen for offices and households, 115 yen for railroads, and 200 yen for key industries. Subsidies to the coal operators were revised to 346 yen.[43] The costs of mining coal continued to rise, and the subsidies climbed with them. The subsidy was reset in July 1947 at 956.08 yen per ton, and prices were raised to 1,208.58 yen. Despite these efforts, coal prices increased again in April 1948 to 3,344.86 yen and the subsidy was hiked to 2,388.53 yen, based on average cost estimates of 2,290 yen and a per-ton profit of 98.50 yen.[44]

The subsidy system was designed to encourage higher production from marginal producers rather than from those with the best natural conditions. Consequently, it increased the volume of coal but not the efficiency of production. The subsidies were figured on the basis of average mining costs. This system worked just like the pricing systems of the past to enrich low-cost producers whether their savings were due to efficient production or to better natural conditions. While *average* mine costs were higher than the government calculations, the large spread between the best and worst mines meant that the low-cost producers could make a profit. The major operators could either work their least attractive seams at cost while saving the better ones for future profit, or they could exploit the good ones for an instant windfall. The incentive to sell poorer coal was enhanced by the fact that, in those years, the price difference between grades of coal was very small. Since a "reasonable profit" was included in the price paid to producers, they could afford to sit back and wait for the Occupation to end while the government paid their bills through the subsidy system.[45] The coal operators themselves acknowledged their lack of investment, arguing that, since "these [subsidy] payments were very mechanistic and standardized, without allowing for coal quality or production efficiency, we have no incentive to rationalize production or *to lower costs of production.*"[46] While the subsidy system, like the allocation program, sustained the marginal producers, it also enriched the ones with high-quality mines. SCAP directed its criticism of Japanese coal policy to this fact—that the subsidies did not encourage production in the big mines.

Despite its mammoth proportions, the subsidy program was neither large nor flexible enough to meet industry's need for capital. Therefore, Ishibashi created the Reconstruction Finance Bank (RFB) in August 1946 to provide an additional source of funds. The RFB became a pillar of the priority-production policy by providing funds to firms in the priority industries.[47] It disbursed 18 percent of *all* loans in Japan in 1947 and 19 percent in 1948, figures that illustrate its influential position.[48] It accounted for a much larger share of loans to the heavy industries, since they found it difficult to get loans from ordinary banks. This "mecca for fund-thirsty industrialists" provided 79.9 percent of the electric-power companies' financing and 66.4 percent of the mining industry's long-term debt in those years.[49]

This RFB money went overwhelmingly to firms in the coal and electric-power industries, consistent with their positions as priority industries. In April 1949, when RFB loans were sharply curtailed, loans to the coal industry accounted for 47,500 million yen or 36 percent of the total 109.4 billion yen owed the RFB by industry. The electric-power industry was the second largest industrial recipient of RFB funds with 22,400 million yen or 20 percent of the three-year total. Other heavy industries accounted for most of the rest of the RFB loans until SCAP ordered the RFB to desist from lending in March 1949. SCAP officials were deeply critical of the RFB as an inflationary and corrupt institution.[50] Closing it down was a key component of the U.S. economic-stabilization plan, which forced the Japanese to reevaluate their economic plans.[51]

CONTRIBUTIONS OF THE PRIORITY-PRODUCTION POLICY

The priority-production policy began as a sister policy to the Ishibashi line and depended on some of the same expansionary and capital-accumulation institutions, including the subsidies to industry and the RFB. Yet, the priority-production policy went beyond the Ishibashi line and represents a separate important innovation. It stands out as a landmark of postwar economic reconstruction. First and most important for initial influence in the political economy, the priority-production policy provided more coal, steel, fertilizer, and electric power. In a nation starved for these basic commodities, delivery of goods and services was a respected pledge of sincerity and commitment to the common good.

Second, this policy set the tone for all subsequent postwar economic policies. It was based on the assumption that Japan would embark immediately on the path toward becoming a high-wage economy, exporting sophisticated goods. This was consistent both with labor-union visions and the Ministry of Foreign Affairs group's assessment that Japan could not expect a strong postwar textile market. It differed, however, from Ishibashi's policies, which emphasized business recovery, and from contemporary Occupation plans, which vaguely imagined that Japan could manage on exports of textiles, porcelain, and bamboo products.

Third, this economic reorientation was to be achieved by concentrating first on a few basic industries, of which the most important was coal. This aspect of the plan pleased both Ishibashi and the Occupationaires, who had both paid special attention to the coal industry. It also took advantage of the structural changes that had taken place in the Japanese economy since the early 1930s as part of the adjustment to fighting the China and Pacific Wars. With the priority-production policy, the Japanese began to build on the positive economic legacies of the war and so overcome the devastation it had left behind. Nor was the strategy of raising the level of a few designated industries at a time abandoned after the priority-production policy ended. It remains a key feature of Japanese economic policy to this day, although the specific industries themselves have changed over time.

Priority-production had a fourth important function. It acted as a shrewd compromise among all the competing economic ideologies. It defused a variety of tensions rather than exacerbating them. The policy managed to revive the economy without challenging private enterprises; at the same time, it enlarged the allocative and distributive functions of the state. It also provided funds to pay wage increases from the Treasury rather than from the pockets of employers.[52] It gave labor high wages, but also channeled funds to existing management. On the political level, the policy meant that the government lobbied for joint labor-management production drives. The subsidies and RFB loans were used by the government to keep workers on the job even when their plants were not producing, to prevent a "politically unfeasible growth of unemployment."[53] The priority-production policy institutionalized the concerns of labor but at the same time strengthened those aspects of the existing economic structure, notably private enterprise, that the unions hoped eventually to eliminate. The plan held enough flexibility to be compatible with a wide variety of grand designs for the political economy and, therefore, was acceptable to individuals with a commensurately wide variety of political programs.

The common thread tying these diverse individuals together was an acceptance of economic planning. The fifth and probably most enduring legacy of the priority-production policy was that it promoted long-term economic planning over a straight market approach to the economy. This was a conscious, careful act. The authors of the Ministry of Foreign Affairs report stressed the need for national planning, better technical and managerial training, and improvements in the collection and use of statistics. In Japan, the economic planners, like union leaders, could draw from a number of different sources, including socialist and fascist theory, to justify their commitment to economic planning. The variety of these sources suggests widespread support for economic planning. The most common rationale for support of planning was scarcity; resource-poor Japan simply could not afford the luxury of uncoordinated development.

The priority-production policy has been evaluated in a variety of ways. Koji Taira has called it a "socialist step" because of its emphasis on basic heavy industries.[54] He also has suggested that this was a conciliatory response to worker organization. "Workers' control of production demonstrated how far workers' militancy could go, even at the risk of brushing with the law. The effectiveness of the workers should have suggested to every political leader that major concessions to the labor movement were in order. Those 'socialist' measures taken by the Yoshida Cabinet . . . were adopted during the most active year of the labor movement—1946."[55] Some contemporaries criticized the priority-production plan as a cooptive response to the leftist and labor critics of the government. They argued that the policy acted as emergency surgery to reconstruct monopoly capitalism through infusions of capital and supplies at a moment when it might have collapsed. In this view, the priority-production policy represented a "new political consolidation of authority" against threats such as nationalization.[56]

These two analyses are not mutually exclusive. The subsidies and loans unquestionably bought labor peace in the mines and industries at a time when Japanese workers, backed by the Occupation

Army, were demanding greater economic and political power. This represents a new level of concessions to the labor movement by the government and by management. The priority-production policy allowed new compromises within the existing economic system. At the same time, however, the loans and subsidies were also used to shore up bankrupt private companies that would not have survived without government aid. Simply permitting rampant inflation allowed firms to survive that otherwise would have been unable to pay back their munitions-related war loans.

The RFB was most often cited as an avenue for government favoritism to business. Not only did the volume of its loans go overwhelmingly to a few industries, but they were also concentrated in a few firms within those industries. When the RFB was closed, only 5.1 percent of its loans (5.681 billion yen) were paid out to small firms, despite the fact that aiding small companies had been one of its original mandates. In fact, 87 percent of all loans went to only 97 firms.[57] In the coal industry, the leading 18 firms won 74 percent of the loans to coal (39.5 billion yen).[58] Mitsui Mining alone had received 3,015 million yen in loans by the end of 1947.[59] This is the aspect of the priority-production policy most vulnerable to the charges that the government was aiding the regeneration of a few large firms in favored industries at the cost of inflation, and depriving other sectors of needed capital.[60] Individual RFB loan recipients were not necessarily chosen on the basis of merit, either. In 1948, revelations that the Shōwa Denkō Corporation had used bribery to acquire RFB loans caused the fall of the Ashida Cabinet.[61]

The priority-production policy did not solve all of Japan's pressing economic problems. Important issues still unresolved included controlling inflation, finding capital, and developing sophisticated export industries. The ESB officials estimated in 1947 that Japanese manufacturing output would have to rise to at least 125 percent of prewar levels simply to regain prewar standards of living, because of the growth in population.[62] The ESB did try to address these problems in 1947 and 1948 in two credible economic plans, but the first was rejected by SCAP because of its reliance on foreign aid and the second was vetoed by Yoshida who was then in a strong enough position to express his antipathy to economic planning.[63]

Another major unresolved question was whether or not to adopt state control and nationalization of key industries. This basic issue was not laid to rest until after a battle over the establishment of state control in the coal mines. The Japanese fought out the coal debate in the Diet, where it quickly became a vehicle for control of the legislative body. The coal bill became entangled with a power struggle among the political parties for control of the Diet, heightening the intense polarization over state control of the mines.

DEBATE ON CONTROL OF THE COAL MINES, 1945-1947

The fight over state control of the coal mines was, in many ways, a fight to determine the nature of the postwar Japanese economy and the role of the state within it. Because of the coal industry's central position in the economy and its unparalleled dependence on the National Treasury, the mines became the single most important focus for discussions about industrial reconstruction. The proponents of state control, including the Japan Socialist Party and the coal miners' unions, wanted to establish state-controlled industries for a variety of reasons. They believed the state could most effectively provide the materials, technology, and capital that were so scarce throughout Japan in 1947. They also had larger social goals in mind. The most important of these was widening the base of economic power in Japan to include organized labor and ordinary citizens. Economic equity was fundamental to their definition of economic efficiency. In contrast, the coal operators argued that narrowly defined efficiency, that is, rates of production, were unlikely to be affected by a change in management. Furthermore, state control would only create bureaucratic red tape that would hamper production efforts. SCAP actions supported the coal operators in that they sanctioned their definition of economic efficiency—one divorced from any consideration of the social base of coal mining.

The debate came to a head after 24 May 1947, when Katayama

Tetsu, a Socialist, took office as Prime Minister in a shaky coalition government. His Cabinet, the only Socialist-led Cabinet in Japan's history, was never able to consolidate power and fell the following March. The Socialist Party had only one ambitious economic program—to establish state control in the coal mines. Securing state control of the coal industry had been a platform promise of the Japan Socialist Party since 1945, and was also endorsed by the coal miners' unions. Katayama chose this as the top economic goal of his own Socialist Party within the ruling coalition. He tied his personal prestige and that of his party to establishing state control of the mines. Unfortunately for Katayama, the Socialist Party did not have a strong enough position within the ruling coalition to impose its economic agenda, and the coal-control bill was not only a spectacular failure, but also a crushing political defeat for himself and for his party.

The proposal to nationalize the mines was originally raised in November 1945 by the Japan Socialist Party, which incorporated nationalization of the coal and fertilizer industries into its inaugural platform. This was part of a general pledge to socialize and democratize the Japanese economy. Later, the coal miners' confederation, Tankyō, and the Japan Communist Party also supported state takeover of the mines. Every major political party published an opinion on the subject in 1946–1947.[64]

The issue did not become a controversy, however, until early September 1946, when MacArthur asked the Allied Council on Japan to deliberate on the problem of "policy with regard to ownership of coal mines and subsidy financing of coal production." After two sessions, the British Commonwealth, Soviet, and Chinese delegates all made statements favoring nationalization of the industry, although they differed on points such as compensation of former owners.[65] Their conclusions and the national coal shortage were important catalysts for the movement toward nationalization.[66]

SCAP clearly leaned toward some kind of state control of the mines at this stage. A SCAP representative told the Allied Council at the 16 October meeting that "SCAP has conceived no plans for the nationalization of the coal mines in Japan. SCAP neither recommends for nor against nationalization of coal mines. SCAP invites comments on the subject."[67] It is significant, however, that SCAP asked the Allied Council of Japan to deal with the issue at all, since the relationship between the two bodies was always strained. SCAP opinion was made clearer by a plan to raise coal production announced by the Economic and Scientific Section's Rationing and Price Division Chief, W.S. Egekvist, on 24 September 1946. This plan limited subsidies to the coal mines and profits to owners, while setting quotas for each mine and establishing bonus payments for any mine that met 75 percent of its quota. The plan also included a provision that "the Japanese Government will operate any idle mine or those not producing a reasonable percent of former production." SCAP's numerous published criticisms of the mine managers indicate their belief that the coal operators were deliberately delaying production recovery. The Americans wanted higher production rates and were willing to accept a larger state role to achieve this.[68]

Within the conservative Yoshida Government, opinion was divided over the merits of nationalizing the coal mines. The first official statements, in September 1946, were favorable. The Director General of the semi-autonomous Coal Bureau, Yasukawa Daigorō, told reporters that "development of new coal mines by the State and readjustments and control of all coal mines were advisable for increasing coal output." On the following day, the Director General of the ESB, Zen Keinosuke, told Diet members that he personally believed that soon the coal industry would be "managed by government officials." However, this opinion was quickly reversed. Only a few hours later, Zen joined the Minister of Commerce and Industry, Hoshijima Nirō, in an official statement before a Diet committee stating that the government was *not* planning to nationalize the coal industry because it would not lead to higher coal output. Hoshijima explained that "coal production is currently on the increase, and I wish no misunderstanding . . . because these talks about nationalization of the coal industry are likely to cause unrest among the circles concerned, thus hampering productivity." The Yoshida Government rejected the idea of nationalization, but it did adopt a position of formal, if unenthusiastic, support for state control on the condition that it lead to higher efficiencies of production.[69] On 26 September, Hoshijima announced a new coal-production plan based mainly on the SCAP plan issued one week earlier. It contained the following provision: "New mines will be developed by the projected [state-owned] Industrial Reconstruction Corporation and others on the basis of state management." Ishibashi Tanzan has written that this Yoshida-era plan was the basis for the first draft of Katayama's coal-control bill.[70]

Later that week, the Coal Mining Industry Association (representing coal-mine owners) issued a statement opposing state control. The Association's position was that, if the problems of food, materials, and funds were solved, production would increase. They maintained that changing the form of management in the mines would not lead to more coal. The threat of change did seem to have some effect, since the coal operators suddenly had a strong incentive to raise production in order to avoid state control. This partially explains why they were willing to cooperate in the Coal Reconstruction Committee, organized by Sōdōmei and Keizai Dōyūkai as the flagship body of the Economic Reconstruction Conference movement.[71]

On 16 September, the Japan Socialist Party published its "Policy for Socialist State Control of Coal based on the Premise of Nationalization." The Socialists had called for state control of industry in late 1945, but this was the first time they or anyone had spelled out a plan for achieving it. Their statement affirmed that, "since the feudal quality of the labor system is most severe in coal mines, nationalization is the only alternative."[72] Despite the party name, the Socialists hedged on the socialist goals of this policy. At their national meeting on 28 September, they explained that they were not trying to nationalize the coal industry in the sense of changing ownership, but to increase state control by prioritizing and concentrating state aid to the mines. The private management form would be transformed from within the corporation by bringing labor into the decision-making process and then by fitting the companies into national state economic plans.[73] Eventually, the coal mines would evolve into a truly nationalized industry. This was a compromise position, revealing deep strategic and ideological divisions within the Socialist Party. In January 1947, the left wing of the party published its own "Policy for State Control Based on State Ownership," which took a much stronger position.[74]

The priority-production policy of the Yoshida Government was begun in the context of this debate. Part of Professor Arisawa's contribution in articulating this policy was that he was able to find a way to delay decision on the politically volatile issue of state control while still acting to resolve the economic crisis. Although priority production, administered out of the ESB, did not include state management of the coal mines, it did make coal the linchpin of economic recovery. The priority-production policy benefited from the operators' desire to raise production without losing managerial control of the mines. However, the idea that the state should step in and take control of the mines was consistent with priority production, and, in fact, the ESB endorsed this.[75] The implementation of the priority-production policy left open the possibility of state control of the coal mines, but this issue may not have resurfaced if the Yoshida Cabinet had not fallen in April 1947 and been replaced by a fragile coalition government, headed by the Socialist Party Chairman, Katayama Tetsu.

KATAYAMA'S ECONOMIC POLICIES AND THE COAL-CONTROL BILL

The Katayama Administration continued the priority-production plan as its dominant economic policy, but it also strove to add several distinctive elements of its own. In general, the Katayama Government worked harder than previous governments to control inflation, to institutionalize economic planning, and to enlarge the role of the state in the economy. His "Emergency Economic Plan" of 11 June 1947 sought to strengthen the priority-production policy by tightening economic controls on commodities, wages, and prices.[76] On 5 July 1947, the government published a more detailed wage-price plan, which attempted both to bring down official prices and squeeze the black market out of existence. The ESB designated several basic industrial goods as "stabilization-belt" commodities and set their prices at 65 times that of the 1934–1936 price level. Wages were officially set at 1,800 yen per month, or 28 times prewar levels. This comprehensive economic policy retained "slanted" production recovery as a goal, but took far more active measures to control inflation than had Ishibashi.[77]

In this second phase of the priority-production policy, the Katayama Government *reimposed* economic controls that had been lifted by the three previous postwar administrations. This breaks up the "tōseiki" or period of economic control cited by Japanese economic historians to explain the 1937–1949 period, and rendered as the "transwar period" by some American political scientists.[78] Although government controls of the economy formally existed throughout this period, the issues surrounding them changed markedly in the Occupation era. There was ideological continuity with the war years, but also important conceptual dissonance in two ways.

First, the goals of control differed in that the Katayama Government worked toward building a non-military economy, while previously controls had been instituted specifically as part of Japan's war effort. The basic reason for reimposing control in 1947 was to bring as many economic transactions as possible into the official economy and out of the black market. This economic policy emphasized allocations and rationing as much as price controls. Second, there was also a significant administrative hiatus in the government control system. The first three postwar cabinets all tried to limit government economic controls, despite SCAP orders to maintain them. Those cabinets would have preferred to leave allocating and price-control functions in the hands of the wartime control associations, with their strong zaibatsu domination. The intensification of control in 1947 represented the loss of power of those associations, a fact Keidanren recognized when it hastened to transmit its criticism of the new controls. SCAP records from the first twenty months of the Occupation frequently mention American efforts to force a recalcitrant Japanese government to strengthen allocations controls.[79] This is one of the ways in which the Japanese had abandoned economic policy in the first postwar months.

The orientation toward peacetime economic planning became institutionalized under the Katayama Administration through the ESB and the introduction of annual reports on the economy. SCAP had previously tried to establish a technocratic, non-political economic planning body within the Japanese government. In SCAP's estimation, this was preferable to Cabinet action (determined by the political party in control) or private control associations. The Americans' efforts resulted in establishment of the Cabinet-level ESB in August 1946, but Yoshida never gave the new agency enough staff or money to be effective. Katayama made the ESB into a viable organ, creating 10 bureaus and 48 sections, and increasing the staff from 316 to 2,000 persons.[80] The ESB became the administrative center for economic planning until the end of the Occupation, when Yoshida, back in power, gutted it once again. By that time, however, MITI had taken over many of the planning functions pioneered by the ESB. Many of the authors of the Ministry of Foreign Affairs report become either ESB staff or advisors under Katayama.

In July 1947, the ESB published its first "White Paper" on the national economic situation. Its release to the public was the most startling departure from tradition. The idea that "every one of the people must be given an adequate knowledge of the national economy as though it were matters of their own household economy"[81] was unusual in Japan, where the phrase, "Revere the officials, despise the people" had been famous for hundreds of years. Within the bureaucracy, it also was pathbreaking in that it provided a means to circulate and share the statistics and information gathered by each ministry.[82]

The economic policy that became the political key to the Socialist Party's fortunes, however, was the drive to establish state control of the coal mines. This bill, the "sole socialist measure" of the administration, became a proxy for a debate on the future of the entire Japanese political economy.[83] The Minister of Commerce and Industry in the new cabinet, Mizutani Chōsaburō, announced on 1 June 1947, that the new government would designate 5 important industries for state control: coal, steel, fertilizer, electric power, and shipping. Following the recent example of the British Labour Party, the government would concentrate first on state control of the coal mines, while the other 4 industries would be reorganized later. Before the Cabinet was formed, the Socialists had managed to reach an agreement over state control, not only with the other members of the coalition, but also with the opposition Liberal Party. Mizutani also carefully checked with senior SCAP officials in early June before embarking on this project.[84] The joint party position was that, "as necessary, state control of important basic industries will be imposed in order to increase production, which is the overriding industrial policy." Just before Katayama assumed the prime minister's post, however, the Liberals pulled out of the coalition and ended their never-deep commitment to state control of industry at the same time.[85]

In the summer of 1947, the government argued that state control of the mines was efficient and fair. On 3 June 1947, Minister of Commerce and Industry Mizutani told the Diet that coal mines would be brought under state control in order to develop new mines, provide funds for coal mining, ensure smooth distribution of materials, and promote greater efficiency in both production and management. He also stressed the notion of "fairness." Since the state was allocating a large proportion of the nation's scarce resources to the coal industry, the latter should be required to use them efficiently. Because the coal industry received priority for funds and materials, Mizutani explained, "it is quite natural that [the government] should assert the adoption of a system, by which it assumes direct responsibility for the management of coal mines in order to see that the funds and materials acquired by the said priority operation are properly used."[86] The ESB head, Wada Hiroo, put the same idea more bluntly: "Under the present circumstances of Japan, we cannot afford to tolerate such social dissipation as would be allowed under the laisser faire of capitalism, in which everyone is free to pursue his personal profits and the elements for necessary production are often derouted to socially unnecessary production."[87]

The MCI and the ESB were already working on separate draft plans for state control of the mines. In a 2 June meeting, the two ministries agreed that the final plan would create a democratic Coal

Control Committee to make policy, place zaibatsu mines under direct state control, establish a Coal Mine Commodities Purchasing firm *(kōdan),* and make development of new mines a state responsibility.[88] Both plans also proposed a mine-level Joint Production Council *(seisan kyōgikai),* to be composed equally of workers and managers to implement the Coal Control Committee's decisions. Both also strengthened state power at the level of individual mines. Not surprisingly, the two plans differed in their structure of command, with the MCI plan emphasizing the role of its semi-detached Coal Bureau, and the ESB placing responsibility—and power—in its own hands. They also differed in that the ESB, which leaned toward the fairness argument, wanted to change the form of enterprise management, while the MCI plan supported the existing one on the grounds of greater efficiency. In the ESB plan, the state would exert control directly at the mine level, rather than delegate it to private mine managers.[89]

On 28 June 1947, after many meetings and further negotiation with the budget-conscious Ministry of Finance, the two bureaucracies drafted a joint "Outline Plan for State Control of the Coal Mines" *(Sekitan Kokka Kanri Yōkō).* It retained the 4 main points agreed on on 2 June except that the object of control was changed from "zaibatsu-owned mines" to "major mines," a change of more symbolic than practical importance. Otherwise, it resembled the MCI plan for a complex dual chain of command which relegated the Joint Production Councils to advisory status and left decision-making power with the traditional managers. This draft still contained many unclear areas, such as the duration of the control period, responsibilities of the controller, source of operations planning, character and rights of the Joint Production Council, and the precise role of labor.

This plan generated enormous controversy. Within the ruling coalition, the members of Ashida's Minshu party did not want to include labor in management decisions at all, while the left Socialists wanted an overt commitment to socialism. They were able to patch together a fragile compromise and send a draft bill based on the MCI plan to the Diet on 15 August. Both the Cabinet and the

Diet were immediately pressured from all sides to change the legislation.[90]

The Liberal Party and the Kyushu Coal Operator's League were the strongest foes of the draft bill. The League, highly reminiscent of the prewar Mutual Aid Society, provided an ad hoc forum for owners of smaller Kyushu mines to express their opposition to state control. They argued that it was inefficient, redundant, unnatural, and would create a bureaucratic monster. A U.S. State Department analyst concluded in 1948 that the coal operators "conceive of the government's proper role as largely one of paying subsidies, freeing restricted funds, and granting liberal loans and bounties."[91] Opposition to state control was strongest among small and medium-sized mine owners, who believed that state intervention would resemble the wartime control committees, when the government had helped the larger operators keep their oligopolistic market position. The large mine owners opposed the bill too, but they were more sanguine about their position, even if it passed.[92] The rest of the business community was far less agitated by the proposal. One of the two forerunners of Keidanren, Nihon Sangyō Kyōgikai, issued a more guarded opinion on state control of the coal mines on 29 July 1947. It did not oppose state control outright, but stressed the need to avoid rigid bureaucratic control.[93]

The Kyushu Coal Operators' League soon teamed up with Yoshida's Liberal Party, which was in ideological agreement with them. Yoshida also recognized a golden opportunity to embarrass the Minshu party by painting the Liberals as the only "pure" conservative party. He could remain in lofty opposition, while Ashida's party acceded to socialism in the coal mines.[94]

This alliance of the Liberal Party and the coal operators heralded a new pattern of business funding of political parties. Yoshida was personally tied to the coal industry through his son-in-law, Asō Takayoshi, one of the most important Kyushu coal operators. Two Kyushu Diet members, themselves owners of coal mines, Takano Tatsuo and Nishida Okano, were the most active opponents of the bill. By all accounts, a great deal of money passed from the coal

operators to receptive politicians while the bill was under debate.
The Kyushu Coal Operators' League set up headquarters in Tokyo,
lavishly entertaining Diet members nightly while making their case.
The money for this purpose came from a secret levy of 10 yen on
each ton of Kyushu coal produced. In this direct way, the coal
operators were able to use production increases by miners to protect
their own position in the industry. They also reportedly used government largesse in the form of RFB loans to bribe Diet members
to cripple the bill.[95] Later, several Diet members were convicted of
accepting bribes to vote against the coal bill, including Tanaka
Kakuei, although his conviction was overturned on appeal. Kiso
Shigeyoshi, the Kyushu coal-mine owner who was convicted of paying Tanaka 1 million yen, is widely believed to have channeled
money to Yoshida Shigeru through Asō as well.[96]

   The important point here is not the venality of the Diet members
but the emergent pattern of political funding and the fact that the
coal operators, *as an organization,* became much more closely involved in the political process both at the level of informational
lobbying and of payments. The Kyushu Coal Operators' League's
involvement in politics is an early postwar example of political lobbying by an organized industry association. This was a new pattern.
Before the war, the leading zaibatsu had each supported "their"
political party, rather than participating in industry-based endorse-
ments. The coal industry also set the standard for political contributions in the postwar years. In 1952, the Coal Mining Industry
Association donated 26 million yen to the Liberal Party, by far the
largest sum of any contributor.[97] The coal operators would remain
politically powerful long after they were marginalized economically, partly because they had, early on, cemented their political
alliances.

   There was a second and equally significant legacy of the coal-
control-bill controversy. At the same time that the coal operators
were drawing closer to the Liberal Party and learning to manipulate
the political system, they were sharpening their objections to government authority within their industry. The proposal to nationalize the coal mines was a political threat that raised their level of

distrust of the government and spurred them to demand limits on state involvement in coal mining. This distrust was already well developed as a result of the wartime battle over economic control, but the specter of state control under a *Socialist* government was far more terrifying. If the government continued to be run by conservatives, then the unpleasant aspects of state control were balanced in the minds of many businessmen by the conviction that only the government could raise the resources necessary to modernize Japanese industry. However, the coal industrialists felt they had narrowly escaped control by Socialists, which was a much riskier proposition. This explains why few coal operators shared the assumption that state control was unavoidable, although industrialists in *other* fields sometimes considered coal a prime candidate for development by the state.

The debate over state control of the coal mines raised two equally horrifying specters for the coal operators: usurpation of management authority by the state and by labor unions. If enacted as originally proposed, the state-control plan would have done both. The Hokkaido mine owners had already banded together to protect themselves against Zentan, but now they redoubled their efforts to regain management prerogatives. These mine operators were the first to form a postwar management organization and were an integral part of the national resurgence of employers' groups in 1948. Their participation explains much of "fighting Nikkeiren's" zeal against the labor movement over the next three years. After successfully warding off effective state control in the mines, these managers turned to the problem of labor in 1948, backed by increasingly sympathetic Occupation and Japanese government authorities.[98]

While the issue of state control and its attendant threat of labor control galvanized the mine owners, it helped splinter the mine workers. The coal miners' unions were in a difficult position, since they supported state control in the mines and participation by miners in management planning. They realized the limitations of the government plan, however, and were reluctant to support a bill that gave them such limited powers. Their relationship with the new government had already deteriorated in June, after the Katayama

Cabinet enforced strict wage controls for government workers as part of its Emergency Economic Policy. Although a valiant attempt to stem inflation and government deficits, this policy embittered the labor unions. Politically it was a suicidal move on Katayama's part. By enforcing wage controls and allowing a weak coal-control bill out of committee, Katayama alienated his natural constituency without gaining any other support. This narrowing of public support, combined with the tenuous nature of the coalition that had brought him to power in the first place, led to the collapse of his Cabinet in February 1948. It also stripped the coal miners' unions of clear alternatives in the state-control debate.

After the government proposal on state control of the mines was announced, the confederation of all the coal miners' unions, Zen Tankyō (composed of Zentan, representing 28 percent of unionized miners, the Sōdōmei federation, Nikkō, representing 17 percent, and an independent group of unions, Tanren, representing 55 percent) published the opinion on 8 July that state control should be perpetual and extend to all mines regardless of size; that all private property rights in mines should be abolished; that management should be democratized and separated from ownership; that a management body centered on labor unions should be established; and that state subsidies and capital should be given to workers themselves to use.

Zen Tankyō was so dissatisfied with the cabinet bill that it submitted a separate bill to the Diet incorporating these ideas on 21 August 1947. It also called for precise definition of the term *state control*. However, this bill was not seriously considered in the Diet, and conservative members began to water down the provisions of the already-weaker government bill. The union federation responded by demanding a tougher bill, and, in September, Zen Tankyō withdrew from the Coal Reconstruction Committee in protest over the operators' resistance to democratizing the mines. Zen Tankyō noted that the organization had failed as a forum for democratic management of the mines, and was only a device for raising production. The failure of the Coal Reconstruction Committee disillusioned the miners about working jointly with management, which also affected their attitude toward the coal-control bill. In the case of the Sōdōmei and the independent federations, Nikkō and Tan-ren, the unions began to think of bureaucratic control under the government bill as the lesser evil, since management could not be trusted. However, in Zentan's case, it just confirmed the union's belief that the existing bill was too weak to create change in the mines. The all-union federation split over this and other disagreements, and, in the ensuing weeks, the conservatives in the Diet were able to weaken the law.[99]

At this point, MacArthur issued an extremely ambiguous statement on SCAP attitudes toward state control of the coal mines. His letter to Katayama of 18 September 1947 on the Temporary State Control of Coal Mining Law stated that "there is no objection to its presentation to the Diet for consideration on its merit, without prejudice of any kind from this Headquarters. If the emergency measure under which the Government temporarily assumes the responsibility heretofore resting upon private enterprise is adopted, the Government must raise the production goal previously set to a level consistent with the added resources which alone would justify the change." The letter also spelled out specific measures the government was expected to take to raise production, such as placing the mines on round-the-clock shifts. MacArthur's dilemma was a simple one. He and most of his staff disapproved of state control but he did not want to countermand the democratic decision of a freely elected Japanese government. Moreover, in the absence of any directives explicitly prohibiting state control (or nationalization) of industry, he preferred not to consult Washington on this question.[100]

This letter forced Katayama to do two things. It locked the Socialist Party onto a course that they had already partially chosen: justifying the bill on narrow grounds of efficiency in the coal mines, rather than larger visions of social justice and economic reconstruction. In late September, Mizutani told the Diet that the coal bill was being proposed as a way to check inflation through higher production. In essence, it became merely an extension of the Ishibashi Line. He stressed that "state control of coal mines was conceived purely as an emergency measure in order to meet the actual needs under the present circumstances, and was not an attempt in any way whatsoever to infuse any specific ideology into the minds of the people." In Katayama's own description of the coal bill, "As a socialist industrial policy, it was a very tepid affair."[101] This letter also forced the Cabinet to implement production-raising measures immediately rather than incorporating them into the State Coal Control Bill. These became the "Emergency Measures to Raise Coal Production" of 3 October 1947. Coal production increased as a result of the emergency measures, and the sole remaining rationale for state control grew less and less valid.[102]

After months of debate, the bill passed the Diet on 20 December 1947, as a temporary three-year law which included no enforcement measures. Management representatives dominated the Coal Control Committees through "consumer" positions filled by representatives of the steel, ammonium sulphate, gas, and electric-power industries, plus a bureaucrat from the Ministry of Transportation.[103] Administrative orders based on the law were rarely issued, and, in May 1950, the Liberal Party abrogated it before three years had passed. By that time, coal production had substantially increased. More important, the Japanese were no longer trying to supply their energy needs entirely from domestic sources. American policy had shifted to allow a major petroleum-refining industry in Japan, and imported coal was once again supplying some of Japan's requirements. With the restoration of international trade, the Japanese could afford to buy their energy supplies rather than rely on domestic resources.

In the final analysis, the controversy was won by the proponents of private enterprise. Passage of the anemic coal-control law represented the victory of their definition of economic reconstruction. The original questions raised by the proponents of state control—questions of economic democracy and labor participation in management—had been marginalized to the edges of political discussion during the debate over the coal bill. The issue of state control of the coal mines began as a serious attempt to redress inequalities of the past and the present, especially between mine owner and miner. It was used as a vehicle to raise grand questions about what kind of economy postwar Japan needed. Gradually, however, it became a discussion of productivity, and the earlier issue of economic democratization faded from consideration. At the same time, the coal operators were able to assume the mantle of production recovery—still the key to legitimacy for any economic program. By the end of 1947, they claimed to be the ones who were primarily concerned with increasing supplies of fuel, while the miners talked about who would sign their pay stubs.

State control of the coal mines was increasingly justified as an isolated case, due to the extreme problems and importance of that industry. Originally, labor planned to establish state control in all the important industries, beginning with the mines. By converting only the coal industry, the experiment with state control was doomed to failure, as the coal miners argued at the time.[104] The debacle in the coal mines prevented any serious discussion of extending state control to new industries, although the question of retaining state control over electric power was still unresolved. As the planners at the Ministry of Foreign Affairs had warned in early 1946, it grew increasingly difficult to make radical changes in the economic system. When debate over coal ended, the option of using state control as a means to social and economic democracy was closed. Thereafter, planning moved in new directions.

SIX

U.S. Austerity Policy and Rationalization Theory

By 1947, World War II had receded from the minds of American policymakers, replaced by growing concerns about international security and world trade. These larger shifts led to a new American commitment to revive the Japanese economy and its foreign trade. Rebuilding Japan as the future "workshop of Asia" meant the Americans reassessed and rejected their earlier analysis of Japan as a fundamentally flawed political economy.[1] They turned their energies in late 1948 and 1949 to promoting Japan's economic recovery rather than its demilitarization and democratization.

At first, the Americans planned to give Japan economic aid as a transitional solution to encourage foreign trade. Like Marshall Plan aid to Europe, Japan would receive direct dollar grants and loans from the U.S. government to revive foreign trade. In January 1948, the U.S. representative to the Far Eastern Commission, Major General Frank McCoy, announced that the United States would provide "assistance . . . for a temporary period" to help Japan become self-supporting. A 1948 SCAP document called for 1.3 billion dollars in aid for 1949 and 1950, because "the pipelines of the economy must be filled with the necessary raw materials" and because it would take time to build up Asian sources of industrial materials and food. This policy eventually materialized in the form of aid for Economic Recovery to Occupied Areas (EROA). In early 1948, Congress authorized 165 million dollars in EROA aid to Japan for April 1948

through July 1949, and authorized 180 million dollars for economic recovery in Japan the following year.[2]

The Japanese were quite pleased with the American policy shift
in this first incarnation. In many ways, the American plans were
conforming to Japanese economic assumptions. By mid-1948, the
Americans agreed with the Japanese on several key points: that the
economy should be rebuilt, that it should center on heavy industry,
that exports should be promoted, and that Japan should sell manufactured goods to Southeast Asia and buy raw materials in return.
They were also delighted that the United States seemed willing to
finance Japan's recovery with foreign aid.[3]

Recovery through foreign aid was unquestionably the most pal-
atable of the U.S. policies to the Japanese.[4] The implicit assumption behind the deficit-spending policies of the Yoshida, Katayama,
and Ashida Cabinets was that the United States would continue to
provide economic assistance in Japan. The ESB Economic Rehabilitation Plans of 1947 and 1948 emphasized government investment
and foreign government aid, which the ESB planners regarded as
the only likely source of non-government capital available in Japan
for the next few years. This aid, they hoped, would help raise the
domestic standard of living, thus establishing a peaceful, domestically oriented economy. United States government and private aid
was also deemed essential by business groups. Keizai Dōyūkai, for
example, published a report on 2 July 1948 which shared most of
the key assumptions of the ESB's Economic Rehabilitation Plan but
stressed even more emphatically the importance of U.S. foreign aid
in achieving self-sufficiency by 1953. Keidanren also endorsed this
plan. Japanese planners wanted to redevelop overseas trade but were
not willing to finance it through drastic reductions in domestic
consumption, which they were convinced was the only alternative
to foreign aid. They planned to use American aid as they had Jap-
anese-government subsidies and loans—to calm social tensions by
raising general living standards.[5] The Japanese hoped for an Asian
Marshall Plan; instead they received economic stabilization and deflation.[6]

To the horror and disappointment of the Japanese, by late 1948 the Americans had rejected aid as the primary way to promote Japanese economic recovery. It was simply too expensive. Congress was not enthusiastic about spending American tax dollars abroad and demanded visible and rapid results from EROA aid. More critically, the policy did not work. Aid alone was not enough to revive Japan's foreign commerce, both because of global trade difficulties and high inflation in Japan. The Americans grew convinced that the Japanese economy had to be stabilized before it could survive in international trade. Thus, in late 1948 they began to intervene directly in the domestic economy. The Washington policymakers grew more insistent that Japan implement strict austerity measures to curb inflation and squeeze all economic surplus into the export sector. An early herald of this policy, Under Secretary of the Army William Draper, warned that economic recovery required both political stability and economic austerity within Japan: "The Japanese people will have to work hard and long, with comparatively little recompense for many years to come."[7] These were the new parameters within which the Japanese had to operate.

Japanese planning was in disarray too. The austerity program forced the Japanese to give up the loans and subsidies that undergirded the priority-production policy. Austerity also appeared just after a shakeup within the Japanese government. Yoshida regained the prime minister's post in October 1948, when the undistinguished Ashida Cabinet fell after only seven months in office. The ESB had developed some important plans under Ashida, but Yoshida abandoned them when he returned to power. Since he did not have any clear alternative, this act threw economic planning into confusion. The Japanese were thus neither unified nor prepared when the austerity orders arrived.

The Japanese were loath to abandon all their earlier ideas. Indeed, they retained much of the strategy developed with the priority-production policy—the focus on production, on heavy industry, and on maintaining a government presence in planning, particularly in electric power. This put them in direct conflict with the austerity program, which not only caused general economic decline, but struck heavy industries particularly hard. Government planning was piecemeal and disjointed in 1949 and early 1950, partly because American prohibitions on new government loans and subsidies weakened Japanese state control of the economy. United States policy not only undercut postwar Japanese policy. It also once again cut against the structural changes that had taken place in the economy during the war (although some shifts, like ending reparations, eased Japanese economic recovery). Most galling to the Japanese, the austerity program failed to revive the economy. The year 1949 and early 1950 were times of great hardship, while coal, still the linchpin of reconstruction, was the greatest disappointment.

The Japanese still had major economic problems left to solve. They had not settled on what goods to export or even whether or not to maximize exports or minimize imports. They had neither obvious trade partners nor sources of capital. Nor had they decided how to address these problems. The Japanese tried different approaches in various sectors of the economy, hoping that trial and error would lead them to a new strategy. Economic planning developed out of the experiences of industries such as coal, electric power, and petroleum, rather than dictating their development. Indeed, the Japanese tried three different approaches in these three industries in 1949. They struggled over which—if any—seemed both economically viable and politically feasible.

One new approach, first pursued in coal and steel, was rationalization. This involved using technological advances to improve both domestic standards of living and industrial productivity. Rationalization policy would become a key and lasting part of postwar strategy, but its promise did not show immediately. Without capital or overseas markets, it remained little more than an idea on paper. The Japanese originally imagined wrongly that, if they concentrated technological development in a few designated industries, this automatically would upgrade the whole economy. Their reasoning progressed logically from priority production to priority-productivity policy. Only later did they develop an appreciation of the complex effects of one industry's rationalization on that of another. Rationalization efforts in the steel industry offered some reason for hope, but rationalization in the coal mines failed miserably.

Given this record, few Japanese were confident that rationalization could solve their vast economic problems. Many of the positive aspects of rationalization policy were still invisible in 1949. Nor were all its consequences intended. Rather, its greatest contribution to economic development—the energy revolution—was unanticipated by Japanese planners.

Gloomy assessments of rationalization in 1949 meant that the Japanese continued to pursue other paths to reconstruction. They tried to retain state control of electric power in a bitter and amazingly lengthy struggle with the Americans. The fight over reorganizing Hassōden, which meant that the industry was neither rationalizing nor pursuing any alternative recovery strategy, probably was the single largest obstacle to economic recovery in Japan. The Americans simply did not allow the Japanese to pursue this route to reconstruction, despite Japanese wishes and the real costs to U.S. policies in Asia. This was not the only time the United States would adopt policies detrimental to Japanese economic recovery. They also forbade Japanese trade with Northeast Asia in 1951, despite strong Japanese lobbying for such trade on the grounds that it would ease the transition to more sophisticated exports.

The Japanese also pursued a third strategy for development—using foreign investment to reconstruct. This strategy worked in the petroleum-refining industry, one of the very few to thrive in Japan. Many Japanese looked to recovery through foreign investment as a model in 1949 and 1950, although they would reject it later. Japanese business and government leaders worked hard to attract private foreign aid, but found few interested foreign investors beyond oil. Japan seemed a poor business risk at the time to potential investors.

In hindsight, one can see the foundations of some of Japan's later economic success in rationalization theory and in some specific developments of these years. Rationalization policy provided the key to the conundrum of how to improve both productivity and living standards, still a goal in the present drive to develop "knowledge-intensive" industries. Rationalization policy developed out of the interplay between Japanese government planners, businessmen, organized labor, U.S. austerity planners, and SCAP technical advisors, although in a climate much more hostile to labor than in the first postwar years. This diversity would eventually be a source of strength, although these groups fought bitterly over rationalization's meaning. Other important developments included the emergence of the *keiretsu* (bank-oriented) business structure, methods to control the foreign-exchange budget, use of advisory councils to make and disseminate policy, modernization of the oil industry, careful attention to infrastructure, and the further entrenchment of economic planning. The intense debates of the era themselves brought the various economic strategies into public discussion. Many of these developments, however, came about as by-products of attempts to solve other problems. The Japanese had not yet found an economic strategy that brought reconstruction. They would not do so until the international context radically changed once again after the outbreak of war in Korea.

ENFORCING AUSTERITY

American stabilization-policy plans began with a critical evaluation of Japanese economic policy. While the priority-production policy raised production levels in designated industries, it was not sufficient to revive the Japanese economy. Nor did priority production work to halt inflation and develop international trade. In many ways, the crux of the problem was to develop the foreign-trade sector. Japan could never produce enough food and basic raw materials to support its population, and so had to find ways to pay for these imports. However, Japan had neither viable exports nor cash to develop any. American "economic-recovery" policy thus referred particularly to export recovery.

Japan's economic problems were symptoms of a global trade imbalance between the United States and all other parts of the world. America's enormous economic strength in the late 1940s meant that it could provide the goods other countries needed but, in turn, there was no demand in America for foreign products. To put it simply, although nations all over the world wanted to buy American goods, few could afford to pay for them. This "dollar gap" was a crucial obstacle, not only to the reintegration of Japan, but to the stability of the whole postwar economic edifice.[8]

Within the general trade crisis, Japan had some particularly difficult hurdles to overcome. Japan had lost its main sources of inexpensive imports when its colonies were shorn away. Imports had to come from a longer distance and were correspondingly more expensive. Worse, most postwar imports came from the United States, paid for in precious dollars. Nor was it clear what goods Japan should try to sell abroad, since the future for Japan's important prewar exports, silk and cotton products, seemed bleak. It was equally unclear *where* Japan should try to ship its goods, partly because the Japanese needed to be paid in dollars; since they had to repay *their* creditors in dollars, they could not afford to accept weaker currencies such as the pound sterling. Currency inconvertibility exacerbated the trade problem, rather than creating it, but was a major obstacle in its own right.[9]

In Japan, the austerity policy invalidated a broad range of Occupation as well as Japanese policies, including the reparations, economic deconcentration, and labor programs. These were now evaluated more on the basis of their contribution to Japan's rapid economic recovery than on principles of democracy or retribution. Pauley's reparations plan was reevaluated three times in 1947 and 1948, and diminished each time. Finally, in May 1949, the program was canceled after only a small amount of goods had been shipped overseas. This action was of great symbolic (and some practical) importance for general Asian economic development. While Pauley had worked from the principle that Japan should relinquish its role as the most industrialized country in Asia, the later reports were based on the assumption that the United States should not only strengthen the Japanese economy, but also reemphasize its asymmetrical trade pattern with other Asian countries of buying food and raw materials and selling finished products.[10]

The economic deconcentration program fell into disfavor in 1948 for similar reasons. A special Deconcentration Review Board (DRB), which arrived in Japan in May 1948, reversed the spirit of the Deconcentration Law; it required evidence that a firm had "restricted competition or hindered the opportunity for others to engage independently in any business" before a deconcentration order could be issued. Such behavior is notoriously difficult to document, and the DRB drastically reduced the scale of the deconcentration program.[11] Later, one member of the DRB explained that their role was "to provide a balance wheel against over-decartelization." He explained that, "by the early months of 1948, those responsible for our Far Eastern foreign policy had become aware of changes in the international situation and deemed it unwise to pursue longer a policy of pulverizing companies representing the backbone of Japanese commerce and industry, at least to a point where it might inhibit recovery of the Japanese economy."[12] By the time the DRB finished its review in July 1949, only 18 firms were reorganized under the Deconcentration Law. In addition, the DRB found the electric-power industry to be an excessive concentration of economic power, but a ruling on that case was deferred "because the issue was political as well as economic."[13]

SCAP had already become dissatisfied with labor-union activity in early 1947 when it banned a general strike, but, during 1948, American attitudes toward the Japanese labor movement grew steadily harsher. On 11 December 1948, the Chief of the Labor Division of ESS elaborated 3 wage principles. The first forbade the Japanese government practice of using subsidies in wage disputes to resolve the problem of low real wages and fixed prices. Loans for this purpose were also prohibited. Finally, SCAP announced that it would not approve any wage increases that could cause a rise in the general price level.[14] This statement, issued in response to requests for wage increases by Densan and the coal miners, repudiated one of the basic functions of the priority-production policy—to use government resources to ease tension between labor and management in essential industries. This action set the stage for the industrial confrontations that were to take place over the next two years.

SCAP officials also took several actions to strengthen the hand of management against the unions. They allowed employers more freedom to coordinate their labor policies, initiating a "rising consciousness of their role and a greater class solidarity" among management. The most important symbol of this new policy was SCAP sanction of Nikkeiren as a national employers' organization in April 1948. Nikkeiren sought to reestablish managerial control over management decisions. This meant denouncing production control and, eventually, reducing labor-management councils to consultative bodies, changing contracts to limit the right of the union to intervene in decisions, and breaking the power of radical unions. Nikkeiren remains the most important voice for management in Japan today.[15]

The Americans consolidated their austerity policy in December 1948, when they *ordered* the new Yoshida Administration to begin economic-stabilization measures. For the next eighteen months, the Americans directly controlled the Japanese budget and economic policy. On 19 December, MacArthur directed the Japanese government to implement the Nine-Point Economic Stabilization Program.[16] The main features of the program were curtailment of all loans and credit, a balanced national budget, and abolition of the government subsidies and loans that had protected Japanese industry from the harsh rigors of the free-enterprise system. The 3 wage principles—no loans and no subsidies for wages, and no increases that contribute to inflation—were incorporated into the stabilization policy. When the Japanese government, which was not at all pleased by these harsh measures, dragged its feet, Washington sent Detroit banker Joseph Dodge to implement an austere "stabilization" program. American policymakers in Japan understood and accepted the impact of this policy. In January 1949, the Chief of ESS, Major-General Marquat, chillingly quoted MacArthur as saying that the stabilization program "will call for increased austerity in every phase of Japanese life and for the temporary surrender of some of the privileges and immunities inherent in a free society."[17] Demilitarization and democratization policy had been reversed.

Dodge's agenda consisted of two main items: controlling inflation to give the yen a stable value against the dollar, and slimming the government budget to minimize the need for U.S. public aid. The goal of these combined measures was a competitive export industry that could eventually pay for imports to Japan, making the country "self-sufficient." The term *self-sufficiency* referred to the reintegration of Japan into the world economy rather than to a separation from it. It really meant reorienting Japanese economic institutions, especially government-controlled ones. Dodge planned to break down the institutions that held the Japanese economy apart from the global one, that is, U.S. aid and Japanese government subsidies, or the two legs of the artificial "stilts holding up the economy."

Dodge's priorities were based on his rejection of Ishibashi's argument that inflation was the result of commodity shortages. Rather, Dodge laid the blame for inflation squarely on Ishibashi's policies. He was especially critical of the RFB's loan activities and shut down that institution in 1949. He also slashed producer subsidies and export subsidies, although import subsidies were continued for some time. These moves effectively smashed the stilt of direct government aid into matchsticks. They also curbed inflation, and the economy was sufficiently stabilized by May 1949 to set an exchange rate for the yen at 360 to the dollar.[18]

Dodge derided the priority-production policy because it placed the burden of Japanese recovery on "the American taxpayer's back." He attacked this other "stilt" by organizing a revolving fund to handle U.S. aid money to Japan. This counterpart aid fund differed from earlier assistance accounts in that it was controlled by SCAP rather than by the Japanese government. U.S. aid arrived in Japan in dollars, which were used to buy needed imports. Then the yen equivalent of the aid dollars was placed in a special fund, which could be withdrawn by SCAP as needed. Dodge used the counterpart aid fund to retire the Japanese government debt created by the RFB and help balance the budget. After that function had been fulfilled, the counterpart aid fund could also be used as a lender of industrial rehabilitation funds like the RFB, but the Americans were much stricter in their definition of eligibility than were the Japanese.[19]

Dodge hoped these stilt-smashing measures would force Japanese firms to streamline their production operations through "rationalization," that is, higher productivity and other forms of cost cutting. Private industries had neglected efforts in this direction since they could get free government aid, Dodge argued. He hoped economic adversity would stimulate the efficiency created by a competitive environment. The medicine of economic orthodoxy would impose hardship on the Japanese people, but Dodge believed in its efficacy.

The stabilization program cut domestic spending drastically, just as it was designed to do. For many Japanese, this meant a return to the hungry conditions of 1945. Balancing the budget meant that, between February 1949 and February 1950, 419,000 government workers lost their jobs. When subsidies and controls ended, services such as railroad fares and postal rates shot up in price. In private industry, too, the general economic slump meant mass discharges, and estimates of the number of unemployed ranged as high as 2.4 million people.[20] In the coal industry, 37,053 miners were laid off between February 1949 and June 1950.[21]

Dodge would have been satisfied with this effect if it had been balanced by rising exports. Economic recession within Japan should lead, by his reasoning, to less domestic consumption and greater production efficiency, thus lowering the prices of Japanese exports, expanding Japan's overseas markets, and eventually bringing prosperity back to Japan. However, the Dodge plan was not successful in this goal. The stabilization plan could make Japanese goods cheaper, but it could not create markets for them. The Japanese government commented in late 1949 that it was no longer "raw materials and capacity but effective demand which determines the level of production."[22] The constriction of the domestic market was part of the stabilization plan, but the lack of world markets was both unanticipated and fatal to its success in making Japan self-sufficient.[23]

JAPANESE RESPONSE TO STABILIZATION MEASURES

In Japan, the period of the stabilization program is referred to as the "stabilization panic," a term that captures the contemporary mood about the economy. The Japanese were horrified when the stabilization program replaced aid-based recovery in American plans. They agreed with the Americans that inflation had to be controlled and that the Japanese economy had to be aligned with the global economy. They recognized that Ishibashi had been overly optimistic about inflation, and that the priority-production policy was better suited to increasing production than it was to improving the efficiency of production.[24] However, they disagreed profoundly over priorities, degrees of enforcement, and timing of these policies.

Japanese economic policymakers were deeply divided over the austerity program. The ESB was probably the most opposed to it, while Dodge's strongest supporters were the men most like himself—bankers and Ministry of Finance officials. Others, such as Yoshida Shigeru, back as prime minister, saw the Dodge Line as a way to implement unpopular policies that would consolidate his hold on office.[25] However, all of them feared that Dodge would go too far, plunging Japan into economic disaster. This was because they disputed several of his basic assumptions about the Japanese economy.

CAPITAL-ACCUMULATION DEBATE. The point of greatest friction between the Japanese government and Dodge was the problem of capital accumulation. Dodge firmly believed that this was a secondary issue, to be addressed after fiscal stabilization had been achieved. He was equally firm in his belief that accumulating capital was the job of the private sector, either firms or banks, but not the government. The Japanese government officials, who could reflect on a long history of aiding businesses financially, never accepted either part of this analysis. They argued that industrial recovery was still a greater problem than fiscal stabilization in 1949. and that halting inflation without boosting production would create a disastrous depression.

They argued further that the government needed to retain policy control over investment in order to best use scarce financial resources. Despite Prime Minister Yoshida's personal opposition to any government economic planning, his key lieutenants, notably

Ikeda Hayato, Minister of Finance from 1949 to 1952, believed in indicative planning. Ikeda and the bureaucrats at the ESB justified the need for planning on the scarcity of resources in postwar Japan. They compared their task to that of a tailor who has not quite enough material to make a suit according to a standard pattern and has to plan how to use every scrap of cloth before making the first cut.

The ESB wanted to attract capital partly out of concern for *future* economic problems. In the tradition of the 1946 Ministry of Foreign Affairs report, these men were charting a long-term course for the Japanese economy. They were far more concerned about the damaged infrastructure of their nation than were the Americans, and they criticized the stabilization plan for not allocating funds to improve Japan's energy industries and agriculture. They warned that, if more money was not allocated to these basic long-term projects, future economic projections were unrealistic; it "will be the same as to ask a juggler to take out a rabbit before the audience while furnishing him a top-hat that has room only for . . . a rat."[26] Energy thus remained central to their plans.

Most Japanese businessmen were equally sure that Dodge's policies were inappropriate for a poor country like Japan. Keidanren issued gloomy warnings that the Japanese economy and social structure were too weak for such drastic action, although it formally supported Dodge. Keizai Dōyūkai called the 9-point stabilization plan "one big alarm bell" for Japan and published a steady flow of reports over the next eighteen months, all equating the deflation with economic stagnation.[27] Although many businessmen feared bureaucratic "meddling" in their firms, they were still interested in receiving government funds. Since little private capital was available in postwar Japan, most managers recognized that investment could come only from the government or from foreign sources. Kei Hoashi, the managing director of the Japan Federation of Industries (Nissankyō), spoke for business in 1949 when he wrote that, "for the present, however, it is utterly impossible to finance these projects with normal accumulation of national savings. For the reconstruction of the Japanese economy, therefore, it is necessary, in the first place, to make efficient use of the Counterpart Fund and other financial aids from foreign countries, and, in the second place, to obtain financial aid from the State, as advance credit within the limits of [the policy of] not aggravating inflation." Hoashi was openly critical of Dodge's refusal to use the counterpart-aid fund more freely for industrial rehabilitation.[28]

STANDARD-OF-LIVING DEBATE. The second most important problem, as the ESB saw it, was the political instability caused by unemployment. From the ESB point of view, successfully applying the stabilization plan would require a politically dangerous suppression of the domestic standard of living: "The army of the unemployed thus swollen is bound to give rise to serious social unrest."[29] Keidanren echoed this concern in its warnings about Japan's "weak social structure." The ESB, however, was sympathetic to Dodge's goal of limiting domestic consumption for the sake of the health of the total economy. The ESB planners, like Dodge, wanted to create deferred consumption (that is, savings) which could be used to revive Japanese industry.[30] The ESB hoped to raise the Japanese standard of living back up to the 1930–1934 level, but increase the production level to a higher, perhaps 1937, level. The difference between the industrial production level and the consumption level would provide the capital which they were so earnestly trying to accumulate.

The difference was really one of degree rather than kind, but it was an important one, nonetheless. Dodge was willing to hold the standard of living down to a much lower level than were the Japanese. This was clear in many small decisions. For example, when the Japanese proposed raising freight rates by 100 percent but not passenger fares on Japan National Railways, Dodge changed that to a 60-percent increase for passengers and none for freight. Japanese policymakers at the ESB believed that it was in the best interests of Japan as a nation to raise the average wage, consumption, and technical level of the Japanese people. In their 1949 White Paper, the ESB economists argued that "the stagnation of living at such low level will, in the long run, deteriorate labor power, render mainte-

nance and development of technical and intellectual ability difficult, and hamper the development of [the] economy. . . . [T]he
low level of living shrinks [the] domestic market, thereby arresting
the sound expansion of production and export."[31] They feared that
Dodge's drastic surgery would kill the patient.

At the same time, the ESB planners realized that domestic consumption could not be allowed to rise to the point where it hindered
capital accumulation. The ESB, despite its relatively strong defense
of general living standards as compared to Dodge, firmly supported
the "production-first" strategy that characterized Japanese economic
policy at least until the 1960s. This attention to both standard of
living and savings was a natural development from the 1946 Ministry of Foreign Affairs report. While it had boldly argued for substantially expanded domestic markets, the 1946 report also recognized that this trend had to be paralleled by increases in exports if
Japan was not to bankrupt itself. Conceptually, this was straight-
forward, but difficult to attain in practice.

MAXIMIZE EXPORTS OR MINIMIZE IMPORTS? There was a third debate
taking place among the Japanese within the context of the Dodge
plan—whether to emphasize natural-resource development within
Japan or export industries. Dodge himself was not included, as all
the parties to this debate agreed on the need for greater state planning of the economy. Arisawa Hiromi, Tsuru Shigeto, and the ESB
argued that import-minimization projects, like the Tennessee Val-
ley Authority in the United States, should have priority. They based
this argument on two main points. First, the disruptions in the
world economy, the dollar gap, and Japan's special disadvantages
meant that a primary reliance on exports was simply too dangerous.
Japan should try to minimize its dependence on overseas commodities. Second, Japan needed to develop its infrastructure, if it hoped
to grow economically in the future. This attention to the foundations of the future economy—with its implicit acceptance of planning—continues to be an important element of Japanese economic
policy. Arisawa took this reasoning one step further, arguing that
this kind of development, using government funds and public over-

sight, would build a more broad-based economic socialism. He was operating out of a very similar set of assumptions to those used by Densan officials when they suggested reorganizing their industry in 1946 and 1947. Planning was not only more efficient, Arisawa believed, but also fairer.[32]

The other side of this Japanese debate was that the nation should focus first on expanding exports, because that was the quickest path to self-sufficiency. Nakayama Ichirō spoke for this position when he argued that Japanese economic conditions were very like those of nineteenth-century Britain.[33] He recognized the limitations of a large population and few natural resources, but thought these were best resolved by embracing foreign trade rather than limiting it. Like nineteenth-century Britain, the Japanese economy would be sustained by processing imports and selling manufactured goods.

This debate was eventually resolved in Nakayama's favor by a major coal-mine strike in 1952 and the physical limits of the domestic resource base. Although the Japanese developed their hydroelectric potential (for example) as far as they could, it simply could not support the burgeoning economy of the 1960s. In the meantime, however, the Japanese settled on a plan broad enough to incorporate both positions. This was rationalization policy, used to pursue both goals of export maximization and import minimization. Rationalization, they hoped, would also create capital and raise both productivity and standards of living. It was to become the main Japanese response to the failure of austerity.

INDUSTRIAL RATIONALIZATION POLICY

Rationalization, or more efficient production, was one of Dodge's major goals and is one of his most important legacies. But only the *goal* of rationalization can be considered a direct bequest from the stabilization planners. The *meaning* of rationalization changed in the hands of the Japanese at the ESB and MITI to a different and much more dynamic program. Industrial rationalization in postwar Japan far surpassed any prewar project in both scale and content. It became a shorthand expression for promoting both economic efficiency at every level of the economy and greater integration between economic sectors. The goal of this effort was to encourage a healthy flow of more sophisticated exports and so create a self-sufficient economy. This was the historic core of Japan's famous industrial policy.

By this time, the two key insights of the 1946 Ministry of Foreign Affairs report were accepted as Japanese policy. Since postwar Japan could not produce enough food to feed its growing population, the Japanese had to export to survive. Moreover, the traditional strategy of exporting inexpensive, low-quality goods was no longer appropriate to Japan's new postwar conditions. This was both because traditional overseas markets had shrunk and because Japanese businessmen could no longer enforce low wages at home. "In the prewar years, Japanese products had extensive overseas markets, but these were mainly for low-technology, low-wage goods which had the reputation of being 'cheap and poor quality.' Now that Japan is reborn as a democratic state, we absolutely cannot use dumping supported by low wages, as in the past. Thus, the only effective method to promote exports left to us is industrial rationalization, especially enterprise rationalization," the government argued.[34]

Again and again, the Japanese planners referred to rationalization as one of the only effective choices available to them in the effort to strengthen the economy. This perception bolstered their opposition to Dodge on the questions of capital accumulation and living standards. The ESB planners attacked the stabilization program directly, arguing that rationalization would be easier with high levels of production and high employment than during a depression. The ESB warned that "stagnant production caused by insufficient purchasing power has set a limit to the rationalization."[35] They pointed out that the most serious problem for Japanese firms was lack of access to capital rather than poor management. While fiscal restraint might force managers to become more efficient, it further shrank the financial resources available for rationalization.

Government officials also hoped that rationalization could act as the key to the dilemma of how to raise both domestic consumption and exports. This concept was invoked to resolve the same problems the Japanese had been grappling with since 1946. They needed a plan that would deliver a better standard of living *and* generate export income. They hoped that greater economic efficiency could resolve the social tensions that would develop if domestic standards of living were forcibly kept low. By moving the economy toward production of more sophisticated goods (and exporting those goods) the Japanese could hope both to improve consumption at home and pay for imports. This concept included the assumptions that high rates of employment and high levels of production were the best preconditions for technological improvement. It drew heavily on the ideas of the 1946 Ministry of Foreign Affairs report, which had argued that the Japanese had to upgrade their domestic economy in order to find a comfortable niche within the international one. This was in contrast to the traditional conservative opinion that domestic consumption was a far less immediate task then raising exports, the attitude of Dodge and of Yoshida Shigeru.

The ESB planners argued that cutting wages was a shortsighted policy, the limits of which were already being reached. As pointed out by Professor Arisawa, a frequent advisor to the ESB, "It has become obvious today that there is no more room left for further industrial rationalization unless it is based on the modernization of technique and equipment. And the advanced technique and equipment cannot be acquired except with the aid of long-term investment. And labor adjustment, an essential factor in free economy, can sometimes become a counteracting factor when misapplied."[36] The goal was not simply to produce cheaper goods, but to improve their quality. That required money and an educated and motivated labor force.

The MITI bureaucrats, who made rationalization policy their special project, substantially agreed with the ESB on all these points. There was a slight difference in tone between MITI planners and their colleagues at the ESB, however. MITI officials tended to stress power politics rather than the inherent social and economic inefficiency of cutting wages. They showed great consciousness of the ways in which the growing strength of labor, the impact of the international economy, and restrictions on state intervention limited their choices for economic policymaking. The MITI Enterprise Bureau draft of the basic document on rationalization, which the Cabinet adopted as the Policy Concerning Industrial Rationalization on 13 September 1949, explained:

> Rationalization is crucial for the country's survival as a trading nation and for reintegration of the Japanese economy on a stable basis with the world economy. . . . Given the rise in influence of the working classes, the movement of capitalism in a more socialist direction is inevitable and the present capitalist course of enterprise rationalization, that is, lowering wages—rationalizing—dropping costs—increasing production levels—and raising profits, is not possible. We must instead use the method of guaranteeing real wages—rationalization—production increases—lowered unit prices—and higher profits. To put it another way, we must start from the premise of an assured balance in the national economy, created by expanding the domestic consumer market. . . . The poverty of state finances . . . combined with the loosening of controls and the passage of the democratization legislation, which mean that we must act out of a basis of respect for economic democracy, limits our power.[37]

MITI's tone was more reluctant than that of the ESB, but its conclusions were the same. Japan required an economic policy that would permanently incorporate workers at a higher level and create a strong domestic consumer market.

COMPONENTS OF THE RATIONALIZATION POLICY. From the first, rationalization was seen as a complex phenomenon which had to be integrated throughout the entire Japanese economy if it was to be successful. It had 4 main goals as expressed in the September 1949 Cabinet order on rationalization. First was the rationalization of each firm, "with Japan's future industrial structure in mind." Second was to bring Japanese industrial-product prices immediately in line with international prices. Third, "depending on the initiative and skill of an industry to effect the rationalization of its firms, government efforts will be directed to cultivate an environment conducive to rationalization and to eliminate obstacles to it." Fourth, rationalization was to be actively promoted and planned through higher efficiency and adoption of superior technology.[38]

The first principle, that firms develop on the basis of "future industrial structure," reflected the fact that the rationalization program grew out of the realization that Japan's traditional products of cotton textiles, silk, and tea could no longer bring in much revenue. This had been recognized in Japanese circles as early as the 1946 Ministry of Foreign Affairs report, and was a basic assumption of the three ESB White Papers after that. Rationalization was the chosen method to develop new industries, mainly heavy and chemical industries, to fill the gap. In other words, rationalization was a way to improve the efficiency of the entire economy rather than just of individual industries. This followed the ESB argument of 1948 that rationalization of production was the key to raising efficiency and lowering production costs in Japan generally.[39]

MITI added another element to this idea in 1949—that rationalization performed an integrative economic function. Their rationalization policy statement contains the first mention of the concept of "industrial structure," and it documents the origin of the postwar Japanese definition of this as a dynamic process that changes in response to international market conditions. The MITI drafters of this policy divided rationalization into 3 levels: enterprise rationalization, industry rationalization, and whole-economy rationalization as a way of defining MITI's own relationship to industrial structure and guiding firms toward a consistent development path. This was to become an important analytical tool for the Japanese through the decades to come.

The second goal reflected the immediate impetus for the rationalization plan. If Japan hoped to become economically self-sufficient, then it had to expand its exports. One of the major obstacles to self-sufficiency was the low quality and high prices of Japanese goods compared to those of foreign competitors. The government officials also tied rationalization closely to a shift to more sophisticated exports, or the new "industrial structure." In practice, this meant concentrating on basic industry as much as on export industries directly. This twin approach would simultaneously maximize exports and minimize imports, it was hoped. As in 1946, the first two industries chosen were coal mining and steel making, both basic industries.[40] By 1952, the government defined rationalization as including "judgments based on the rate for foreign-exchange profits, the amount of goods exported, the condition of industries in foreign countries, and deciding what kind of industries and in what proportions Japan should encourage," and specifically tied it to promotion of exports.[41]

The third principle is, I suspect, expressed in a deliberately vague manner. The government needed the cooperation of industry for a successful rationalization drive, but industrialists were wary of allowing the government free rein within their factories. On 12 April 1949, Nikkeiren published its "Views Concerning Enterprise Rationalization." This document set out a 7-point program for a government industrial policy which it deemed necessary for survival in the competitive world economy. It started from the same premises as the bureaucrats did, namely, that "our country's reconstruction and self-sufficiency is dependent on encouragement of export trade, which cannot be achieved without enterprise rationalization. The problem of rationalization is not just the problem of a single firm but also of the government and the citizens." The Nikkeiren proposal attacked the government for imposing economic controls during and after the war. "It would not be an overstatement to say that the result of being under the sway of the Japanese government's control policies was that the firms are inefficient and irrational. Control is inappropriate to modern times and a deep-rooted evil."[42] However, although Nikkeiren made it very clear that it did not want the government to interfere within individual firms, it did see a role for the state in guiding rationalization policy. According to Nikkeiren, appropriate actions for the government included establishing an effective national production plan, developing a national capital financing and investment plan, and coordinating these two plans. Appropriate government behavior also included price policy, improvements in the tax system and tax-collection methods, minimization of state controls, and a substantially new policy toward failed businesses. Nikkeiren opposed past forms of administrative guidance in which the state had reached within a firm to control prices or distribution of goods, but it did not object to aid to a whole industry or to unified production and financing policies.

MITI seems to have taken these suggestions to heart and promised to concentrate on "establishing goals, removing environmental obstacles to rationalization, and offering information and guidance."[43] There was certainly plenty to do in these areas. The most important "obstacle" was the capital shortage, but the government also pledged to improve quality standards, ease restrictions on technology imports, provide information about foreign markets, assure a stable, balanced national budget, and improve transportation and communication networks. This avoided direct government involvement in rationalization within firms, which the business community would have found intrusive.

By 1957, MITI had realized that this system of leaving rationalization decisions within a company to its management encouraged tremendous and stimulating competition among Japanese firms and was a major boon to economic development. Japanese firms in the petroleum, electric-power, steel, electric-machinery, and many other industries chose to invest heavily in modern equipment in order to seize new market shares from their competitors. In 1949, however, this situation was not clear to MITI officials nor to anyone else.[44] The decision to concentrate on environmental obstacles was based more on a desire to avoid a major battle with Nikkeiren than on a clearly defined policy.

The 1949 policy statement also laid the cornerstone of an institutional framework for joint government-business policymaking by establishing an Industrial Rationalization Council as an advisory commission to MITI in the autumn of 1949. This is one of the first and most important of the *shingikai*, composed of industrialists, financiers, academic or other "outside experts," and government officials, that have received attention as important policymaking vehicles in Japan.[45] The Industrial Rationalization Council organized many private exchanges of technical information, such as study-abroad programs for Japanese, in cooperation with SCAP and the Japanese government. The council set up demonstration projects, translated and published articles, and hosted conferences on technical subjects to hear Japanese and foreign experts.

The fourth goal of the rationalization policy simply established priorities. Importing technology seemed like the fastest, least disruptive type of rationalization. It emphasized positive social change, as opposed to rationalization through lay-offs or speed-ups—in short, the aspects of the rationalization policy that were most popular. It also could be applied directly to either the export or the domestic natural-resource sectors. Finally, this priority took advantage of the fifteen-year technology gap between Japanese and Western industries.

PRECONDITIONS: TECHNOLOGY GAP. The massive gain in productivity envisioned by the Japanese was possible because new technologies were available in a wide range of fields in the United States and Europe. Since the early 1930s, the Japanese had gradually lost contact with scientific and technological developments in other countries. Not only did World War II isolate Japan; it also stimulated rapid technological experimentation elsewhere, especially in the United States. This accumulated research experience was just becoming available for commercial exploitation in the postwar years. The decade from 1945 to 1955 was one of tremendous technological innovation in areas as diverse as miniaturization and plastics—just at the point when the Japanese were in the market for new equipment and processes.

It is often argued that American bombers cleared the path for Japan's economic success by destroying old and out-moded plants As other battlefields around the world attest, this is hardly a sufficient explanation of Japan's later prosperity; but there is a grain of truth to the observation that the loss of old equipment forced the Japanese to rebuild just at a time when rebuilding would provide the greatest returns in speed of production and quality of product. Moreover, the *experience* of being bombed was an important factor in creating a national consensus on the need to develop technologically. Losing the war was a graphic demonstration to the Japanese of the importance of technology.[46]

Timing is not the only factor that set the Japanese apart in their quest to upgrade their industries, however. Despite the fact that Japan produced mainly cheap and shoddy goods for export in the prewar years, its citizens had a solid base of presurrender education and technical experience to draw on. This developed partly from the same stimulus as in America: War preparations and armaments manufacture provided a crucial training ground for postwar engineers and technicians.[47] As in the Meiji period, the high education level of the Japanese people allowed them to move quickly into new economic activities. Ironically, although it was the gap between Western and Japanese technology that allowed Japan to grow so fast in the postwar decades, it was only because that gap was comparatively narrow that this is true.

The effort to improve Japanese production by introducing new technology was warmly supported by the Economic and Scientific, Civil Communications, and Natural Resources sections of SCAP and by U.S. officials in Washington. In January 1949, an ESS division chief wrote to Marquat that "production experts in GHQ all agree that substantial increases in production, both in quantity and quality, can be achieved through a concerted drive to raise the level of technology in Japanese industry. . . . The returns from the program will come in the form of increased quantity and quality of exports, more efficient utilization of imported materials and added production for domestic consumption." Like the Japanese, this SCAP official tied the issue of technology to Japan's ability to export. He suggested that emphasis be placed on acquiring technology, knowhow, and licenses, and that first priority go to projects "that will provide more immediate results in relation to the foreign trade program or domestic industrial reconstruction."[48] Meanwhile, the Natural Resources Section established a large, well-funded Japanese Technical Visitor Program to send Japanese petroleum, mining, and manufacturing experts to the United States to study advanced techniques. SCAP officials were instrumental in drafting the 1 June 1949 Product Standards Law, which improved assessments of quality and standardization in Japan.[49]

In early 1950, 50 Japanese business executives assembled in Tokyo for a special 10-week seminar on product standards and quality control. Each of them had been personally invited by the Science and Technology Division of SCAP's Economic and Scientific Section, which hoped that lectures by four American experts would "heighten the interest of Japanese industrialists in raising product quality and uniformity." SCAP officials also encouraged technical experts to explore these problems themselves. In mid-1950, SCAP arranged for the Japanese Union of Scientists and Engineers to invite a crusty American statistician, W. Edwards Deming, to Japan. Deming's creed of quality control, that quality must be built into a product rather than inspected in after completion, seemed to speak precisely to the problems the Japanese were facing. His careful, step-by-step approach offered concrete ways to implement the rationalization policy which had been ratified by the Cabinet in September 1949.[50] SCAP officials' willingness to help the Japanese break free from their "technological sloth" was an important stimulus to rationalization in Japan.[51]

THE REALITIES OF RATIONALIZATION PLANNING. Despite its promise, rationalization remained more coherent in theory than in practice. The very factors that made rationalization important—Japan's lack of natural resources, the puny domestic or Asian markets for industrial goods, the uneven development of various production sectors, the lack of capital, the superannuation of production equipment and technology, the shortage of funds under the stabilization plan, the new influence of labor and prohibitions on cheap labor, and the democratization of the domestic economic system—also made it difficult to implement.

In practice, this meant that rationalization was often achieved the old-fashioned way: by cutting wages, firing workers (*kubikiri gōrika*), and allowing smaller firms to go bankrupt. These were far more typical ways to cut costs in 1949 and 1950 than technological and mechanical innovation. Because of this, labor unions and small businessmen were ambivalent about the rationalization program. They shared in the goal of expanding exports but not at the cost of their own livelihood. Under the stabilization program it was too easy for rationalization to mean just that. In the short term, it was most important to cut production costs of export industries, and so the old, traditional kind of rationalization was used extensively. Indeed, where industries were short of investment capital or had difficulty obtaining new technology or machinery, this was the only available avenue for cutting costs.

The rationalization program contained absolutely no safeguards for labor. Even seemingly unrelated aspects of the austerity program directly jeopardized jobs. For example, when Tōshiba Corporation tried to get a 600-million-yen loan from a private bank in 1949, the bank insisted that the company close several small, debt-ridden plants and fire the workers there. The bank was responding to a Dodge directive forbidding loans to companies that consistently lost money (a category that included nearly all Japanese firms in 1945–1948). At the same time, cutbacks in government and electric-power-company purchases, due to SCAP actions, further weakened Tōshiba's financial position. The Tōshiba management had been looking for an excuse to fire union activists for some time and was able to take advantage of the bank and government pressure to remove over 4,500 people, including much of the union leadership.[52]

The labor unions did not respond quickly to the broad issue of rationalization. In 1949 and early 1950, labor-union members were overwhelmed by the problems posed by the austerity plan: direct attacks on their organizations by the Japanese government, SCAP, and Nikkeiren, and by internal conflict. The hostile attitudes of both SCAP and the Japanese government rocked the labor movement, since the unions had faced much more receptive policies from SCAP earlier and from the Katayama Cabinet. In contrast, the Yoshida Government enthusiastically enforced rules that restricted labor unions and took a firm stance against its own public-sector workers. Yoshida's administration fired many thousands of employees, including about 11,000 who were dismissed in a special "Red Purge" of suspected Communist government employees.[53] SCAP began intervening regularly in labor disputes, deploying the power of the Occupation against the unions. In the spring of 1948, SCAP's labor chief publicly told the miners they had to settle within six days.

Shortly thereafter, he threatened to liquidate Densan as a "political alliance" if it did not come to an agreement with Hassōden immediately. The unions were forced into defensive postures—fighting against wage cuts and job losses rather than for new gains, unlike 1945-1948. Broader issues of economic democratization were set aside, as the unions fought for the immediate livelihood of their members.

The new pressures on the labor movement led to its polarization into left and right wings. Thus, internal dissension within the labor movement prevented it from protesting the austerity policy effectively, or evaluating the rationalization policy in the way the unions had studied earlier economic plans. This was especially true in Sanbetsu-affiliated unions, where there were many Communist members, and the polarization was most intense. Sanbetsu itself was destroyed as a meaningful organization by this struggle, while infighting in its member unions sometimes went so far as to cause a split and the creation of a separate union. These second unions often quickly destroyed any remaining chance of labor unity by signing a "sweetheart contract" with employers in order to gain recognition as the official union.

The appearance of second unions was not a spontaneous event. They were encouraged by both SCAP and Japanese employers to wrest power from existing union leaders. The Americans were primarily motivated by anti-communism. They encouraged "democratization leagues" (*mindō*) within various unions, as a way to weaken the Japan Communist Party. One contemporary observer called these leagues "essentially SCAP-sponsored anti-Communist 'cells'."[54] The Japanese employers supported the *mindō* both out of anti-communism and because the existing labor leadership had been uncomfortably effective. The Sanbetsu unions had been particularly skillful, not only at winning higher wages, but also at redefining the rights of labor to participate in economic decisions. The democratization leagues provided an opportunity to minimize the effect of their activities. Nikkeiren both supported *mindō* labor groups and also coordinated layoffs and plant closures among employers in its first years. In late 1949, Nikkeiren began to develop a new system of

industrial relations, which stressed the need for cooperation between management and labor in order to modernize and rationalize
industry. Nikkeiren sought to establish clear rules in which the
rights and obligations of both labor and managers were specified. It
also sought to limit the range of topics that had to be discussed
with unions to personnel-related issues only.[55] This was a conscious
attempt to prevent unions like Densan and Zentan from winning
changes in industrial structure or management.

The union leaders had been quick to challenge business definitions of labor's rights. This was partly *because* many of them were
Communists, and therefore ideologically at ease with notions of
worker control. It was also because they were experienced in the
labor struggles of the past three years. They recognized that decisions about control were more important than wage increases, which
could be wiped out in a month by inflation. Both Densan and the
coal miners were to fight bitterly over the next few years for the
right to establish a standard wage across the industry, to base that
wage on need, and the right to bargain with all employers jointly.
Densan and Zentan members understood that these issues, rather
than a higher wage packet, were the keys to their future influence.
In 1949 and early 1950, however, both unions were locked in internal battle between the democratization leagues and earlier leadership, as well as harassed by outside pressures. Their influence had
sunk to its postwar nadir. For many workers, rationalization looked
very like austerity.

SEVEN

Austerity and Rationalization in Practice:

The Energy Industries

For economic planners—and their historians—there always comes a moment when it is necessary to step down from the lofty heights of theory into the gritty world of implementation. It is usually only then that the precise meaning of any policy is hammered out. Often, as in Japan in 1949, this is because there are not enough resources to improve every field simultaneously. In practice, although not in theory, rationalization policy was a crucial impetus to the energy revolution in Japan. It was an unintended result of a policy that centered on reconstructing the coal mines and relegated oil to a secondary position as a service to more important industries. The rationalization planners concentrated on a few industries—including coal, steel, and electric power. Coal and steel, the first two rationalization-policy industries, were chosen for essentially the same reason as in the priority-production years. The planners hoped that improvements there would have a ripple effect on the entire economy, since they were still two of the greatest supply and price bottlenecks. Development of electric-power, transportation, and communication networks also received highest priority, in order to build a solid infrastructural base for export industries. This set of priorities was in accordance with the government's pledge to upgrade infrastructure so that firms in all industries could rationalize. Despite this assistance, however, neither industry rebuilt then. Elec-

Table 5 Japanese Primary Energy Supply Structure, 1935–1960 (percent)

	1935	1940	1945	1946	1947	1948	1949	1950	1951
Hydroelectric	18.1	16.1	32.7	40.6	35.5	33.6	34.3	32.7	28.3
Coal	61.7	66.2	49.0	42.1	46.0	48.9	50.5	51.2	54.1
domestic	52.5	54.2	48.1	42.1	45.8	46.2	48.4	49.6	50.5
imported	9.2	12.0	0.9	—	0.2	2.7	2.1	1.6	3.6
Petroleum	10.4	7.0	0.9	2.1	3.7	4.5	4.3	6.2	8.7
Other	9.8	10.7	17.4	15.2	14.8	13.0	10.9	9.9	8.9

	1952	1953	1954	1955	1956	1957	1958	1959	1960
Hydroelectric	28.9	29.4	30.2	30.5	29.0	27.8	30.3	27.6	22.7
Coal	51.3	48.7	45.5	44.0	44.6	44.4	40.9	37.9	38.1
domestic	45.9	43.5	41.7	40.3	40.3	38.9	36.8	32.2	31.9
imported	5.4	5.2	3.8	3.7	4.2	5.5	4.1	4.7	6.2
Petroleum	11.4	13.7	16.5	17.9	19.7	21.6	22.5	29.4	34.7
Other	8.4	8.2	7.8	7.6	6.7	6.2	6.3	5.1	4.5

Source: Tsūshō Sangyō Shō, *Enerugī Tōkeishū 1962*, pp. 74–75.

Note: "Other" consists of lignite, natural gas, charcoal, and firewood.

tric power would get another opportunity but King Coal's time was running out (see Table 5).

Once the Japanese adopted rationalization policy, national economic strategy depended on providing low-cost materials to industry, especially to export industries, while keeping wages reasonably high. The government officials hoped to achieve this goal by using more domestic resources, and so save on import bills, following Arisawa Hiromi's rather than Nakayama Ichirō's strategy. For energy, this meant stressing coal rather than oil. Export industries could not compete for sales in international markets unless they were assured inexpensive and steady supplies of high-quality raw materials. At that point, simply supplying industries—at any price—was still a grave problem. As one ESB official commented, "The biggest obstacle to this [high-production] policy was the ceiling placed on economic expansion by the availability of raw materials imports."[1] This problem was most acute for energy; coal shortages and power blackouts were chronic through 1952. Thus, development of those industries was of greatest concern to Japanese economic policymakers.

In 1949 and 1950, the two goals of promoting domestic energy and providing cheap and stable supplies seemed compatible. The dearth of foreign exchange, moreover, meant that the Japanese had little choice but to reinvest in domestic coal. Nonetheless, debate on this point had already begun—at the theoretical level between Nakayama and Arisawa, and at the practical level between the steel and coal industries. The debate gradually was to become more acrimonious over the next years. The coal industry was never again able to provide fuel to its customers at a price they were content to pay, and the 1950s saw the coal industry's inability to conform to national rationalization policy. It is ironic that, although the coal industry was the first and most important target industry (together with steel), it was the most conspicuous failure of the rationalization policy.

In 1949 and 1950, however, most Japanese still expected the coal industry to resume its central place in the economy. The steel industry's complaints that coal was just too expensive are, in hindsight, an omen of deeper problems, but this was not yet obvious. The abiding problems of the coal industry—physical deterioration of the resource base, labor-intensive processes, and undercapitalization—were simply the problems of Japan writ small. At the time, they did not seem to be different in kind from those faced by every other industry in Japan. Coal was still the archetypal industry for Japanese economic planners, and the experience of the coal mines merely bore out Japanese arguments that the austerity plan was too hasty and too harsh. Since reviving coal was a basic goal of rationalization policy, Japanese government bureaucrats devised new programs to channel capital to the coal mines, mainly through intensifying the ties between the Bank of Japan and private banks. This began the bank-centered *keiretsu* economic pattern. Government officials also helped coal operators import new machinery and offered technical assistance. These capital- and knowledge-accumulating techniques, while insufficient in the coal industry, were to be used again more effectively later.

The electric-power industry was slow to rationalize because it was immobilized by the reorganization struggle in the early 1950s. Although it later became a leader in importing new machinery and new technical processes, in this period the reorganization problem overshadowed all other considerations. This delay occurred even though development and rationalization of electric power was a very high priority for the government and for most industry. Reorganization also discouraged potential foreign investors in the electric-power industry, to general Japanese dismay.

It is interesting—and surprising—that SCAP allowed the political impasse over reorganization of the electric-power industry to continue for so long, since Occupation policy was to press for economic recovery. There were a number of reasons for this anomalous behavior, but the Americans held out for reorganization mainly from determination to limit the role of government in the Japanese economy. This was both the product of free-market ideology and of stubborn bureaucratic commitment to their own plan. By 1949, the role of the state had become the main focus of electric-power industry reorganization, rather than either Densan's concern for worker participation or the original deconcentration order. In fact, the union, weakened by internal conflict, had been elbowed out of the reorganization debate. The American intervention to prevent state management was crucial. Without it, the Japanese would almost certainly have chosen to keep Hassōden or a similar state-managed electricity-generating body. In this instance, American policy reoriented the Japanese economy away from state planning and control, directing Japan along specific lines of development and not just promoting quantitative economic growth.

The oil industry presents an interesting contrast because it developed with the aid of foreign capital, precisely as the Japanese had hoped in 1949. Under the austerity plan, foreign investment was one of the few possible capital sources for Japanese firms, and officials and businessmen alike hoped to attract it. In 1949 and 1950, the 50-percent foreign-capital tie-ups in the oil refining industry were not only welcome but were also seen as models for other industries. The assistance was also vital to the development of the postwar refining industry. With the wealth and technical assistance of their foreign partners, the Japanese refiners were able quickly to build one of Japan's most sophisticated industries. This relative success when compared to coal was enhanced further by the gradual closing of Japan's traditional trade ties to Northeast Asia and its mines.

The Japanese were still groping for any solution that might revive their economy. American austerity policy limited their choices and made the earlier priority-production policy unworkable. The Japanese rejected Dodge's willingness to cut spending and living standards but had few practical solutions to their economic problems. Rationalization seemed theoretically workable. In practice, however, it created new tensions like those between the coal and steel industries. Meanwhile, the Japanese pursued other strategies whenever they could.

RATIONALIZING THE COAL MINES

Even before the stabilization plan appeared, the solvency of the coal industry had become a matter of general concern, although most Japanese expected that the coal mines eventually could recover to their prewar level of profitability. The financial distress of the coal industry in 1949 derived from several causes. The national problem of tight credit was particularly acute in the coal mines because of the huge debts the mine owners had incurred since the end of the war. In July 1950, one estimate put the combined debts of the coal industry at 16,350 million yen.[2] This meant that, even when the mine operators could get loans, interest costs were high. Moreover, these costs were expected to rise further as the coal operators began developing new shafts and seams, a task that had been neglected since the war began. Underlying these problems was the physical depletion of the mines. At the end of 1949, coal seams were thinner, mine shafts deeper, and underground distances to coal

Table 6 Natural Conditions in Fifteen Large Mines
        (meters)

	December 1934	December 1949
Average shaft depth	222	275
Average distance from mouth of mine to face	1,616	1,983
Average length of coal face	17,535	15,347

Source: Nihon Sangyō Kōzō Kenkyūkai, *Nihon Sangyō Kōzō no Kadai* I, 550; original data from Sekitan Kyōkai.

faces all farther than in 1934. This translated into more expensive mining conditions (see Table 6).

The single biggest reason that coal mining was less profitable in 1949 than before the war, however, was the higher labor bill. Coal production increased rapidly from 1945 to 1949, but this was achieved almost entirely by hiring more workers, an effective but not very economical method. The changes in working conditions and labor legislation meant that miners had to be paid more than in prewar years. Labor costs were 55.1 percent of all mining costs in 1949, rather than the 34.3 percent of 1940. Meanwhile, labor efficiency, measured in man-hours per ton produced, was still only 50 percent of the 1935 level in 1951. A major reason for this low productivity was that, in accordance with the Labor Standards Law of 1947, the number of actual working hours in a day was cut by about 30 percent. These were still not especially short. In 1950, pit workers averaged 176 hours per month or 7.5 hours per day during a 6-day week, while surface workers spent 193 hours on the job each month, or 8 hours each day.[3]

The changes in labor conditions had greater impact in the coal mines than in most industries for two reasons. First, mining is a comparatively labor-intensive activity. Second, the prewar working conditions and wages in the mines had been far worse than average. The Japanese probably could not have dug coal profitably in the prewar period with comparatively benign postwar working conditions. The only way the coal operators could overcome the problem of rising labor costs was to mechanize their mines. Often this meant something fairly simple (although expensive). For example, in some mines workers had to walk up to two hours underground simply to get to the coal faces.[4] Employers now had to pay them from the moment they entered the mine. Elevators or conveyor belts could drastically reduce those unproductive hours. Japanese mines also lacked any of the sophisticated long-wall mining techniques that were already standard equipment in Germany and had the advantage of improving both productivity and safety. Labor had become more valuable, but the operators had not yet started to use it efficiently.

Conditions varied considerably from mine to mine, however. The smallest mines simply could not survive without the subsidy and allocations systems. Under the priority-production plan, the subsidies and material goods had gone to all firms within a priority industry, regardless of size. When these two programs were ended, it forced the smallest mines to shut down. Many of these marginal producers had been closed by the government as inefficient during the Pacific War and were reopened during the priority-production years. The number of working mines in Japan went from 623 in 1941 to 392 in 1945, and then back up to 628 in 1948. Most of the shift was in the smallest class of mine, each of which produced less than 50,000 tons annually.[5] As in the prewar years, the structure of the coal industry was tiered, with the major mines controlled by large companies and the small mines by tiny independent firms. The natural condition of the major mines were vastly better than those at the "badger holes," or small independents. For example, the coal seams at Mitsui's Miike were over 2 meters thick, while at small mines in Sasebo the seams were only 62 centimeters thick.[6]

The differences in physical conditions between the mines of the 20 largest companies and all the others meant that the two groups were actually facing very different market conditions. The large-mine operators were carrying a very high debt, but they still received a good price for their coal, since they retained a monopoly on higher grades of coal, as in the prewar years. Special coals, such as those used in steel making, did not fall in price, whereas general coals did. Moreover, even before the subsidy system ended, the coal-price structure had been modified to price good-quality coal higher per calorie than average coal. From 1949, the large companies also moved back toward the prewar system of name-brand coal, which favored their products. This bias in the pricing system was maintained through the 1950s by an informal price cartel, which the largest firms set up in 1949 when official price controls ended. Since they had no enforcement powers, this broke down occasionally, but they were always able to create an artificially large range for coal prices. Ultimately, this meant that the low-quality coals were reasonably competitive with imports while the higher grades were not. In the short term, however, when imports were still a luxury, it meant that the larger firms were still enjoying monopoly rents.[7]

The rest of the mine operators were in a difficult position. They suddenly faced the prospect of price decontrol, no subsidies, and economic depression in late 1949. The smallest mines began to go out of business from 1949 because they could not get loans. Counterpart aid funds to the coal industry went only to the largest firms, and private bank loans were not available at all. The response of the medium-sized mines was to cut back on their largest cost—labor. This meant firing workers, cutting wages, setting higher productivity targets, and sometimes not paying wages at all.[8] The coal operators suddenly became much better organized and more hostile in their stance toward the unions. From 1949, they cooperated to deliver coal for brother companies who were being struck, hired ostensible miners whose real jobs were to disrupt the union, and brought their views to the nation through Nikkeiren.[9]

These changes were equally difficult for the coal miners' unions. Zentan had gone through several reorganizations, and, from October 1947, became known as Tanrō.[10] Like the rest of the Japanese labor movement, Tanrō spent 1949 in a defensive and largely unsuccessful battle on two fronts: protection of wages and industry-wide bargaining. In March 1949, the coal employers' bargaining unit, Nihon Kōgyō Renmei, asked for 15 percent more work for the same wages as the standard agreement, and the right to amend that agreement at mines where "physical conditions were poor" or "operations rationalization" was underway. Both these points were totally unacceptable to the union, which countered with a proposal for a wage increase, to be decided in general bargaining only. The two sides were unable to come to an agreement, particularly on the issue of industry-wide bargaining, which each party considered vital.[11]

After reaching a complete stalemate, (and working without a contract for a month), Tanrō began waves of 24-hour strikes (3 May in Hokkaido, 4 May in Kyushu, and so on). This "wave" tactic had been invented to bypass the increasingly restrictive Occupation rules about strikes in key industries. But, by mid-1949, with the austerity plan in full swing, this tactic was not acceptable to the Americans. MacArthur requested that the Labor Minister and the head of the Central Labor Relations Board, Suehiro Izutarō, mediate the coal dispute. Suehiro ruled that the employers had to keep standard wages and productivity requirements at the level of the last contract, but that individual mines could revise this agreement with their workers. This was only a minute gain for the union (especially since Suehiro's ruling only covered a three-month period) and a major victory for the mine operators. Tanrō tried to fight on for industry-wide bargaining, but Occupation officials intervened unofficially twice more, and the issue was settled along the lines of Suehiro's proposal. In March 1950, SCAP officials intervened again, this time officially, ordering the government to force the miners to submit to arbitration.[12]

By June 1950, Tanrō's power to enforce industry-wide bargaining was greatly weakened. Wages and working conditions for workers in the big mines stayed about the same, but deteriorated in smaller mines. In Yamaguchi prefecture, where the mines were all small, wages fell 10 to 20 percent.[13] Tanrō also suffered from internal dissension. As its general meeting in May 1949, a democratization league, which criticized Tanrō leadership as too political, nearly gained control of the union. The league was not successful, but it won enough votes to show that the union had to stick to economic issues if it hoped to maintain any unity. Thus, for about three years, the fighting coal miners became much more timid, willing to strike over wages but not other issues.[14]

MIXED SIGNALS FROM BUSINESS. Leaders within one of the major business organizations, Nissankyō (which merged with Keidanren in 1952), began to study the problem of coal-industry finances as early as July 1948. This group, headed by Nagano Shigeo, a key spokesman for Japanese big business until his death in 1984, found that the coal operators needed to receive higher prices to improve the financial standing of their companies. Nonetheless, as representatives of major coal-using industries, they preferred to raise government subsidies rather than allow higher prices. This meant continuing economic controls, which the coal operators also wanted to retain. The Japanese government, however, was split on the question of subsidies. The ESB, the Price Agency, and the Ministry of Commerce and Industry wanted to keep them to aid their consumer and industrial constituents. The ESB held that, if fixed coal prices were maintained and more special measures to encourage domestic output were created, Japan would need to import less coal in 1949. The Ministry of Finance, however, aware of the impact of the subsidies on the deficit, agreed with Dodge that they should go.[15]

This debate was purely academic, since the Japanese were not free to make a decision. Dodge ordered coal prices decontrolled, the state coal wholesaling agency closed, and subsidies abolished from 15 September 1949. Because general economic activity and demand for coal had decreased due to the stabilization plan, the immediate result was that average coal prices plummeted. Nissankyō members opposed this rapid decontrol. Although inexpensive coal was, at first glance, good for their own factories, they feared that bankruptcies in the mines would spark a deflationary crisis in all Japan. On 10 August, Nissankyō submitted a policy statement to SCAP, which contained this warning. It also argued that Japanese industry should help the mines mechanize, while the government should take responsibility for redeveloping the disrupted coal-distribution system and expanding the market for general coal.

One market that Nissankyō hoped to develop was China. On 7 November, the organization called for barter of Japanese coal for high-grade Chinese coking coal. The businessmen argued that this would address both the problems of the Japanese coal mines and diminish the need for expensive dollar-area coking coal. Nissankyō put considerable effort into this, and the coal barter actually began in May 1950 but was abruptly terminated after the Chinese entered the Korean War in October.[16] China was also the preferred source of industrial materials for Japan. Its non-dollar raw materials could be shipped relatively inexpensively to Japan. Moreover, since these raw materials had originally been developed for Japanese industry, rail and shipping lines were already in place. Since Japanese plants had been built specifically with Chinese grades of coal, iron ore, and other materials in mind, using Chinese resources could bring down the cost of Japanese imports and so help exports become internationally competitive.

The China trade would have allowed the Japanese to ease more gradually into their strategy of shifting to a more capital-intensive industrial structure and more sophisticated exports. But the eventual embargo of China by the United States meant that the Japanese had to focus entirely on their plan to build a self-sufficient economy through industrial rationalization.[17] The Japanese continued to pursue industrial rationalization, now convinced that that was the only open escape route from their structural trap of high-cost Japanese goods and the need to export. This, with its many ramifications, was the main goal of domestic Japanese economic policy through the 1950s.

Early business support of the coal industry reveals the extent to which coal was still a central part of the economy. Nissankyō feared that collapse of the coal industry would be disastrous to the entire Japanese economy. Through 1950, business leaders searched for ways to shore up the coal industry. They were joined by prefectural and municipal officials in coal-mining regions. For example, in April 1949 the Mayor of Takahagi City in Ibaraki prefecture called for a meeting of all the local government officials to find ways to keep the Takahagi mine operating, because, "the town will disappear if the mine fails."[18] The austerity measures threatened to bankrupt all Japan; to most Japanese, the coal companies seemed to be only a little more vulnerable than the rest of industry.

Among coal consumers, the steel companies were much more critical of the coal industry than was Nissankyō. The steel companies spent the months from March 1950 studying their future export potential, expected to be bleak when the industry was scheduled to lose its special subsidies in July 1950. The pessimistic steel companies published a Steel White Paper in July to publicize their plight. This document called for more state aid and more subsidies as the first steps toward achieving an internationally viable steel industry. The steel manufacturers also severely criticized the "high-cost coal problem," arguing that "Japan's steel plants have many advantages as to location, and the technology is not too backward, but the root cause of our inability to bring prices down is the high cost of coal."[19] The steelmakers issued a challenge to the coal operators:

> If we only could pay with hard currency, we could easily get fuels. . . . Moreover, heavy oil has a higher fuel efficiency than coal, it is easier to regulate the heat level of oil than of coal, if we use oil it reduces the amount of fuel we need, equipment and transport are simpler, it requires fewer of our employees to handle it. In short, if it can bring down the cost of producing a steel ingot, then the steel makers find it appropriate to switch to heavy oil.[20]

The steelmakers were less sympathetic to the coal operators than were other business consumers for a number of reasons. First, high-quality coal prices did not fall with those for general coal, and soon began to rise. Second, the steel companies, with the help of SCAP technical experts, had just completed a study of steelmaking in other countries. They realized that their comparatively high coal bill was a big disadvantage in the international market. Third, the steel companies had imported their own coking coal from Northeast Asia before the war and so did not have a longstanding trade relationship with the coal companies; the steel companies were outsiders.[21]

Steel was an outsider in another way too. It did not enjoy as close a relationship to the zaibatsu as had the major coal companies. The prewar role of the coal mines as zaibatsu "money boxes" had given them great power and prestige, which they retained well into the postwar period. After the Occupationaires' democratization programs, the tightly knit zaibatsu were replaced by much looser *keiretsu* groupings. These were the former subsidiaries of the dissolved zaibatsu holding companies, and still did considerable business with each other. Although the banks were the real centers of the new *keiretsu* groups, the coal-mine-company presidents chaired *keiretsu* meetings until the late 1950s.[22]

GOVERNMENT RESPONSE. The government responded to the plight of the steel and coal industries with its first specific rationalization plan. On 24 June 1950, the Industrial Rationalization Council presented the Three-Year Coal and Steel Rationalization Plan to the MITI Minister. This plan concentrated on bringing the price of coking coal down to 3,300 yen per ton by fiscal 1953 through mechanization and technological improvements.[23] The main slant of the plan was to lower the cost of coal to steel firms, and to provide state subsidies to steel rather than force rationalization within the steel industry itself. The committee had listened sympathetically to the arguments of the steel manufacturers that "high-cost coal" explained the expense of their products.

The government pledged special measures for capital and import guarantees to the mine owners and steelmakers to achieve this. These included low-interest rates on government loans of 42 billion yen to the steel and 40 billion yen to the coal companies, special depreciation rates, tax and import-duty exemptions, lower railroad fares on coal bound for steel plants, and discounts on electric-power costs, although not so large that they angered other industries. The government also promised to provide special assistance in importing machinery and technology to the two industries. Other recommended measures were state guarantees of needed imports of coking coal and anthracite, more emphasis on pig-iron production, and increased use of heavy oil in the steel industry. Finally, the committee suggested that the government set up demonstration equipment in several important factories and mines. This plan was passed by the Cabinet on 18 August 1950 but was shelved shortly afterward because of the Korean War boom. Although this plan was not implemented in 1950, its provisions would reappear in all Japanese rationalization policies through the next decade, including later ones for the coal and steel industries.

The government also worked to channel *private* bank loans to coal and the other basic industries. These were the areas that suffered most when the RFB was closed down. Without the guidance of the Japanese government, the private banks gave most of their funds to light industries such as textiles and food processing, because those industries could be expected to turn a profit more quickly than coal mines or electric-power plants and probably would earn larger returns. MITI historians explain that total industrial capital supply actually rose from 385,839 million to 527,410 million yen (a 36-percent increase) in 1949 over 1948, but the nature of these funds changed from long- to primarily short-term investment. The 17 largest coal mines were able to raise only 32 percent of the funds they needed in fiscal 1949, while the textile industry enjoyed 126 percent of what it required.[24]

In the face of this problem, the Bank of Japan took several steps to see that the money it loaned to private banks went to serve heavy industry. Advances by the central bank and the Ministry of Finance to private banks totaled 92.1 billion yen during 1949 and the Bank of Japan also reduced interest rates in July 1949 and again in February 1950, two moves that expanded the money supply.[25] The government also instituted a much-needed policy allowing businesses to revalue assets, which increased depreciation allowances and reduced taxes. This primarily aided industries with high equipment costs, foremost of which was the electric-power industry. The Bank of Japan established preferential treatment for loans secured by corporate debentures and expanded a program that had been established in 1947 to bring several banks together so that they could combine their resources for large loans to big enterprises. One of the first results of this was that the Bank of Japan arranged for a loan of 2.5 billion yen from the city banks to 19 large coal companies in June 1949.[26]

The reliance on bank loans was a significant turn of events for Japanese postwar industrial structure, since it allowed banks to develop their central role in the modern *keiretsu* financial groups and initiate the "over-loan" policy, (in which increases in banks' lending rose faster than their total assets) that characterized Japanese banking through the 1950s. Previously, most major industrial loans were either made within the zaibatsu conglomerates to fund their own projects or through special government banks. Both these sources were disrupted by Occupation deconcentration policies. Thus, there was no viable credit system in place after the war, until the banks began their "over-loan" practices. The ratio of bank loans to total assets increased from 52 percent in March 1949 to 67 percent one year later. The heavy reliance on loans also increased the dependency of private banks on the Bank of Japan, another important feature of the *keiretsu* system.[27]

The Economic and Scientific Section of SCAP, which had worked closely with the ESB, agreed that money should be channeled through private banks to lend to industry, and, therefore, aided the Japanese in these maneuvers, despite the austerity program. Dodge himself saw this as the least objectionable method of credit expansion. Expanding credit through private bank loans was compatible with the economic structure Dodge wanted to build in Japan, although he did not want to use that tactic until inflation was controlled. Thus, he did not fight as hard as on other points. This exemption from deflationary policies, in Bronfenbrenner's phrase, "left a gap wide enough for the proverbial team of horses, and also wide enough to nullify the policy in the long run under the best of circumstances."[28] Americans and Japanese alike regarded "over-loaning" as a temporary practice until the economy grew stronger. Later, they realized that this practice had helped the economy grow faster, but contemporary discussions all apologized for its unorthodoxy.

In general, SCAP supported Japanese rationalization efforts within the coal industry. SCAP hosted technical experts in Japan, sent

Japanese mining engineers on tours of U.S. coal pits, screened training films on mine safety, and imported state-of-the-art machinery from the United States and Europe.[29] Nonetheless, SCAP remained highly critical of the coal operators and of what it considered to be Japanese government laxity toward them. In March 1949, SCAP issued orders that coal operators should be policed more carefully to insure that they paid their workers in full and "immediately eliminated fictitious overtime payments." If they did not reform their accounting systems by 1 April 1949, SCAP threatened to take control of all revenue from coal sales. In the analysis of a senior ESS official, the large coal operators "were guilty of wasteful use of manpower and new equipment as well as unbusinesslike squandering of public loans and subsidies. The responsible Japanese ministries responded sympathetically to the operators' plight and abstained from undertaking any forceful measures to increase production."[30] Coal already had a few critics.

These bitter SCAP comments and the steelmakers' complaints were still the exception in 1949 and early 1950. Most Japanese considered the American austerity plan too harsh, and so did not fault the coal operators for not strictly adhering to it. At that time, the coal industry was generally considered the rightful center of the economy. By the mid-1950s, however, the steelmakers would represent the dominant opinion of the coal operators in Japan.

ELECTRIC-POWER INDUSTRY REORGANIZATION, 1948–1949

In the electric-power industry, the stabilization plan and national economic policy were completely eclipsed by the struggle over reorganizing Hassōden and the Haiden. This battle, which raged on until it was finally resolved in May 1951 with the creation of 9 private, regional electric-power companies, prevented any of the sorely needed development work in electric power. The political debate was long and divisive enough to seriously threaten Japan's economic recovery.

The contours of this debate changed over time; at the beginning, Densan was an active participant, and "economic democratization" was an important reorganization goal. By 1949, however, Densan had been pushed out of the decision-making process. Neither the Yoshida Government nor SCAP supported the union's proposals or demands to participate in the reorganization decisions. Their joint indifference to Densan (and to the original goals of the deconcentration policy) was, however, their only point of convergence. Japanese official opinion, supported by the majority of the business community, was that Hassōden, or a similar, government-managed body, should handle electric power. They believed that this format would best encourage industrial rationalization. They were especially concerned that smaller, private companies would fail in 3 areas: technical ability to supply power at standard prices, new development, and fund raising. The Japanese conclusion—reached in 1948 and in 1950—was that a state-controlled company would be better equipped to meet these 3 needs.

The only major Japanese dissenters from this view were the men who had run their own private electric-power companies before Hassōden was created in 1938. They wanted to regain control of the industry. This group could never have succeeded without the support of Occupation officials. As in labor-management relations and the coal-nationalization debate of 1947, SCAP actions were pivotal to the outcome of the electric-power-industry reorganization issue.

SCAP officials did not decide this problem on the basis of its relevance to their own economic recovery policy. Indeed, their actions in prolonging the debate undoubtedly hampered Japan's economic revival. Nor were SCAP actions a holdover from earlier economic democratization policy, which had been directed at breakup of *private* concentrations of economic power. In the political realm, too, MacArthur's summary rejection of the wishes of the Japanese majority on this issue contravened the democratic process. Rather, SCAP officials seem to have been motivated mainly by an antipathy to state control of important industries. In 1948, the economic deconcentration program was used to attack the government presence in several industries, including electric power. State control of industry offended the Occupationaires' assumptions about the superiority of free-market enterprise, despite the fact that America's major allies in Europe were moving toward greater state control in the postwar years. SCAP opinion was also probably swayed by the lobbying of the prewar power-company owners, as well as by SCAP infighting.

When the Holding Company Liquidation Commission (HCLC) designated all 10 power companies as excessive concentrations of economic power in February 1948, the debate over reorganization shifted from the Diet to the HCLC and SCAP, as all the interested parties submitted petitions detailing their preferred method of reorganization. The Japanese government bureaucracy had already vigorously but unsuccessfully lobbied SCAP to exempt the electric-power industry from deconcentration measures. In August, the ESB submitted a lengthy argument to exempt all public utilities; and, in September, Prime Minister Katayama sent MacArthur a formal letter asking that public utilities and financial organs be omitted from the deconcentration lists.[31]

Densan was the first to submit a plan, on 9 March 1948. Its proposal was very similar to the one filed at the Diet during the previous autumn. The union explained that, although its goal was a state-owned, state-operated industry, because "we have not yet achieved thorough political and economic democracy and since the bureaucrats and finance capitalists still have a strong hold on power, simple state management is dangerous." Therefore, Densan proposed a complex system of advisory committees to act as a check on any resurgence of undemocratic behavior.[32]

The electric-power companies had their own ideas about reorganization. Hassōden and the Haiden, however, offered radically different plans for the industry's future. Hassōden, supported by the Electric Power Bureau of the Ministry of Commerce and Industry (MITI from April 1949), put up a spirited defense of the existing system, while the Haiden attacked it. They did agree on one point, however. This was to reject the agreement reached with Densan in late 1946 and concurred in by the Yoshida Administration. Densan had won a promise from the managers of the 10 companies to honor the principle of labor and consumer oversight of a single firm. However, at a 13 April 1948 meeting, management insisted that the deconcentration order had rendered the agreement unenforceable and unilaterally abrogated it.[33]

Hassōden's proposal, submitted in April 1948, was for a single, integrated, national company, publicly owned and privately operated. This was essentially a plan to absorb the Haiden into itself. It resembled Densan's plan, except that it reserved the rights of management to professional managers. From a technical perspective, the single nationwide generating and transmission company was probably the best option.[34] As Hassōden and Densan officials argued, a single company could compensate for the fact that the richest hydroelectric sites (namely, Tōhoku, Chūbu, and Hokuriku) were very far from the major consumption centers. Partition would create some chronically power-hungry and some over-supplied regions. The Vice-President of Hassōden, Shindō Takezaemon, also felt that a single company was in a better position than a sectioned industry to attract desperately wanted foreign capital. The majority of Japanese businessmen agreed with Shindō.[35]

The Haiden were weak organizations and had fallen under the sway of another group that was trying to engineer the reorganization of the electric-power industry, the former private-power-company managers. This group was epitomized by Matsunaga Yasuzaemon. As the ex-president of one of the prewar Big Five electric-power companies, he was interested in returning to the profitable days of the early 1930s, when the big firms had wrested the industry from their competitors and before the creation of Hassōden. This group was working through the structure of the 9 wartime Haiden, who were eager to get out from under Hassōden dominance. Thus, the "Haiden" proposal for reorganization began by criticizing the state-managed form. This proposal was for privately owned, privately managed, regional, integrated generating and distribution companies. These regional companies were to be fully independent of each other, and power rates were to be based on the actual cost of production in each area. They belittled the problem of regionally different rates, although this was one of the most serious flaws in their plan. Instead of a single company, Matsunaga proposed a self-regulated power "interconnection" system among the regional companies. This would take advantage of the fact that peak loads in Hokkaido occur in winter, while southern Japan uses the greatest amount of electricity in the summer.[36]

The former private companies made it clear that they only wished to return to the system of centralized private power companies of the early 1930s, not the highly competitive era of the 1920s: "At the time the electric-power industry was suddenly merged into one centralized company under the National Mobilization Policy, the industry had already begun to consolidate on its own initiative. The electric-power firms had realized that the flood of suppliers created by uncontrolled competition in the prewar years was a problem, and had begun to cooperate to rationalize operations and increase efficiency. Thus, our proposal for 9 bloc companies meets the necessary conditions for profitability." Another document argued that the prewar companies already had been absorbing smaller firms for the purposes of "rationalizing management and enhancing efficiency, and. . . . [t]he mobilization policy merely happened at this juncture."[37] This group used the opportunity of the SCAP deconcentration policy to recapture management control of their industry from the MCI officials. These men also fended off Densan's demand for labor participation in management decisions. They were still the nominal owners, and reaped a stable profit from the government-operated firms all through the war, at a considerable loss to the Treasury. They fought a battle on two fronts: to weaken Japanese government control and to prevent Densan's socialization plan. To Matsunaga, the bureaucrats and the union were "the tiger at the front gate and the wolf at the rear."[38]

Their plan also won favor with SCAP, and the reorganization mandated by MacArthur in 1950 was very similar to this Haiden proposal. The ESS officials were very cool toward the Densan plan, and consistently ignored it.[39] They were willing to consider the Hassōden proposal, since it was favored by the majority of Japanese. The Haiden plan, however, most closely resembled the American pattern and economic philosophy. Moreover, there was a personal rapport between Matsunaga and the American officials. Matsunaga spoke English, had traveled abroad, and had excellent connections with American businessmen, with whom he had worked in the prewar years. After the Sino-Japanese War began, he had insisted on repaying loans to foreign banks taken out by his company, and so had the best international credit rating of any individual in Japan at the end of the war. He was also a great admirer of the American "frontier spirit" and business system.[40]

The process of reorganization itself was both protracted and complex. The Ashida Administration, recognizing that this was going to become a major controversy, established a committee to study the matter, and the Committee for the Democratization of the Electric-Power Industry (Denki Jigyō Minshuka Iinkai) was established on 30 April 1948 to advise the MCI. Ōyama Matsujirō, a Tokyo University professor, was the chair of the 21-person committee. It included electric-power-company heads, other industrialists, labor representatives, local autonomy group members, a bank president, and a representative from each house of the Diet.[41]

This committee issued its final report on 1 October 1948. Its recommendations were a compromise, reflecting the wide variety of plans espoused by its members. The keynote was the one issue that all parties could agree on—the need to increase electric-power service. Thus, they framed their recommendations in terms of what would best encourage electric-power development. They suggested turning Hassōden into an ordinary private company, although the government would be empowered to direct the industry. (The nature of the directives was not specified.) The facilities on Hokkaido and Shikoku were each to be consolidated into a single "bloc" company, but the other 7 Haiden would remain unchanged. In addition, the committee recommended that rates not be allowed to vary significantly from region to region, a position supported both by the regional autonomy groups and by consuming industries.[42]

The report did not, however, address a number of unresolved problems. The administrative structure of the industry, improvements in service, pooled accounts, electric-power development, and appropriate scale of firms were all fiercely debated without resolution. These issues were never addressed by the committee, because

SCAP rejected the plan on 7 October and the committee was disbanded when the Ashida Cabinet fell on 14 October 1948. When SCAP vetoed the Ōyama Committee plan, it left the Japanese hopelessly divided on the reorganization problem. They had just barely been able to come up with that compromise. For over a year, no new proposals were offered from the Japanese side and the initiative passed to SCAP.[43]

The next proposal was submitted by the special Deconcentration Review Board (DRB), sent out to Tokyo to minimize the impact of the Law to Eliminate Excessive Concentrations of Economic Power. One of the 5 members, Edward Burger, was a public utility company vice-president from Ohio. Burger felt that Japan should have a privately owned, publicly regulated, regional electric-power structure as in the United States. The DRB came out in support of an ESS proposal to split the industry into 7 separate private companies. Burger sent an informal memo suggesting reorganization into 7 units to Mr. Mori, Hassōden Director, on 10 May 1949. The 7 units would be Hokkaido, Tōhoku, Kantō, Kansai (including the former Chūbu and Hokuriku regions), Chūgoku, Shikoku, and Kyushu. Each region was to be a "bloc" generating, transmission, and distribution area.[44]

The DRB was not the final arbiter in the electric-power-industry case, but its observations were the basis for the eventual decision. The DRB's finding that the industry was an excessive concentration of economic power was based largely on the fact that the industry was government-controlled. The Electric Power Bureau appointed the officers of the 10 companies and made decisions directly on accounting procedures, rates, material and fuel allocations, and many other matters. Although the companies were nominally privately owned, the national and local governments owned 19 percent of Hassōden's stock and 11 percent of the Haidens'. The DRB was deeply critical of the relationship between Hassōden and the Ministry of Commerce and Industry/MITI. It wrote:

> Men selected by political appointments to top positions in Hassoden must of necessity serve two masters—they must first express their loyalty to their appointers and secondly to the company. . . . the Electric Power Bureau

which constitutes the administrative link between the Japanese Government and Hassoden should be eliminated and in its stead a National Utilities Commission composed of capable men on a ministry level be created.[45]

These criticisms were as much about government control of the industry as they were about oligopoly. In its final report, the DRB commented that eliminating government security holdings in Japanese enterprises was "an essential feature of the deconcentration program and substantial progress has been made toward this end. . . . In reviewing the cases, the Board gave consideration to the fact that under the broad program government interests in the companies should eventually be liquidated."[46] With this final comment, the DRB disbanded in early August 1949, leaving the electric-power industry still in limbo.

This final report is remarkable for the fact that eliminating government holdings was by no means "an essential feature of the deconcentration program," despite the assertions of the DRB. Rather, the original law had specified deconcentrating *private* enterprise as its object. The involvement of the government in the company was added, without any discernible legal basis, as a reason to order the dismemberment of the company. In fact, from a legal point of view, the situation was ironic; the law to eliminate private monopoly was used to turn a state-operated firm into 9 regional private monopolies on the slender legal claim that the state did not own the firm outright, but continued to pay the owners handsome dividends. Thus, since Hassōden was state-managed but not state-owned, it was technically eligible for deconcentration.

After the DRB left, Mr. T.O. Kennedy was sent by the Army to advise ESS on the electric-power reorganization problem. In a 27 September 1949 memo to the Japanese government, Kennedy laid out a plan for reorganization along the lines suggested by the DRB. He was very critical of the strong government role in the industry, but left room for negotiation on the issue of the number of new private firms.[47]

Yoshida responded to the ultimatum of the Kennedy memorandum by creating a new study group to prepare recommendations.

This Electric Power Industry Reorganization Commission (Denki Jigyō Saihensei Shingikai) was sworn in as an advisory body to MITI on 4 November 1949. The 5 members were Matsunaga Yasuzaemon, Chair and former head of Tōhō Power Company, Koike Ryuichi of Keio University, Kudō Akiyorō, Vice-President of the RFB, Miki Takashi, President of Nippon Seitetsu K.K. and a member of the Ashida Committee, and Mizuno Shigeo, Vice-President of Kokuseki Pulp K.K. Matsunaga was suggested to Yoshida by the former head of the Mitsui zaibatsu, Ikeda Seihin, an old ally from prewar days.[48] This move bought Yoshida some political breathing space from SCAP; on 17 January 1950, Marquat informed Chief of Staff Major General Edward Almond that MacArthur himself had insisted that the Japanese government be allowed to submit its own plan and "specifically that the Japanese Government not be directed to break up the power monopoly into any specific number of plants."[49] SCAP temporarily lifted its pressure on Yoshida to "voluntarily" disband Hassōden.

This moved the initiative back to the Japanese and the new body. What is most striking about the Yoshida commission on reorganization is the diminution of the range of debate. Labor and local autonomy groups were conspicuously absent from the discussion. Densan, which had initiated the debate, had disappeared, as had its demands for labor and consumer oversight. Hassōden representatives were also omitted. By the end of 1949, the reorganization debate revolved only around the problem of whether or not Hassōden, and by extension the economic bureaucracy, would have an important role to play in the management and operations of the electric-power industry.

This narrowing of the terms of debate reflects the new balance of power within Japan *and* shifts in SCAP policy. The Dodge-induced recession of 1949–1950 was accompanied by restrictions on labor and recentralization of economic and political power in the name of efficiency. In the electric-power industry, Densan complained that "there are comparatively many who maintain it is necessary to reorganize the electric-power industry by splitting it up for the purpose of weakening our union."[50] This new pressure on labor leaders was condoned by SCAP, which issued repeated warnings to the union members to depoliticize their movement.[51]

DENSAN IN RETREAT. Densan's plan to socialize its industry grew increasingly ephemeral. Densan's ideas were too close to the path rejected during the debate on state control of the coal mines. Moreover, the political climate had, by 1949, veered farther away from socialization. The union was no longer able to mobilize support for its plans. Keidanren's official history blandly commented that Densan's nationalization plan had become inappropriate because it would have hindered foreign capital and outside financing of electric-power development.[52] This stark lesson in power politics was a blow to Densan leaders, who had continued to work actively for democratization and reorganization of their industry.

Like other unions, Densan was also suffering from severe schisms. The democratization league, or *mindō*, within the electric-power workers' union was very strong, and, by the end of 1948, the union was polarized into opposing camps.[53] From the first days of the union, there was tension between its rural and urban members. Ōkōchi characterized the rural members as "half-agricultural, half-industrial" in consciousness, while the urban workers were much more ready to describe themselves solely as industrial workers. They were also much more likely to be Communist or Left Socialist Party members. In the intensely political environment of postwar Japan, these differences within the union acted to widen gaps among members and define them as political disagreements—primarily Communist versus anti-Communist. This focus on politics was intensified by pressure from the government and the employers.[54]

In the electric-power industry, the *mindō* movement included a right-wing group, the Midorikai, which saw itself more as a patriotic society than as a union. The Midorikai began in Tōhoku after the October 1946 strikes and gradually gained followers, mainly in rural Chūgoku and Kyushu. This anti-urban group, reminiscent of prewar agrarian radicalism, allied in early 1948 with other disaffected Densan members to oppose the existing leadership. These people, many of them Socialist Party activists and strong believers in the union movement, were not natural allies for the Midorikai. However, they opposed the Densan leadership for such reasons as anti-communism, anger over specific decisions, frustration at the slow pace of change, and encouragement from SCAP and Japanese government officials.

The biggest strategic dispute at that time was over Densan's regional strike tactic. Similar to the "wave" strikes in the coal mines, this was Densan's response to Hepler's three wage principles and prohibitions on national strikes in the power industry. The *mindō* group opposed this tactic as too provocative of the Japanese government and SCAP, and as fomenting negative public opinion. Ironically, since the regional strikes emphasized local action, they worked to bring the rural, more conservative groups to the fore.

Another bone of contention was the plan for industry democratization itself. This was a high priority for the union leadership, but, because it involved many complex and technical issues, rank-and-file union members were not involved in the reorganization planning. Thus, it came to be seen as an elite preoccupation of the union officials. Later, a Densan leader ruefully commented that this issue was "way over the heads" of the general membership.[55]

These issues combined to bring the *mindō* group to union leadership in May 1949, when they won union elections by a slim margin. Densan's experience in this regard was typical of all Japanese unions in 1949 and 1950. In the electric-power industry, again typically, the democratization-league members were unified only by their anti-communism; once they had achieved their goal of toppling the Communists, they had difficulty agreeing, which diminished their effectiveness. The union temporarily retreated from its earlier strong stand on the issues of democratization and state control of electric power and concentrated on less controversial wage problems. It also began to disintegrate; in October 1949, the Kantō local, the most militant, split off and formed a separate union.

ELECTRIC-POWER REORGANIZATION: THE NEXT STAGE

Despite the marginalization of Densan and the municipalities, deep divisions remained over reorganization. On 4 February 1950,

Yoshida's Electric Power Industry Reorganization Commission submitted its final report in the form of majority and minority opinions. The majority opinion, written by Miki Takashi and signed by 4 of the 5 commission members, scaled down the existing system, but essentially retained it in diminished form. It called for 9 regional bloc companies and an inter-regional "power circulating company" which would balance supply and demand requirements. It was to be formed out of 42 percent of Hassōden's assets and perform the same functions.[56] Like the earlier Ōyama Commission proposal, Miki left vague the precise government role in directing this firm.

In an unusual move, Matsunaga Yasuzaemon also submitted a separate opinion. As chairman, Matsunaga had tried to bully the commission into supporting his position, earning notoriety as "the Communist Party of the business world" for his dictatorial ways.[57] His proposal called for 9 privately owned and privately operated plants. He also raised a proposition that was to be bitterly contended in the months ahead: to award developed and undeveloped hydropower resources to the company that would ultimately distribute the power to the consumers, rather than to the region in which the plant was located. This "pragmatic" approach was opposed by SCAP, which firmly held to the "regionalist" view that electric-power resources should be owned by the local company. This was the only significant disagreement between the Occupation officials and Matsunaga. This issue also splintered the alliance based on the 9 Haiden that had operated since 1947. The urban Kansai, Kantō, and Chūbu Haiden rallied behind Matsunaga and his "pragmatic" analysis. Now that the principle of private ownership and operation seemed attainable, the representatives from the major consumption centers began to demand concessions from the rural areas, which had little besides hydroelectric resources to bargain with.[58]

The Japanese government sent a draft bill based on the Miki plan to SCAP on 6 February, but it was rejected on the grounds that it was too much like the existing system. Then, in a Cabinet reshuffle, Ikeda Hayato became Minister of International Trade and Industry for two months from 11 February. This was a stroke of luck for

Matsunaga, since Ikeda was the only major politician who supported his plan. Ikeda thought that the technical problems could be resolved later and that it was pointless to resist SCAP on this issue. Therefore, he submitted a proposal to the Diet calling for 9 bloc companies without the circulating company in April 1950. The Yoshida Administration was not at all enthusiastic about the proposal, however, and, when Ikeda left the MITI post soon after, no one worked for its passage in the Diet. According to SCAP, "It appears that there is a concerted effort on the [part of the] Japanese Government to delay action on this problem as long as possible."[59] Yoshida's attitude is not surprising, since the commission roughly represented Japanese attitudes toward reorganization, that is, 4 to 1 against privatization.

Ikeda's bill met a stormy reception in the Diet. Miki expressed the opinion of the business world when he pleaded for minimal disruption of the electric-power industry. He was concerned about the effect on economic recovery given the ongoing recession. He also feared that, if the electric-power industry was split into regional groups and allowed to set its own rates, factories such as his own steel plant in high-cost regions would pay higher electric bills and might even suffer power shortages. This was of particular concern in drought-prone Kansai, where 5 business organizations issued a joint criticism of the government bill in April 1950. Finally, the majority of industrialists and MITI were convinced that reorganization would hamper new electric-power development; that regional companies would not be able to mobilize the (foreign or domestic) financial and technical expertise needed to begin new hydroelectric projects. Without these hydroelectric projects, the rationalization policy was unlikely to succeed.[60]

Matsunaga had little support elsewhere. The *Mainichi* and *Asahi* newspapers came out against him, as did the academic community. Within the Diet, the Ōno Bamboku faction of the Liberal Party and all the opposition parties fought the plan. Diet debate widened as the regional groups repeated their earlier requests for local public operation of power distribution, the Japan Socialist Party called for state operation of the industry, and Densan denounced the Matsunaga plan as an attack on labor unions. The Diet was not able to reach a compromise, and the session was adjourned on 2 May without settling the issue.[61]

Once again SCAP stepped in. ESS members were by now firmly in favor of the type of solution advocated by Matsunaga. They were no longer willing to consider any government involvement in the electric-power industry except as regulator. This was far more extreme than America's allies in Europe; France, for example, had centralized the electric-power industry under state control in 1946. T.O. Kennedy explained the ESS position: "Experience shows most economic and efficient construction and operation results from private ownership as compared to government ownership. Elimination of government control of business is desirable especially in Japan where there is too great a tendency for all business management to look to government for financing, direction and subsidy."[62] The Americans wanted the Japanese government to privatize the electric-power industry, but Yoshida could not—and did not want to— take such a politically unpopular step.

SCAP became more threatening on the matter, cutting off some counterpart-fund aid that had been designated for electric-power development in May 1950, in order to force the Diet to vote on the reorganization of Hassōden. This was a serious blow to Japanese rationalization because the electric-power development program was already two years behind schedule. The ESB had drawn up a 5- year hydroelectricity development program in 1948 to increase power capacity by 970,000 kilowatts, but virtually none of this plan had been carried out. Originally it was to be funded through the RFB. When that bank closed, the plan was stalled until the first counterpart aid funds became available in December 1949. By March 1950, loans from this source had reached 7.9 billion yen, and the power companies were at last able to start construction and repair work. When the funds were abruptly held up two months later, it meant very real pressure on the industry and on Japanese government policy. Suddenly, the reorganization had become an economic as well as a political problem.

The Japanese would have preferred to modify the existing situation, but not to change it drastically. They continued to believe that a state-managed, centralized electric-power industry was the best alternative for Japan. However, SCAP used the full force of its authority to prevent that settlement. For the SCAP officials, it was both a matter of ideology and of bureaucratic pride. They sincerely believed that a system of private, regulated power companies, as in the United States, was the best choice for Japan. Their desire to prevail delayed expansion of the electric-power system, despite the clear need. Japan's 1950 electric-power output of 39,914 million kilowatts was already inadequate, even in the depressed economic conditions of the first half of that year. Japanese government economists estimated in January 1951 that, even with a major development program, the electric-power shortfall would come to 3 billion kilowatt-hours annually over the next few years.[63] The situation was approaching crisis proportions.

REVERSAL IN U.S. PETROLEUM POLICY

American demilitarization policy was especially harsh in the petroleum industry, forcing closure of nearly all Japanese refineries. This decree lasted until July 1949 when SCAP policy toward oil underwent a dramatic reversal, from banning all refining of imported crude to supervising the redevelopment of a modern, expanded industry. At that time, SCAP decided that the world no longer needed this safeguard against Japanese industrial remilitarization.[64] This was a surprising move, because the policy of forbidding Japan an oil industry had been reaffirmed several times.

Both the Strike and the Overseas Consultants, Inc. (OCI) reparations reports, otherwise generally lenient, suggested harsh restrictions on oil. In his 1947 report, Strike advised that "the Japanese war potential in this industry can be sufficiently curbed by volume control over crude imports and it is considered less practical to resort to control of refining operations." He suggested limiting Japanese refining capacity to 12 million barrels per year and storage facilities to 6 million barrels. Existing capacity over that amount could be used for reparations, although Strike estimated that only a few storage tanks would be available for this purpose, because of war destruction.[65]

The OCI report is interesting because it suggested a solution to the problem of the postwar Japanese oil industry based neither on the strategic considerations of earlier thinkers nor on the then-developing economic self-sufficiency argument of Dodge or the U.S. Army. The OCI consultants were extremely critical of the outmoded, inefficient Japanese refineries, none of which had incorporated new cracking technology. They recommended closing down those facilities, explicitly not for reparations, but because "it would be more economical for Japan to sell its crude oil for refining in the modern plants of the Dutch East Indies than to continue its present wasteful practices."[66] Their anomalous suggestion was ignored, but it cast the Japanese oil industry into deep gloom.

In 1948, the policy of closing the Japanese refining industry came into question for several reasons. First, the major international oil companies had changed their global marketing strategy in 1947. Realizing that overseas petroleum markets would grow, they moved from refining mainly in the United States and exporting petroleum products to building refineries near the ultimate points of consumption. This new policy grew out of the intensive development of the Saudi Arabian oil fields and was further encouraged by the availability of Marshall aid funds to finance oil refining projects in Western Europe. In East Asia, Japan emerged as "the logical staging area for exploiting a vast potential market" in addition to Japan's own lucrative domestic market. The international oil companies switched from lobbying for eliminating Japanese refineries to rebuilding them.[67]

The nascent push to revive the Japanese economy provided another reason to rebuild the refining industry. It was much cheaper in foreign-exchange terms to import crude oil and refine it locally than to import more expensive petroleum products. Under Secretary of the Army William Draper was one of the main articulators of this policy, and he contradicted OCI on this point, arguing that the oil-refining industry should be reconstructed.[68]

The Americans, however, still saw petroleum as a vital security issue as well as an economic one; many SCAP personnel still wished to close the Japanese oil-refining industry on security grounds. A report by SCAP/ESS in January 1947 suggested that economic control over Japan be continued indefinitely and that it be centered on two industries—steel and petroleum; that steel and petroleum were the best choices because they are basic to waging war, easy to monitor, and, since they are capital rather than consumer goods, controls are less highly visible. Their analysis was based on the assumption that economic control of resource-poor Japan could be achieved simply by "decentralization" of the economy and indirect and unseen controls of a few key strategic points.[69] After that, debate shifted to whether to control Japanese oil supplies at the dock or at the refinery, rather than forbidding refining altogether. Colonel Harold Eastwood of SCAP/G-4 opposed reopening the Pacific Coast refineries as a security risk as late as May 1949, but H. Noel, the technical representative to SCAP of Standard of New Jersey, argued with the majority that there could be no security problem as long as the Japanese had no significant source of crude petroleum under their own control.[70] Both sides agreed that the United States should maintain some economic constraints on Japan through the oil industry.

Noel shaped the new policy when he was invited to Japan by the Army in December 1948 to evaluate the petroleum-refining industry in relation to Japanese economic self-sufficiency. He distorted the postwar concern over security by recasting the "war menace" as the "possibility of Japan's falling into the hands of an unfriendly power."[71] Having thus ignored the original fear of renewed Japanese aggression, he proceeded to argue for reopening and enlarging the refineries for "a saving to the world economy of about $70,000,000."[72]

This debate reached at least as far up into the American policy-making establishment as George Kennan, who argued in October 1949 that, if the United States created "controls . . . foolproof enough and cleverly enough exercised really to have power over what Japan imports in the way of oil and other things as she has got from overseas," then "we could have veto power over what she does need."[73]

Since, by October 1949, the decision to reopen the refineries had already been made, Kennan's remarks suggest a possible long-term agreement between the U.S. government and the major oil companies to control Japanese access to crude oil.

The Noel Report was the turning point in the decision to reopen the refineries. Accordingly, on 13 July 1949, SCAP issued permission to reopen and repair the Pacific Coast oil refineries (excluding ex-military plants) and authorized imports of crude to supply them.[74] By that time, the Japanese oil companies and major international companies had already begun negotiations for joint operations.

REVITALIZING THE OIL REFINERIES. Wartime bombing followed by five years of neglect meant the oil refineries had to be almost completely rebuilt in 1949–1950. Rebuilding proceeded quite quickly after permission to begin repairs was granted in July 1949; by the end of 1951, crude throughput capacity was greater than the pre-surrender peak, at 94,539 barrels per day. Oil refining quickly became one of Japan's most technologically advanced industries; a 1956 MITI publication cited "the high degree of automation and continuity of the various processes. . . . In this way the petroleum industry in Japan is probably the most highly automated of all manufacturing operations in the country."[75] The speed of recovery was possible because, unlike most other industries, the oil refiners had ample capital available from the international oil companies.

In 1949 and 1950, both the Japanese government and Japanese industrialists were perfectly willing to work with the international oil firms in order to rebuild the refining industry for many reasons. The Japanese had been trying to convince SCAP for several years that reopening the refineries would provide important savings in foreign exchange. Crude oil was less costly than petroleum products; more important, the foreign-exchange costs were much lower. Products came almost exclusively from United States refineries and had to be paid for with scarce dollars, while crude oil could be purchased with "softer" currencies.[76] Moreover, the Japanese hoped the majors would use their advanced technology to discover oil off the Japanese coast.

Perhaps most important to the Japanese oil companies was access to crude oil. At that time, the 7 major oil companies controlled the international oil market. Any refiner that spurned a crude-oil contract with one of the "seven sisters" risked a sudden cutoff of all supplies. The Japanese, both refiners and government officials, needed the international firms for other reasons too. Most crucially, they wanted capital assistance to rebuild their plants and access to new refining technology. All the Occupation studies on the oil industry agreed that Japanese equipment was outmoded as well as old. The Japanese refiners had been severely shocked by the OCI reparations report, which had singled them out as too backward to rehabilitate. The international oil companies could offer crude oil, exploration and refining technology, and financial assistance to the Japanese firms. Finally, the Japanese hoped they could generate exports by "re-exporting refined products to Korea, Okinawa, China, Formosa, the Philippines, etc." But the *Oriental Economist* probably summed up the attitude of the Japanese refiners most succinctly: "There is little wonder that Japanese oil firms have no alternative than to seek the collaboration of foreign interests, as it is now quite impossible for them to compete with the latter, either politically or economically."[77]

Between 1949 and 1952, the 5 most important oil refining companies in Japan signed contracts giving 50-percent control to one of the international companies (55 percent in the case of Tōa Nenryō and Stanvac).[78] These arrangements were later criticized for subordinating the interests of the Japanese partner to those of the foreign one. However, at the time they were not only initiated by the Japanese partners but were greeted with pleasure by the rest of the Japanese business community. "Great interest is now concentrated upon the industry which, as one of the first to establish contact for obtaining financial aid from abroad, will be looked upon as a test by Japan's economic circles so eager for foreign assistance,"[79] reported the *Oriental Economist* in 1949.

Japan is commonly thought of as a country that views foreign capital with suspicion and erects legislative barriers against it, but this is not strictly accurate for the years 1948 to 1952. There was active debate over the desirability of capital from abroad, and business journals and government papers from those years were full of pleas for foreign funds.[80] The debate on foreign capital hinged on two questions: whether it was forthcoming and whether it meant loss of control. The ESB officials expressed a pessimistic view in a March 1949 document. They would have preferred to rely on domestic spending "while at the same time advancing our economy by greater planning," rather than on private foreign capital, because they did not expect to attract enough foreign capital. As the ESB planners remarked, "Japan is not a paradise for foreign investors."[81] This was one of their main arguments for instituting a more gradual policy than the Dodge line.

Even if foreign investment did come to Japan, the ESB planners feared that it would actually be a drain rather than an asset. That was because "most of the foreign capital likely to come in is in manufacturing and service industry, and not in the basic industry which Japan desires to rehabilitate." In the short run, this would also force Japanese capital away from basic industry to service the new foreign capital. This is a sophisticated point that attests to the careful analysis of the ESB planners. Their concern that the infrastructural base be developed first explains why the Japanese government was anxious to have policy control over capital, not just more money.[82]

The Foreign Investment Council within the ESB acted on this concern in 1949 by holding up foreign applications for investment. They were severely criticized by Japanese businessmen for "operating as a throttle valve impeding the flow of foreign investments into the Japanese economy" and reversed this policy in January 1950.[83] Moreover, the Japanese government had already taken several steps to attract foreign capital. The Diet revised the Anti-Monopoly Law in 1949 to encourage foreign investment. Restrictions on international agreements, stockholding, and mergers were all removed, and, most important, prohibitions on exclusive international contracts with foreign entrepreneurs were dropped. This change meant that patents on foreign technology had greater protection. The Foreign Exchange and Foreign Trade Control Law of December

1949 empowered the government to establish an annual foreign-exchange budget in order to protect its balance of payments. At least until the end of the Occupation, foreign-exchange allocations were awarded on a first-come/first-served or a lottery basis. The main purpose of the law was to regulate foreign transactions so as to maintain a balance-of-payments equilibrium that would help increase foreign trade.[84]

In May 1950, the Law Concerning Foreign Investment set up more precise criteria for investments involving transfer of earnings out of Japan. Five areas were brought under government regulation: foreign acquisition of stocks of Japanese companies, beneficiary certificates, corporate bonds, loans, and technical-assistance contracts. The law also guaranteed remittances abroad, which had not been the case in earlier regulations.[85] It was passed in order to encourage more foreign investment, but it also gave the government broad powers over that investment.

Under the 1950 law, each proposed transaction was evaluated and approved only if the government felt the foreign capital investment "contributed to the self-support and sound development of the Japanese economy as well as to the improvement of the international balance of payments."[86] By international standards, this was a fairly restrictive law, but it seemed appropriate to both Japanese and SCAP officials, because the Japanese economy was still in a precarious condition. Even the International Monetary Fund (IMF), the last bastion of international free trade, studied the Japanese economy in late 1949 and recommended strict controls on international currencies through a foreign-exchange budget "to prevent a flight of capital and assure that all exchange is returned to authorities."[87] The point was to encourage the controlled entry of foreign capital into Japan.

Over the next two decades, however, the Japanese used these laws to protect a wide range of domestic industries, despite considerable pressure from the United States, other trade partners, and international organizations such as GATT and the IMF. The Foreign Exchange Law became an effective tool to encourage some firms and industries and discourage others. The historical consequences of this policy have been to limit foreign investment and channel it into only three patterns—loans, licensing agreements, and joint ventures with Japanese partners.

The Foreign Exchange Law and the Foreign Investment Law were originally designed to *encourage* foreign capital. The restrictive clauses in the two laws were written in to protect the fragile postwar economy. It was this fragility rather than Japanese opposition that discouraged potential investors in the first few years. Suspicion toward foreign investment existed in the late Occupation years but it was superseded by the frantic desire to rebuild. In those years, nearly all Japanese firms were in desperate need of capital. As a researcher at the Mitsubishi Economic Research Institute commented in 1949, "It is of urgent necessity that Japan has a firm basis for attracting foreign investors."[88] Only later could Japan enjoy the luxury of rejecting capital from overseas.

Petroleum refining was the first and most important industry to attract foreign capital. Sixty-five percent of all foreign capital investment to May 1950 involved petroleum; in the following year, 38 percent of new foreign investments went to that industry. Thus, the petroleum industry was carefully watched as the foreign capital bellwether for all Japan.[89]

The first agreement was negotiated between Tōa Nenryō and Stanvac in 1948 after Tōa Nenryō approached the American company and received final approval in March 1949. This was very early, even before SCAP permitted the Japanese refineries to reopen. In exchange for 55 percent of Tōa Nenryō stock, Stanvac pledged to supply crude oil, refining technology, and a construction loan of 20 million yen to the Japanese company. Stanvac insisted on more than 50 percent of Tōa Nenryō's stock because its facilities were in such poor shape. Stanvac also kept the rights to market the petroleum products. The American firm pledged future loans for expansion when needed, as in February 1952, when Tōa Nenryō borrowed 3.5 million dollars. Mitsubishi Oil Company, the only oil firm that had a prewar capital agreement with a foreign company, reestablished its links to Tidewater-Associated Oil in 1949 in a similar agreement, but for only 50 percent of its stock. While eager to develop capital ties, most of the other firms thought Tōa Nenryō should have kept 50-percent ownership.[90]

Caltex (Japan) Oil Company signed a more limited sales agreement with Kōa Oil in July 1949 in which Caltex paid Kōa to refine its crude and marketed the refined products itself. Then, in November 1950, Caltex traded pledges of financial and technological assistance and a guaranteed crude-oil supply for 50 percent of Kōa stock. The introduction between Kōa and Caltex was made by a personal friend of the President of Kōa Oil, Nomura Komakichi, who had represented first Mitsui Bussan and then Mitsubishi Shōji in San Francisco and Seattle, and later worked for Mitsubishi Oil. Kōa Oil also negotiated with Gulf Oil Company in 1949, but the Japanese decided to choose Caltex, because Gulf wanted to sell only crude oil and Caltex was willing also to sell them petroleum products.[91] Kōa planned from the beginning to move toward a capital tie-up, but wanted to do so gradually.[92]

In 1948, Nihon Oil Company and Caltex began negotiations for a simple exchange of crude oil for storage facilities, but this gradually developed into a more long-term agreement. Unlike any of the other oil compacts, the two companies established a new firm, the Nihon Petroleum Refining Company, as an equally shared joint venture in May 1951. Otherwise, the agreement contained the same general features as the earlier ones. Nihon Oil retained managerial control over the new company while Caltex provided crude oil, technological assistance, and start-up funds. A little later, in fall 1952, Shōwa Oil Company and Shell Oil negotiated an agreement modeled on the Standard-Tōa Nenryō and Caltex-Kōa ones.

Idemitsu Sazō and his oil-refining company, Idemitsu Kōsan, are best known for their long battle against the international oil majors, but he too considered a sales agreement with Caltex. Meeting secretly at the Kabuki theater, he negotiated in mid-1947 with the Caltex man in Japan, L.M. Carson. This was about nine months before negotiations began with other oil companies, but Idemitsu and Carson, then of Texas Oil, had discussed a sales agreement in China in 1941. They had just reached the final stages when the

Pacific War intervened. The postwar negotiations also ended in failure, when Carson's superior arrived in Japan in May 1948 and decided to pursue an agreement with Nihon Oil, rather than with Idemitsu.[93]

The Nihon Oil-Caltex agreement sheds some light on prevailing attitudes toward foreign investment in 1951 during the Korean War boom. The agreement to set up Nihon Petroleum Refining Company had been proposed several months earlier, but had been challenged by Japan's Fair Trade Commission (FTC) on the grounds that it violated the Anti-Monopoly Law. The FTC had the support of the Bank of Japan, which argued that the agreement was inflationary. However, "practically all . . . bankers and industrialists welcomed the project," which, at 6 million dollars, was the largest postwar investment in Japan. They put tremendous pressure on the government, which finally resolved the issue in July 1951 in a special Cabinet ordinance, limiting the applicability of the Anti-Monopoly Law to foreign investments. Caltex (Japan) was also required to transfer its holdings in Kōa Oil Company to its parent firm, California Texas Corporation, a largely cosmetic adjustment. Japanese industrialists expressed hope that the decision on the Caltex case would "pave the way" for future investment in the oil-refining, rubber goods, and electric-power industries.[94]

The international oil firms had been poised to take advantage of the short span of time—from 1948 to 1952—when the Japanese actively encouraged direct foreign investment (see Table 7). No other industry came close in its degree of foreign ownership, because few foreign firms found Japan attractive for investment at the time. In the electric-power industry, for example, potential investors waited for the reorganization issue to be resolved. Many large U.S. firms were busy in Europe and so had little time to spend on Japan. Others considered Japan too poor a risk to pursue. Perhaps foreign companies might have become more interested in later years, but, when the Japanese economy grew stronger, the government made such investment more difficult. In the early 1950s, however, the Japanese were grateful for all the assistance they could get to rebuild

Table 7 Japanese Oil Company Affiliations with Foreign
        Companies (31 December 1952)

Company	Affiliated With	Ratio (%)	Affiliation Date
Mitsubishi Oil	Tidewater Oil	50	February 1931(b)
Tōa Nenryō	Standard-Vacuum	55	March 1949
Kōa Oil	Caltex Oil Products	50	November 1950
Nihon Petroleum Refining	Caltex Oil	50(a)	May 1951
Shōwa Oil	Anglo-Saxon Petroleum (Shell)	50	December 1952

Source: Derived from Inokuchi Tōsuke, *Sekiyu,* pp. 387–403.

Notes: (a) Other 50% is held by Nihon Oil.
       (b) Reaffirmed March 1949.

their weakened economy. They were far less fearful about dependent economic development than they were concerned with the opportunity to develop at all.

Despite Dodge's efforts to reintegrate Japan into the world economy, the island nation remained isolated and poor. It still had no reliable trade partners. Notwithstanding civil war, China remained the most promising partner. The United States was too expensive a market. Few people elsewhere had any interest in trading with Japan. Recovery of the domestic economy proceeded equally slowly. The Japanese were most concerned about rebuilding basic infrastructural industries, such as coal, steel, and electric power. Yet these were precisely the areas hardest hit by the austerity program, bringing the Japanese economy and economic planning to a standstill. Without capital, the Japanese could not rationalize and, without control of the budget, government officials could not provide easy credit, as they had during the priority-production years. The Japanese had run out of solutions until new opportunities arrived from overseas in the form of the Korean War.

EIGHT

Post-Austerity Rationalization: Japan in the

World Economy

In the half-decade between 1950 and 1955, the Japanese began establishing the institutions that would support the concepts developed in the preceding five years. The postwar Japanese economy acquired most of the features that buttressed high-speed growth by 1955. Japan now had the resources and freedom of movement to explore the ideas of rationalization and "self-sufficiency" and to test them against real-world problems. Perhaps the most thorny of these was energy, which the Japanese struggled to resolve through the 1950s. The Korean War confirmed the growing Japanese commitment to self-sufficiency through rationalization and export promotion. From that time, Japan developed into an important producer and exporter of heavy industrial goods with an economy organized to expedite economic growth.

As in the previous five years, U.S. policy in Asia defined the parameters of this development in both great and small spheres. From the point of view of the Japanese economy, the most important aspect of American policy was the renewed decision to encourage expansion of Japan's heavy industry and its foreign trade. By early 1950, building a strong Japanese economy had already become a major preoccupation of American policymakers, who linked it to global containment of communism and regional Asian economic and strategic integration. This meant moving away from the harshest aspects of the stabilization program and toward more active material assistance to Japan. It is unclear how well this policy would have succeeded in the absence of the Korean War—a crucial stroke of luck for U.S. policy toward Japan as well as for the Japanese. Certainly, the outbreak of war provided an opportunity for the U.S. government to use its military purchases to help Japan. These "special procurements" boosted Japanese export levels and provided a pivotal infusion of dollars to Japanese industrialists. They were the first postwar solution to Japan's enduring search for stable markets.

From the Japanese point of view, the Korean War provided a happy and unanticipated opportunity to move toward their previously adopted goal of economic self-sufficiency through rationalization. American military purchases and American technical and financial assistance made rationalization much easier to implement. The flood of dollars ended the period of austerity, which had forced down Japanese wages and living standards. American policy also continued to shape the nature of Japan's economic relations with the outside world. For example, the United States government fostered a World Bank loan to three electric-power companies in 1953. Not coincidentally, this loan gave an unusually favorable position to Westinghouse and General Electric and assured them an early position of superiority in the postwar Japanese market.

The Americans also continued to shape relations domestically. Again in the electric-power industry, one of SCAP's last acts was to force the privatization of the industry. Direct pressure on labor unions by the Americans (and the Japanese government) remained significant, too, notably the SCAP-approved "Red Purge" in private industry during the second half of 1950. This combination of improved economic conditions and attacks on political activity pushed the labor unions a little closer to the image cherished by the Americans of a "bread-and-butter" labor movement that avoided national political issues but shared to some extent in increasing prosperity.

Despite the sudden improvement in their economic position when the Korean War began, the Japanese remained pessimistic about their long-term economic prospects. They realized that the Korean conflict was a temporary solution, unlikely to provide the vast amount of capital Japan needed or a permanent export market. Japanese leaders assumed that U.S. government support would remain essential for many years to come, especially for expensive development projects such as new hydroelectric plants. Thus, the advent of war did not significantly change Japanese economic thinking, although it did put them in a better position to implement the existing rationalization policies. The future for Japan still seemed uncertain and impoverished—as it had before the Korean War began.

This pessimism reconfirmed Japanese commitment to rationalization, the only economic strategy available to the Japanese that responded both to the new postwar international context and to the democratic reforms that had taken place within Japan. In the international sphere, American support and the availability of foreign technology and financing made the rationalization plan feasible. The Japanese benefited from a historic moment when this type of policy could be particularly effective. Meanwhile, American embargo of trade with China and abolition of Hassōden closed off alternative paths to development.

Within Japan, positive government economic policies and lively competition among Japanese firms aided productivity increases. Rationalization also provided a basis for compromise with the new labor unions by promising a higher standard of living for their members. Moreover, rationalization eventually meant that more and more imports became available for domestic consumption. This rise in the standard of living—transmitted through the medium of higher wages and higher employment levels—created a domestic consumption boom which in itself solved Japan's most pressing economic problem—lack of markets. The larger market at home allowed Japanese producers to enjoy economies of scale that paid for an increasing proportion of ever-essential imports. The Japanese people were finally prospering along with their economy.

Although this was the national story, at more local levels, like coal-mining regions, rationalization's promise was empty. Living standards did not rise and, perhaps worse, they fell in relation to the new Japanese norm. Modernization drives in specific industries or companies also became excuses to break radical unions, including

Densan. Rationalization became the vehicle by which labor was elbowed out of national economic policymaking. It always presented a two-fisted image to labor, grasping both a threat and a promise. This ambiguous message is one reason why rationalization never seemed the perfect solution.

Another problem with rationalization, as the experience of the coal industry showed, was that considerable American and Japanese policy assists in the early 1950s were not always enough to ensure prosperity. Although at the heart of Japanese rationalization policy, the coal industry proved a dismal failure and was already becoming Japan's "sick man" by the end of 1954. The generous incentives offered to the coal industry were insufficient to revitalize the mines. At bottom, this was due to factors outside Japanese control: a depleted resource base and plummeting world oil prices. Other factors contributed as well, including the resistance to rationalization by both the coal operators and the miners' unions. These two groups rarely cooperated, but their separate opposition—and their endless battling—combined to prevent all but minimal technological development in the mines. The failure of the coal industry to fulfill the pivotal role it was assigned in economic reconstruction caused new problems for the Japanese. It raised dilemmas of unemployment, regional destitution, and foreign control of energy supplies— all problems that would have remained dormant if the mines had rationalized as originally hoped and planned.

It would be a mistake to attribute the successes of rationalization policy or economic prosperity to prescient government or business planning. Government policies did make it easier for firms to purchase and import foreign technology and to accumulate capital, both crucial elements of postwar economic growth. Yet, an examination of specific industries reveals a variety of patterns diverging from the model envisioned by the rationalization planners. Some industries—most notably coal—failed to respond to the Japanese government's rationalization plans. Others, including electric power, grew rapidly, just as the economic planners had hoped, but were stimulated by unanticipated factors. Still other industries, among them petroleum refining, became leading sectors despite the fact that they were neither targeted by the government as key to the economy nor offered special rationalization incentives. These varied and unexpected developments reveal the ad hoc nature of Japanese industrial planning. The Japanese had by no means discovered a secret blueprint for economic success.

The Korean War, or more accurately, American use of the war, had an enormous impact on the Japanese economy in practical terms. It is hard to overestimate the importance of that timely influx of money, technology, and willing customers for Japanese industry. Not least, the war forced the first real commitment to oil by fuel-user industries, presaging Japan's energy revolution. The war had no commensurate influence, however, on Japanese thinking about their economy. It served only to confirm the Japanese in their support of rationalization policy, of coal and the import-minimization approach, of cautiously reflationary monetary measures, and of economic planning. It cemented Japanese ties to Western firms through capital and technological agreements and permanently linked Japanese economic development to United States military priorities in Asia. As with U.S. foreign policy, all these ideas developed before the Korean War, which merely provided an opportunity to implement them. Nonetheless, new, unanticipated developments during the Korean War would have major implications for grand economic policy. One of these was the persistence of labor unions, despite setbacks to their influence, partly because rationalization strategy itself embodied a commitment to raising standards of living and education for workers. Another development was the abysmal failure of coal to respond to rationalization. This ushered in the energy revolution.

THE AMERICAN POLICY CONTEXT AND JAPANESE ASSESSMENT, 1950–1954

While the Japanese wrestled with the dilemmas created by Dodge's austerity plan in early 1950, the Americans began reconsidering policy in Asia, especially in regard to the fledgling People's Republic of China. During the first six months of 1950, Washington policymakers discussed various means to contain communism in Asia. The keynote of American foreign policy was the fashioning of regional alliances, so their discussions centered on analyses of Eastern Asia as a whole, rather than country-by-country policies. In the economic sphere, the Americans resolved to more closely integrate the Japanese economy with the economies of other non-Communist Asian countries, and continued to debate the value of economic ties between Japan and China. This discussion, in stark contrast to the Pauley reparations plan of only five years earlier, centered on Japan's needs and how best to organize Asia to support the *Japanese* economy.

Japan's dearth of markets was an enduring problem, laid bare by the effects of the stabilization plan. By early 1950, this problem had to be addressed directly, and Southeast Asia was the obvious place to begin. The United States government had discussed this issue as early as 1948, but the founding of the People's Republic of China gave it new urgency. As Michael Schaller revealed, the desirability of economic ties between Japan and Southeast Asia was one of the few points on which the State Department and U.S. military leaders could agree. Although many officials remained deeply pessimistic about developing such ties, discussions about economic aid centered more on the East Asian region and less on each separate country. American policy increasingly was designed to work regionally to tie Japan and Southeast Asia together.[1]

The Americans also discussed a different kind of integration, that is, combining economic, political, and military objectives in Asia. The Army coordinated military and economic aid within Japan, in a concept pioneered by Under Secretary of the Army Tracy Voorhees. In early 1950, Voorhees used Japanese construction firms instead of American firms to build U.S. military bases in Okinawa. The dollars the Army paid the Japanese firms directly enriched Japan's foreign-exchange holdings and also eased the strain on economic aid to Japan. In Voorhees's phrase, the aid dollars could do "double duty" as economic pump primer and as contributor to military preparedness. Moreover, the Army could show Congress that Japan needed less economic aid each year, since the military budget was figured separately. The Army bureaucrats had discovered that, while it was difficult to winkle appropriations out of Congress on economic grounds, arguments based on security cracked open the lawmakers' hard shell. Men like Voorhees and his predecessor, William Draper, who had returned to his civilian job as Vice-President of Dillon, Read & Co., successfully argued that, if the U.S. government paid the Japanese for supporting the Occupation (out of the military budget) rather than expecting the Japanese to pay Occupation costs and then granting economic aid, this would have the same "double-duty" effect. Voorhees was proposing one more step toward transforming Japan from vanquished foe to ally. Voorhees argued further that "United States military forces themselves are potentially a much larger dollar market for Japanese products than they have been heretofore."[2] This was the modest start of a general militarization of U.S. economic aid to Japan and other nations after the Korean War began.

By early 1951, these efforts to integrate Japan and Southeast Asia economically and to incorporate Japan's economy more fully into U.S. containment policy in Asia had coalesced into a "U.S.-Japan economic cooperation" plan. In this concept, Japanese industrial development would be encouraged by the United States so as to buttress the "economic stability of the non-communist countries of Asia." Japanese Self-Defense Forces would cooperate with the Americans in the garrisoning of Japan, while Japan would produce "low-cost military material in volume for use in Japan and in other non-communist countries of Asia." The formal culmination of this multilateral military-economic policy in Japan would be the Mutual Security Agreement of 1954. This general policy was still on the drawing board or in only the first stages of implementation when the Korean War began, but it is important to note that its salient features—Japanese rearmament, post-treaty U.S. bases in Japan, industrial remilitarization, and designation of Japan as producer of manufactured goods for Asia—were developed before 25 June 1950, and were not a response to the war. Rather, they developed out of the deeper problems of reconstructing the shattered Japanese trade structure and of containing communism in Asia.[3]

There is no doubt, however, that the Korean War speeded up implementation of these policies, as well as negotiation of the peace treaty with Japan. Economically, the war was a tremendous boon to the Japanese. It provided a crucial spurt of income and of hard currency at a time when Japanese industry was desperate for foreign exchange to import new machinery and to purchase raw materials. The war stimulated global trade of all kinds; the volume of world trade increased in 1950 by 34 percent, or $19 billion over 1949. Japan shared in the global prosperity, with both production and export figures jumping past the prewar levels for the first time. The value of Japanese exports went from $510 million in 1949 to $820 million in 1950 and on up to $1,355 million in 1951 and $1,273 million in 1952. At least temporarily, the Korean War had solved the problem of finding export markets for Japanese goods. It also solved the dollar problem, since the main new customer was the U.S. government's offshore procurement program. This special procurement program accounted for 60 to 70 percent of Japanese exports in 1950 through 1952. Dollar payments to Japan for these goods and services totaled $590 million in 1950, and over $800 million in both 1951 and 1952. Non-official but related dollar sources, such as GI spending in Japan, were also significant. In October 1951 alone, American servicemen spent $3.5 million in Japan. Imports were still from expensive dollar sources, but that did not matter as long as exports were reimbursed in the same powerful currency. Business improved in a wide variety of industries; leather, rubber, textiles, steel, trucks, cement, and lumber all reported brisk sales.[4]

Despite the strong American commitment to rebuilding the Japanese economy, and the subsequent assist toward this goal created by the Korean War boom, "U.S.-Japan economic cooperation" was not a well-defined concept. Probably the most important blurry area was in Sino-Japanese trade. Eisenhower himself remained convinced throughout the Korean War years that the United States would have to allow such trade to shore up the Japanese economy. There were quirks in other aspects of the U.S. position on Japanese economic recovery as well. Although American planners were dedicated to Japanese recovery in a broad sense, attempts to control certain aspects of the Japanese economy did not work toward general reconstruction. For example, Japanese oil supplies were a continuing sore point for U.S. officials. This was more a reflection of the gap between American acceptance of Japan and lingering Allied suspicions than of splits within American policy. Discussion with the other Allied countries about restricting Japanese access to oil continued into 1951, even though other American documents of the same period stress the need to provide Japan with raw materials. Once again, the problem was whether to define petroleum as a strategic good, and thus potentially dangerous in Japanese hands, or as a necessary economic one. This confusion lingered for a surprisingly long time. Other battles were fought within the Occupation structure, where the Allies had little influence. One was the drawn-out and surprisingly ideological debate over reorganization of the electric-power industry, described in the preceding chapter. This was not resolved until late 1950, well into the Korean War, and was one of the main reasons for the extreme shortage of electric power in 1951. It also revealed inconsistencies within American policy in Japan.[5]

The Korean War itself did not affect Japanese analyses of their economic problems very much. Even after the boom was well underway, the Japanese remained pessimistic about their economic future. In Japanese eyes, the Korean War did not adequately address Japan's fundamental economic problems, particularly its lack of trade partners. The Japanese recognized that continued U.S. government aid, or even ingenious methods of tying that aid to Southeast Asian purchases, would not suffice to create an overseas market for Japan. They were acutely conscious of the fact that the military market was a temporary one and might disappear as rapidly as it developed. Even if it lasted for a few years, this artificial export market could not resolve the long-term problems of stable capital formation and peacetime markets.[6]

In January 1951, at the height of the war boom, the ESB warned that "Japan's economy is still being supported by U.S. aid amounting to hundreds of millions of dollars per year and is far from being self-supporting. Therefore the highest objective of our economic policy should be the attainment of a self-supporting economy and we should do our utmost so that we may quickly be able to get along without foreign aid."[7] Three months later, the ESB published a plan for post-treaty Japan estimating that Japan would still need at least $140 million in U.S. aid in order to balance its foreign-exchange account. Even this pessimistic forecast was branded by the Japanese business community as "too ambitious." Self-sufficiency through economic rationalization remained the most important goal in Japan. The Korean War provided a timely boost, and was certainly appreciated, but the Japanese feared it was too temporary to generate enough capital or long-term overseas markets.[8]

The Japanese, experienced in the effect of wars on their economy, also feared that a postwar economic slump would wipe out the gains of the Korean War boom. From mid-1951, anxious reports on economic slowdowns and especially unemployment became more common. The Japanese worried about the fact that one-third of their industrial capacity was unused even at the height of the Korean War boom. This, and growing inflation, shadowed Japanese assessments about their economic future. Their attitude was epitomized by Yoshida Shigeru's comment that the Korean War was a "gift from the gods"—to be accepted gratefully without expecting repeat performances.[9]

Japanese pessimism was based partly on the fact that war demand also *caused* new problems for their economy. Inflation, a sudden shortage of raw materials, and distortions in their economy due to abrupt and uncoordinated procurement orders threatened not only to cancel out any gains made by higher production but also to endanger the industrial rationalization effort. Inflation was perhaps the most pernicious, given the long struggle against it in postwar Japan. This was a global phenomenon over which Japan did not have much control, although it was more severe there than elsewhere. Global price increases were especially high in raw materials and shipping, two areas in which Japan was already at a comparative disadvantage. A year after the Korean War began, Japanese commodity prices had increased by an alarming 50 percent, a far greater increase than in the United States or Great Britain, where prices rose about 20 percent. One ESB official warned in 1951 that "the return of inflation with increased production cost will be a fatal blow to the preservation of the export industry. . . . any further price rise will depreciate its competitive strength to such an extent that most of the outlets to the world market will be closed to the Japanese goods." [10] At the same time, the Japanese were reluctant to reduce credit or take other anti-inflation measures, since that would further restrict already-scarce capital resources. These conflicting requirements—to restrain inflation and provide capital—made financial policy decisions very difficult indeed. The Japanese chose to continue more liberal credit policies but worried about the consequences of this choice. In late 1951 and 1952, many Japanese feared they would have to devalue the yen as far as 500 to the dollar before inflation could be controlled. [11]

The Korean War also strained supplies of natural resources traded internationally. Previously, the Japanese had worried about producing and selling enough exports to pay for imports, but had not needed to search the four corners of the globe for supplies. Now there was a sudden dearth of metals and other ingredients for industrial production, not all due to the conflict in Korea itself, but to the Korean War's spur to the worldwide remilitarization that American planners had discussed in early 1950. This large-scale rearmament fed upon itself when the U.S. Army instituted stockpile programs of strategic materials for America and its main allies in 1950 and again in 1952. This kept supplies of some resources tight for several more years until the stockpiles were completed. [12]

The shortages of natural resources caused by the Korean War and related policies forced the Japanese to consider an import as well as an export policy. Their discussions covered both developing domestic supplies and methods for securing resources from abroad. These were seen as alternative tactics within the same general strategy, but the main emphasis was on developing domestic resources. The import problem was first discussed in detail in the ESB's "Basic Ideas underlying Economic Self-support Program," of 4 October 1950. This document redefined economic self-support as a state in which "international payments are balanced, a reasonable standard of living is secured, and higher economic self-supply is attained through the development of indigenous resources." Another ESB document defined the "three pillars of the plan" as securing or substituting for imports, achieving self-sufficiency, and accumulating capital.[13]

The lack of imports turned attention once more to domestic resources. It also revived Arisawa's formulation of the export-import problem, that the uncertainties of international trade and Japan's lack of foreign currency made it imperative to emphasize domestic energy, as foreign mineral and energy resources became harder to obtain. As Arisawa had recognized, however, this strategy required an aggressive domestic resource-development program, given the postwar energy crisis in Japan. Both domestic coal and hydroelectricity were in critically short supply in 1950 because of the lack of development over the previous decade. Compounding this problem, in the early 1950s securing natural resources from abroad was not an easy task, since the same problems beset the Japanese in their quest for imports as for exports. The lack of currency convertibility, finances, and favorable trade agreements blocked the flow of goods both into and out of Japan. Identifying the problem was simple: Japan was not yet financially and diplomatically reintegrated into world trade systems. The solution, however, was more difficult.

The Korean War boom also unbalanced the tottery Japanese supply structure. The sudden spurt of large special procurement orders caused spot shortages of certain goods, such as fertilizer. Japanese officials repeatedly asked that the various U.S. bodies that spent in Japan (for example, each of the military services) work together and notify the Japanese government in advance of large purchases. Because the Americans did not do so, the domestic as well as the imported "supply lines" to Japan's export industries were repeatedly disrupted.[14] Moreover, when the Chinese entered the war in October, the Americans made the final decision to require a complete embargo of Sino-Japanese trade, suddenly cutting off that source.

All these problems made greater coordination of the economy

appear increasingly necessary. The Korean War seemed to intensify the need for rationalization of industry rather than to eliminate it. Most official Japanese papers on the economy in 1951 and 1952 warned that the government might have to reimpose controls on imports and perhaps consumption of scarcer domestic items. The ESB suggested that the government directly import strategic materials and either build its own stockpiles or subsidize private traders to do so. Dodge himself, although a die-hard advocate of free trade, told Finance Minister Ikeda in late 1951 that the Japanese government should institute controls over imports and raw materials.[15]

Planning seemed necessary to Japanese officials because the problem was not simply one of scarcity but also of misallocation of resources. As they had during the Dodge Line period, private businessmen still chose to invest in immediately profitable industries, such as paper and textiles. They did not put money into basic infrastructural development of energy and transportation networks, projects that offered only slow and small returns. This omission threatened to hobble all Japanese economic activity. In fact, the faster industrial activity grew, the sooner these bottlenecks would be reached. The thinking behind Japanese economic plans was not changed by the advent of the Korean War nor by the American "U.S.-Japan economic cooperation" policy. Rather, the disruptions associated with the war boom intensified Japanese commitment to their earlier plans. These were still based on a concept of "self-sufficiency," and rationalization and export promotion were still Japan's main methods of achieving that goal.

Assessing the actual impact of the Korean War on these programs was difficult. Even within single industries, the war boom had an unpredictable effect on rationalization efforts, and it was hard to discern a dominant trend. Many Japanese firms, including the steelmakers, used their wartime earnings to purchase new machinery and upgrade their plants. This timely infusion of money was a key factor in the later success of the important steel, shipbuilding, and automobile industries. In hindsight, we know that the intense spurt of investment in these and other industries helped propel the Japanese economy to prosperity and made the rationalization policy possible. However, not all industries responded to the war in the same way. Some, such as machine-tools manufacturers, simply did not experience boom conditions. Their products were inferior to foreign designs, and, when firms in other industries had money to buy new machine tools, they preferred to shop abroad. Government incentives to rationalize by buying this foreign technology only exacerbated the plight of the machine-tool industry, a contradiction within rationalization policy that will be discussed in more detail later. The relevant point here is that the Korean War prosperity was not shared by the machine-tool makers.[16]

Other industries did well, but did not use the boom conditions to rationalize. The most significant example was the coal mines, where the revenue generated by the war provided the first opportunity to put rationalization plans in practice, but also acted as an obstacle. Suddenly, demand was so great that Japanese collieries did not need to cut costs or raise quality to sell their coal. Although equipment investment was active, it was often directed at expanding immediate *production* rather than at rationalizing operations or raising *productivity*. The advent of the Korean War and its promise of high profits during the boom deflected business interest from rationalization to raising production in the short term. MITI, which was very concerned about this, argued in a contemporary policy paper that, "if these internal and external conditions [created by war demand] prevent active promotion of future rationalization, it will gravely weaken the basis on which to build a self-sufficient economy in the future."[17] They feared that failure in the mines would jeopardize national reconstruction.

Although the content of Japanese planning did not change, within the Japanese bureaucracy the locus of economic planning shifted from the ESB to MITI. From about 1951, the mainspring of economic planning was MITI, while the Ministry of Finance remained key for fiscal policy. The ESB had been the intellectual and policy center for economic issues during the Occupation, but, by late 1950, it was an open secret that Yoshida would weaken it as soon as the peace treaty came into effect. Meanwhile, MITI had been formed in May 1949 out of the MCI and the Board of Trade in order to strengthen the international aspects of Japan's economy. Yoshida, who did not like MITI either, wanted to minimize the power of all the professional economic bureaucracies rather than strengthen MITI. He represented an older generation of gentleman-diplomat and had little respect for what he saw as mere technicians.

The two agencies worked together without much discord until the ESB was dissolved in August 1952 and was replaced by the much more modest Economic Deliberation Agency. The new young MITI was ready and ambitious to take over the ESB role and chose rationalization policy as one of its principal vehicles to that end.[18] The ESB and MITI essentially agreed on the need to expand exports and establish self-sufficiency. Both emphasized development of domestic energy, transport, and communications networks and recommended extensive imports of foreign technology. Perhaps the most important difference between the two agencies was their fundamental attitude toward labor unions and workers. The ESB officials consistently struck a more worker-oriented note in their comments on industrial relations. They stressed the need to train workers as technical experts in order to increase their contribution and, therefore, their wages. This contrasted with MITI's and the Rationalization Council's language, in which workers were described as a comparatively abundant resource. This bureaucratic transition provides one more reason why the climate for labor unions became more hostile toward the end of the Occupation.[19]

Japanese government officials took a number of steps to strengthen their rationalization policies across the entire economy during the Korean War years, particularly in the areas of finance and technological expertise. The government pioneered a variety of methods to help firms in key industries accumulate capital. The most important were tax exemptions, loans, foreign-exchange allocations, exceptions to the Anti-Monopoly Law, and shouldering the responsibility for infrastructural development. The government was equally assiduous in helping firms attract new technology with import licenses, more tax exemptions, mediation with overseas firms, and guarantees for foreign loans. These government actions were well organized and deserve credit for improving the efficiency of Japanese industry.

The officials also devoted considerable effort to getting assistance from abroad, especially from the American government. Throughout the early 1950s, the Japanese looked for capital from U.S. government loans or credits, the World Bank, and American private investment. They did not hesitate to lobby hard for funds even before the Korean War began. In May 1950, in the midst of delicate negotiations between the Japanese and American governments over a peace treaty and post-treaty bases in Japan, Ikeda told Dodge that the Japanese were prepared to offer bases to the United States. He immediately went on to comment that "substantial amounts of private capital investment from the United States would tend to make the Japanese people less skeptical about their own future." The offer of bases in Japan was a major concession, and the Japanese hoped for some direct financial return in addition to their main goal of ending the Occupation as quickly as possible.[20]

The Japanese returned to this theme again several times after the Korean War began. Yoshida asked for a major U.S. government loan for electric-power development in mid-1951 and followed with a second request in December. He argued that "a loan from the United States would kill two birds, one political and the other economic, with one stone. It would demonstrate in a dramatic and unmistakable fashion American intentions and policy toward Japan." Yoshida argued that a loan would help the Japanese government consolidate political support for the war effort in Korea and for the alliance with the United States, as well as finance production of materials to use in the conflict. The U.S. Ambassador to Japan accepted Yoshida's hints that the electric-power loan was a fair return for Japanese remilitarization. He wrote to the Department of State arguing for the loan because it "might be helpful in pressing govt to accelerate its lagging armament effort." In 1954, Yoshida again linked American economic assistance, this time for road building, to Japanese rearmament in a conversation with the U.S. Secretary of Defense.[21]

This intensive effort to attract U.S. government (and World Bank) loans and private foreign capital is worth noting, because it clarifies the nature and limitations of Japanese "self-sufficiency." Attaining independence did not mean ending all assistance from the U.S. government; rather it meant gaining more policy control over that assistance. Similarly, it did not mean excluding private foreign investment, although the Japanese government wanted to keep 50-percent control of any joint ventures in Japanese hands. "Self-sufficiency," even as a concept, recognized the dependence of the Japanese economy on American financial assistance in the 1950s. Nor did Japanese self-sufficiency mean independence from American military strategy in East Asia. Rather, on several occasions, the Japanese traded military concessions for financial rewards, forging direct and lasting links between their economic prosperity and American military power.

The Japanese economy remained closely tied to the U.S. military for the rest of the decade and beyond. Direct Korean War spending, and general U.S. military procurement in Asia were both larger and more enduring than the Japanese imagined. In the five years between 1952 and 1956, procurement income came to $3,381 million, equivalent in value to over one quarter of Japan's commodity imports during that period. In 1958–1959, the value was still equivalent to 14 percent of imports. The United States also underwrote most of the early expenses of the Self-Defense Forces as well as those of its own troops in Japan, and helped the Japanese develop valuable new skills so that they could produce more sophisticated goods. "U.S.-Japan economic cooperation" institutionalized military demand by welding together economic and military aid. In fiscal 1959, the Americans still paid millions of dollars in aid: They provided Japan with $168.6 million in direct military procurement; $108.3 million in non-military procurement; $54 million in direct military assistance; and $2.5 million in technical assistance; plus an additional $208.3 million spent by U.S. personnel in Japan. The U.S. overseas military in Asia had become a semi-permanent market for Japanese goods, while the original plan to develop Southeast Asia itself as a trade partner remained a more long-term solution.[22]

COAL: BEGINNING THE LONG SLIDE

The government continued to develop rationalization plans for the coal industry, but none of them ever fulfilled their promise. This failure was due to new pressures from foreign energy sources and physical depletion of the mines. It was further accentuated by the growing technical preference of Japanese consumers for petroleum and the sluggish response of the coal industry to outside calls for lower prices. The Japanese coal industry would never have been able to sustain the rapid growth of the 1960s, but the speed of the coal companies' decline was due in part to their failure to rationalize in the early 1950s. Given the poor natural-resource base, one can certainly make the argument that this was a blessing in disguise for the Japanese economy as a whole, since the failure of the coal industry to keep up with the economic expansion of the late 1950s meant that Japanese fuel-consuming industries switched over to petroleum early. Thus, they began to use the world's most advanced technologies as soon as they were developed. The Japanese also profited from the historic moment when petroleum prices were low, and could rebuild their economy at relatively low cost. This assessment, however, can only be made with benefit of hindsight. At the time, the long-term effect of the energy revolution was not understood. Moreover, it was a disaster for the coal industry itself.

The failure of the coal industry also indicates the limits of Japanese industrial planning. The rationalization policy was designed to revive the coal industry, and its collapse was unquestionably an unplanned event. Although other targeted industries, notably steel, became world leaders in the 1950s, the original rationalization plans envisioned a sturdy domestic coal industry underpinning the Japanese economy. Japan's comparatively early move to petroleum represented a failure of policy, even though the *unintended* consequences may have been beneficial.

As the years went by, the rationale for the various coal policies changed. At first, programs for the mines were designed to raise productivity and lower prices as part of industrial rationalization. By 1960, however, it gradually became clear that shifting from primary reliance on domestic coal to imported fuel—as advocated by Nakayama Ichirō—was the energy policy most consistent with the "production first" self-sufficiency policy. This policy was half-heartedly chosen in 1955, but it raised new issues of unemployment, social welfare, and national security. The coal operators and the organized coal miners stressed these issues, but were only moderately successful in getting a hearing. They also failed to work together, and angered other economic policymakers by their lack of cooperation.

Profits from special procurement orders during the Korean War provided the first opportunity for most Japanese industries to import new machinery and improve technologically. This pattern was most obvious in the steel industry, which began an ambitious modernization program. The Korean War boom was the key stroke of luck for the steel companies, which needed only a timely infusion of capital to take advantage of the improved technology available in other countries. They received this when the price of steel tripled during the Korean War boom. In the fall of 1950, both Yawata and Nihon Tekkan steel companies set up 3-year rationalization plans which required 10 times the investment level of the previous three years. Kawasaki Steel Company had an even more ambitious plan. Its Chiba Bay factory, the world's first ore-to-steel continuous casting plant, began operating in 1953.[23]

The government then coordinated the plans of the steel companies into the February 1952 steel rationalization plan. Government assistance included huge loans to the steelmakers, imports of new technology, generous foreign-exchange allocations, a special 50-percent depreciation on new machinery, and other tax and tariff exemptions. The government provided another crucial but indirect form of assistance to all firms by heavily subsidizing the "environmental obstacles" to their rationalization. The 1952 Enterprise Rationalization Promotion Law pledged state responsibility for improvements to road and rail lines, harbors, telecommunications, and water supply.[24] Since these are the most expensive components in constructing a new plant, this policy allowed firms to put their own money into new equipment instead. This kind of assistance is not unique to Japan, but it was a key element in the postwar success of Japanese industry. Kawasaki Steel's 1953 plant was on newly reclaimed land in Chiba Bay with new water, gas, electricity, harbor, and road facilities, all provided by the government.[25]

The Korean War did not have the same effect in the coal mines. This was partly because the coal companies had more severe problems than most Japanese firms. Coal is an extractive industry, and Japanese coal reserves grew more expensive to exploit as the best seams were consumed. This problem was aggravated by the ten-year gap in mine development, which meant that the industry faced huge expansion costs without any immediate return in sales. The coal operators avoided these problems during the Korean War. Temporarily, they had no difficulty selling their coal. The general economic upturn meant a stronger coal market while the severe drought of 1951 meant that electric-power plants were buying more than usual. Unlike the steel firms, they did not have to worry about competing in the international market in the future. Moreover, spiraling freight costs drove up the costs of imported coal. In short, the coal companies enjoyed conditions under which they could sell their coal at any price.

There is some difference of opinion among researchers as to whether the coal companies honestly tried to mechanize their mines; most argue that they did not. It is clear that the smaller mines were not able to cut unit costs, but the actions of the largest mine owners are debatable. The mine operators insisted they spent all that they had available, and showed statistics of steadily increasing tons per man-hour to support claims to have invested in their mines. They also mechanized some of the coal faces and installed conveyor systems.

Other researchers, however, have calculated that the sum invested by the 18 largest firms between 1950 and 1956, an average yearly amount of 13 billion yen, was approximately equivalent to the financial breaks the firms received in the form of lowered taxes, deferred loan repayments, and accelerated depreciation. The coal operators either wrote off or repaid their debts rather than incurring new ones. This relatively minor level of reinvestment was in sharp contrast to other Japanese industries such as steel and electric power and also in contrast to the coal mines in Europe during the same period. These researchers argue that the major coal operators expected to enjoy continued high profits from their monopoly control of the best mines rather than from lowering costs, and that the productivity improvements were achieved with outside funds. Certainly the mine operators were overconfident about their importance. In early 1952, the coal industry rejected requests from consumers for lower prices.[26] Instead, the largest firms continued to collect their "marginal rents" and use them to finance new, non-coal ventures just as they had before the Pacific War. As one Japanese researcher commented, "At the height of the Korean War boom, when foreign energy posed no threat, the coal companies probably wanted to maintain their high prices and high profits, and disregarded the government's strong demands that they accumulate capital."[27] In the early 1950s, this seemed a safe strategy.

Why was the response of the coal operators so different from that of the steelmakers? Through 1956, the coal operators resisted all rationalization attempts. Some did so because they saw no future in further investment; their mines were small or inappropriate for machinery. However, many still thought in prewar terms of autarky and monopoly control, attitudes that had been surprisingly unshaken by postwar changes. The major coal operators were well insulated from change during the Occupation and were forced to respond to new pressures only from 1953. They were largely exempt from SCAP deconcentration and democratization programs in order to raise coal production. They received the lion's share of state funds during the RFB years and so stayed ahead of inflation.[28] They had beaten back an attempt to establish state control of the mines, and had grown closer to the leading political party in the process. Even during the Dodge deflation, the large coal companies enjoyed a protected market because Japan did not have the foreign exchange to buy fuel abroad. The Korean War brought new prosperity and a raw-materials shortage, and so the coal operators did not have to face their critics until 1952. Even after the Occupation ended, the big coal companies continued to be protected to some extent from market pressures. They felt secure under the self-sufficiency policy, which stressed domestic energy sources. Japan's weak balance-of-payments situation made energy imports a luxury, and so the domestic coal operators retained their monopoly powers. The large coal operators were further able to protect themselves by exerting pressure on the small, high-cost producers, many of whom became subcontractors to the 18 largest firms.[29] In interviews, the adjectives most commonly used to describe the coal industry executives in this period were old-fashioned, backward (*okurete*), traditional (*dentōteki*), and stubborn (*ganko*).[30]

These attitudes went unchallenged by other business groups during the first postwar years. The steel industry demanded lower coal prices from 1950, but even this protest was muted by the outbreak of the Korean War. After the war boom ended, the steel companies repeated their demands, but the war had given the coal industry another period of respite. The government protected the coal industry too. Ironically, this was partly because so much emphasis had been placed on coal since 1945. As Arisawa remarked, "Precisely because we had put so much effort into reaching the 300-million-ton goal, we continued to support the coal industry."[31] Thus, the major coal companies were in a remarkably privileged position, not subject to discipline by the market, nor by the government, nor by SCAP. Ultimately, however, these privileges led to the failure of the coal companies to adjust to the competitive postwar environment. Also, coal's favored status did not last forever.

The big coal companies continued their longstanding custom of extracting wealth from the mines, but higher wage costs and the gradual depletion of natural resources after the Pacific War meant that the traditional "money boxes" were emptying out. Meanwhile, huge petroleum discoveries in the Mideast and the steady development of oil-based technologies abroad were eroding the competitive edge of coal all around the world. Japanese coal operators no longer enjoyed either the low labor costs or the monopoly market position that had brought them wealth in decades past. These problems were already visible in 1950 but the coal operators were not yet aware of the depth of the difficulty. They did not realize it until about 1957, when the rest of the Japanese economy began to prosper, leaving the coal industry behind in permanent depression.

INDUSTRIAL RELATIONS IN THE COAL MINES. The old-fashioned atmosphere in the coal mines extended to industrial relations, among the most acrimonious in Japan. While industrialists in other fields were searching for new, more "harmonious" work forms, the coal operators relied exclusively on old, confrontational tactics such as wage cuts and lockouts. For their part, the coal miners' union was among the most doctrinaire and stubborn. The postwar era is punctuated with many long and bitter labor struggles in the coal industry, attesting to the dogged strength of both management and labor. The intensity of this conflict precluded any joint solution; neither side was strong enough to destroy the other.

Tanrō recovered from the *mindō* schisms relatively quickly. This was largely because outside pressures forced the coal miners to put aside their internal feuds. This pressure arrived in mid-1950, in the form of an anti-Communist sweep of the labor movement in private industry. About 11,000 people lost their jobs in this second Red Purge.[32] The Red Purge came late to the coal industry, which gave Tanrō time to work out a counter strategy. After most of the major coal firms issued identically phrased purge notices on 14 October 1950, the union petitioned both SCAP and the courts, arguing that the issue of communism was being used opportunistically by the managers to weaken the union. Tanrō agreed to remove disruptive members, but criticized the Red Purge on two counts: It gave unilateral power to the management and was directed at people's beliefs and party affiliation rather than their actions. Tanrō was able to reduce the size of the purge list to about 2,000 people and, although in absolute numbers the coal miners lost more individuals to the purge than any union but Densan, this was only 0.5 percent of the membership, as opposed to Densan's 1.5 percent.[33]

The Red Purge was recalled by one Tanrō official as the worst blow to union morale in the postwar period, but the shock had a catalyzing effect on the union. As in other unions, at first many people were willing to let the radical leftist leadership of their unions be cleared away through political dismissals and new legislation. However, after the Red Purge ended, Japanese unionists grew apprehensive that they themselves might become the targets of the same tactics. Tanrō members were dismayed to discover how vulnerable they became when they quarreled among themselves, and, by 1952, they were known again for their union solidarity. This was mirrored in the national labor movement as well, when a new inter-industry labor federation, Sōhyō, emerged from the Red Purge as the undisputed center of the labor movement.[34]

This new federation had been encouraged by Occupation officials, who wanted to leave with a strong but anti-Communist Japanese labor movement in place. This new federation, to replace Sanbetsu and Sōdōmei, was to be anti-Communist, and that was SCAP's primary concern. Like the earlier federations, it was an attempt to create some national coordination for the loosely organized enterprise unions. It was formed out of the left wing of Sōdōmei, some independent unions, and the *mindō* groups in Sanbetsu unions. Both Tanrō and Densan were active members. Accordingly, Sōhyō was established in July 1950 with about 3 million members.[35] At first, Sōhyō was very cautious, but the experience of the Red Purge and the economic distress caused first by the austerity program and then by inflation meant that union leaders were pressed by the rank-and-file to take more aggressive action. By 1951, the previously moderate elements were gradually becoming more militant.

Tanrō's internal cohesion and its importance to the Sōhyō federation were both demonstrated in 1952, when Sōhyō returned to the wage policy concepts suggested by Densan five year earlier. Sōhyō argued for a new principle for determining wages, the "market-basket" formula. This guaranteed a minimum wage for all workers and tied wage rates to the standard of living as calculated by the union federation. Sōhyō hoped to reset the main portion of wages at a higher level, or a "base-up" strategy. This strategy would have made permanent the link between the right to a livelihood and the job, a link that had characterized the Densan wage system. It would also have regained a place for labor at the center of economic policymaking.

Sōhyō's wage formula was invented to counter concurrent attempts by employers' groups to redefine wages on the basis of productivity, and to establish more job classifications, each with a different wage scale. It was an attempt to control the relationship between wage scales and rationalization. Employers' groups like Nikkeiren wanted to link wage hikes to increased productivity as part of the rationalization movement. At the same time, Nikkeiren hoped to remove decisions about pay increases as much as possible away from the union and into the boardroom. In the Nikkeiren concept of rationalization, even its more positive aspects, as well as "employee-centered rationalization," worked to limit the power of labor unions. When this interpretation prevailed, measures and definitions of an individual's productivity increasingly became a management prerogative.

A second aspect of this struggle was that the unions wanted to maintain industry-wide bargaining, or at least uniform wages and working conditions for the enterprise unions in each industry. The managers, in contrast, wanted to separate the negotiations between each firm and its union from all others. This issue was particularly controversial in industries like coal and electric power in which the union had achieved some degree of industry-wide bargaining.

Thus, it was not surprising that the two industries chosen to test out the new "market-basket" wage formula were coal mining and electric power. These two unions had led the fight for industry-wide, standard wage rates since 1946. However, by 1952, both had been hobbled by changes in their industries and the Red Purge of the unions. Bitter strikes failed to establish the Sōhyō wage system. This weakened both unions, Densan fatally, and also hurt Sōhyō, which did not fully recover until 1956.

Tanrō opened negotiations in July with 4 demands. First, that the method of negotiation follow the "diagonal bargaining" technique Tanrō had developed the previous year. This involved central Tanrō members alongside enterprise union leaders at the bargaining table and enforced some continuity among the settlements. Second, that wages be set according to Sōhyō's "market-basket" formula. This meant a wage increase, but, more important, it would have established a wage formula based on Sōhyō's consumer price index.[36] Furthermore, the miners wanted to prevent management demands that wage increases be linked to productivity increases, and specifically pledged to defend the 8-hour day.

The Japan Coal Mining Association, representing big coal operators, and the Japan Coal Mine Federation, representing small and medium ones, rejected all these demands. Moreover, despite the recent increase in coal prices, the joint-management committee demanded a program of "deferred wages and a raise in standard levels of production," or a speed-up. They had unusually large stockpiles and could afford to wait the union out. The two sides reached an impasse, and on 17 October all the Tanrō affiliates went on strike. They coordinated their strike with Densan, which sought the same goals of nationwide bargaining and wage levels determined by the cost of living rather than productivity. The links to national issues politicized local issues and deepened the bitterness of the struggle within the mines.[37]

The main issue tactically that emerged during Tanrō's strike was over participation by workers in charge of safety in the mines. As the strike dragged on, the union decided to pull these workers, claiming that mine safety was the responsibility of management alone. The coal operators and the government disagreed, and, on 31 October, the head of the Safety Bureau of MITI's coal division ruled that the miners were required to maintain safety standards. Meanwhile, there were no changes at the negotiating table. The union was able to stay out by organizing the families of the striking workers, but, by mid-December, they were suffering from two months without pay. The unions in one region, Jōban, settled locally and pulled out of both the strike and the union federation; that was the only defection.

This strike was notable for its sheer size and duration; it lasted for 63 days, and, every day, 110,000 tons of coal went unproduced. It also revealed the impasse that had been reached between the union and the mine owners. The strike continued until it was halted by the Yoshida Government on the grounds that safety was threatened. The government imposed mandatory mediation in the Emergency Termination Order of 16 December 1952. This was basically an intervention in favor of the mine owners and electric-power-company management, and should be seen as state endorsement of rationalization without investment. After the union was forced to end its strike, the coal miners settled for a small raise and dropped all other demands. In the following August, the Yoshida Government passed a special Law Concerning Control of Methods of Acts of Dispute in the Electric-Enterprise and Coal-Mining Industries. This "Strike Control Law," as it was popularly known, restricted the right to strike in these two industries, "in order to protect public welfare." It was hailed by Keidanren as an appropriate measure to reverse the effects of the Occupation, that is, too-militant labor unions. In general, however, the coal operators were considered to have been the unreasonable party. Even the *Oriental Economist* criticized the coal and electric-power management for their "high-handed policy" which "aggravated labor relations more than anything else."[38]

As recognized at the time, this was a major defeat for the labor movement. Sōhyō lost its bid for routine labor participation in national economic policymaking in 1952 when the Densan and Tanrō strikes failed in their objectives. The combined opposition of management, Japanese government, and U.S. Occupation policy made it an unequal struggle. Yet it would be inappropriate to dismiss the labor unions at their 1952 nadir. The militancy of the labor movement did not disappear at that time. Sōhyō was able to regroup after its disappointments over the 1952 strikes. The union federation learned from this experience and was far more successful with its "spring wage offensive," or *shuntō* tactic, which the federation developed in 1955 and 1956. Unlike the 1952 labor drive, the *shuntō* actions were coordinated among *all* Sōhyō member unions, rather than delegated to only two unions. During the *shuntō*, the unions boiled down their demands to a few key points, usually wage increases, which they tried to win for all participants, rather than including long-term political demands. In this way, the victories of the strongest unions quickly became standards for all the unions in that industry and for other industry federations under the Sōhyō umbrella. This usually has meant across-the-board annual wage increases for most organized Japanese workers.[39] The *shuntō* became an alternate method for enforcing industry-wide standards and overcame some of the greatest drawbacks of the enterprise union form. This new institution ensured that, each spring, labor increased its wages. Moreover, the economic strategy adopted by the Japanese—rationalization policy—itself required that labor receive a growing share of the national wealth in the form of higher living standards.

Higher standards of living for Japanese working people had become a basic assumption of industrial planning by 1952. Rationalization itself was rooted in acceptance of a transformation of Japanese workers into a highly skilled and highly paid labor force. Japanese wage earners were also needed as consumers to create domestic demand for Japanese industry. As had been argued in the 1946 Ministry of Foreign Affairs report, greater domestic purchasing power would generate funds for Japanese firms to expand production, provide economies of scale, and increase export sales. This much larger domestic market made the postwar economy fundamentally different from the prewar one, with, of course, equally significant implications for political and social life.

In both business and government circles, the expectation crystallized in the 1950s that workers' standards of living would rise steadily over time. This striking contrast to prewar assumptions represents a victory for the labor movement and must be ranged against the defeats of 1948–1952 in any historical analysis of Japanese industrial relations. Densan's early attempts to win a guaranteed minimum standard of living had been institutionalized as part of economic policy by 1952. Although the rate at which real wages rose decreased, Japanese workers never sank back to pre-surrender levels. The labor movement had also gained several other important goals by the end of the Occupation. Workers had far more legal and

customary protections from management exploitation, better working conditions, and a systematic method of improving them. While
the heady victories of the early postwar years had been limited, and
sometimes reversed, by 1952, the labor unions successfully had leg-
itimated themselves as participants in economic decision making,
although their influence was uneven. They were most successful in
areas that directly concerned unions, such as wage and labor policies, and less influential in other areas of economic planning.

This explains why many Japanese unions accepted the argument
that their industry needed to rationalize in the 1950s. These workers feared that, if their plants did not modernize, they would close.
The specter of foreign control of the Japanese economy, raised by
both employers and Socialist Party intellectuals, threatened to destroy their jobs permanently. This impelled many unions to cooperate with employers to introduce new technology.[40] The employers, for their part, needed the good will of workers to install their
expensive new machinery, and were willing to compromise a little,
too. Rationalization did not necessarily mean an attack on workers'
wages and living standards. It is also important to note that some
unions, including Densan, were greatly weakened just before rationalization measures began, and could not prevent these changes,
even when they so desired. Ugly stories of punitive, negative rationalization continued to punctuate the history of rationalization
through this period.

The acceptance of rationalization by most Japanese unions had a
number of implications.[41] Most relevant to this study is the fact
that, as rationalization efforts bore fruit and productivity in Japanese factories soared, wages declined in relation to productivity.
This was a victory for management, but it was possible only because
real wages were rising too. Between 1950 and 1955, real wages rose
by one-third, although productivity gains were even greater. Over
the next decade, real wage increases were larger.[42] Management
groups fought to break labor *control* of the wage system in the early
1950s in order to reserve productivity gains for investment, but
they recognized that labor's *share* still had to grow. Only an improvement in the standard of living would ensure the cooperation

of Japanese workers to build the economy. This was a mutually reinforcing cycle, since employers wanted new machinery in part because wages had already risen. Machinery was now often less expensive than unskilled workers. Thus, rationalization provided a true basis for accommodation in most Japanese industries.

RATIONALIZATION AND LABOR IN THE MINES. This compromise between labor control and labor's share did not extend to failing industries, however, and the coal mines were the most prominent of these. Tanrō opposed the rationalization movement because it threatened greater unemployment, devaluation of traditional skills, and loss of control over the work process. The miners looked at the actions of the coal operators and of Nikkeiren and decided that rationalization measures were primarily a fancy title for cutting the work force and diminishing the power of the union. Since this was an accurate reading of conditions in their industry, it is not surprising that bitter labor struggles around the issue of rationalization continued to erupt in the mines.

Rationalization, even more than wages, was the vital issue in the mines from 1953. Unsold coal stockpiles had already grown alarmingly in 1952, but the 63-day strike had temporarily resolved that problem. For smaller mines, 1953 was a very bad year. Of the 940 members of the Japan Coal Mine Federation, 149 had closed by mid-June, and floods in western Japan forced many more to close in the autumn. The 18 largest mines, with their monopoly of high-quality coal, had greater freedom of movement. They responded to the poor market by curtailing production by 10 percent. These events, plus the importation of some new machinery meant a sharp reduction in the mine work force. In all, 72,000 miners were laid off in 1953.[43]

Cutting costs through layoffs created a vicious circle, just as the ESB and Arisawa had predicted. Since the mines relied so exclusively on labor for production, they could not use productivity increases as the basis for wage hikes. Despite the fact that wage costs were rising, the coal operators did not try to upgrade labor productivity through mechanization. Instead they hired more workers when the market was good. "The postwar recovery of coal production was completely dependent on the labor force. This is related to low productivity levels. Although quantitative recovery was visible, fundamental developments in production were impossible without active investment in new equipment to rejuvenate the antiquated production strength—that is, to break free of the old outer husk of reliance on the labor force."[44] When the coal market soured, these miners were laid off.

This strategy did not even succeed in lowering immediate costs, since Tanrō effectively organized against this "labor-centered rationalization" and was able to prevent it in many large mines. Unlike most industries in Japan, because the owners defined rationalization as primarily a method of cutting labor costs, the union was very suspicious of all rationalization attempts. For a decade, the union opposed mine mechanization as nothing but "a dagger constantly brandished at us."[45] Tanrō had ample evidence to show that the major mine operators thought mainly in terms of cutting wages and laying off workers. This employer strategy both reflected and perpetuated the antagonism between the union and the coal-mine owners. The mine operators avoided capital investment because they feared any profits generated by them would get swallowed up in wage hikes. This represented the attitude of most industrialists immediately after the end of the war—that it was better to minimize reconstruction than to allow labor unions control of the economy. By 1952, however, only the coal operators still maintained this stance.

The union also did its part to prevent rationalization of any sort in the mines. Tanrō's strength, combined with the companies' attitude, contributed to the late mechanization and the instability of the industry. Ironically, by periodically striking, the union cut production for the mine owners, eliminating the need for owners to do this themselves. Temporarily, the actions of the union benefited the operators and buttressed their strategy of creating artificial scarcity to propel coal prices back up. However, the ongoing struggle between labor and management in the mines meant unstable coal supplies and continued high prices, which steadily drove off customers.

This is another way in which the coal operators and coal miners were "traditional." They were simply following the pattern they had established in the 1930s.

Tanrō won its greatest victory over "labor-centered rationalization" at Mitsui's Miike mine in late 1953. The dispute began when the Miike mine operator suddenly announced that he was firing 6,000 employees from a list that included all miners over 50 years old, all those who had worked less than three years at the mine, miners with poor productivity or poor attendance records, miners of "bad character or conduct," and women and children miners. The two most controversial categories were "those who do not cooperate with the company," which in practice meant union activists, and "those of unsound mind, body, or low intelligence, or those who cannot perform their duties up to expectations." This last criterion included, in order: the color-blind, epileptics, alcoholics or amphetamine addicts, schizophrenics, the chronically mentally ill, and the sick and injured, beginning with tuberculosis victims. Since many of this last group were workers who had been injured in the mines, their inclusion was considered especially callous.[46]

The mine operator refused to negotiate with the Tanrō affiliate at Miike, and the union went on strike in August. Tanrō organized not only the miners but also their families and the population of the local towns. This wide base of support for the strikers within the region allowed them to stay out for 113 days. By mid-September, other Mitsui companies that had contracts with the Miike mine were beginning to run out of coal. Finally, the company "gave up the idea of designated dismissals," and the strike was ended on 27 November 1953. The mine operator signed an agreement promising to consult with the union before firing anyone in a rationalization move. Thus, the union was able to prevent any layoffs and remained very powerful until another, and devastating, strike at Miike in 1960. This decisive 1953 victory also forced operators at other large mines to be more cautious in their discharge measures.[47]

"Labor costs" were not always as high as the companies made out. Kinoshita reported that, in 1954, the 18 major coal operators disguised profits as reserve funds. The big 18 companies in the latter half of 1950 had a reserve fund of 1.3 billion yen which grew to 22.2 billion yen by the second half of 1954. Within this, the fund for worker retirement bonuses grew particularly fast, significant because it was tax-free and so an especially good place to hide profits. The labor unions criticized this retirement fund sharply because it was added into labor costs in calculations of coal-production costs.[48]

Since the union was strongest in the big mines, the strikes were most disruptive there. In other words, the labor struggles acted to limit the advantage the large mines had over the small ones, which was one historic basis for profits. Labor costs were higher in the best mines, where Tanrō could enforce higher wages and better working conditions. For a long time this difference contributed to the passivity of the big mines toward mechanization. It seemed easier to the owners of the best mines to try to match the poor wages and working conditions of the small mines than to mechanize.[49]

Meanwhile, the union was being forced out of the medium-sized and smaller mines, which were able to stay in business only by cutting labor costs. This distinction was already noticeable in 1952, when the workers from Jōban left Tanrō. They were all employees of small mines that simply could not offer the same benefits as large ones. The enterprise unions there preferred to settle for as much as they could get and return to work quickly.[50] There was a gradual weakening of the union presence in smaller mines through the 1950s. One medium-sized coal-mine operator, Kiso Shigeyoshi, described his involvement with the failing Nakajima mine in Kyushu in 1954.[51] When the "obnoxious" (*yakamashii*) union struck for higher wages, he fired all the union leaders (*warui yatsu*). After the legal advisor and the labor specialist of the Japan Coal Mine Federation told him that was illegal, he closed the mine to pressure the union. Kiso recalled that he had 5,000 leaflets printed up and pasted on the miners' homes so that they would feel the full force of his decision. Then, about 7 members of the union who were critical of the leadership came to Kiso and promised to cooperate if he would reopen the mine. He set those 7 people up as a second union and negotiated with them to reduce the labor force by 40 percent without decreasing production levels. Since there were about 530 employees, that meant a cut of 200 people. Kiso made selective dismissals of all the union activities *(warui mono)*. The following year, he recruited a new labor force.

RATIONALIZATION PLANS. The lack of interest in rationalization on the part of the coal operators stands in sharp contrast to the government, which continued to develop plans for the coal industry and to provide numerous incentives. In March 1952, the coal subcommittee of the Industrial Rationalization Council revised its June 1950 plan as the Three-Year Plan for Coal Mine Rationalization. It encouraged the 18 biggest mining companies to invest 55.6 billion yen in machinery from fiscal 1952 to 1954, to raise the efficiency rate from 12 tons per miner per month to 17 tons, and to lower the price of coal from 4,318 to 3,875 yen per ton. The state provided a moratorium on interest on debts as well as tax breaks on internal capital reserves in this plan. The government also made loans for coal-miner housing retroactively interest-free and deferred repayment on the operating capital and equipment loans from the RFB until the industry could pay them.[52] However, the firms were expected to promote rationalization through self-investment. This is where the plan broke down. The coal companies refused to add to their already very high debt burden of over 48 billion yen in outstanding loans from the RFB.

The coal industry was eligible for these measures—debt moratorium, interest-free loans, and special depreciation allowances—because it had been named a "key" or "priority" industry in the original 1950 coal and steel rationalization plan. In 1951, electric power and shipbuilding were also designated as key industries. Shipbuilding was added because, if Japan could carry out its foreign trade with its own ships, that would tip the international balance of payments in its favor. In February 1951, the Industrial Rationalization Council stated as one of its ten fundamental points that "special efforts should be made to develop electric-power and shipping resources, and to finance coal and steel rationalization, which are at the heart of the industrial rationalization plans."[53] In practical terms,

Table 8 JDB Loans to the Four Priority Industries, 1951–1953
(million yen)

Industry	1951	1952	1953	Total
Electric Power	2,457	14,767	43,963	61,187
Shipbuilding	4,707	5,740	21,461	31,908
Iron & Steel	3,605	5,778	3,915	13,298
Coal	3,116	3,521	4,376	11,013
Subtotal	13,885	29,806	73,715	117,406
Other JDB				
Loans	6,711	12,905	9,412	29,028
Total	20,596	42,711	83,127	146,434

Source: Nihon Kaihatsu Ginkō. Jū-nen Shi Hensa Iinkai, ed., *Nihon Kaihatsu Ginkō Jū-nen Shi,* pp. 71, 142–143.

this meant priority for government loans and special financial and technical assistance of the kinds offered to the coal mines in 1952. For example, the key industries were almost assured of import licenses and foreign exchange for any foreign technology they wished to purchase.[54]

MITI's Coal Bureau made another attempt, again unsuccessful, to win the support of the coal operators in October 1952, in the midst of the "high-cost coal" period. This was the Five Year Coal Shaft Development Program. In addition to the benefits provided in the earlier plan, it included direct loans from the Japan Development Bank (JDB) to 22 coal operators to develop 719 shafts in existing mines and to improve mine equipment, mine conditions, and safety measures.

The JDB, which opened its doors on 15 May 1951, was created to provide long-term, low-interest financing to priority industries. It took over the last functions of the RFB and the U.S. aid counterpart fund and was begun with 2.5 billion yen from the counterpart fund. Later it acquired funds from the government-operated postal-savings system. In the first 75 days of operation, the bank granted 1,025 million yen in loans to coal, electric-power, steel, and chemical firms, and to the fishing industry (see Table 8).[55] The JDB wielded considerable influence beyond its actual lending capacity through the 1950s because of its respected research staff and its sources of government information. In later years, when the private banks had more loan money available, the JDB often extended small loans as a flag to attract private money. These loans signaled that the Ministry of Finance considered certain industries or firms to be good risks.

The specific goal of the 1952 coal rationalization plan was to lower the price of coal at participating mines to 3,069 yen per ton.[56] In theory, the new shafts would eliminate long walks for miners within the mines and provide ventilation for new machinery. The plan also allowed the coal operators to write off on their taxes much of the cost of sinking the shafts. This was done by redefining mine shafts as fixed assets and allowing accelerated depreciation on them.[57] However, the coal operators were unenthusiastic about this plan too, since they were still expected to contribute a larger share than they were willing to pay. Moreover, in 1953, the government had to cut the JDB contribution as part of its general fiscal retrenchment, and the plan expired.

The government continued to develop rationalization plans for coal through the next decade, but, by 1955, these plans already had begun to take on the connotation of managing decline rather than planning improvements in the industry. All the problems that would plague the mines were already visible, but their severity was not yet recognized. These problems—high prices, resource depletion, changing technology preferences, constant industrial strife, and low levels of investment by the large coal operators—all prevented the Japanese coal industry from playing an important role in the modern economy. Moreover, the international environment was not as lucky for the coal industry as for the Japanese economy generally. The Korean War boom did provide windfall profits, although it did not move the coal industry to produce more efficiently. More important, however, the international price of crude oil declined steadily during the 1950s, making coal less competitive every year. This was an unexpected blow to Japanese policymakers, who had chosen coal as a central plank of postwar economic development. Coal had begun to part company with the rest of the Japanese economy.

In sharp contrast, both the electric-power and petroleum industries expanded dramatically during the 1950s. They, rather than coal, became the building blocks of the modern economy, precisely because rationalization succeeded in those areas. As the years passed, Japanese government and business leaders developed an increasingly sophisticated understanding of economic growth through experience with rationalizing industries. By the time they developed atomic power and petrochemicals, they had learned how to manipulate policy measures to speed up rationalization. This sophistication would lead them on to high-speed growth, but first they had to face the terrible imbalances created by their continued reliance on unrationalized coal.

NINE

Electric Power: Reorganization, Rationalization, and Expansion

Development of the electric-power industry eventually became one of the most dynamic areas of the economy, but it began slowly. The lengthy debate over reorganization of the industry was the first obstacle to reconstruction. This disagreement had hindered the industry's recovery since early 1948. At last, in November 1950, SCAP resolved the deadlock with the unusual step of ordering reorganization into 9 private companies. This flouted the wishes of most Japanese, although they were pleased to have the way finally cleared for rationalization in the power industry.

After six years of only minimal reconstruction, the electric-power firms initiated a huge expansion program in the mid-1950s, first in hydroelectricity, but quickly embracing thermal power as well. The electric-power industry was a leader in importing new machinery and new technical processes and acted as a catalyst in the rationalization of other industries. The government-sponsored hydroelectric project at Sakuma, for example, revolutionized the earth-moving and construction industries in postwar Japan by demonstrating the superiority of many types of new equipment. Private electric-power companies stimulated similar development among heavy-machine producers with their demands for the most up-to-date thermal generating equipment.[1] However, before the electric-power industry could develop as intended by the Japanese economic planners, some lingering problems raised during the reorganization debate still had to be solved.

The first and largest was money. While the reorganization issue was still being wrangled over, the Japanese government had committed itself to developing 40,100 million kilowatts of new electric-power capacity by 1952 in response to Korean War-induced increases in demand. The need for reservoirs and water control was underscored by the severe drought of 1951.[2] The basic government assumption was that, from 1951, when reorganization could be completed, the Treasury would invest heavily in electric-power development. At that time, there was no other domestic source of funds for electric-power development (although three companies had already begun negotiations for loans from the World Bank and the U.S. Export-Import Bank). All parties within the business and government communities agreed that the Japanese government should provide funds to alleviate the power shortage.

The second major issue was industrial relations. This changed in 1952 when the union was subordinated within the separate firms and lost its power to shape industry policy. Like Japanese unions generally, organized labor in the electric-power industry was still strong when compared to the pre-surrender years, but limits of union power were firmly reestablished by the companies between 1950 and 1952. In electric power, again typically, the union lost much of its *control,* but its members continued to enjoy a rising *share* in the form of steadily higher wages. Densan collapsed, and the new union, Den Rōren (Zenkoku Denryoku Rōdō Kumiai Rengōkai), represented a group of workers who were more willing to give up a voice in economic policy as long as their standard of living continued to rise.

The third problem was redefining the relationship between government and business in the electric-power industry. Like management and labor, this was institutionalized in 1952, but the power relationship was resolved in a very different way. This was a partial reconcentration of the industry under government control through the new Electric Power Development Corporation. Although this superficially looked much like the Hassōden-Haiden relationship, it differed in that the 9 power companies had far more fiscal independence and the right to develop their own generating facilities.

Finally, there was tension among the 9 companies over water rights and the high cost of thermal generation relative to hydroelectricity. This acted to spur the power companies, especially the large, urban ones, to introduce new thermal technology as quickly as possible, eventually leading to a primary commitment to thermal generation. This exemplified how government rationalization policy was translated into practice by competition among private firms, although in a way unintended by either the Japanese government or SCAP. Rapid rationalization of the power industry also raised a new challenge for Japanese equipment manufacturers. They had to modernize equally rapidly if they hoped to win contracts away from foreign firms for new electric-power equipment.

This modernization process within one Japanese industry directly relied on American military and economic policies in East Asia. Both during and after the Occupation, American financial and technological assistance made development possible. Various 4-cornered business arrangements between private American firms, private Japanese firms, and the two governments illustrate the growing complexity of "U.S.-Japan economic cooperation" in practice. Specific examples of this included Japan's first World Bank loan (adding a fifth, transnational element), and an atomic-power program from the mid-1950s. Each step in Japanese economic recovery served to strengthen rather than weaken these bonds.

ENDING THE REORGANIZATION STALEMATE

The outbreak of the Korean War and consequent economic boom in Japan galvanized the Americans into action on the lingering reorganization stalemate. SCAP officials stepped up pressure on the Japanese to accept privatization of the electric-power industry. On 12 August, Major General Marquat forbade the electric-power companies to increase capital or to issue corporate bonds, effectively stopping all but routine work. The *Oriental Economist,* no friend of Hassōden, laconically remarked that "there is not the slightest doubt that the restrictions impose considerable inconveniences upon the power industry." The magazine estimated that Marquat's move would cost the electric-power companies 5,336 million yen and put between 23,300 and 23,800 people out of work.[3]

Japanese officials took a number of steps to resolve the electric-power stalemate or, more precisely, to remove the restrictions on the counterpart fund, but they were not successful. MITI sent repeated requests for funds, arguing each time that it was an urgent exception. ESS hung grimly on to its strategy of refusal. Then Yoshida fired the President and Vice-President of Hassōden in August, since they adamantly opposed the reorganization plan. Nonetheless, the Diet still refused to accept it.[4] It was precisely at that point that the electric-power companies carried out the Red Purge in their industry. On 26 August 1950, over 2,000 people were fired, the largest number of any industry in the private sector. This mass firing was possible only because the government, the managers, and the new union leadership all supported it.

The power struggle between the *mindō* group and the original leadership in Densan came to a head in July 1950, just after the Korean War began. The *mindō* group, which had achieved control of the central union standing committee in May, decided to get rid of all those who had supported the former union leadership. Citing the "threat of international red fascism," the central committee charged that "enemies of democracy" within the union, especially from Kantō and Kansai, were working against the interests of the union, of Japan, and of democracy. Officially they were disciplining a group that had disrupted a general meeting in Nara in May 1950. They went through the union membership rolls, affirming 108,095 names and investigating 19,282.[5]

The union leadership then did something it was to regret later. It met with the employers' association on 16 August and promised not to object if any of the people on their investigative list were to be fired. The union itself disciplined only 578 people, but the announcement that it would not protect its members had much wider results. At the end of August, the employers discharged 2,137 people, most in Kantō and Kansai, without any protest from the union leadership. About 86 percent of them were Communist Party members, but all were union activists. Later, the new union leaders were to discover that they had weakened the union almost fatally by this action, but at the time they saw the Red Purge as a way of removing their immediate opposition. The electric-power companies, unlike many Japanese industries at the time, were *not* overstaffed and these firings were clearly political.[6]

This Red-Purge maneuver was successful for a number of reasons. The Korean War had prompted a general attack on Communists in Japan by Japanese and American officials, so the Densan action did not stand out qualitatively, although it involved more people than in most organizations. The Communist Party of Japan was itself badly split and unable to wage a concerted effort against anti-Communist activity. Within Densan itself, the same two factors of increased pressure and internal disunity prevailed. From the time the Diet began to consider an electric-power-industry reorganization bill in early 1950, the Haiden, with the help of local police, had stepped up pressure on Densan because of its history of left-wing militancy. In the areas where the Midorikai, the right wing of the *mindō* movement, was strong, the police worked with them *and* the employers. Elsewhere, this combination of employer and police pressure was too powerful for a divided union to withstand. Moreover, the Communists had alienated other left groups within Densan and could not count on their support against *mindō* or outside attack.

As the reorganization issue continued to drag on, the consequences of not resolving it grew larger. By autumn 1950, most of the Japanese economy was caught up in the Korean War boom. Only electric power, potentially the most severe constraint on the economy, stagnated. Marquat's ban on acquiring money meant that the power companies could not make needed repairs nor stockpile coal, despite warnings of both a coming drought and coal shortages. This was to haunt Japan in 1951 and 1952, when restrictions on power use had to be reimposed nationwide.[7]

These extreme SCAP measures were intended to force Yoshida and the Diet into quick passage of an electric-power reorganization law, but, in the end, it was the American forces that gave in. On 24 November 1950, SCAP resorted to the Potsdam Declaration giving supreme power to the Commander of the Allied forces and compelled the Cabinet to pass two ordinances. One created 9 generation, transmission, and distribution companies. The other established an independent Public Utilities Commission (PUC) under the jurisdiction of the Prime Minister's office to replace the Electric Power Bureau of MITI (effective 15 December 1950). This was one of only two times a "Potsdam directive" was invoked; the other had been the general strike ban of January 1947.

The PUC was to have extensive regulatory powers over the electric-power and gas industries, but absolutely no authority over the management of any of the utility companies. The home for the PUC was worked out in a compromise between SCAP and Finance Minister Ikeda Hayato, since SCAP had originally wanted the PUC to be attached to the Diet. However, the Diet's inability to decide the electric-power-industry reorganization problem may have softened SCAP's resolve on that point. The establishment of 9 private companies and the PUC was an important step, but it did not end the wrangling over reorganization. The new electric-power companies did not start operations until 1 May 1951, and very little development work went on in the meantime. Even then, there were more delays.[8]

The use of a "Potsdam directive" at that late date was extremely controversial, and SCAP had been reluctant to take such a drastic step. Yoshida pushed for it, however, in order to avoid making a politically unpopular move himself.[9] Many Japanese sources assert that SCAP was pressured by American electrical-equipment manufacturers, especially General Electric, to resolve the reorganization problem quickly and in favor of private companies. No direct evidence of this has emerged, but it is quite plausible. Certainly, Westinghouse intervened with American officials on two other occasions to get similar concessions. The company petitioned SCAP in support of its prewar partner, Mitsubishi Electric, in early 1950, and spoke to the Assistant Secretary of State for Economic Affairs in support of its loans to three power companies in 1953.[10]

Unquestionably, the reorganization ordered by SCAP was a victory for the prewar private power companies. Their demands for a return to private enterprise and the exclusion of the state from their industry were in conformity with SCAP policy to build private capitalism in Japan. Matsunaga and the SCAP officials forced their vision of a free-enterprise economy on a Japan that was still deeply divided over this issue in the electric-power industry and in general.[11] Although the final arbiters were the officials at ESS, they were in some ways tangential to the political struggle raging around them.

FUNDING ELECTRIC-POWER DEVELOPMENT, 1951–1954

Once the reorganization problem had been resolved, the next enormous task was to find money for the power industry. Electric power was the single largest recipient of official rationalization aid in the 1950s. Through direct and indirect means, the power companies reaped enormous sums from Treasury coffers. Most of this money went to expand the electric-power network until such time as the power companies could raise their own funds. The Japanese government—and the U.S. government—also spent a considerable amount of time helping the industry attract capital from overseas. The power companies grew more solvent from about 1955, after which government aid to the electric-power industry was increasingly concentrated in the area of atomic-power development. The most important sources of funds were rate increases, direct government sources, and foreign loans.

The first official step was to approve large rate increases of 31 percent in August 1951 and of 28 percent in May 1952. The rate structure was also amended to lower rates to industry relative to ones for households and to encourage large-scale power users.[12] The Rationalization Council had argued for several years that electric-power rates were too low to allow the power companies to pay off their debts and to accumulate funds for further development. Also, since electric-power rates had been tightly regulated since the war years, they were very low compared to the price of other indus-

Table 9 Electric Power Rates and General Price Indices, 1946–1952 (indices = 1.0 for 1934–1936)

	1946	1948	1950	1951	1952
Electric rates	5.3	48.6	86.5	111.1	143.6
Wholesale index	16.3	127.9	246.8	341.9	357.2
Retail index	18.9	149.6	239.1	309.5	308.3
Consumer index	—	168.6	192.2	227.3	244.7

Sources: Nihon Kaihatsu Ginkō. Jū-nen Shi Hensa Iinkai, ed., *Nihon Kaihatsu Ginkō Jū-nen Shi,* p. 167, original data from Prime Minister's Office, Statistical Division.

trial or consumer goods. The Rationalization Council, along with the electric-power companies, wanted to bring the price of electric power back in line with the price of other raw materials. The Public Utilities Commission, which approved the increase, agreed (see Table 9).

The rate increases were very controversial at the time. Industrialists from electricity-consuming industries and some bureaucrats wanted to keep electricity prices low as an indirect subsidy to other industries. Household consumers were also angered at the large jump in their power bills. The controversy was partly over questions that had kept alive the reorganization debate. Should electric power be treated as a private commodity or was it a public good? Did anyone have a right to make a profit on electricity? Should funds for electric-power development come out of rates or from some other source?

Since the government had already agreed to finance electric-power development, the argument was in part about the autonomy of the power companies. If they raised their money through internal capital accumulation, they had more control over how to spend it than if the funds were provided directly from the government. Also, as the power companies argued, they were more likely to handle money responsibly if they had control over it. With the sloppy example of Hassōden in everyone's mind, this was a strong argument.

Most important was the fact that attitudes toward state control

Table 10 Distribution of State Capital to the Electric-Power
Industry, 1946–1955 (100 million nominal yen)

Year	I Total Construction Capital (a)	II 9 Companies	III State Capital to Hassōden /EPDC (b)	IV State Capital to All Electric Power Companies	V State Capital to Electric Power as Share of Total Construction Capital (%) (c)
1946	7		1	1	14.3
1947	42		22	22	52.4
1948	195		185	185	94.9
1949	150		101	101	67.3
1950	269		100	100	37.2
1951	511	232	—	232	45.4
1952	1,082	366	58	457	42.2
1953	1,621	403	180	672	41.5
1954	1,589	322	265	681	43.1 (d)
1955	1,708	224	299	622	36.4

Source: Kurihara Tōyō, *Denryoku,* p. 469. Original data are from the Bank of Japan and the Denki
Chūō Kenkyūjo.
Notes: (a) Includes both public and private construction capital.
(b) EPDC is the Electric Power Development Company, established in 1952.
Earlier figures in this column are for Hassōden, abolished in 1951.
(c) Column IV divided by Column I.
(d) Discrepancy is in original.

were changing. Businessmen, even those who wanted cheap electricity, wanted to maintain the principle of autonomy from the
government. Government indicative planning and funds were desirable, but Japanese industrialists wanted free rein within their
firms. Yoshida and his party supported this principle too, and no
direct clashes occurred, since the government's self-sufficiency policy meant fostering economic growth through private enterprises.
Even when a Hassōden-like generating company was established
under state control in late 1952, the 9 private companies did not
lose any autonomy.

The 9 companies did, however, accept substantial funds from the
government (see Table 10). This was primarily in the form of loans
from the JDB, although, from 1949 to 1952, money from the U.S.

counterpart aid fund was also important. This state money was about 40 percent of all funds provided to the electric-power industry through 1951, when it gradually declined to 26 percent by 1954.[13] This great infusion allowed the electric-power companies to accumulate capital within their firms and so become solvent. Internal reserves for the 9 companies increased at an annual average of 34 percent in 1951–1954. In 1954, the government cut its payments to the electric-power industry by 17 percent as part of its fiscal austerity measures. By that time, however, the companies were able to withstand the loss.

To compensate for smaller government funds, the power companies were granted a third rate increase in October 1954. The primary reason was that the industry's interest and depreciation costs were very high, since the companies were growing fast and introducing expensive new technology at the same time. This situation created a cash shortage, despite the many special government policies to ease high capital costs. The 1954 rate increase provided the electric-power companies with the internal capital to grow. From 1955, they were able to generate much more of their necessary funds without direct government loans.[14]

The electric-power industry was a major beneficiary of the many tax, tariff, and depreciation exemptions enjoyed by industry in general. It became a "key industry" in 1952 in order to be eligible for maximum aid. In addition, the government invented other ad hoc ways to help certain favored industries accumulate capital. For example, in 1955, the Ministry of Finance allowed the electric-power companies, coal operators, and export-import traders to convert their short-term loans into long-term debts in a special one-time move. The 9 electric-power companies were allowed to transform $140 million worth of loans from private financial institutions into company debentures (at 8.5 percent interest for 5 years) in early 1955. The due dates of RFB and counterpart fund loans were also extended.[15]

The Yoshida Administration was a major champion of foreign loans, especially for the electric-power industry. The power companies needed so much money that they could not expect adequate loans from private foreign sources, and Japanese attention soon concentrated on U.S. government and international banks. Yoshida and his lieutenants lobbied extensively for loans and credits from the U.S. government both during and after the Occupation. This was not purely for the good of Japan as a whole; Yoshida frequently told the Americans that "a financial gesture" on their part would help his own political position.[16]

In the early 1950s, the Yoshida Administration made several requests for electric-power loans to both the Export-Import Bank of the United States and the International Bank for Reconstruction and Development, better known as the World Bank. At first the Japanese asked for a major hydroelectric loan. They developed a plan for two hydroelectric projects they hoped would not only reduce the electricity shortage but also increase national income by 10 percent by 1957. The Japanese government estimated this would cost $320 million. In a neat insight into the private American interests involved in assisting Japanese reconstruction, OCI, which had first studied the industry in 1948 to make reparations recommendations, was hired to draw up plans for the new power-plant sites, first by SCAP and Hassōden and then, after the Occupation ended, by the PUC. Yoshida initially asked the American government for a loan for this purpose, but Dulles told him to apply directly to the Export-Import and World Banks. He did, and the World Bank completed a site study of Japan in the autumn of 1952. At least one private firm also took the initiative on hydroelectric loans. Executives of Chūgoku Electric Power Company went to the United States in 1951 to talk to Westinghouse and Export-Import Bank officials. None of these loans went through, however, mainly because the electric-power industry and the Japanese economy were still too unsettled.[17]

This changed in 1953. The U.S. Export-Import Bank discussed a joint loan with Kansai, Chūbu, and Kyushu Electric-Power Companies in 1952 and 1953. The 3 companies worked together to request a loan of $40.2 million ($21.5, $7.5, $11.2 million, respectively) to import thermal-power generation equipment from Westinghouse and General Electric companies. The first move actually came from the U.S. firms involved. In 1952, Westinghouse initiated talks with the Kyushu and Kansai power companies. Then General Electric approached Chūbu in fear that Westinghouse would capture all of the Japanese market. However, just as the negotiations were nearing completion in April 1953, the guidelines for the Export-Import Bank were changed to limit it to smaller, short-term loans, and the power-loan decision was handed over to the World Bank. This was partly the result of World Bank insistence that the Japanese not be allowed to borrow from both banks. The Japanese government, dismayed by the delay this created, asked the U.S. Department of State to speed up the decision on the power companies' request.[18]

The World Bank had stricter terms for guaranteeing the loan, which were announced on 18 September 1953. Japan's loan ceiling was also lower than the Japanese had hoped. It was set at $100 million, which meant that the thermal-power projects claimed 40 percent of Japan's total credit at the World Bank. The loan agreement actually consisted of 3 separate agreements, variously between the JDB and the World Bank, between the power companies and the World Bank, and between the Japanese government and the World Bank. This arrangement was very controversial, especially the extent to which it involved the Japanese government.

First, the contract involving the 3 power companies gave the World Bank the right of direct participation in their management and subjected their equipment and books to inspection by their creditor.[19] More inflammatory, the Japanese government became a "debtor in the first degree" for payment of principal and interest of the loan. Since the government was an actual member of the World Bank, it was legally responsible for repaying the loan. That meant that, whenever the Japanese government or its agencies desired to contract future foreign loans, they had first to get the approval of the World Bank, which retained the right to claim the mortgages for such future loans. Nor was the Japanese government allowed to dispose of state property without the World Bank's approval. These clauses were seen as infringements on the sovereignty of Japan by many Japanese. On 18 September, Takashima Seijirō, financier and member of the Bank of Japan policy board, expressed the opinion of most bankers: "It would be national humiliation to have to seek the World Bank approval to the disposition of State property in exchange for a loan of a mere $40,000,000. Contracting a foreign loan of this nature is a matter for the Diet to decide."[20]

The controversy delayed the agreement but did not change it. Since the orders for equipment had already been placed, the Japanese government was in a difficult position. The negotiations were nearly completed by the time they became public, and the Japanese officials involved decided not to break them off, especially since they themselves had not considered the loan requirements especially harsh. They did become more cautious over negotiating further loans that too obviously involved the government.[21]

The loans were typical of World Bank loans, in that they were for infrastructural development. Most contemporary World Bank loans were for electric power, land reclamation, irrigation, or transportation. They were also typical in that the government was required to be the formal borrower, but the money actually went to a non-government entity. The World Bank, as a matter of policy, "frequently insisted" that government projects be entrusted to an autonomous group before it would fund them. As policy, it did not want to encourage direct government intervention in the economy. However, this autonomous group was usually a semi-public body rather than a private firm, since most governments were not willing to guarantee loans to a single firm for domestic political reasons. Thus, it was slightly unusual for the World Bank to lend to wholly private firms. At the end of 1953, only $200 million out of $1,800 million in World Bank loans had been to private companies. The conditions imposed on the Japanese government were also standard procedure. The World Bank insisted on extensive study and oversight of any recipient nation's full economy before it would extend a loan.[22]

What was far more unusual about the loans was the participation of the American supplier companies. Westinghouse and General Electric actually provided about $6.1 million of the World Bank loans themselves. This was *not* standard bank procedure, since a basic condition of World Bank loans was that they not be "tied" to purchases in any particular country. It was not, however, unique; in 1952, Chase Manhattan Bank participated in a similar World Bank loan to KLM, the national Dutch airline. In the electric-power case, the World Bank told the Department of State that it would "waive its usual requirements for competitive bids in view of the fact that Westinghouse and General Electric are the logical suppliers of the highly technical equipment involved."[23]

This arrangement was more typical of Export-Import Bank loans, whose primary function was to encourage American exports. Earlier, when negotiations for the hydroelectric power plants had still been alive, Japanese officials at the Washington Embassy had disparaged these "Westinghouse loans" and indicated that they preferred a direct bank-to-government arrangement. However, by 1953, this was the only request still likely to be funded, and its success was due largely to official U.S. government lobbying for a loan.

Although the World Bank was an international organization, its decisions were closely tied to American foreign policy. The bank officials were reluctant to extend loans to impoverished Japan, but Vice-President Robert L. Garner privately indicated to the Department of State that, if the United States would guarantee long-term support of the Japanese economy, the bank would change its policy. After extensive discussions within the State Department and with Treasury officials, something very close to a guarantee was given confidentially to high World Bank officials *of U.S. nationality*. Then, in a series of written questions and answers, the Department of State explained why the loans were important to U.S. policy in Japan. They would serve a 3-fold function, the officials argued. First, the expression of support would have implications "of a psychological and political nature . . . out of all proportion to the economic importance. Conversely, refusal to loan would be taken as a rejection of Japan and an indication of lack of confidence in Japan's future." Second, the loans would strengthen those groups within Japan most closely allied with American foreign policy. In particular, they would undercut the argument that Japan had to cooperate with "the Soviet bloc" to thrive. Finally, World Bank loans to Japan and to Southeast Asia would help development of those countries in ways that would stimulate greater Pacific trade and non-dollar raw material imports to Japan.[24] Thus, these loans, a key element in the Japanese power companies' reconstruction efforts, were also an integral part of American policy in Japan. They were not obtained easily and probably would not have been granted at all if Japanese economic recovery had not been a high priority for American officials.

Despite the political turmoil, the loans were an excellent deal for the power companies. Kansai Electric's Tanagawa plant cost 1,120 million yen to construct, of which 780 million yen came from the World Bank. The company could not possibly have raised that much money within Japan. Moreover, the terms of the loan were very good. Instead of a 5-year loan at 9 percent interest, as available from Japanese banks, the World Bank offered 5.5 percent interest and repayment over 20 years. The President of Kansai Electric Power Company remembered winning this first postwar loan as a big victory.[25]

After that loan, the power companies were able to deal directly with Westinghouse and General Electric. The two American firms, which provided almost all the new Japanese equipment, were anxious to cultivate these valuable customers. The purchases Kansai and Kyushu power companies made with their World Bank loan, for example, included the first 75,000-kilowatt equipment ever to be exported to any country. The American power companies were able to secure the Japanese market from 1954 by providing "maker's credits" that allowed the Japanese companies to buy new machinery on credit. General Electric was the first to do this, in a 1954 agreement with Tokyo Electric Power. Under this system, the American company borrowed $9 million from the U.S. Export-Import Bank and allowed Tokyo Electric to buy the machinery on credit. The JDB stood as guarantor for this loan too, but it did not evoke controversy because there was no direct contact between the Japanese and U.S. governments. After 1954, this became the main method of financing new power plants, and, later yet, was important to the development of atomic power. Westinghouse and General Electric were able to maintain their dominant position in the

Japanese market over their European competitors and extend it to atomic-power equipment largely because of this early start.[26]

INDUSTRIAL RELATIONS IN THE POWER INDUSTRY

Finding capital for electric-power development was difficult but relatively uncontroversial. Establishing the balance of power between management and workers was much harder. The years of 1950 to 1952 were just as important for management-labor relations as for management-government relations in the electric-power industry. Both ended as real victories for the private managers, but, while the relationship with the government remained amicable, the one with labor was strife-filled and ended in decimation of the union. The electric-power workers re-formed into a new union, Den Rō-ren, but they did not maintain Densan's tradition of innovative union activity.

The reorganization into 9 private companies was devastating to Densan, which had enjoyed a rare industry-wide position among Japanese unions. Although Densan was formally divided into separate units for Hassōden and the 9 Haiden, all the enterprise unions bargained for wages together. This was partly because the 10 companies had pooled budgets and could be treated as a single accounting unit. Moreover, Hassōden and the Haiden, on opposite sides of the reorganization issue, were much less unified than the Densan locals. After reorganization, the new power companies were determined to end the joint bargaining system. They also attacked Densan's living-wage concept by arguing that each company should set wages on the basis of its ability to pay.

This was bitterly but unsuccessfully opposed by the union, to the point of a 86-day strike in late 1952. There were several issues involved, but the future of joint industry-wide bargaining was considered by all parties to be the most important. The first issues raised were the wage system and raises. Densan wanted to move to Sōhyō's "market-basket" wage formula, which would have meant an immediate average wage increase from 12,800 to 20,055 yen per month. The companies refused to grant any increases and demanded that the union settle with each company separately. The two sides deadlocked over this point until the government sent them to compulsory mediation on 15 November 1952.

At that time, the management made four demands. These were: (1) Some of the power companies would pay nearly all of the CLRB-recommended wage increase of 15,400 yen, but the Shikoku, Kyushu, and Hokkaido companies would not, thus destroying the industry-wide wage concept. (2) The work week should be increased from 38.5 to 42 hours. (3) The number of paid holidays would be reduced. (4) Wages should reflect more job classifications. The union rejected all these demands but reduced their wage request to 16,200 yen. In the end, the union got only the compromise wage increase and lost what they considered to be the more important issues of unified bargaining and work hours. They lost after unity on their own side crumbled. In early December, the employees of Chūbu Electric Power Company were the first to settle separately with their company; Kansai and the independent Tokyo union both followed soon after. The strike formally ended on 18 December, just after the government Emergency Termination Action.[27]

Densan's experience was a magnified version of all Japanese labor experience in the early 1950s. The new balance of power between management and labor was based on the premise that labor unions were powerful and had a right to participate in decisions that specifically related to labor. However, labor had lost its bid to directly participate in larger issues of economic policy. Densan's ability to do so was already eroded by 1950 and decisively lost in the strike of 1952. The new contract after the 1952 strike, which varied by company, was based on job classifications and skill levels as well as base pay. This defeat shattered Densan's tenuous unity, and the union ceased to exist as a viable organization.[28]

There were a number of reasons why Densan collapsed in 1952. First, it was weaker than it appeared at first glance. The collaboration by the *mindō* group in the Red Purge frayed the last remaining strands of unity within Densan. The union also faced stronger opposition from the new private power companies. Until the reorganization, Densan dealt with very weak managers, who were caught

Table 11 Changes in Size and Calculation of the Densan Wage
Base, 1947–1951

Wage Base	April 1947 ¥ 1,854	March 1948 ¥ 5,358	January 1949 ¥ 7,100	April 1950 ¥ 8,621	January 1951 ¥ 10,316
Standard wage	100.0%	100.0%	100.0%	100.0%	100.0%
Worker's needs	47.5	47.5	43.4	47.7	44.4
Family needs	20.7	20.7	17.6	17.8	18.1
Length of employment	3.7	3.7	2.2	1.9	1.8
Ability pay	19.4	19.4	24.0	23.8	28.4
Regional allowance	8.0	8.0	11.4	8.8 (a)	7.3 (a)
Winter allowance	0.7	0.7	1.5		

Sources: 1947–1949 data reprinted in Rōdō Sōgi Chōsakai, ed., *Densan Sōgi*, p. 67. 1950–1951 data from Akita Nariyoshi, Arizumi Makoto, and Tosaka Ranko, "Denki Sangyō Rōdō Kumiai (Densan)," in Ōkōchi Kazuo, ed., *Nihon Rōdō Kumiai Ron*, p. 94. Original data from Densan Chōsabu, ed. *Chōsa Jipō*, IV, 2 and Rōdō Chōsa Kyōgikai, *Chōsa Geppō*, July 1952.

Note: (a) A combination of regional and winter allowances.

between the state and the union and had little autonomy. Also, because the Haiden had opposed Hassōden in the reorganization debate, relations among the managers of the firms deteriorated to the point where it was very difficult for them to put up a unified resistance to Densan demands.[29] After reorganization, the managers became much more aggressive. When the new 9 companies took the offensive against uniform contracts, Densan could not protect them.

Densan had already lost some key battles before the 1952 strike. The points on which management most actively pressed for change were seniority and severance-pay systems. This first came up in the fall of 1951, when the Kantō Electric Power Workers' Union, which had broken away from Densan, struck over these issues. The Kantō union lost the strike and disintegrated as an organization, foreshadowing the fate of Densan exactly one year later. Another big issue was the wage structure—Densan's contribution to the labor movement of 1946. After the Red Purge, the industry management association and Nikkeiren pushed to change the wage structure to emphasize ability pay (see Table 11). The growing importance of this wage category illustrates the increasing strength of managers, since this was the area over which they had the most discretion. They controlled wage raises more, and the differences in wage rates among firms grew. Densan was not able to prevent management from gradually introducing non-uniform elements into the contract, weakening the principle of a unified wage across the industry.[30]

After Densan collapsed, the electric-power workers formed 10 new enterprise unions to represent them, federated as Den Rōren. These unions were politically far less assertive than Densan and did not play a leading role in the Japanese labor movement. They also elected not to join the Sōhyō federation. They did, however, enjoy rising real wages through the 1950s. Moreover, wage differences between companies in their industry began to diminish from the late 1950s, because new equipment purchased by the electric-power companies meant that productivity rose each year so management could afford to be generous with raises. Real wages in the electric-power industry increased 21 percent between 1952 and 1956. Despite this, labor's share of value-added fell from 76 to 52 percent.[31]

Given steady improvement in wage levels, it is not surprising that the electric-power workers embraced rationalization. In stark contrast to the coal miners, they were "in principle" willing to accept new technology. Unlike the coal mines, higher productivity in each power plant did not mean electric-power workers lost their jobs, since the total number of power plants was growing rapidly. Den Rōren spokesmen also pledged to work together with management on changes associated with rationalization, citing the "strong public nature" of their industry as a special impetus for this cooperation. In fact, Den Rōren was the first union to develop explicitly a new set of criteria for wage raises based on increases in worker productivity and national economic growth rather than on living standards. This 1959 concept was noted among labor circles as a startling new departure in union thinking because of its total acceptance of rationalization as a basis for labor-management cooperation.[32]

This situation, in which labor reaped some of the benefits of greater productivity, but left an increasing share of it available to management for investment, was precisely the sort of division of profits imagined by the Keizai Dōyūkai and other progressive business groups. It was also consistent with the postwar vision of the ESB officials. In their plans, rationalization and technology induction were *supposed* to achieve both a higher standard of living and new sources of investment capital. Moreover, as far as Den Rōren members were concerned, this settlement was satisfactory. In rapidly developing industries, such as electric power (and oil refining), this goal was obtainable, but it was harder to achieve across all Japanese industry. Compared to most other Japanese industries, the electric-power companies could relatively painlessly meet the workers' economic demands.

The direct attack on Densan was, however, part of the older tradition of negative rationalization. These great gains in productivity also would have been possible with Densan representing the electric-power workers. The management campaign against the union was based more in fear of Densan's political philosophy and its desire to help set economic priorities than in economic hardship. It was a rejection of labor demands to participate in economic policy-making.

HYDROPOWER DEVELOPMENT

There were also a number of ostensibly technical obstacles to development of the power industry that had to be resolved. These were presented as problems of hydroelectric, thermal, and atomic-power development, but several highly political issues were embedded within them, including the proper role of the state within the industry. Not only was the government involved in mediating with foreign lenders and vendors; it directly took over the expensive task of hydroelectric development from 1952. Moreover, the electric-power companies soon realized that their development strategy profoundly influenced the fortunes of related Japanese industries, particularly heavy- and electrical-equipment manufacturers and machine-tool makers. These debates also masked an internal struggle within the industry between hydro-rich rural regions and ambitious urban power companies. At each of these levels, then, highly politicized battles raged, emerging first in debates over hydroelectricity.

As soon as reorganization was completed, an old struggle over underdeveloped hydroelectric resources resurfaced. It had first appeared in 1949 in Matsunaga's proposal that hydropower resources be awarded to the company that would ultimately distribute the resultant power to consumers rather than to the region in which the plant was located. This plan, known as the "pragmatic" approach, had been opposed by SCAP, which together with Hokuriku and Tōhoku supported a "regionalist" view. Almost as soon as the SCAP officials embarked for home, the old quarrels between the "pragmatists" and the "regionalists" cropped up again. Although the final reorganization plan had officially adhered to the "regionalist" philosophy, the question of as-yet-undeveloped sites was left for the new Public Utilities Commission to resolve.

The Matsunaga plan, which had used the criterion of prewar ownership, was the strongest statement of the "pragmatist" position that electric-power resources should go to user-region companies. This meant, in particular, that Kansai would own undeveloped water resources in the Hokuriku region and Tokyo would regain its old rights in Tōhoku. This issue harked back to the days before Hassōden, when the two industry leaders, Tokyo Electric Light Company and Matsunaga's own Tōhō Electric Power Company, had staked out water claims in undeveloped regions. The PUC found in favor of the "pragmatist" argument. This was not especially surprising, as Matsunaga himself was on the 5-person PUC. The result was to "reconcentrate the industry in Tokyo and Kansai, indicating the resurgence of vested interests—the prewar powers of Tokyo Electric Light and Tōhō Electric Power."[33] In other words, after this ruling the major urban power companies had an advantage over the rural ones in hydropower development (see Table 12).

In fact, the difference in scale among the 9 companies was larger than had existed among the prewar Big 5. This created a serious problem of weak versus strong companies, just as Hassōden and

Table 12 Changes in Electric-Power Resource Ownership due
to Reorganization by the Public Utility Commission
(kw)

Region	Size of Area	PUC Plan	Loss/Gain
Tōhoku	1,287,850	808,240	(−) 478,610
Kantō	742,280	1,406,820	(+) 664,540
Chūbu	1,363,640	699,600	(−) 664,040
Hokuriku	926,860	336,420	(−) 590,440
Kansai	185,280	1,254,830	(+) 1,069,550

Source: Denki Jigyō Saihensei Shi Kenkōkai, *Denki Jigyō Saihensei Shi,* p. 860. (Tōhoku discrepancy in original.)

Densan had predicted. This disparity tended to increase over time as urban demand, especially for higher-priced household use, meant high revenues for Tokyo and Kansai power companies, while rural Shikoku Electric Power had the shakiest economic position. This imbalance was enhanced by the PUC decision to award undeveloped water resources to the urban areas, and by the two major rate increases approved by the PUC in 1951 and 1952. Finally, as the comparative advantage of hydroelectricity disappeared in the face of new thermal technology, the urban companies were increasingly able to compete with the water-rich rural ones.[34] By 1960, Tokyo Electric Power had become the largest and Kansai the second largest privately owned power company in the world. (The other companies were among the biggest firms in their own regions and thus wielded great *local* power, even though they were dwarfed by Tokyo and Kansai.)

The drive by these two companies to win control of hydroelectric resources *and* develop new thermal plants generated rapid rationalization in the electric-power industry. It was motivated more by a desire to prevail over the other power companies than by a national strategy. This effect certainly had not been foreseen by the Japanese government, which had opposed reorganization. Nor had it been intended by SCAP, which had unsuccessfully argued for a "regionalist" division of hydroelectric resources. While government policy made these technological improvements possible, it did not anticipate the process by which they were actually incorporated by the electric-power companies. Rather, the government concentrated on removing risks to industry profits by taking over the expensive task of developing hydroelectricity.

THE ELECTRIC-POWER DEVELOPMENT COMPANY. Although no one argued against the need for government funds in the power industry, there was disagreement on how to provide and administer those funds. Matsunaga and a large segment of the banking community wanted to set up a bank that would channel money only to the 9 regional companies. The companies would be solely responsible for planning, building, and operating the new generating sites. In contrast, the chairman of the PUC, Matsumoto Jōji, industrialists such as Miki Takashi, and the Diet preferred a special semi-governmental corporation that would guide the industry's development. They argued that central control was necessary to decide on rival water claims, afforestation, and flood-control problems related to hydroelectric-power development projects. Moreover, they affirmed that only a nationwide corporation could attract the additional capital necessary to carry out the ambitious development plan. This led to the creation of a special company to move government funds into large-scale electric-power development projects. The Ōno Bamboku faction of the Liberal Party submitted a bill to the Diet for the formation of this company in March 1952.

As it was less than a year since the final demise of Hassōden and this plan was highly reminiscent of the Miki plan's "power-circulation company," this proposal was hotly debated in the Diet. The bill was eventually passed, creating the Electric Power Development Company (EPDC) on 16 September 1952. Its initial capital came jointly from the government and from the 9 power companies, but the government appointed the corporation's officers. The EPDC, which is still active, is administered through MITI and is not itself a policymaking body. MITI also controls the flow of money to the EPDC. The EPDC wholesales the resulting power from its developments to the 9 companies at cost but does not sell directly to consumers. When it was first established, the plan was to turn generating facilities over to the 9 companies after they had been built, but in the end it was decided that the EPDC should retain title to them.[35]

The most important casualty of the debate over the EPDC and the concurrent controversy over rate increases was the PUC, attacked by the Liberal Party for helping the power companies at the expense of other Japanese on the grounds that it had too speedily granted the 1951 and 1952 rate increases. The general public perception was that the PUC was aiding, rather than regulating, the electric-power industry. Moreover, the PUC suffered from a poor image as an unwanted stepchild of the Occupation. The result was that it was abolished on 1 August 1952, and responsibility for electric power was handed back to MITI.[36] It would be inappropriate to see this as a victory by MITI over business, however. Rather, there was a congruence of interests that smoothed the way for this transition. Government plans to expand electric-power facilities closely coincided with industry ambitions, and the electric-power companies continued to receive favorable treatment.

The abolition of the PUC, transference of jurisdiction over the 9 power companies back to MITI, and establishment of the EPDC all brought the companies under tighter government oversight. After regaining independence, the Japanese moved back toward a structure more like that of the war years, in which the government had greater policy control over the electric-power industry. However, the private companies were now much more powerful than before the war, and the balance between government and *zaikai* in this field was fairly even. Although electric-power-company officials were still nervous about the possibility of state control, they did not seriously fear its recurrence for several reasons.[37] First, the private companies were able to operate independently of the EPDC, unlike their predecessors under Hassōden. Second, the postwar government was far more comfortable than the wartime leaders with a modified form of capitalism. Third, the electric-power industry was increasingly incorporated into international structures, like the World Bank, which prevented the Japanese government from taking precipitate action against them. Finally, all the involved parties shared the goal of rapid expansion of the electric-power grid, and so there was a strong basis for mutual adjustment among the individuals involved.

The EPDC was part of a larger government policy to expand electric-power capacity and lower costs. By 1952, the government agreed that this meant healthy and relatively autonomous private firms. The idea that electric power was a basic right lingered on, but it had been combined with the conviction that this was best achieved through private enterprise. Enhancing the profit base of the power companies was now patriotic, since it allowed them to develop new facilities. This was the reverse of the prewar concept— that profit obscured responsibility to rural citizens.

The Liberal Party had its own political reasons to favor a development corporation. The Ōno faction, which would have preferred regional development packages rather than a single focus on electric power, was fully aware of the pork-barrel opportunities the plan would create. When this group introduced the Electric Power Development Promotion Bill into the Diet, the project was quickly dubbed the "law to develop financial resources for the Liberal Party." The private electric-power-company executives were very close to the Liberal Party as well, notably the new President of Tōhoku Power Company, Shirasu Jirō, one of Yoshida's most important advisors. A 1953 article reported that Shirasu's "alleged ambition now is to help his Tōhoku Electric Power Company freely to the resources of the Tadami river . . . , to induce foreign capital into the company, and make of it a money-bag for Mr. Yoshida and his lieutenants."[38] The 9 electric-power companies' joint management association contributed 10 million yen to the Liberal Party in 1952, second only to the coal operators, who donated 26 million yen.[39] The electric-power industry had indeed become an important source of funds for Yoshida's political needs. The government's willingness to support the autonomy of the private companies was to some extent related to the companies' willingness to support the ruling party in government.

The activities of the EPDC after its creation clearly were in no way antagonistic to the private companies. While the formation of the EPDC itself and the impetus for creating it can be interpreted as a government attempt to curb the autonomous power of business in a basic industry, the terms of its establishment were quite beneficial to the private companies. The most important role played by the EPDC was to lead the way in induction of foreign hydroelectric technology, that is, to take big risks. The use of new technology was pioneered by the 9 power companies in the less risky and less expensive area of thermal-plant technology. The EPDC essentially was limited to development projects that the 9 companies did not want to undertake themselves, and to a wholesaling role that strengthened the private firms financially. It developed these projects with the aid of special low-interest loans from the government banks.[40] In this way, the 9 companies shifted the risk of large-scale development to the government, while assuring themselves the use of the resultant power at cost. The creation of the EPDC eliminated the need for the firms to tie up funds in slow-moving projects and created an entity that could mediate between power companies on lingering jurisdictional disputes, as at Tadami River, which had been claimed by both Tokyo and Tōhoku Power Companies since the prewar years.

The EPDC also helped rationalize the Japanese construction industry as well as hydroelectricity production. This process took place through close cooperation with public and private American groups. Three EPDC hydroelectric projects begun in 1954 (Okutadami, Tagokura, and Miboro) cost $175 million to build. Of this, the EPDC borrowed $8 million for construction equipment and $2 million for technological assistance from the World Bank, and used the money to import American construction machinery, such as 15-ton dump trucks, bulldozers, plows, and cement mixers.[41] The EPDC and its construction company subcontractors justified importing this equipment on the following grounds: It was unavailable in Japan, especially in equivalently large and efficient models; where comparative Japanese equipment did exist, it was "not mechanically reliable," had a shorter service life, and was made from inferior equipment; moreover, use of foreign machinery would shorten construction time by a full year and reduce costs. It was also cheaper. Most of the American equipment was priced at 50 to 75 percent of domestic models.[42] The imported equipment acted to introduce many new techniques to the Japanese construction business and immediately stimulated faster and more durable construction. On another occasion, this process was set in motion with private funds. The EPDC also borrowed $7 million from the Bank of America in 1953 and 1954 to build the Sakuma hydroelectric dam. The money specifically went to hire an American engineering firm, the Atkinson Company, on a technical-assistance contract and to import construction machinery.[43]

The EPDC also served to draw official American technological assistance into Japan. In an interesting insight into the workings of "U.S.-Japan economic cooperation," the presence of the U.S. Army considerably aided the task of disseminating this technology in Japan. The American military provided training and initial experience operating the construction equipment to the Japanese. One hundred Japanese employees of the Hazama Construction Company, a subcontractor to the EPDC, spent three months learning how to use and repair the equipment. They were taught by five men who had been trained at a U.S. Army heavy-machine and equipment school in Tokorozawa. Another subcontractor, Kumagai-Gumi, used personnel who had learned to operate American equipment while working on U.S. Army construction projects in Okinawa. Both subcontractors rented the machinery from the EPDC.[44]

Thus, the EPDC illustrates the close congruence of interests among government officials, Diet leaders, and private electric-power companies. All agreed—for a variety of reasons—on the need for a major, government-funded body to undertake risky, long-term projects. The EPDC clearly helped the electric-power industry to develop and to stimulate development in other industries. The EPDC also helped attract World Bank loans and American technological assistance to Japan, and tied Japan more closely both to U.S. foreign policy and U.S. private firms. Yet, this was not a carefully planned outcome of rationalization policy, nor a manifestation of enormous government power. Rather, the EPDC was a negotiated settlement between public and private control of the electric-power industry after the varied experience, first with Hassōden, and then the 9 private companies.

RATIONALIZATION PLANS AND THERMAL POWER

Through the first postwar decade, official Japanese policy was to develop hydroelectricity as the main power source and use thermal plants as backup. By 1953, this was a way of amalgamating Arisawa's argument that Japan had to develop its domestic economy with Nakayama's concern for raising the level of net exports. Water is one of Japan's few abundant resources, and the Japanese wished to take full advantage of this gift. However, from 1955, two trends led to a change in this policy; at the same time that hydroelectric sites were becoming more remote and more expensive to build, new American thermal technology was improving. Plants built with this technology were much larger and far more efficient than earlier models. They also could be built near consumption centers, and generally could be erected far more quickly than large dams, thus saving on transmission and construction costs. Matsunaga Yasuzaemon was the first to recognize this. He argued in four reports issued between 1955 and 1958 that the industry and government should switch from a strategy based on primary use of hydroelectricity to one centered on thermal-power plants.[45] Although hydroelectric plants would remain important as peak-load suppliers, the base-line supply would come increasingly from the new thermal plants. These not only burned coal more efficiently but also required a lower grade of coal, thus cutting fuel costs per kilowatt considerably. The 9 power companies needed 0.834 kilograms of coal to produce one kilowatt-hour in fiscal 1952, but had cut this to 0.547 kilograms by 1959.[46] The Japanese power companies were able to buy these expensive plants through the "maker's-credit" system pioneered by General Electric and Westinghouse, and through U.S. Export-Import Bank loans.

CONTRADICTIONS IN THERMAL-POWER DEVELOPMENT. Thermal-power development raised a new and difficult problem for national industrial rationalization policy, however. The American loans and "maker's-credit" arrangements promoted U.S. exports as they were designed to do. Certainly, without them, the capital-poor Japanese power companies would have been unable to shop in the United States. Since this encouraged quick development of the electric-power industry through foreign technology, it was totally within the framework of the Japanese government rationalization policy, and the power companies had no difficulty getting their import requests approved. Nonetheless, buying abroad hindered reconstruction of Japanese electric-machine and machine-tools producers, which were themselves prime potential export industries. These Japanese companies needed the very customers who were shopping in America. This internal contradiction in rationalization policy was one of the most difficult problems to resolve. The same problem developed for the heavy-equipment manufacturers who sold dam-building equipment. These firms, which were in a similar position to the electric-machinery makers, had to scramble to update their products. Just as in thermal power, the U.S.-financed development of hydroelectricity forced Japanese producers to improve their products or lose their best domestic customers. This conflict between rationalization of different sectors of the economy is a classic problem of development, and Japan is by no means the only country to wrestle with it.

Other Japanese industries struggled with this problem too. The machine-tool industry, suffering from a terrible dearth of markets in the early 1950s, lobbied the government to create incentives for other Japanese industries to buy from them, resulting in a February 1953 administrative regulation, which provided financial aid to business that replaced old machinery with new Japanese equipment. However, simultaneous government programs that assisted firms to replace old machinery with state-of-the-art imports completely negated the value of this more modest plan.[47]

In postwar Japan, the deciding factor was the superior technology of U.S companies, which was developing very rapidly. This was important both for national economic policy and for the corporate strategy of the leading power-company executives. New high-efficiency thermal plants allowed the electric-power companies to use less coal and to lower electric bills for export industries, as the government officials wanted. The urban power companies badly wanted the new thermal technology, to bring their rates down to the levels charged by the hydro-rich rural regions, in order to compete for new industrial customers. They did not want to lose business to their country cousins.

The fact that the power companies were expanding rapidly and competitively forced the machinery companies to modernize as quickly as possible, since they hoped to win the contracts to supply the electric-power companies. This battle among the power companies became a powerful indirect spur to the Japanese manufacturing firms. Faced with a demand for the best technology from their consumers, the Japanese machinery companies aggressively sought loans abroad from 1953 so they could modernize in time to provide the high-quality power equipment. They generally needed two or three years more than their American competitors to bring out new types. In practice, the solution to the conflict with the electric-machine manufacturers was for the power companies to buy the first new plant of each type from abroad, then switch to Japanese producers. If one looks at the record, this is exactly what happened.[48]

The main Japanese electric-machine manufacturers used the same American sources to upgrade. They had longstanding ties to the American companies (Toshiba and Hitachi to General Electric and Mitsubishi to Westinghouse), established just before and just after World War I and reaffirmed in late 1949. The American firms were happy to sell technological licenses to their Japanese counterparts. Like U.S. government officials, they never expected serious competition from that quarter.

Thus, power-company orders directly led to rationalization in the electrical-machinery industry. This shows concretely how the development of new technology abroad and the ability of Japanese companies to absorb it rapidly were the crucial gambles that paid off for Japanese reconstruction policy. Not a clear strategy, this was indeed a gamble.[49]

DREAMS FOR THE FUTURE: ATOMIC ENERGY

By the mid-1950s, the Japanese began to look to a new electric-power source—atomic energy. They hoped this ultramodern energy would someday replace not only declining hydroelectric resources but also coal.

Nuclear research began again while Japan was still under occupation. The United States Atomic Energy Commission decided in November 1949 to allow Japan to purchase radioisotopes for research.[50] As in so many other areas, this was an about-face in Occupation policy motivated by global Cold War concerns. After World War II, the Americans forbade all atomic-energy experiments and destroyed Japan's existing cyclotrons. By 1954, however, Eisenhower was launching an international nuclear-power program called Atoms for Peace. Despite the name, Atoms for Peace was a Cold War weapon, as were nuclear bombs. The new American policy specifically extended to Japan. In September 1954, American Atomic Energy Commissioner Thomas E. Murray urged that the United States build a nuclear power plant in Japan to disprove the Soviet claim that the United States thought only in terms of weapons. He argued that the gift of an atomic reactor would be a "lasting monument to our technology and our good will." The underlying Cold War motivation was revealed in his second argument, that such a gesture would "go a very long way toward nullifying what has been lost at Dienbienphu and Geneva."[51] In January 1955, the U.S. government unofficially offered the Japanese access to 20-percent enriched uranium and told them that 30 American firms were capable of supplying the fuel. Representatives of some of those firms soon appeared in Japan. In May 1955, the President of General Dynamics and the officer in charge of atomic energy for the Chase Manhattan Bank gave public lectures in Tokyo on the virtues of atomic power, while a representative of Westinghouse visited Japan in December to discuss nuclear reactors.[52] The U.S. government also invited important Japanese to study various aspects of nuclear-power development in America, culminating in the United States-Japan Atomic Energy Agreement. The agreement, signed 14 November 1955, meant that the Japanese could buy nuclear fuel and technology for peaceful purposes from the United States.

In 1954 and 1955, atomic-energy development seemed to many people to be an attractive long-term solution to Japan's growing energy problem. Bureaucratic, Diet, business, and academic leaders enthusiastically began work toward an atomic-energy program. In the Diet, this issue was nearly unique in that it had support from both the newly merged Liberal Democratic Party and the Japan Socialist Party. The Cabinet established the Preparatory Council for the Peaceful Uses of Atomic Energy in May 1954 to plan for the development of atomic power. It also authorized an amendment to the 1949 Mining Law, which required that claim holders actively prospect for ore, to include uranium. The Geological Society began a nationwide uranium survey in 1954, but Japan's natural endowment proved to be negligible, and the Japanese were forced to go abroad for atomic fuel.[53]

Most of the legal framework for the atomic-energy program began operating in 1956. On 1 January 1956, the Basic Law for Atomic Energy went into effect. A companion law provided for an Atomic Energy Commission, set up under the jurisdiction of the Prime Minister's Office (as the short-lived PUC had been), chaired by Shōriki Matsutarō, President of the *Yomiuri* newspaper, who had become a great champion of nuclear energy. He used his newspaper and many other forums to popularize the idea of atomic power in Japan and disassociate it from weaponry.[54] The other members were Ishikawa Ichirō, another key nuclear enthusiast and President of Keidanren (until February 1956), two noted Japanese physicists, Yukawa Hideki and Fujioka Yoshio, and Arisawa Hiromi. Two other laws were passed in May 1956, the Atomic Fuel Corporation Law and the Nuclear Material Resources Development Promotion Law, to help promotion of nuclear research and development. In June of the same year, the Japan Atomic Energy Research Forum was established to study ways to generate electricity with nuclear power. The Forum functioned, then and now, to coordinate research in Japan, study developments in foreign countries, and publicize findings on the subject of atomic energy. It was organized as a special corporation with an initial investment of 250 million yen from the government and 248 million yen from the private sector, mainly electric-power companies and heavy-machine manufacturers. In August, construction began on the first atomic-power site, a research center at Tōkai Mura in Ibaraki prefecture.[55]

Business groups had already organized themselves into 5 consortia to develop nuclear energy. These were organized along *keiretsu* lines, one each for the Mitsubishi, Mitsui, and Sumitomo groups, the fourth set up by Hitachi and Fuji Banks, and the fifth organized around the Furukawa and Kawasaki manufacturers and the Daiichi Bank.[56] The electric-power companies also began internal research on atomic power. Kansai Electric Power Company sent employees on study tours to Westinghouse and other centers in Canada, England, and France from 1957. The electric utilities generally followed the technology-purchasing patterns they had established with conventional power equipment. Thus, Kansai bought conventional and atomic-power equipment from Westinghouse, while Tokyo Electric Power consistently chose General Electric.[57]

Atomic-power development was set up from the beginning to conform to the rationalization pattern the Japanese had worked out through trial and error over the past six years. Ventures with commercial potential were allotted to private firms, which competed with each other for profits. This competition was designed to force them continually to rationalize. In order to build the industry quickly, the government generously assisted all these firms with tax breaks, special permission to import technology, and loans. The government also tried to strike a balance between the needs of the electric-power and the heavy-machinery industries—that is, between operators and builders of atomic technology. Reflecting the compromise achieved in conventional power-plant machinery, the electric-power firms were permitted to import advanced foreign nuclear plants for the time being, in order to get immediate experience operating them. However, the government helped heavy-machinery manufacturers develop a domestic industry for future power-plant purchases. The government also shouldered the riskier task of basic research. Some of the techniques for stimulating technological development that had been discovered during the previous years in other industries were consciously applied to this new industry. These included pitting Japanese firms against each other, while offering them all financial inducements to incorporate new machinery and ideas. Although the firms were not guaranteed profits, they were protected from the worst effects of failure by government guarantees.

Atomic-power development policy contained an internal contradiction from its inception. The Japanese hoped to use nuclear technology as an independent Japanese energy source, which would eventually limit Japanese economic dependence on foreigners. This goal encouraged them to devote considerable resources to the atomic-energy program and to basic research on atomic power. Japanese heavy-machinery firms were urged to develop expertise to build nuclear power plants. Yet the nuclear-energy program never was independent. Like rationalization policy in general, Japanese nuclear planning was based on the assumption that American technology would continue to be available. Their atomic-energy strategy was possible only because of the American Atoms for Peace program and American willingness to share nuclear technology. Once again, this created new ties between the Japanese economy and American military strategies in East Asia. Moreover, like crude oil, Japan never had power over its uranium supply, which was largely controlled by the United States.[58] Energy "self-sufficiency" existed only within the context of the continuing relationship with the United States, just as the domestic Japanese economy could not be separated from its international context.

TEN

Coal versus Oil: The 1950s

In the 1950s, King Coal occupied an uneasy position as titular head of the energy sector, while its actual role in the economy steadily declined. By the end of the decade, like the emperors of feudal Japan, coal reigned but did not rule. From the vantage point of the late 1980s, coal's replacement by oil as Japan's main industrial fuel is without question the most important energy fact of that period. While it was taking place, however, the Japanese were aware of neither the dimensions nor the implications of this trend. They assumed that various barriers to development of oil refining, particularly lack of foreign exchange, would prevent such a shift. They generally anticipated that oil use would grow, but only as a supplement to coal. The Japanese expected the coal mines to respond positively to rationalization measures and continue their traditional role as an economic base. Many Japanese hoped that new exploration and extraction techniques would yield greater coal reserves than previously charted, while others feared that international oil supplies would dwindle. These were all reasonable concerns, which closely mirrored the thinking of energy planners in other parts of the world at that time.

Although coal's long-term decline seems obvious now, it was difficult then to pick out the long-term trend. The coal industry was extremely volatile in the postwar years: in a boom until 1949, then in decline until 1951 when it enjoyed two very good years until another slump in 1953–1954, and then another boom in 1956–

1957. These constant changes made it hard to know when a down-turn was due to a short-term fluctuation in the economy and when it signified a permanent decline. The best single year for the coal mines was 1957, just before the industry began its final collapse. Short-term fluctuations in the prices of coal and oil made compari-son between them very difficult, while the lack of adequate surveys of domestic coal reserves made future projections even less certain. Proponents of coal were also heartened by the report of a French firm, hired by the Japanese government in 1957 to study Japanese coal resources, costs of future production, and means of increasing productive capacity in large and small mines. Their April 1958 report was very optimistic about future development of the mines.[1] The varied findings of Japanese commissions, fact-finding missions, and industry surveys throughout these years added to the confusion. In short, the Japanese reliance on coal through 1959 was more rea-sonable than it seems in hindsight.

Although the Japanese were fairly typical in their assessment of energy problems in the 1950s, Japan withdrew particularly rapidly from the coal industry, due to developments that, while not specif-ically intended as measures to replace coal with oil, had this effect. Foremost among these was the general focus on technology transfer in an age when new technology was American-made and based on oil. This extended as far as an entirely new industry—petrochemi-cals—that relied exclusively on petroleum and natural gas. Further-more, the oil-refining industry was increasingly able to meet indus-trial demands for cheap and stable energy. The refiners had responded to foreign-exchange limits with aggressive rationalization measures, which not only reduced the price of oil but also had the unintended effect of encouraging technological rationalization within the oil-refining industry. This trend, of course, further widened the price gap between the two fuels. In both price and technology, coal was losing ground to oil. Moreover, the oil refiners' efforts further high-lighted the sluggishness with which the coal operators responded to calls for improvements in mine productivity.

The Japanese were by no means eager to become dependent on oil, although they wanted stable supplies of inexpensive energy.

They would have preferred to rehabilitate the coal mines. This preference became clear in 1955 when Japanese government officials and business leaders tried to limit the shift to oil with a series of legal measures. These were designed to maintain coal's central place in the economy but still provide oil to industrial customers.

The 1955 settlement was designed to support coal, but it also included provisions that encouraged the shift to oil. The Japanese were by and large unaware of the conflicting implications of these decisions. Two elements that, in retrospect, emerge as clear breaks with the past are the decision to promote petrochemicals and the new use of the concept of a declining industry to justify policy toward the coal industry. However, these flags signaling a new approach were coupled with several measures to protect the coal industry. These included extra incentives to the coal industry to rationalize, the use of a tariff on petroleum to support the coal industry, and restrictions on conversions of boilers from coal to oil. This internal ambivalence, and Japanese lack of clarity about their stance, in part explains the failure of the 1955 settlement. In fact, the Japanese did proffer a new potential solution in 1955. They hoped atomic energy would eventually provide the unifying element in this internally inconsistent policy. This was the seat of their hopes for future energy development.

The growing importance of petroleum to the Japanese economy and the decline of the coal industry elevated other issues to prominence. Foremost was foreign investment, greater in the oil industry than in any other. This foreign presence did not threaten national economic strategies as long as oil remained a second-rank industry, but it became a more urgent issue when oil claimed a more central place. Perhaps inevitably, expressions of concern about this economic problem recalled the language used earlier to discuss oil's importance as a military commodity. The coal industry was quick to frame its competition with petroleum as a matter of national security. Other problems, such as regional stagnation and unemployment, also developed as coal declined.

These arguments for retaining coal gained prominence when it became obvious that there was no *economic* justification for doing so.

The failure of the 1955 compromise forced the Japanese finally to reexamine their commitment to coal in 1959 and 1960. Only at that time did they fully accept Nakayama's argument that it was economically more sensible to import cheap and stable energy than to try to develop it at home. From that time, they made a conscious commitment to rely on imported oil as the energy base of their economy.

PETROLEUM REFINING

In late 1952, the government increased allocations of foreign exchange to oil refiners in order to pressure the coal mines into a quick settlement of the protracted strike. This was to have long-reaching consequences for the domestic coal industry, since many fuel-consuming firms never returned to coal. In an early intimation that King Coal's hegemony was threatened, petroleum imports rose rapidly from 5.5 million kiloliters in 1952, to 8.7 million kiloliters in 1953, and then to 10.4 million kiloliters in 1954.[2]

This strike was the first time that petroleum began to play a significant role in the Japanese economy. Although the newly refurbished refineries had started opening in 1950, oil sales were strictly rationed until April 1952. The foreign-exchange-allocations system created a mechanism for indirectly continuing rationing after that. Since nearly all Japan's petroleum had to be imported, this was quite effective.

The events of late 1952 helped break down the automatic assumption that "self-sufficiency" required reliance on domestic fuel. The 1952 strike demonstrated that the stability of coal supplies was as problematic for customers as price. Coal was still cheaper than oil for most applications in 1952, but supply interruptions made it very hard for other industries to meet their contract deadlines. Indeed, this strike was an early turning point intellectually for Japanese industrialists and government officials regarding the coal industry. Nakayama Ichirō's argument that self-sufficiency was easier to achieve through importing fuel gained new adherents, and, from this time, sympathy for the coal industry distinctly declined.[3] In

1954, Inaba Hidezō succinctly set out the problem: "The real point is that the coal companies have to bring costs down. The industry is important as our only domestic natural resource, as a major employer, and as a regional mainstay, but prices have to come down."[4] At that time, however, most Japanese still thought this was possible. They did not realize the precariousness of the domestic coal industry's position.

Moreover, few people imagined that petroleum could supplant the venerable coal industry, because foreign-exchange shortages posed a real limit to growth for oil refining. After allowing higher allotments to oil refiners during the strike, in 1954 the Japanese government cut these back again as part of a general budget-tightening move. This was not done from a desire to curtail the oil industry (although the coal industry had lobbied for lower allocations) as much as it was a response to a short-term crisis in the foreign-exchange supply. The problem of balancing the foreign-exchange budget dominated policy toward the oil industry, because the Japanese economy was very sensitive to fluctuations in world trade; when international trade levels fell, so did Japan's capacity to export and, therefore, to import.[5]

Thus, the problem of foreign exchange was inextricably twined with oil policy. Since the 1952 strike, some bureaucrats and industrialists who wanted to expand export markets had argued that the real issue was *net* foreign-exchange receipts. If oil imports improved the competitive ability of Japanese industry in international markets, they were well worth the original foreign-exchange outlay. As Inaba Hidezō explained, "It is not necessarily bad that we become more dependent on foreign energy sources. The main issue with oil is the foreign-exchange rate and our foreign-currency position. Moreover, the real issue is net foreign exchange. If greater oil imports bring costs down and exports up, then they are worth it."[6] Despite this insight, sometimes there simply was not enough money in the foreign-exchange account to purchase imported goods. This problem had to be resolved before Japanese industry could rely on oil.

The mechanism of foreign-exchange allocations allowed the Japanese government considerable control over the oil industry, since MITI could adjust the flow and distribution of petroleum imports. This power was used to *foster* oil refining within the confines of the foreign-exchange problem. It was also used to spur competition among the oil importers and refiners in order to keep petroleum prices low. This was a creative use of the foreign-exchange-allocation system that had not been part of its original purpose.

The foreign-exchange-controls budget was a complex system. Twice a year, the Cabinet Council decided on a total foreign-exchange budget and allocated specific sums for each commodity to be imported. Petroleum refiners and foreign-trade importers were allowed to submit requests for foreign-exchange quotas up to the total amount allotted for oil purchases. Allotments were granted on the basis of actual past sales, a key feature in spurring competition among the importers. The oil importers then had to deposit collateral at a foreign-exchange bank and be approved by the bank before receiving any foreign currency.[7]

The Japanese government officials wanted to expand and rationalize the oil-refining industry in order to provide cheap, abundant energy to key industries. It is probably more accurate to describe their conception of petroleum at that time as a *service* to other industries rather than as an industry in its own right. Thus, MITI allowed several new companies to import oil and open refineries between 1952 and 1954. The bureaucrats hoped that competition among them would keep oil prices down.

MITI's encouragement of a fragmented oil industry sharply contrasted with its concurrent campaign to reconcentrate key industries such as coal and steel. It also differed notably from the MITI efforts of a decade later to merge several small oil refiners into Kyōdō Oil company. Although the popular image is that MITI abhors "unnecessary" competition, it is more accurate to think of MITI's overarching economic policy as one of strengthening the key industries as much as possible. In the early 1950s—unlike ten years later— petroleum was not a member of this select group. This interpretation of "service-industry" policy does show an interesting evolution from prewar thinking. In the 1930s, electric power was similarly seen as a vital service to industry, the military, and households. At that time, however, the bureaucrats sought low prices through greater centralization and official fixed prices rather than more competition.

The organized business community, heavily represented by individuals from the key industries, was amenable to this policy. In contrast, the oil-refining industry had never had close ties either to government or to national business organizations—unlike the coal or electric-power companies. The plans of both government officials and organized business groups tended to reflect either the interests of the coal industry, oil's competitor, or, more often, the interests of fuel consumers, particularly "key" industrial consumers, such as steel and ship manufacturers.[8] Keidanren, for example, supported the early expansion of oil use, but also represented the interests of the coal industry and of fuel users.

These two positions—of the coal operators and fuel consumers—were deeply conflicting, but they did intersect on some points, one being opposition to a strong cartel in the oil-refining business. This meant enthusiastic support for government policies that were directed toward keeping the oil-refining market crowded and fragmented. The coal operators would have also liked to raise oil prices artificially through high tariffs and restrictions on the use of petroleum, while petroleum users wanted low oil prices and free access to oil. Since the latter position was in line with both Japan's grand economic policy to expand exports and American free-trade precepts, it was the one that ultimately prevailed. This thinking affected the decision to allow the oil industry to grow rapidly. MITI encouraged new refining capacity, on the theory that competition would keep fuel prices to industry low. It was hoped that low petroleum prices would also nudge the coal companies toward lower prices. Throughout the 1950s, the government and major business organizations still considered coal the basic energy industry of Japan. Both government and business pursued fuel policies they hoped were compromises but eventually were revealed to be contradictory. Thus, they aided the growth of the refining industry and, at the same time, protected the coal industry against the inroads of petroleum.

Meanwhile, the Japanese oil refiners concentrated on expanding and improving their industry. Interestingly, the foreign-exchange-allocation system not only spurred expansion of the refineries but also played a decisive role in their technological improvement. The challenge for the refiners was to win greater market shares despite fixed foreign-exchange allocations. Since the foreign-exchange-allocations system limited the dollar amount of petroleum purchases but not the volume, Japanese companies searched for ways to get the most value from their foreign-exchange allotments. This became a major impetus toward technological rationalization for the oil refiners and importers.

One way was to scour the globe for inexpensive crude oil. The independent Japanese companies, notably Idemitsu, were the most enterprising in this regard. The foreign affiliates, which had generally signed long-term "tied-crude" contracts with one or more of the majors in return for technological and financial assistance, were unable to take advantage of low spot-market prices. Idemitsu Sazō, unhampered by long-term contracts, was one of the few people anywhere to defy a boycott of Iranian oil by the majors in February 1953. Over the course of the 1950s, the "domestic" firms increased their market share, mainly by scavenging for cheaper crude oil. Idemitsu also led the pack in a second dollar-saving measure—building and operating his own tankers. Since shipbuilding was a priority industry, this operation was heavily subsidized by the government. Idemitsu was the first Japanese oil man to order a tanker (in a move the spurred development of the shipbuilding industry), and his flagship, the *Nisshō Maru,* was launched in May 1952.[9]

A third way for refiners to get more high-quality results, and so minimize imports of expensive petroleum products, was to improve oil-processing techniques. The Japanese did not eliminate the need to import some refined products until about 1960, so investment in crude processing continued for about a decade. Their efforts centered on increasing the octane rating of gasoline by importing catalytic converting technology. They continued to rely on imported American capital and technology, as they had from 1949.[10] Yet another avenue for enhancing the value of the fixed foreign-exchange allotment was to incorporate different processes that allowed refiners to use lower-quality crude oil. Refiners who were able to handle cheaper grades of crude could buy more with their set allocations and so could have more finished products available for sale. This point increased in importance in the late 1950s for two reasons. First, as the years went by, the government wanted to diversify crude sources to include oil from Russia, Southeast Asia and a Japanese firm operating in the neutral zone near Kuwait. It was willing to offer larger allotments to refiners that accepted these harder-to-handle inferior grades. Second, the market for low-grade heavy oil grew faster than any other due to rapid construction of oil-fired thermal-power plants.[11] It was wasteful to use premium Arabian oil for this purpose. (Later technical refinements from about 1960 allowed the electric-power plants to run on crude oil itself. At that point the Japanese pioneered the *kombinato* concept, which linked oil refining, electric power, and heavy-industrial production at a single site.)

The government policy of encouraging new entrants into the refining business did succeed in keeping innovation high and prices low. Continued control of the foreign-exchange budget also prevented the refiners from unbalancing the Japanese foreign-currency account. Through the 1950s, oil prices dropped continuously, especially gasoline, while, simultaneously, technical capability and the volume of refining both grew steadily. This was not necessarily ideal for the oil-refining industry itself. The refiners were engaged in a major price war through much of this period and nearly all their earnings were dedicated to rationalization investment.[12]

The steady decline in oil prices caused fuel users to complain to the mines about their high-priced product. Other customers quietly bought new oil-burning equipment, and coal sales declined. The slump in the domestic coal industry had become severe enough by 1954 to constitute a major social problem. Allowing the industry to die would mean great local unemployment in Kyushu and Hokkaido at a time when jobs were still very scarce. The prefectural government in Kyushu's Amagi area told the mine owners, "We have no unemployment money so it is best if you don't fire any more people. If you do, it might lead to real social unrest." The mine owners responded by refusing either to pay or fire their workers. As a December 1954 article explained: "The hardest hit are the workers employed at the small- and medium-size mines in Kyushu. They are not paid their wages; but, since they are not discharged yet, they are unable to collect unemployment allowances. Nor do they wish to leave, as several months' wages are due to them, still unpaid."[13] This "old-fashioned" response to pressure was typical of the coal-company executives, who relied on political clout. As they had in the prewar era, they turned to production restraints and political pressure (to limit foreign-exchange allocations for petroleum) to solve their economic woes. They were able to win considerable support, but the fuel-user industries demanded that any protection be accompanied by efforts to lower coal prices through rationalization.

1955: THE COMPROMISE THAT FAILED

The problems of the coal industry became severe enough that government officials developed a new set of measures for the energy industries in late 1954 and 1955. Their main concern was coal-mine rationalization, since they had not yet wavered from their expectation that coal would remain central to the economy. MITI introduced a proposal in late 1954 that would become the Coal Rationalization Law the following year. The Coal Rationalization Law was designed to stabilize the Japanese coal industry by trimming it to a level competitive with imported fuel. The government officials hoped to build yearly coal output to 49 million tons and lower coal prices by 20 percent in five years. MITI chose to do this by aiding large mines and shutting ones that could not bring the cost of production down to a competitive level.[14] This was the first formulation of the famous "scrap-and-build" policy, although this phrase was not coined until about 1957.[15] This policy, which continued in various guises until 1965, was to shut down the small, labor-intensive mines, recognizing that there would be less demand for coal in the future, and simultaneously to help mines that had the capacity to rationalize production. The "build" portion was a carryover of the plan to reconcentrate production that had worked in iron and steel, in shipbuilding, and in many other export industries. The "scrap" portion, however, was a response to the pressure by miners and politicians from coal-mining regions to minimize the social impact of mine closures. When the government "scrapped" a mine, it provided funds for severance pay to all employees and settled the mine's other outstanding debts. From late 1952, the coal miners had successfully fought to include this issue in coal policy-making, rather than simply letting the mines close.[16]

As part of the Coal Rationalization Law, coal companies were encouraged to cooperate with each other through a 1953 amendment to the Anti-Monopoly Law which allowed "orderly reconstruction" through production restraints.[17] This amendment allowed "recession and rationalization cartels" in foundering industries, and was usually used to protect weaker industries rather than to encourage strong ones. As such, it represents a wider interpretation of "rationalization" to include support for declining industries. This was a conceptual breakthrough for industrial policy, which earlier had not included the possibility of structural barriers to industrial growth. This interpretation of rationalization was originally invented in 1953 for the textile industries, but it became very important to the coal industry, which went directly from support on the basis of its growth potential to support on the basis of its unprofitability.[18]

As a "recession cartel," the coal companies were allowed to set prices, although the MITI Coal Bureau officials tried to reserve this right to themselves. The mines were also encouraged to cut their labor force from 277,000 to 220,000 workers, and to reduce transport costs by 20 percent. Traditionally, the coal operators had restricted coal supply and maintained high prices and high profits without reducing production costs. MITI hoped that, if it controlled coal prices, the companies would be forced to mechanize. In fact, MITI was never able to enforce its "standard prices"; they were simply ignored by the coal companies.

Money was allocated by the government in two ways to buy up

inefficient mines from 1955. The first was a new tariff on heavy oil (6.5 percent) and crude oil (2 percent), a source first proposed by Keidanren.[19] The second was through the Japan Development Bank and the Small and Medium Enterprises Bank. These two banks set aside some of the interest payments they received to buy out inefficient coal firms. The coal-legislation package also included sizable loans and grants for potentially efficient mines to encourage higher investment and rationalization. Meanwhile, a new law restricting the use of heavy oil as boiler fuel was included to assure the coal industry a stable market. MITI allowed higher levels of oil imports, however, so that the coal industry would not be unduly protected and in response to pressure from petroleum-consuming industries.[20]

Meanwhile, the domestic petroleum industry was expected to grow soberly but steadily, spurred by both rising industrial demand and the new petrochemical industry. The move into petrochemicals committed Japan to the development of a major oil-refining industry. Petrochemicals were launched as a national-policy industry in July 1955, in an update of the 1952 "key-industry" concept. Diversification into petrochemicals represented a new level of sophistication in the use of petroleum. As such, it was an important step in the transition to an oil-based economy in Japan and undercut the goals of the Coal Rationalization Law. Yet, this step was taken blindly when most Japanese still believed that the slimmed-down coal industry would dominate their energy supply structure for years to come. The Japanese worried that international petroleum reserves could run dry. As late as 1956, a respected Japanese energy expert wrote that "world petroleum consumption is itself increasing so rapidly that there is anxiety over dwindling supplies."[21] The Japanese also recognized early the vulnerability of their oil supply to foreign wars.

The Japanese government gave petrochemicals a high priority for several reasons, chiefly because of the promise of retained foreign exchange. The *Fuji Bank Bulletin* calculated that petroleum consumption by the petrochemical industry should account for only 1 percent of total national consumption, and that its basic fuel would be gas waste created by petroleum refining. Thus, petrochemical-based exports would more than compensate for increased petroleum needs. Another study by the same magazine forecast $100 million in foreign-exchange earnings in 1960, half of which would be petrochemical exports to Asia.[22] The designation as a national-policy industry made petrochemical firms eligible for special financing, tax exemptions, and import privileges, including an exemption from oil-import duty. Most Japanese refiners immediately applied to the government to open a petrochemicals division.

The Japanese refiners had a specific technical reason to expand into petrochemicals. They hoped this move would solve their persistent problem of unbalanced demand for the various petroleum products. Despite the great expansion of the oil refineries, 23 percent of Japan's oil still was imported as products in 1954 (mainly heavy fuel oil), rather than as crude oil.[23] Although the Japanese wished to reduce this category, they were stymied by a structural incompatibility between the refining industry's supply capacity and Japanese demand. When the Japanese oil refineries were rebuilt in 1949 and 1950, they were redesigned to the most efficient U.S. specifications. Catalytic cracking plants built in the early 1950s produced between 40 and 50 percent gasoline from a given amount of crude oil, a ratio that almost exactly corresponded to the demand structure in the United States. In Japan, however, where heavy oil was the basic industrial fuel and automobiles rarer, gasoline accounted for only about 24 percent of demand. The American refining technology, transferred to Japan without adequate review, was not particularly appropriate for the Japanese market. As a result, the refiners had a constant shortage of fuel oil and a glut of gasoline (creating an endemic gas-price war). As production levels rose, the greater the imbalance became and the faster gasoline prices plummeted. The refiners hoped that diverting gasoline-like naptha to the petrochemical industry would create new demand for the lighter fuels and correct the chronic product imbalance.

Development of the petrochemicals industry illustrates inter-industry rationalization, since it was encouraged partly to help out the refineries. Expansion of the refining industry had caused fresh economic problems, which could only be resolved by judicious application of even newer technology. Thus, the *problems* created by rationalization of one industry became harnessed to rationalization in another. By 1955, inter-industry rationalization had taken on new importance to economic planners as the methods of encouraging intra-industry rationalization became more routine. The Japanese were beginning to think consciously about the ways that upgrading one industry would affect another, also visible in their plans for atomic power development. Thus, by the late 1950s, rationalization planning gradually focused more on links between industries than on development within each one. Like the concept of declining industries, this revealed a new level of sophistication in Japanese industrial planning.

The final element of the 1955 energy settlement was the new commitment to atomic energy. This ultimate technological solution to the energy dilemma would, the Japanese hoped, finesse their need for petroleum. When coal reserves eventually dwindled, they could be replaced with nuclear power. Japanese dreams of a post-coal Japan centered not on oil but on the atom.

The policy developed in 1955—to rely primarily on coal, while developing petroleum for short-term and atomic power for long-term expansion—did not succeed. The first setbacks arose in the coal industry. As with previous rationalization plans, the coal operators' response was disappointing. The Coal Rationalization Law had attempted to address the issue of coal-price structure by wresting control over prices from the large coal-mine operators and by eliminating the high-cost mines altogether. It was not successful in either regard. Since the "scrap" portion of the plan was voluntary, MITI could not force inefficient mines to stay closed. Instead, the large mine owners bought up small mines with their rationalization funds and collected the government compensation money to close them down. Then, when the coal market improved (temporarily) in 1956, they reopened them. From 1956, the number of small mines went down only very gradually, but the number of independent small mines dropped much more rapidly. The 18 big mine operators preferred to operate the small mines, with their non-union, low-wage labor force, instead of developing their own mines.[24] They

Table 13 Changes in Prices of Coal and Heavy Oil
per Calorie, 1955–1958
(1/100 yen per calorie)

Year	1955	1956	1957	1958
Coal	92.3	96.6	114.2	99.8
Heavy oil	97.0	119.9	114.0	88.1

Sources: Sonoda, *Sengo Sekitan Shi,* p. 63. See also "Coal and the Government," *Japan Quarterly* 10.1: 7–11 (January–March 1963).

continued to work the big mines but avoided expensive preparation of new seams.

One fact that supports the theory that the coal-company managers were deliberately withholding investment was that the situation suddenly changed in 1957. Investment jumped from all capital sources, including rapid growth in the size of government loans from 1958, increases in bank loans, and in internal capital investment. After a decade of neglect and overconfidence, the coal operators suddenly became scared. At that point, they thought mechanization could slow the demise of coal.[25] In Arisawa's words, "The ten years of postwar energy planning were completely wasted as far as rejuvenating coal production was concerned. But, by the time the coal companies realized this, they were already a 'setting sun' industry."[26] The coal industry had waited too long.

Other obstacles to the 1955 settlement were outside Japanese control. The most important was the steady decline in international petroleum prices. No one had expected oil prices to drop as far or as fast as they actually did. By late 1959, after several important petroleum discoveries in the Middle East, it was clear that global petroleum supplies would not soon run out. These new discoveries, together with changes in the structure of the international oil market and cheaper tanker transport, meant that oil prices fell substantially below prices of domestic coal in 1958. The domestic coal industry never again was able to match the cost of imported heavy oil (see Table 13).[27]

The problem was not simply one of lower oil prices, something that conceivably could be reversed, if, for example, the Suez Canal were to close permanently or war break out in the Middle East. More fundamentally, the rationalization movement itself was gradually destroying the Japanese market for coal. Concretely, rationalization in a particular industry often meant switching from coal to oil. Sometimes this was precisely because oil burns more efficiently than coal; sometimes because newer, more advanced designs from America happened to use oil-fired engines. In the world of the 1950s, general industrial technology was increasingly oil-based. Since government economic policy emphasized rapid absorption of new machinery and processes, this automatically enhanced the power of oil to draw new customers. Petroleum's technical features meant that Japanese industrial users often were interested in converting even when oil's per-calorie price was still higher than coal's. The first industries to switch to gas or to heavy oil were consumers of high-quality coal, such as chemical producers. The ammonia-base fertilizer industry found that it was cheaper to use natural gas than coal, even when fertilizer was produced near the coal fields in an integrated plant, like Mitsui's conglomerate at Miike.[28] This was because the newest, most efficient Western machinery ran on oil. In addition to these traditional coal consumers, oil use expanded in new areas, such as gasoline for cars. The market for coal in Japan grew steadily more narrow and specialized. Soon two industries, steel and electric power, were buying over one-third of all Japanese coal.[29]

The transformation of the chemicals sector in 1955 was a crucial element of this shift to oil. At first, the Japanese hoped to develop new industries based on coal, and, as late as 1954, commented hopefully about coal-based chemicals and "the Neo-Coal Age."[30] When the government decided to emphasize petrochemicals in July 1955, it drove the most important nail in the coffin of the coal industry, since it assured that future technological linkages and developments would be connected to oil or gas, rather than to coal. This was also the point when the coal industrialists began to treat the oil industry as a serious competitor, according to the President of Hokutan Mining Company.[31]

The progress of the rationalization efforts in the electric-power industry illustrates the problems technological development created for the coal industry. At first, the thermal-generation strategy was very beneficial to the coal mines. The power companies rapidly increased their use of coal in the mid-1950s as they shifted to primary reliance on thermal-power plants. The electric-power companies were required by the Heavy Boiler Law of 1955 to use coal, acceptable to them because they were able to buy domestic coal and still turn a profit. Electric-power plants were being built so rapidly that total coal use rose even though the coal needed per kilowatt-hour produced declined. This was important to the coal industry, because these higher purchases by the power companies partly offset the general decline in the market. Yet, when oil prices dropped below those of coal in 1958, the power companies resisted their assigned role as the main consumer of Japanese coal.[32] By this time, moreover, the newest electric turbines were oil-fired. The electric-power firms too wanted to switch to cheap oil. Clearly, the premise behind the 1955 Coal Rationalization Law—that the coal industry was economically competitive—was no longer valid.

The shift toward oil also destroyed the historic advantage enjoyed by the big over the small coal operators. Unlike prewar Manchurian coal, the major Japanese mine operators did not own these imports. Nor could they continue to control the market through their monopoly of high-grade coals, since it was precisely these coals that were being supplanted by petroleum and natural gas. Thermal-power generation was one of the few areas in which coal-based technology was holding its own, but power plants burn poor-quality coal. Although the electric-power companies were buying more coal, they did not want the grades on which the industry leaders depended for profit. The growing importance of low-grade coal for electric-power plants meant that the existing coal-price system was less and less defensible.[33] In other words, the major coal companies were challenged for their most profitable sales. For the first time, they were unable to manipulate the coal market to benefit themselves.

The point about technology is important, because it contradicts the assumption that price was the only crucial determinant in coal's defeat. Like the problem of stable supply, technology also affected fuel-users' calculations. Most accounts of the decline of coal versus oil (in any country) stress resource depletion and prices, but this does not sufficiently explain the shift. It was the historic rise of petroleum-based technologies in a wide range of fields that did the most damage to the Japanese coal industry. International technical contracts and technological imports show an intensely practical side of the new level of Japan's integration into the global economy. From the mid-1950's, this was overwhelming petroleum-based.

The new technology entering Japan handicapped the coal industry in other, less obvious ways, most important in comparative transport costs. The ambitious "environmental rationalization" plans to improve port facilities meant that oil shipping and storage grew steadily cheaper. Tanker transport also declined in price through the 1950s and 1960s. Moreover, as the shipbuilding industry recovered, more of the tankers were Japanese, which eliminated a foreign-exchange drain. Coal, which had to come from Kyushu or Hokkaido to the population centers in central Japan, did not enjoy corresponding reductions in transport costs.

These changed circumstances raised the specter of dependence on a foreign energy source, an issue that became increasingly sensitive as imported petroleum enlarged its share of the Japanese energy market. Both the coal operators and the coal miners' unions began to stress the *domestic* nature of their industry. They still were unable to work together on other issues, but their interests converged on this point. More and more, they argued that Japan should sustain the coal industry for reasons of national security as much as for economic reasons. This new justification for support of coal was highlighted by the Suez Crisis of late 1956, which blocked the flow of oil to Japan temporarily. This event actually cut two ways: Although it raised the possibility of an oil shortage, it was not nearly as serious a disruption as had been feared, which encouraged many new coal consumers to switch to oil. Even so, the trend toward greater Japanese dependence on foreign oil resources disturbed many Japanese. Foreign control of the oil-importing and refining firms similarly emerged as an issue of increasing concern.

FOREIGN INVESTMENT, "INDEPENDENCE," AND THE OIL INDUSTRY

Gaining independent Japanese control of the oil industry was a distinctly secondary goal for MITI in the early 1950s, after promotion of competition. MITI encouraged 4 oil importers who did not have foreign stock ownership to enter the oil-refining business between 1952 and 1954. In welcoming Idemitsu, Maruzen, Daikyō, and Tōa Oil Companies, MITI had two goals in mind. First, it hoped to decrease the influence of the foreign oil companies in the downstream portions of the oil industry, that is, marketing and sales. It publicly called for a goal of 30-percent control of market shares by non-foreign affiliated companies. Foreign ownership was not, however, the primary issue. More important, MITI was increasing the number of oil refiners in order to raise the level of competition among them. The real threat from the foreign-affiliated companies was that they would use their independent power to raise oil prices, drive up the cost of Japanese manufactured goods, and so jeopardize Japan's self-sufficiency policy. Non-affiliated firms were weaker and hungrier—and more likely to strive for lower prices, MITI reasoned. This is consistent with the fact that the government allowed *several* new firms to enter the refining business. Fear of foreign domination undoubtedly did play a part in the decision to keep the oil-refining business weak and fragmented. Although this fear contributed to policy, the primary concern was to keep oil prices to industry low.

There are other indications that national control of the oil industry was a low-priority issue for the Japanese in these years. For example, the Japanese oil companies did not make serious efforts to engage in the "upstream" activities of prospecting and extracting oil abroad in the 1950s. They did not have the resources to do this, and probably the majors did not encourage it. There were a number of other reasons why Japan did not pursue oil development. Traditionally, major Japanese financial groups had invested in coal mining rather than oil. Moreover, Japanese upstream and downstream petroleum operations were separated in 1941 when the Teikoku Petroleum Company was established, a division that was never reversed. Finally, the development of the Mideast fields in the 1950s caused an oil glut and low prices, which discouraged risky exploration by all potential developers.[34] These various obstacles meant that, to most Japanese, it seemed foolish to challenge the powerful international oil companies in their area of greatest strength. If energy independence in oil had seemed feasible, probably the Japanese would have pursued it more enthusiastically.

The single exception was the maverick entrepreneur Yamashita Tarō. Yamashita, who had been involved in the development of Manchuria during the 1930s, was motivated by the prewar conception of oil as a strategic commodity. He thought that Japan should develop overseas sources of crude oil in order to protect its national security. After the Suez Canal crisis of 1956, he established the Arabian Oil Company, signed agreements with Saudi Arabia and Kuwait to prospect in their territory in 1958, and eventually discovered the Khafji oil field there. Yamashita's point of view became more popular in the 1960s after Japan had become overwhelmingly dependent on its oil supplies, but in the mid-1950s, he had great difficulty financing his project. Yamashita eventually found backers from the electric-power and steel companies, but neither other oil industrialists nor the Japanese government showed much open interest in his plans.[35]

"Domesticating" the Japanese oil industry was not a realistic goal in the 1950s. Although, at first glance, the government policy to shift 30 percent of market share to "domestic" firms appears to have been successful, this did not mean that the international majors lost their influence in the Japanese oil industry. On the contrary, the pressure to compete among refiners in Japan increased reliance by local firms on the international majors during the 1950s. The endemic price wars meant that the Japanese companies had very little internal capital. Increasingly, the "domestic" as well as the foreign affiliates turned to the international firms for financing and technology to carry out their expansion plans. The majors tied their assistance to long-term crude contracts (to their benefit in those days when the price of oil was declining), so dependence on them for crude grew along with financial and technical dependence.[36] Between 1951 and 1960, the difference between affiliated and non-affiliated companies became one of degree rather than of kind.

The reliance of the Japanese oil refiners on the majors increased most sharply in the late 1950s and early 1960s, when all the Japanese companies introduced new catalytic cracking, alkylation, and hydro-desulphurization plants. The Japanese refiners were eager to get this new technology, available only through the major oil companies. However, this investment boom plunged them into debt. The funds needed, amounting to about $1 billion, came from the international oil companies and U.S. banks, particularly the Bank of America. In 1961, the Japanese oil refiners could provide for 56 percent of construction costs from internal funds, but only 36 percent in 1963 and a mere 15 percent in 1964.[37]

In particular, the non-foreign-affiliated Japanese firms borrowed heavily from these overseas sources. They simply were not able to raise money any other way. Maruzen Oil Company, for example, was a "domestic" producer, but it renegotiated a contract with its prewar sales partner, Union Oil Company of California, for crude oil supplies, technology, and sales agreements. In the late 1950s, Maruzen borrowed heavily from American banks to finance expansion. By March 1963, the company was 520 million yen in debt, and had to give 30 percent of its shares to Union Oil to meet its obligations, thus losing its "domestic" status. Meanwhile, Daikyō Oil Company signed technological agreements with two major oil companies, while Idemitsu borrowed abroad. Both firms went deeply into debt, and signed more tied-crude import agreements with the majors. This was significant, because new, independent crude sellers were appearing in the late 1950s, and so the international oil market was becoming freer. The Japanese companies, "domestic" and affiliates alike, were unable to take advantage of these new suppliers because they were committed to their long-term contracts with the majors. These dependencies, on foreign sources and foreign companies, seemed more ominous as they increased in importance to the economy. By 1962, the foreign petroleum companies held long-term supply contracts for 90 percent of Japan's crude-oil imports, enjoyed a major interest in about 75 percent of its refining capacity, and owned 25 percent of the industry directly.[38]

The link between economic development and greater reliance on American oil companies had been foreseen and welcomed by American policymakers. In 1949, representatives of Standard Oil, SCAP, and George Kennan had agreed that controls over Japan's oil industry were desirable as a way of limiting future Japanese actions. American—and Allied—desires to control Japanese war potential through control of the oil supply lingered on, while, at the same time, facilitating Japanese access to oil became a major U.S. policy concern. The trend in American policy was toward acceptance of Japan as a military ally, but there were many among Japan's former enemies who drew comfort from the fact that crude-oil supplies remained outside Japanese control. Hints that this feeling continued to be influential after the Occupation include the withdrawal of a bill before the Diet in 1954 to nationalize the former naval refinery at Yokkaichi (and allow 8 private refiners jointly to operate it) because the Japanese government feared it would jeopardize negotiations over the Mutual Security Agreement.[39] In petroleum, American strategic planning set limits on Japanese self-sufficiency, although not on Japanese economic recovery.

The shift to oil also epitomized the American strategy of "U.S.-Japan cooperation," which emphasized greater volumes of trade and *net* export levels, rather than Japan's scarcity of foreign exchange. The U.S.-Japan economic cooperation plan meant, among other things, that the Japanese could assume stability and access to fuel supplies abroad. This was a measure of the success with which the United States was able to impose its version of order onto the world economy, since petroleum from the Mideast was more stable than coal from Kyushu. The international oil-supply system based on the majors lasted for twenty-five years, quite remarkable given the latent instability of its foundations. Yet, what is important here is that the Americans devoted considerable energy to assuring Japan an adequate supply of imported oil. The Japanese felt some unease about placing themselves in such a dependent position vis-à-vis the

United States, but their choices were limited. According to one Japanese scholar, the Japanese shared the assumption that U.S. world dominance would last indefinitely.[40]

The Japanese were divided over the question of accepting direct foreign investment in the general economy and specifically in the oil industry. They were not as uniformly opposed to the idea as is often believed. Aiichirō Fujiyama, President of the Japan Chamber of Commerce, spoke for a solid block of opinion in a 1953 article which argued that, while increasing Japanese exports to the United States would be a positive move, "it is, however, far more important that the United States should recognize Japan as an investment market for her capital, rather than as a market for her manufactures, so that the unbalance of the payment accounts between Japan and the United States may be adjusted by the export of capital by the latter."[41] Japanese business leaders still saw U.S. private lenders as a key capital source.

Expressions of concern about foreign economic domination started to appear in the business press and in government pronouncements from 1952, along with continuing pleas for investment from overseas.[42] The storm of protest over the World Bank loans for electric-power plants in late 1953 added to the controversy. Japanese bureaucrats were becoming more anxious about using foreign capital as a way to improve Japan's economic health. They correctly feared that this was a remedy that could easily deepen Japan's most serious economic problems rather than solve them. As foreign-owned firms in Japan prospered and profits were remitted abroad, the net result could become a capital drain from Japan. Worse, the remittances were mainly to U.S. owners, which meant that they had to be paid in dollars. Ironically, foreign investment might well lead to less capital and lower dollar reserves in Japan, already two of the nation's most pressing economic problems.[43] Japanese government officials and business leaders also worried that, since most Japanese firms were financed largely by debt, they would be bought up easily by rich foreign companies. Firms that were trying to rationalize should not have to worry about hostile takeovers, they reasoned. This was rarely a concern with domestic firms, because no Japanese

company had spare cash in those years. The official compromise was
to balk at contracts that allowed more than 50-percent foreign control.[44]

The Japanese continued to look for private foreign capital for big
projects like electric-power development, but they grew increasingly wary of it as a general tool for development within the larger
strategy of industrial rationalization. Reliance on foreign capital did
not mean that Japan would automatically have more capital or more
hard currency. It also limited Japanese government control over the
economy, just when resources needed to be coordinated the most.
Although foreign capital investment had seemed to be the only
answer to Japan's problems in 1948 and 1949, by 1952 its drawbacks were more obvious. Yet, in 1951, the ESB argued that "the
inducement of foreign capital must be strongly promoted for the
accomplishment of economic self-sufficiency."[45] The Japanese were
still not sure that they could manage without foreign capital.

This uneasiness about foreign investment affected policy toward
petroleum refining, the industry with the strongest foreign-capital
presence, by introducing an element of ambivalence toward the industry.[46] The Japanese officials feared that a foreign-dominated industry could jack up prices to the key industrial sectors. At the
same time, they knew that Japan was not strong enough to antag-
onize the powerful and united international oil firms. As oil refining
increased its importance to the Japanese economy, its sharp foreign
flavor became more distasteful to the Japanese. This translated into
an uncertain oil policy—alternately nurturing and prohibiting—
throughout the decade. The oil-refining industry demonstrates the
contradictions within the Japanese push to become self-sufficient.
"Independence," in fact, meant much closer ties to the international
economy and to the United States because of Japan's need for capital, technology, and machinery. This dependence deepened as the
economy recovered and the need of the Japanese oil-refining companies for further infusions of capital and technology grew accordingly. The decision to develop petrochemicals in 1955 further accentuated this trend, since that technology had to be imported as
well.

Moreover, development of an independent atomic-power program was disappointingly slow. The Japanese had originally imagined an ambitious development plan, including a fast breeder reactor, but both budgetary and technical constraints showed that they had been too optimistic. By 1959, it was clear that atomic energy was still a long-term solution when Japan needed an immediate response to the sudden decline of coal.[47] Japan's dearth of uranium resources and lack of skills to develop a complete nuclear fuel cycle explain why the Japanese rather wistfully named atomic energy a "semi-autonomous" energy resource. Nuclear power's failure as a domestic energy source meant that, even when it did develop, Japanese energy dependence would grow rather than decrease with the economy. Dependence on foreign oil and atomic technology was a structural problem, built into Japan's postwar economic strategy. This dependence did not necessarily foreclose opportunities for prosperity, but it did limit Japanese independence in both the world and domestic economies.

Through 1959, coal was still officially the main industrial fuel of Japan, although, by then, no one expected annual production ever to exceed 70 million tons, and most projections had been reduced to 50 to 55 million tons. Production at that level would maintain the coal mines as an important industry and regional mainstay, although some smaller mines would have to close. It would also mean that a significant portion of Japanese fuel supplies would be domestically produced. Ongoing rationalization would keep coal prices competitive with imports, it was expected. In other words, the coal industry would not grow with the rest of the economy but would retain a steady and signficant presence. This was the official outlook in the late 1950s. However, the real rationales for retaining the coal industry increasingly related to issues of welfare and national security rather than any hope of economic competition.[48] From 1955 to 1960, the coal industry visibly declined.

ELEVEN

Planning for an Economy Based on Imported Oil

Trained to count in units of ten, we are all quick to confer historic import to the beginning of each new decade and to divide historical trends accordingly. Usually this is misleading, but occasionally history imitates mathematics. Thus, 1960 was a milestone year—the moment when the Japanese economy was poised on the threshold of high-speed growth. During the next twelve years, the economy would burgeon at unprecedented rates, and the Japanese at last would leave behind the physical destruction of the Pacific War.

High-speed growth was made possible by a variety of factors inside and outside Japan. Some were beyond Japanese control, such as the favorable context of expanding international trade during the 1950s and 1960s. The most important of these external factors was U.S. encouragement of Japanese economic development. From 1948 on, American economic and strategic policy in East Asia was focused on reconstruction of the Japanese economy. American economic assistance centered in the three key areas of providing advanced technology, capital, and markets for the Japanese. This assistance continued beyond the Occupation, as is evident both in single industries, such as electric power and oil refining, and in grand economic policy.

Within Japan, economic prosperity was possible only because the Japanese were able to reach a broad political and economic settlement after the catalyzing effects of defeat in World War II. The failure of the pre-surrender national economic strategy forced a re-

evaluation of economic and social priorities in postwar Japan. This
led to a new commitment to economic planning and economic recovery itself, a commitment that grew out of postwar labor-union
efforts as much as bureaucratic or business efforts. Economic policy
in Japan represents the integration of the goals of these (and other)
groups. This integration was uneven and hard-won and reflects the
sometimes intense conflict that surrounded reconstruction. Moreover, economic policy developed only slowly, as the Japanese negotiated each compromise and adjusted to each new change in the
external environment.

The range of participants in discussions about economic policy
widened after the war. Labor unions in particular took the opportunity provided by the partial collapse of the old order to demand a
greater share of wealth and of economic decision making. They also
built on a new set of legal protections established by the Occupation. Ironically, perhaps the American action in Japan that most
contributed to later economic growth was the initial postwar demilitarization and democratization policy. Labor-union power declined after Japanese conservatives regrouped behind Prime Minister Yoshida Shigeru, but the change was still profound when compared
to pre-surrender Japan. The unions had won legitimacy through
their acceptance of responsibility for economic revival at the end of
the war. This legitimacy, workers' rights to a rising standard of
living, and to job security all became tenets of the Japanese economy. In turn, this recognition of the economic (although not all
the political) aspirations of urban workers and tenant farmers was a
key ingredient of high-speed growth. By 1960, higher urban wages
and rural incomes had created a larger domestic market, the last
and knottiest obstacle to economic growth. As the planners at the
Ministry of Foreign Affairs and the electric-power workers had both
argued in 1946, Japan could not thrive without this development.

Government policy was also important. The commitment to production and to rationalization policy, with its strong emphasis on
technology-driven productivity increases, was an important incentive to growth. The fact that the Japanese government provided a

planned and rational framework for businesses clearly had a positive impact on investment. It also created a forum for discussion and compromise among industries. Not only did government policy provide a safety net for risk-taking businesses; it also created channels for the flow of economic information. The annual Economic Stabilization Board White Papers set the tone for information sharing both within and outside of the government from 1947. Most Japanese today probably take for granted the vast quantities of statistics that emanate from government offices, but this legacy of the Katayama months was, in its own modest way, a revolutionary change.

Through its economic plans, the government was able to mediate between its domestic constituents and the foreign-policy experts within the U.S. government. Although the Japanese rejected the United States as an explicit model of development in many respects, the rationalization policy dovetailed with the contemporary technocratic American assumption that economic progress was the high road to American-style democracy. The development of economic planning gave the Japanese an increasingly sophisticated means to evaluate the changes taking place in the international economy, which, in turn, allowed them to reevaluate and improve Japan's place within that larger structure.

This integrative quality certainly characterized the "priority-production" policy and the rationalization plans, the two most important official economic plans discussed in earlier chapters. Examination of these two policies reveals the evolution of Japanese postwar economic thinking. The priority-production policy at last revived production, over a year after the end of the war. It established the official assumption that Japan would embark on a strategy of developing high-wage, high-valued-added goods and the precedent of focusing on a few core industries at one time. Most important, it provided a common basis for bureaucrats, businessmen, and labor organizers to talk about economic recovery. A shrewd compromise among all the competing ideas for reconstruction, the priority-production policy delicately threaded its way through the arguments by elevating planning as the common thread. Thus, the priority-production policy, by promoting long-term economic planning, provided the first basis for a new economic reconstruction.

The priority-production policy, however, left a number of issues unaddressed. One of the most important was Japan's reintegration into the world economy. In 1948, the Americans changed the parameters of the Japanese debate by insisting on a severe economic austerity program, designed to halt inflation, encourage exports, and depress domestic spending. The Americans saw this in terms of the world political economy, but the Japanese were horrified by its domestic implications. Forced to abandon the free-spending priority-production policy, they anxiously searched for a new approach.

Their solution was rationalization policy. This 1949 concept used technology imports as the key to unlock increases in productivity to generate both investment capital and a rise in living standards. This implied improving the quality of Japanese goods in order to promote exports as well as domestic consumption. The policy also involved a reorganization of the banking system and tax structure to encourage technological improvements in industry. It provided a lasting framework for business and government to iron out their differences, and is the core of Japanese industrial policy today.

The implications of rationalization policy for labor were far more mixed. Rationalization provided an opportunity for managers, government officials, and Occupationaires to attack the labor unions and enforce longer hours and lower wages. Many took advantage of this opportunity, and these years were a nadir of influence for the labor movement. Yet, it would be a mistake to dismiss rationalization as entirely an attack on working people or their unions. The need to accommodate the aspirations of organized labor was explicit in the rationalization concept. Although longer hours and lower wages cut the costs of producing goods, this strategy could not contribute to improvements in their quality. Rising skill levels—and worker commitment to quality—were both necessary to rationalization. Japanese workers, like their Western counterparts, responded to these needs by insisting on rising standards of living and improvements in their status. Japanese elite planners hoped that rationalization would lead to higher living standards without any need for redistribution of wealth. In both Japan and America, planners put their faith in technology as the answer to social as well as economic problems. In truth, this faith was justified for the majority of Japanese workers. Real wages did rise steadily through the 1950s, pulled along by larger increases in productivity. This was not true for workers in every industry, however, and conflict erupted where this implicit compact broke down. Acceptance of rationalization policy extended precisely as far as its benefits.

Although economic planning was important in Japan, attention must also be paid to the limits of planning. Rationalization was spurred by unanticipated as well as intended forces. In the energy sector, the bitter squabbling among the 9 new electric-power companies after 1951 was an unexpected incentive to rationalization. So was the ferocious rate at which the oil refineries replaced their equipment in order to squeeze the most out of their foreign-exchange allotments. Subsequently, both government and business became more sophisticated at manipulating this kind of competition to suit policy goals, as in the petrochemicals and atomic-power industries, but this was a later development. Through the 1950s, the Japanese were hesitantly groping their way toward an economic strategy.

Not only were some successes unplanned, but some national plans were dismal failures, preeminently those directed at coal. The Japanese lavished resources on the coal industry through the 1950s, and the rationalization policy itself began with the coal and steel industries. But the mines never fulfilled the role planned for them. This failure eventually forced a major reevaluation of general economic policy as well as of energy policy. Energy posed one of the most difficult problems in the task of economic redevelopment. The search for a dependable and low-priced energy source was a constant theme of the postwar years and the Japanese experimented in turn with coal, hydroelectricity, oil, and atomic energy, attempting to find a mix that would address their needs.

The persistent problem of supplying energy had spurred grand economic policy since 1946. Providing Japan with this most basic industrial commodity was the central task of postwar planners. They could not achieve a sophisticated, high-wage economy without resolving the energy crisis. Energy (and steel) became the key proving grounds for Japan's postwar industrial policies. The Japanese first grappled with their need to upgrade production and then productivity levels in the energy sector. Coal, electric power, and oil refining provided models (and instructive anti-models) for developing other economic sectors. Later industrial policies were more sophisticated, for example, incorporating policies toward declining industries. Indeed, energy itself provided the opportunity to upgrade the whole economy. It was the surge in energy-related technologies, or the "energy revolution," that made Japan's productivity improvements possible in the 1950s. Energy was more than a policy task and industrial development model; it also acted as a technological spur on a grand scale. However, the Japanese could only take full advantage of this last and most powerful economic role by giving up national control of their energy supply. This abandonment of the domestic coal industry was a long and slow process undertaken only reluctantly.

The formal realization that resource-poor Japan had to switch to imported energy when it became cheaper than domestic fuel was one of the last keys to economic growth to emerge. Without this final step, high-speed growth would have been impossible. Taking this step meant embracing the risks inherent in participation in the international economy, and the Japanese would not do so until 1960. In practice, the government had already moved in this direction in 1955, when it decided to encourage petrochemicals production. For the first time the Japanese began to use Japan's oil dependence to national advantage rather than to reduce it, but they did not yet appreciate the implications of the decision. This shift in consciousness did not occur until the Arisawa Report of December 1959.

THE "ENERGY REVOLUTION" RECOGNIZED: THE ARISAWA REPORT

Arisawa Hiromi had continued to advise the government on economic and energy matters since he created the priority production policy in 1946. In 1950, he championed the argument that Japan should minimize its import bill by development of domestic energy resources. Thus, it is significant that it was Arisawa who initiated the shift to reliance on imports. He personified the Japanese nation's shift in thinking. In 1959, Arisawa headed a commission that studied the energy situation in Japan and in Europe. In December, he declared that the decline of the coal industry was a global and historic event, the result of the "international energy revolution." He realized that the rationalization measures of the past ten years were themselves the greatest obstacle to recovery in the coal industry. As he explained in a book published a year after writing this report: "The most important spur to economic growth was the introduction of foreign technology, which allowed great leaps in productivity. This had a major impact on the energy market by introducing 'new' energy—heavy oil, high-quality imported coal, and natural gas."[1]

This insight meant a number of things. First, the coal industry could *never* hope to regain its old dominance, because its decline was due as much to technological changes as to immediate price competition. The Japanese had to learn to accept the "worldwide technological revolution in fluids," since they could not reverse it. Arisawa argued that Japan should rely mainly on petroleum and treat coal as a secondary fuel, while working to develop atomic energy for the future. Second, he accepted the argument that energy and natural resources should be treated like any other candidate for rationalization. If oil was more efficient, Japan should accept oil. He rejected the increasingly popular arguments that coal should be supported for national-security or social-welfare reasons. Arisawa thought that the competitive market should be the mechanism used to determine precisely how important coal would continue to be to the Japanese economy. Price would be the sole determinant of efficiency. In other words, competition should be used as a tool to enforce rationalization, just as had been done previously in such diverse industries as electric power, oil refining, and steel-making. Although some of those earlier applications had been unintended, by 1959 the Japanese had begun to apply the same principle deliberately. They now expected that allowing firms to compete for market share under regulated conditions would encourage technological development.

This decision to rely on market mechanisms to determine the size of the coal industry was the most controversial of Arisawa's recommendations, because it minimized government assistance to coal-mining regions. Arisawa believed that massive government intervention was unnecessary because the coal industry could maintain a "competitive coexistence" with imported oil. Assistance to the coal operators was also undesirable, since it would discourage rationalization, just as subsidies had during the 1940s. He suggested a number of measures to centralize coal mining as a smaller, more efficient industry by 1963, a deadline imposed to force the coal industry to take the rationalization plan seriously. The Commission members calculated that the coal industry could be competitive as a supplier to large buyers like the electric-power industry if it dropped average coal prices by 1,200 yen per ton by 1963. At that price, they believed the industry could sell 50 to 55 million tons a year. This leaner, more efficient industry would be created by tightening the "scrap-and-build" policy. The Commission recommended raising the allowed minimum size of mines from producers of 3 million tons to 6.3 million tons of coal per year, and forcing the 200 mines that were smaller to close. The report further recommended cutting back the mine labor force by 100,000 miners, one third of the total, by 1963. The Commission also encouraged the government to continue funding for rationalization in the biggest mines.[2] Money for this purpose eventually came from an increase in the tariffs on petroleum imports, which were raised in 1960 from 2 to 6 percent on crude and from 6.5 to 10 percent on heavy oil.[3]

The Arisawa Report is often—and correctly—described as the earliest marker of a new era. For the first time, in this report the Japanese officially recognized their massive dependence on imported petroleum. Only in December 1959 did they fully accept the global interdependence inherent in their postwar quest for economic "self-sufficiency" in the energy sector. This was a more sophisticated model of development which allowed—in fact, demanded—greater interaction with the world economy. It was this transformation that allowed the Japanese to prosper and, eventually, carve out a niche for Japan in the international economy, by removing a brake on economic growth that had operated until 1960. The new prosperity of the 1960s was built on the cycle of massive energy imports and exports of energy-intensive goods. This buoyed the economy, as Nakayama Ichirō had predicted in late 1949. At the same time, it was a riskier strategy, in that Japanese vulnerability to international economic fluctuations, political changes abroad, and U.S. policy in East Asia all increased along with Japan's import levels. The Japanese continued to struggle with the problem of this relationship between economic growth and security. As their economy grew, however, the Japanese were also transforming the global economy. More and more resource sellers became dependent on their Japanese customers, who purchased ever-greater amounts. The Japanese had, in effect, shifted a large part of the uncertainty of their energy supply to the international sphere.

This new development in energy policy was closely tied to a concurrent transformation of rationalization policy itself. The recent experience of the coal (and textile) industries had shown that rationalization was not equally possible in all sectors. Coal mining, which could not keep up with the rapid changes taking place in petroleum technology, had become a declining industry. Arisawa, in fact, underestimated the problems of the coal industry in 1959. His "competitive-coexistence" plan failed when the coal industry foundered more rapidly than he had expected.

The success of rationalization policy depended partly on world trade and technology markets, over which the Japanese had little control. The Japanese knew this, but originally they had assumed that new technology would upgrade any industry. The problems of declining industries required a different policy. By 1959, they also had learned to study the effects of rationalization itself, based on their experiences in electric power, oil refining, and other industries. Rationalization of one industry could either help or hinder rationalization in another, and the Japanese were only beginning to understand how to manipulate these inter-industry linkages in the late 1950s. These problems had to be addressed before the Japanese could transform their policy for economic reconstruction into one suitable for growth. Without a larger analysis, they were unprepared for the inevitable shrinkage of the technology gap or for less favorable world-trade conditions.

This analysis emerged out of MITI in late 1959. The new "industrial-structure" policy used the metaphor of a biological life cycle to define and justify criteria for rationalization.[4] Industries at the beginning and end of their life cycle—like infant and aged humans—require more care than mature sectors. From 1960, government assistance was increasingly targeted toward those two classes of industries. This was an important refinement of rationalization policy, which had previously emphasized basic industry. The two original declining industries were textiles and coal, although the mature adult industries of one era are the pensioners of the next, as the oil refiners and petrochemical firms discovered in the 1970s. In an equally important refinement, unlike rationalization, industrial structure is a dynamic concept: Appropriate policies for any given industry will change over time. Moreover, the effects of rationalization within one industry on development of another have become a standard aspect of study for industrial-structure policy, providing an analytical framework for Japanese planners which they continue to use today. Industrial-structure policy also assumes a permanent need for economic planning and government assistance to all industries at some stage of the life cycle. It has permanently incorporated economic planning into the Japanese economy. In theory as well as practice, economic planning has been institutionalized in postwar Japan.

ACCEPTING AMERICA, ACCEPTING LABOR

The Arisawa Report was, indeed, the sign of a new, more sophisticated approach to economic growth. Yet, like any true boundary, it also stands as the last statement of an old policy. Its incisive understanding of the global economic superiority of petroleum was not matched by political sensitivity to two major Japanese concerns: dependence on the United States and the plight of the coal-mining regions. Government blindness to these concerns led to two enormous social protests in 1960.

Although the Japanese consciously chose to favor cheap, imported oil by adopting Arisawa's recommendations, this choice engendered a growing unease about dependence on the United States. This was part of a much larger reevaluation of Japan's political and economic relationship with America in 1960. The U.S.-Japan Security Treaty revisions propelled the political aspects of this dependence into public consciousness, triggering months of protests and riots. This debate forced the Japanese to reconsider the highly emotional and divisive issues of national sovereignty, their place in international Cold War politics, their position on nuclear warfare, and the continued presence of foreign military bases on Japanese soil. Meanwhile, public deliberation over trade "liberalization" made economic dependence equally controversial. The Japanese were due to end trade and foreign-currency restrictions in 1960 to conform with the International Monetary Fund charter, stirring great anxiety within Japan over possible foreign domination of the economy.

Energy policy was directly affected by the loss of currency restrictions since the government controlled the flow of oil into Japan through foreign-exchange limits. The IMF liberalization put new pressures on the coal industry and further curbed Japanese ability to protect it.[5] With these general concerns as a background, the growing reliance on foreign oil disturbed the Japanese more and more. The concern heightened when it become obvious that the Arisawa Commission had erred in its assumption that coal could remain competitive. From 1962, more cheap oil started flowing into the country, seriously cutting into the coal market.[6] International oil prices continued to fall beyond the level anticipated in 1959, and the Japanese went over the same ground again and again in their analyses of this problem.

This concern over dependence is visible in the rhetoric and quick passage of the Oil Industry Law in May 1962, which restored to MITI the powers it had wielded through the Foreign Exchange Law in the oil-refining industry. It authorized MITI to issue permits for plant expansion and mergers, write import plans, and set standard petroleum prices. The Oil Industry Law also expressed the goal of providing 30 percent of Japan's oil needs through Japanese firms rather than the majors. Talk of creating a "Japanese major," eventually culminating in Kyōdō Oil Company, also began at that time.[7]

Nonetheless, the issue of national security was still most important at the level of rhetoric. The Oil Industry Law was welcomed by many of the oil refiners and Keidanren for bringing stability to the viciously competitive market. Its main function was to regulate the domestic Japanese oil market and ensure a steady supply of petroleum as a service to Japanese industry.[8] As such, it cannot be described primarily as an expression of economic nationalism. Rather, it is a potent symbol of the ongoing tension within Japan about its place in the world economy.

Through the 1960s, Arisawa's 1959 conclusions were repeatedly reaffirmed in a series of policy statements. In reluctant response to the steady decline of the coal industry, the Japanese became more pessimistic, moving from an "oil-main, coal-secondary" strategy to "gradual withdrawal" from coal, to "total reliance on oil."[9] Rather than avoiding reintegration, the Japanese slowly began to look for the most attractive niche in the global economy into which to fit themselves. They discussed retaining the coal industry as a national-security move, but this was more symbolic than real. The Japanese had accepted integration into the America-dominated world economy. National control of energy resources beyond a token level was no longer a realistic goal.

The Arisawa Report also failed to anticipate the depth of resistance to its exclusive focus on economic competition. The most concentrated opposition came from the coal miners, and a 6-month miners' strike at Mitsui's Miike mine forced a withdrawal from the implications of the Arisawa Report. The coal miners demanded that the Japanese government reassess the basic assumptions of the report and redesign coal policy to consider regional economies, social welfare, and national-security issues in addition to price. The miners did not stand alone. Their demand that quality of life and equity issues be given higher priority concurred with a more general move away from the overwhelmingly "production-first" mentality of the postwar years toward a more consumer-oriented strategy.

The coal operators recognized the ultimatum in the Arisawa Report and responded with aggressive rationalization measures. Prominent among these were cuts in the labor force, which put them into immediate conflict with Tanrō. At Miike, the Tanrō-affiliated union had won control over lay-off procedures after the 1953 strike, and so the work force had shrunk more slowly than at most mines. Just after the Arisawa Report was released, the Miike mine manager fired 1,277 of the 14,000 miners, including 300 union activists, whom he castigated as "production obstructionists." This procedure violated the agreement worked out in 1953, and the Miike union immediately protested. The mine manager responded on 25 January 1960 by locking out the workers in order to prevent a repetition of the 1953 strike, when only a few miners in key positions officially struck, while the others went to "work."

The Miike lockout and strike lasted 282 days, to 1 November 1960 and took on a symbolic importance beyond the struggle of the miners to retain their jobs. Employers saw it as a way to crush a particularly militant union; Sōhyō, as a crucial battle for labor rights; the Japan Socialist Party and the Liberal Democratic Party, as a forum in which to discredit each other; and Japanese generally, as a conflict over power and political legitimacy in their nation. For many Japanese, the Miike miners came to symbolize a disappearing society, characterized by local loyalties and personal relationships. Their struggle to keep their jobs was compared to Japan's struggle to retain its identity in a global economy which seemed destined to reshape the island country in alien ways. Thus, Miike reflected the myriad economic and social tensions within Japan.

The union lost the battle. It faced formidable problems, primarily the poor economic condition of the coal industry. In addition, Tanrō faced a much stronger opponent. Although the coal operators had little support from other industrialists in their attempt to exclude foreign oil, they had considerable assistance in their capacity as foes of the labor movement. Nikkeiren organized its industrial and power-company members to continue to buy coal at an old price, even though it had just been decreased by 70 cents per ton, to help finance Mitsui Mining Company's lockout. The fuel-user industries wanted to cut back on their coal purchases, but they recognized an opportunity to weaken Sōhyō.[10]

As in earlier strikes, the crucial blow to the union was dissension within its ranks. In March, a break-away union formed with about 4,500 members, mainly from white-collar workers in the personnel and accounting divisions of the mine. This development was encouraged both by Sōhyō's rival union federation, Dōmei, and by the Miike coal manager.[11] The company quickly settled with the second union, but the first union remained on strike and refused to let the members of the second union back in the mine to work. Picket lines grew to 15,000 people, while 13,000 police were dispatched from around the nation to keep the two sides apart. Eventually, the first union was forced to ask for mediation and the Central Labor Relations Board upheld the company position, first in April and again in August. The mine manager was allowed to select 1,277 workers for dismissal, as he had wished, and was only required to increase their severance pay by 10,000 yen.[12] Institutionally, this was a major blow to Tanrō, since many other coal operators took the opportunity of the Miike defeat to fire union members.

If one steps back and evaluates the overall effect of the strike, however, in the midst of their defeat the miners were able to wrest an important victory, to change public perceptions through their protest. Because of their struggle, and the great upheaval it had caused, the Japanese began to reconsider coal policy in terms of its social consequences. This perceptual shift extended to all economic policy, and from 1960 more attention was focused on consumption and employment. The coal miners were able to draw attention to their desperation, more stark when contrasted to the growing comfort in the rest of the economy. The standard of living was rising for most Japanese in 1960, and the Miike strike forced them to recognize that this new prosperity was not shared by all their countrymen. Their shamed realization was epitomized by the instant fame of a 1960 book of photographs, *The Children of Chikuhō,* which depicted the dire poverty of coal-miner children. [13]

The Miike strike influenced Japan beyond the scope of the coal industry because it tapped a number of diverse and powerful tensions within modern Japanese society. The Miike strike was, in part, an expression of tension between a local and the national economy, and between community survival and central-government policy. The miners and their local community together demanded a greater share of Japanese wealth. In 1953, the Miike miners had succeeded partly because they had effectively organized their local region, which remained deeply involved in mine issues through the 1960 strike as well. As in Appalachia, there was little other industry in the area, and major coal-mine dismissals meant local economic hardship. This and other protests forced the Japanese government to consider regional equity as well as economic growth. [14]

This strike was also the final bid by the postwar labor movement to develop a different and autonomous vision of economic development, based on labor control of job tenure. This attempt was not successful, but it did move the Japanese government toward more social-welfare programs and a greater acceptance of responsibility for those Japanese who were left behind in the generally increasing prosperity. Broad questions of social equity were reintroduced into energy policymaking at the urging of the labor unions and the coal-mine regions. Once again, the coal miners asserted their right to a livelihood and the responsibility of the government to ensure it for them.

This shift of attention to the social consequences of energy policy meant withdrawal from the implications of the Arisawa Report in two general areas: relaxation of the "scrap" procedures outlined in 1959, and more direct assistance to miners and mining regions. Both government and business plans changed. One new government proposal called for a mandatory minimum wage law: this was defeated by business opposition. It was also rejected as inadequate by Tanrō, since it was combined with a plan to cut 76,000 coal miners' jobs. [15] Instead, Keidanren negotiated a continuation of the existing agreements between major industrial fuel users in the electric-power, steel, gas, and cement industries, in order to maintain a stable market for coal. The electric-power companies pledged to increase their coal consumption to 18 million tons in fiscal 1963 and 20 million tons in 1967. Similarly, the iron-and-steel and gas industries each promised to buy 12 million tons of coal in 1963 and 13 million tons in 1967. This was a "gentlemen's agreement" but later became a legal arrangement.[16] Keidanren and the user industries agreed that maintenance of Tanrō jobs and social order was worth some loss of profits.[17]

The Diet passed a compromise assistance package on 2 March 1963, which set consumption of coal at the comparatively high figure of 60 million tons, established a special loan system for mine improvements, reconsidered the plan to scrap old mines because of its effect on local economies, raised unemployment benefits to former miners for three years to 600 yen per day instead of the standard 450 yen, and increased taxes or tariffs on heavy oil to pay for this. This bill originally had been introduced in the special Diet session of December 1962 but failed to pass because of political maneuvering within the Japan Socialist Party. In addition, several special laws passed—to aid displaced miners in December 1959, and three measures to promote new industries in coal-mining regions in June 1961, November 1961, and April 1962. These only partly alleviated the coal miners' problems, but the miners had won a "soft landing" for workers in future declining industries.[18] They themselves did not enjoy the full benefits of this policy, but it was largely their efforts that forced the issue into the political arena.

These assistance policies were adopted to ease social unrest rather than to resolve economic problems. As such, they were rejections of the rationalization strategy outlined in the 1959 Arisawa Report. Although not integral to routine economic planning as in the immediate postwar years, the labor unions were still able to initiate major reevaluations of energy policy by publicly invoking the concept of equity. This was because the workers themselves had kept the idea of the postwar settlement alive with their acceptance of production and productivity increases. They also maintained pressure through their unions, the *shuntō* tactic, and political agitation. Miike, the last attempt to win labor participation and control of national economic policymaking, failed, but, conversely, it enhanced the legitimacy of labor claims to share in the growing national wealth. The unions had established themselves immediately after the war as valid participants in the economy who were entitled to the fruits of growth. When this compact broke down, as it did with the coal miners, the ensuing conflict involved the entire nation. The ongoing tension over these implicit promises to the labor unions is an enduring legacy of the first postwar decade.

The historic concern of the labor unions—to raise their members' standard of living—also was institutionalized in broad economic policy in 1960. This was reaffirmed in the new Income-Doubling Policy, inaugurated by Prime Minister Ikeda Hayato in December. This plan concentrated on raising the standard of living and increasing consumption of the Japanese people. It stressed the link between economic growth and consumer spending more directly than had earlier plans.[19] After the upheavals of the Miike and the Security Treaty revision struggles, Ikeda recognized the need to concentrate directly on these issues, in order to *recreate* a broad consensus on economic policy and deflect political criticism of the government. The Income-Doubling Plan did not contain radically new economic concepts: Rather, its importance was political. It recast the existing high-speed growth policy into a more popular mold to win back public support. Like the 1946 priority-production policy, the Income-Doubling Plan was a government response to demands for new directions in economic policy. Consensus on economic policy existed exactly as long as the Japanese people believed the material conditions of their lives were improving. Beyond that moment, it became brittle indeed.[20]

Ikeda also believed that the plan was good economics. It reached back to a basic concept of postwar Japanese economic policy, first articulated in the 1946 Ministry of Foreign Affairs report, that Japan had to increase wages and the domestic standard of living in order to develop a stable economy. Toward this end, the Income-Doubling Plan included a major commitment to education and training.[21] It also contained specific proposals to narrow the wage gap between workers in small and large firms, and raise incomes in poorer prefectures. Moreover, the Income-Doubling Plan reaffirmed government responsibility for social welfare and increased spending considerably in this area, notably by drafting a national social-security program. These efforts would, it was hoped, achieve a dual goal. They would expand domestic purchasing power, which would not only raise general standards of living, but also provide a stable market for Japanese industry. The Income-Doubling Plan contained all the basic premises the Ministry of Foreign Affairs planners had designated as crucial to economic development in 1946: recognition of American dominance in the world economy, the interdependence of politics and economics, economic planning, and guarantees of higher standards of living for the Japanese people.[22]

By 1960, Japan's political economy achieved a new postwar settlement. In the energy sector, from that year, Japan relied primarily on imported fuels; imported coal grew in importance along with oil from 1974. Moreover, energy policy had become more tightly integrated into general economic policy, reflecting the primacy of planning itself within postwar Japan. Economic planning continued to evolve, gradually widening its focus on consumption and equity as well as on production. At the same time, the development of industrial-structure policy helped the Japanese move to a more sophisticated niche in the world economy. The war was truly over.

Notes

Notes

1. INTRODUCTION

1. James Morley, "The First Seven Weeks"; Masahiro Hosoya, "Selected Aspects of the Zaibatsu Dissolution in Occupied Japan, 1945–1952"; Joe B. Moore, *Japanese Workers and the Struggle for Power, 1945–1947*. Hosoya details the ways in which the 4 main zaibatsu did not adequately consider U.S. reform policy when making plans in 1945–1946.

2. Densan Chūō Kyōdō Tōsō Iinkai, 7 October 1946 edition, Densan Yōkyū Kyūyo Minshuka An, quoted in Rōdō Sōgi Chōsakai, ed., *Densan Sōgi,* pp. 70–72.

3. On American economic policy in Europe, see Michael J. Hogan, "American Marshall Planners and the Search for a European Neocapitalism"; Michael J. Hogan, *The Marshall Plan: America, Britain, and the reconstruction of Western Europe, 1947–1952;* Charles Maier, "The Politics of Productivity: Foundations of American International Economic Policy after World War II."

4. One example of this in the energy field was Eisenhower's Atoms for Peace campaign. See Blanche Wiesen Cook, *The Declassified Eisenhower,* especially Ch. 8, for other examples.

5. Nihon Tankō Rōdō Kumiai, ed., *Tanrō Jū-nen Shi,* pp. 173, 183.

6. For the shift in discussion, see speeches in Japan Coal Association, ed., *International Coal Conference, October 1963.* For later commitments by managers to workers in declining firms and industries, see Richard Pascale and Thomas P. Rohlen, "The Mazda Turnaround," and Ronald Dore, *Flexible Rigidities.*

7. See Ira C. Magaziner and Thomas M. Hout, *Japanese Industrial Policy.* Also see Jimmy W. Wheeler, Merit E. Janow, and Thomas Pepper, *Japanese Industrial Development Policies in the 1980's.*

8. There is considerable discussion in the late 1980s about the need to expand the domestic Japanese economy, but this would be to a *new* level of consumption. The Japanese have already made one quantum leap since 1945.

9. Japan was able to absorb technology because of changes that had taken place during the prewar and wartime eras. Takafusa Nakamura, *Economic Growth in Prewar Japan;* For the importance of technology transfer to prewar economic growth, see Ryōshin Minami, *Power Revolution in the Industrialization of Japan: 1885–1940,* and Kozo Yamamura, "Japan's Deus ex Machina: Western Technology in the 1920s."

10. An earlier popular theory of Japanese economic growth attributes it to unique cultural qualities or perhaps arcane knowledge available only to the Japanese. In this model, Japan's success is a miracle that virtually defies explanation. The Japanese people are able to coordinate their desires in some non-rational and unique way. This interpretation, which relies heavily on the assumption that Japan is fundamentally unlike other industrialized countries, enjoyed considerable vogue for some time but has lost ground in recent years to the argument that the Japanese respond rationally, like other people, to common problems. See Herman Kahn, *The Emerging Japanese Superstate: Challenge and Response.*

11. Nathaniel Thayer, *How the Conservatives Rule Japan;* Chitoshi Yanaga, *Big Business in Japanese Politics;* T.J. Pempel, *Policy and Politics in Japan: Creative Conservatism;* Chalmers Johnson, *MITI and the Japanese Miracle;* Johnson, "The Reemployment of Retired Government Bureaucrats in Japanese Big Business"; J.A.A. Stockwin, *Japan: Divided Politics in a Growth Economy;* W.W. Lockwood, *The Economic Development of Japan;* Akira Kubota, *Higher Civil Servants in Postwar Japan;* Gary D. Allinson, "Japan's Keidanren and its New Leadership."

12. But see two articles by Michio Muramatsu and Ellis S. Krauss, "Bureaucrats and Politicians in Policymaking; The Case of Japan," and "The Conservative Policy Line and the Development of Patterned Pluralism."

13. Johnson, *MITI and the Japanese Miracle,* p. 24. In the sources cited in note 11, Yanaga comes closest to the parallel argument that business controls the bureaucracy by looking at the ways that big business groups influence government, although he describes this as a "symbiotic relationship."

14. Works that point out these intra-elite conflicts include Magaziner and Hout; Richard J. Samuels, *The Business of the Japanese State;* Roger W. Gale, "Tokyo Electric Power Company: Its Role in Shaping Japan's Coal and LNG Policy"; David Friedman, *The Misunderstood Miracle: Industrial Development and Political Change in Japan.*

15. The standard source for this is Hugh Patrick and Henry Rosovsky, ed., *Asia's New Giant.*

16. Yasusuke Murakami, "Toward a Socioinstitutional Explanation of Japan's Economic Performance," p. 38. The other essays in the same volume also stress the importance of this consensus.

2. THE ENERGY INDUSTRIES IN THE PREWAR YEARS

1. Gas accounted for the remaining 0.8%. 1936 figures from Lockwood, p. 93; 1940 figures from Takafusa Nakamura, *The Postwar Japanese Economy,* p. 76.

2. Yada Toshifumi, *Sengo Nihon no Sekitan Sangyō,* p. 45; Edward Ackerman, *Japan's Natural Resources and Their Relation to Japan's Economic Future.*

3. Shibagaki Kazuo, *Mitsui, Mitsubishi no Hyaku-nen-Nihon Shihonshugi to Zaibatsu* (Tokyo, 1968), pp. 49–50, quoted in Yada Toshifumi, *Sekitan Gyōkai,* pp. 37.

4. Arisawa Hiromi, *Nihon Sangyō Hyaku-nen Shi,* pp. 184–185; Ueno Hidenobu, *Chi no Soko no Warai-banashi* (Tokyo, 1967), p. 111, cited in Mikiso Hane, *Peasants, Rebels, & Outcastes: The Underside of Modern Japan,* p. 232.

5. Yada, *Sekitan Gyōkai,* pp. 23–24.

6. Figures for 1921 from Arisawa, *Nihon Sangyō Hyaku-nen Shi,* p. 268; 1926 figures from Yada, *Sekitan Gyōkai,* p. 22. The firms were Mitsui, Mitsubishi, Sumitomo, Hokutan, Iwaki, Nittetsu, Okinoyama, Meiji, Kaijima, and Asano; 1937 figures from *Oriental Economist,* no date, cited in George C. Allen, "Japanese Industry: Its Organization and Development to 1937," p. 606; See also Supreme Commander for the Allied Powers (SCAP), General Headquarters. Statistics and Reports Section, Historical Monograph, 45, "Coal" (1952), p. 3, for a similar estimate. This series of monographs is available on microfilm from the National Archives.

7. Arisawa, *Nihon Sangyō Hyaku-nen Shi,* pp. 269–270; Allen, "Japanese Industry," p. 606.

8. Mikio Sumiya, "The Development of Japanese Labour Relations."

9. Nakamura Masanori, *Nihon no Rekishi—Rōdōsha to Nōmin,* p. 143.

10. Allen, "Japanese Industry," pp. 668–669.

11. Nakamura Masanori, p. 417. The miners were among approximately 1 million Koreans and 40,000 Chinese who were brought to Japan to work between 1940 and 1945. At the end of the war, 2,365,000 Koreans were in Japan proper. Ōhara Shakai Mondai Kenkyūjo, *Taiheiyō Sensōka no Rōdō Undō,* p. 27.

12. See Anton Bilek's account of life as a POW at Miike mine in Studs Terkel, *"The Good War": An Oral History of World War Two,* pp. 92–93.

13. *Oriental Economist,* 17.396:781 (29 July 1950).

14. E.B. Schumpeter, "Japan, Korea and Manchukuo, 1936–1940"; Kinoshita Etsuji, *Nihon no Sekitan Kōgyō,* pp. 69–70; Jerome B. Cohen, *Japan's Economy in War and Reconstruction,* p. 163.

15. Ackerman, p. 179, noted that the average energy content of Japanese coal was 6,111 kilocalories per kg. See also p. 212.

16. Lockwood, p. 91.

17. Yada, *Sekitan Gyōkai,* p. 29; Yada, *Sengo Nihon no Sekitan Sangyō,* pp. 12–14.

18. 100 sen = 1 yen. Arisawa, *Nihon Sangyō Hyaku-nen Shi,* p. 270; Schumpeter, "Japan, Korea and Manchukuo," p. 426.

19. Schumpeter, "Japan, Korea and Manchukuo," pp. 426–427. Japan Coal Company was a *kokusaku gaisha,* or national-policy company.

20. T.A. Bisson, *Japan's War Economy;* Jerome Cohen, *Japan's Economy in War and Reconstruction;* Itō Mitsuharu, "Munitions Unlimited: The Controlled Economy"; Johnson, *MITI and the Japanese Miracle;* Kinoshita, p. 90; Lockwood, pp. 570–572; Richard Rice, "Economic Mobilization in Wartime Japan: Business, Bureaucracy, and Military in Conflict"; Takahashi Makoto, "The Development of Wartime Economic Controls"; Richard Samuels, *Business of the Japanese State,* pp. 87–88.

21. Yada, *Sekitan Gyōkai,* p. 27.

22. Minami, *Power Revolution,* pp. 153–157.

23. Arisawa, *Nihon Sangyō Hyaku-nen Shi,* p. 182.

24. Tokyo Denryoku Shashi Henshu Iinkai, *Tokyo Denryoku 30-nen Shi,* p. 82. The electric-power industry accounted for 32% of internationally held corporate debt, and the Big Five accounted for 90% of that. Arisawa Hiromi, *Shōwa Keizai Shi* I, 41.

25. Komamura Yūzaburō, *Denryokukai no Kōzai Shi,* cited in Arisawa, *Nihon Sangyō Hyaku-nen Shi,* p. 273

26. Arisawa, *Nihon Sangyō Hyaku-nen Shi,* pp. 272–273; *Tokyo Denryoku 30-nen Shi,* pp. 75–77; Takafusa Nakamura, *Economic Growth in Prewar Japan,* p. 205.

27. Nihon Chōki Shinyō Ginkō Sangyō Kenkyūkai, *Jūyō Sangyō Sengo 25-nen Shi,* p. 365.

28. Ōsawa Etsuji, *Denryoku Jigyōkai,* p. 65; Arisawa Hiromi, *Nihon no Enerugī Mondai,* p. 52; Arisawa Hiromi, *Enerugī,* pp. 117–118. The Social Democratic Party advocated nationalization of the electric-power industry as early as 1931. George O. Totten, *The Social Democratic Movement in Prewar Japan,* p. 245. For WWI-era debates within the government on this issue, see Samuels, *Business of the Japanese State,* p. 138.

29. As quoted in Arisawa, *Shōwa Keizai Shi* I, 213.

30. Ōsawa, p. 65; Arisawa, *Nihon Sangyō Hyaku-nen Shi,* p. 273; Arisawa, *Shōwa Keizai Shi,* pp. 213–214; Peter Duus, "The Reaction of Japanese Big Business to a State-controlled Economy in the 1930s."

31. Ōsawa, p. 67.

32. Bisson, *Japan's War Economy,* pp. 71–89. The government also assumed the remaining foreign debt previously incurred by the power companies. Arisawa, *Shōwa Keizai Shi,* p. 45.

33. Ōsawa, p. 73.

34. *Senshi Sōsho: Kaigun Gunsenbi—Shōwa Jūroku-nen Jūichi-gatsu made*, pp. 722–728. Jerome Cohen, *Japan's Economy in War and Reconstruction*, p. 141, reports even more rapid decrease in civilian gasoline consumption from 6.3 million barrels (10 million kl) in 1940 to 1.5 million barrels (238,500 kl) in 1941, dwindling to 257,000 barrels (40,900 kl) in 1944.

35. *Oriental Economist* 16.3 17:35–36 (15 January 1949); Arisawa, *Nihon no Enerugī Mondai*, pp. 50, 52.

36. Fujiwara Akira, "The Role of the Japanese Army," and Asada Sadao, "The Japanese Navy and the United States," in Dorothy Borg and Shumpei Okamoto, eds., *Pearl Harbor as History*, pp. 189–196, 225–260; Jerome Cohen, *Japan's Economy in War and Reconstruction*, p. 141.

37. In 1899, Standard Oil Co. of New York established a marketing subsidiary in Japan. New York Standard merged with Vacuum Oil Co. and the Asian operations of Standard of New Jersey in 1931 to form Standard Vacuum Corp.

38. Arisawa, *Nihon Sangyō Hyaku-nen Shi*, p. 277.

39. Ibid.; Irvine H. Anderson, *The Standard-Vacuum Oil Company and United States East Asian Policy, 1933–1941*, p. 75.

40. Anderson, *The Standard-Vacuum Oil Company*, pp. 77–79, 93–95; Mira Wilkins, "The Role of U.S. Business."

41. Jerome Cohen, *Japan's Economy in War and Reconstruction*, p. 25; Arisawa, *Nihon Sangyō Hyaku-nen Shi*, p. 278; Johnson, *MITI and the Japanese Miracle*, p. 122; Anderson, pp. 39, 51.

42. Albert H. Solomon, "Revision of the Japanese Mining Law under the Occupation," p. 236. This is a reprint of a 1951 SCAP document, Natural Resource Section Weekly Summary no. 286.

43. Michael A. Barnhart, *Japan Prepares for Total War: The Search for Economic Security*, pp. 29, 146.

44. Herbert Feis, *The Road to Pearl Harbor*, pp. 49–55, 88–90, 236–239; Anderson, pp. 126–192.

3. WAR, DEFEAT, OCCUPATION AND THE ENERGY INDUSTRIES

1. The total Japanese military and civilian death toll from 1937 to 1945 was about 3 million persons. *Encyclopedia of Japan* VIII, 227.

2. Takafusa Nakamura, *The Postwar Japanese Economy*, pp. 14–15.

3. Charles Maier, pp. 23–50.

4. Recent research on the Japan policy of other Allied countries both confirms their secondary role and provides different perspectives. See Roger W. Buckley, *Occupation Diplomacy: Britain, the United States, and Japan, 1945–1952*; Thomas Burkman, ed., *The Occupation of Japan: The International Context*.

5. The Constitution was passed at the insistence of the Occupation. See SCAP,

Political Reorientation of Japan: September 1945 to September 1948, Vols. I–II; Justin Williams, Sr., *Japan's Political Revolution Under MacArthur: A Participant's Account;* Alfred C. Oppler, *Legal Reform in Occupied Japan: A Participant Looks Back;* John M. Maki, tr. and ed., *Japan's Commission on the Constitution: The Final Report;* Theodore McNelly, "The Renunciation of War in the Japanese Constitution."

6. The Potsdam Declaration is reprinted in SCAP, *Political Reorientation of Japan* II, 413; "Report on Japanese Reparations to the President of the United States," Edwin W. Pauley, 1 March 1946, Dower Collection; and "Pauley Interim Report to the President," 6 December 1945, *FRUS,* 1945 VI, 1004–1009.

7. "Statement by Ambassador Edwin W. Pauley on Japanese Interim Reparations Program," 7 December 1945, in Ministry of Foreign Affairs of Japan, Special Records Division, *Documents Concerning the Allied Occupation and Control of Japan* III, 251–253.

8. See *Political Reorientation of Japan;* SCAP, GHQ, Statistics and Reports Section, *History of the Non-Military Activities of the Occupation of Japan* (1952); Edwin M. Martin, *The Allied Occupation of Japan.*

9. Sodei Rinjirō, "A Question of Paternity," Harry Wray and Hilary Conroy, eds., *Japan Examined: Perspectives on Modern Japanese History,* pp. 354–355, ellipses in original. Also see the image of these two forces as the "warp and weft" of the fabric of reform. Holding Company Liquidation Commission, *Laws, Rules and Regulations Concerning the Reconstruction and Democratization of Japanese Economy,* p. 9. Carol Gluck, in a most impressive interpretive and bibliographic essay, discusses the importance of this issue to contemporary Japanese life in "Entangling Illusions—Japanese and American Views of the Occupation," pp. 189–190.

10. Statement by Ambassador Edwin W. Pauley on Japanese Interim Reparations Program, 7 December 1945, in Ministry of Foreign Affairs, *Documents,* "Basic Directive for Post-Surrender Military Government in Japan Proper," 3 November 1945, reprinted in Ōkurashō Zaisei Shishitsu, *Shōwa Zaisei Shi* XX, p. 168.

11. Ironically, this demilitarization and democratization program, while not specifically aimed at economic recovery, is now considered by a number of economists to have been a key factor in postwar growth. See Eleanor M. Hadley, "The Economic Reforms of the Occupation from the Perspective of 1983"; Yutaka Kosai, *The Era of High-Speed Growth;* Takafusa Nakamura, *The Postwar Japanese Economy;* Harry T. Oshima, "Reinterpreting Japan's Postwar Growth."

12. Edwin Martin, pp. 81–82. See also Takemae Eiji, *Sengo Rōdō Kaikaku—GHQ Rōdō Seisaku Shi;* Miriam S. Farley, *Aspects of Japan's Labor Problems;* Moore; Solomon B. Levine, *Industrial Relations in Postwar Japan;* Levine, "Labor"; Iwao Ayusawa, "Developments in Organized Labor," *Contemporary Japan* 21.4–

6:231–235 (April–June 1952); Andrew Gordon, *The Evolution of Labor Relations in Japan: Heavy Industry, 1853–1955;* Ōkōchi Kazuo and Matsuo Hiroshi, *Nihon Rōdō Kumiai Monogatari, Sengo.*

13. Asahi Shinbunsha Keizaibu, ed., *Asahi Keizai Nenkan, 1955,* p. 214, Okōchi and Matsuo, p. 148. December figures from SCAP, *Summations of the Non-Military Activities in Japan,* no. 33 (June 1948).

14. The general strike ban is often cited as the beginning of the new "reverse course" in U.S. policy toward Japan. E.g. Martin Bronfenbrenner, "Economic History—Occupation-Period Economy (1945–1952)."

15. Marlene Mayo, "American Economic Planning For Occupied Japan: The Issue of *Zaibatsu* Dissolution, 1942–1945."

16. "Report of the Mission on Japanese Combines, Part I" (Edwards Report), was published in May 1946 by the Dept. of State, Publication 2628, Far Eastern Series 14, (Washington, 1946) and an amended version, retitled FEC-230, is reprinted in Eleanor Hadley, *Antitrust in Japan,* and Ōkurashō Zaisei Shishitsu, *Shōwa Zaisei Shi XX,* 339–344. A summary of Part II of the Edwards Report appears in SCAP, Historical Monograph 24, "Elimination of Zaibatsu Control," p. 31. As has been amply documented, however, this program was scaled back from Edwards's original plan to a much tamer program, particularly where it was extended beyond the central zaibatsu organs. The most comprehensive works on this subject are T.A. Bisson, *Zaibatsu Dissolution in Japan;* Eleanor Hadley, *Antitrust in Japan;* Hadley, "Zaibatsu" and "Zaibatsu Dissolution"; Hosoya; and Howard Schonberger, "Zaibatsu Dissolution and the American Restoration of Japan."

17. SCAP, Historical Monograph, #24, *Elimination of Zaibatsu Control,* p. 31.

18. Robert A. Fearey, *The Occupation of Japan, Second Phase: 1948–50,* p. 63.

19. This definition was taken word-for-word from a State-War-Navy Coordinating Committee document, SWNCC 302/2, "Statement of U.S. Policy with Respect to Excessive Concentrations of Economic Power in Japan," 22 January 1947, which was the direct model for the law, and presumably from the Edwards report. For the evolution of this policy, see Hadley, *Antitrust in Japan,* pp. 125–129 and appendix for reprinted document. She makes the point that this was American policy, not autonomous SCAP decisions.

20. Hadley, *Antitrust in Japan,* p. 497. SWNCC 302/2 explicitly stated that natural monopolies and public utilities "may be subjected to purchase by the national and local governments of Japan." Hadley, *Antitrust in Japan,* pp. 503–504. See also pp. 508–509.

21. These 4 were the Teikoku Petroleum Co., Nippon Express Co., Japan Iron and Steel Co., and the Hokkaido Dairy Cooperative Co. Teikoku was allowed to retain its 90% control of domestic oil production, but the government was required to sell its 50% share in the company.

22. Slogan mentioned in *Nippon Times,* "Production Declining in Main Coal Dis-

tricts," 15 September 1945, p. 3; For survey, see Nakamura Takafusa, "Sengo Tōseiki ni okeru Sekitan Kōgyō no Chikuseki Katei" p. 217.

23. Nakamura Takafusa, "Sengo Tōseiki, especially chart 3, p. 211.

24. SCAPIN #29, 15 September 1945 "Production in Non-war Plants," and 17 September 1945, SCAPIN #32. All SCAPINS are reproduced and bound together at the Diet Library, Gendai Seiji Shishitsu. Best sources on Occupation coal policy are Ackerman; SCAP, Historical Monograph, #45 "Coal", Arisawa Hiromi, *Nihon no Enerugī Mondai,* Arisawa, *Enerugī;* Nezu Tomoyoshi, *Sekitan Kokka Tōsei Shi;* Kinoshita; Tsūshō Sangyō Shō, Shōkō Seisaku Shi Kankōkai, ed., *Shōkō Seisaku Shi,* Vol. XXIII, *Kōgyō.*

25. SCAPIN #398, 6 December 1945; SCAPIN #424, 11 December 1945; SCAP officials were especially critical of the zaibatsu mines, which were deemed in 1947 to be "the major problem . . . in the recovery of the coal industry." Memo: "Analysis of Coal Production," Frank A March to W.F. Marquat, 6 December 1947, National Archives (NA), RG 331, SCAP. ESS/Fair Trade Practices Division, Box 8447, folder: Industrial Studies: Iron and Non-Ferrous Mining—Coal (Coke).

26. Japanese translation appears in Arisawa Hiromi and Inaba Hidezo, eds., *Keizai Shiryō Sengo Nijū-nen Shi,* II, 36.

27. See interview with Wakimura Yoshitarō in Andō Yoshio, ed., *Shōwa Keizai Shi e no Shōgen,* pp. 193–195, for effects of the deconcentration policy in the mines. For internal SCAP analysis of economic concentration of the coal industry, see George R. Lunn, Jr., "Coal Industry," in NA, RG 331, SCAP. ESS/Fair Trade Practices Division, Box 8448, folder: Studies of Restraints of Trade of Japanese Industries; see also Kinoshita, p. 75. The zaibatsu mining companies were also adversely affected by the purge of high executives. This was a serious problem for Mitsui and for Hokutan. Interview with Edo Hideō in Andō, p. 147 and interview with Hagiwara Kichitarō in Kondō Kanichi and Osanai Hiroshi, eds., *Sengo Sangyō Shi e no Shōgen: Enerugī Kakumei—Bōei Seisan no Kiseki,* p. 88.

28. Solomon, p. 238.

29. Ackerman, pp. 182, 200. In this estimate, if per capita consumption were half that of the United States, then reserves would last for just under 100 years. See SCAP, Historical Monograph, #45, "Coal," pp. 31–34 on SCAP efforts to improve technical standards in the mines. Also "Memo on a conference to increase coal production," 5 January 1946, NA, RG 331, SCAP. G-4/Administrative Division, Decimal file, Box 394.

30. Memo for Record from SCAP. NRS, "GHQ-8th Army Conference on Coal" 5 January 1946, NA, RG 331, SCAP G4/Administrative Division, Box 394, Decimal File 410.2-560, file: Coal (463.3) 1 January 1946–31 December 1948.

31. Economic Stabilization Board, Second Economic White Paper of July

1948, quoted in Jerome Cohen, *Japan's Economy in War and Reconstruction,* p. 476.

32. Tsūshō Sangyō Shō, Kanbō Chōsaka, *Enerugī Tōkeishu,* pp. 140–141.

33. Ackerman, p. 175.

34. SCAP, Historical Monograph, #46, "Expansion and Reorganization of the Electric Power and Gas Industries," 1950, p. 11. Nagase Shūsen recalled that the reparations problem was disruptive into 1949. Personal interview, 9 August 1984.

35. SCAPIN #6611-A, "Petition for Approval to Start Construction Within 1948 Fiscal Year of Hydro-electric Power Plant Construction Program," 3 June 1949, reprinted in Ministry of Foreign Affairs, *Documents* IV, 88–90. Best sources for this area are SCAP, Historical Monograph #46, "Expansion and Reorganization of the Electric Power and Gas Industries"; *Tokyo Denryōku 30-nen Shi;* Nihon Hassōden Kabushiki Gaisha, *Nihon Hassōden Kabushiki Gaisha Shi;* Ackerman; Arisawa, *Nihon no Enerugī Mondai;* Arisawa, *Enerugī;* Kurihara Tōyō, *Denryoku.*

36. Jerome Cohen, *Japan's Economy in War and Reconstruction,* pp. 133–137, 146–147.

37. Derived from ibid., p. 25.

38. The much smaller refineries that exclusively processed crude oil from the Japan Sea oil fields were allowed to remain open. SCAPIN #134, "Petroleum Refineries," 13 October 1945, Ministry of Foreign Affairs, *Documents* IV, 54. Best sources on oil policy are the PAG final report, SCAP, Historical Monograph, #41, "The Petroleum Industry"; Inokuchi Tōsuke, *Sekiyu;* Nihon Sekiyu Shi Henshū Shitsu, *Nihon Sekiyu Shi;* Watanabe Yōzō, "Sekiyu Sangyō to Sengo Keizai Hō Taisaku"; Ishizaki Juro, *Sekiyu Nikki, Senchū-Sengo;* and see citations in note 34.

39. SCAPIN #1236, "Pacific Coast Oil Refineries," 27 September 1946 and SCAPIN #1404, "Pacific Coast Oil Refineries," 14 December 1946, Ministry of Foreign Affairs, *Documents* IV, 58–60; "Report of Civilian Petroleum Industry in Japan," Petroleum Advisory Group, 21 July 1947, NA, RG 331, Box 388, File (334) folder: Petroleum Advisory Group, p. 5 and SCAP, Historical Monograph, #41, "The Petroleum Industry," pp. 61–63; SCAPIN #640, "Crude Oil Imports," 21 January 1946; SCAPIN #645, "Request to Move Crude Oil from Funakawa to Yokohama," 22 January 1946 for Japanese refiners' and government efforts to keep refineries open.

40. SCAP, Historical Monograph, #41, "The Petroleum Industry," pp. 5, 13; Ackerman, p. 220; "Japan's Oil Industry Reviving: Crude Oil Imports and Foreign Investment, Two Props," *Journal of Finance and Commerce* 3.8: 26–27 (15 August 1950).

41. Request by Petroleum G-4, 28 January 1946, NA, RG 331, Box 388, SCAP. G-4/Administrative Division, Decimal File 333.5-334. Firms represented

on the PAG were Standard-Vacuum, Shell, Caltex, and Tidewater Associated Cos. Union Oil Co. joined later.

42. Memo for Record, "Accommodation of British Members of PAG," 22 July 1946, NA, RG 331 Box 388, SCAP. G-4/ Administrative Division, Decimal File 333.5-334; Memo for Record, H.E. Eastwood, Assistant Chief of Staff, G-4, 6 January 1948, NA, RG 331, SCAP. G-4/ Administrative Division, Box 388, Decimal File 333.5-334, Folder 334: "PAG" and "Letter from Francis Bishop to SCAP," 9 November 1949, Box 397, File 095.

43. Internal Department of State office memo from Mr. Bennett to Mr. Vincent, "Digest of Standard Vacuum Oil Company Memo to Mr. P.P. Claxton of December 2, 1946," 12 December 1946, NA, RG 59, Department of State Decimal File, 1945–1949, Box 7118, file: 894.6363/ 1 January 1945 to 31 December 1949.

44. The oil companies also supplied the Occupation forces in Japan, which allowed them considerable advantages. According to Leon Hollerman, they used this liaison to avoid customs duties and to cut down on inventory costs by storing their oil at Army expense. Leon Hollerman, "Interventionism and Foreign Trade; Statistics in Occupied Japan."

4. ECONOMIC POLICY AND THE LABOR UNIONS

1. This is a major theme of both Andrew Gordon, *The Evolution of Labor Relations in Japan,* and Nakayama Ichirō in Rōdō Sōgi Chōsakai ed., *Densan Sōgi.* See also Ch. 1, note 1.

2. Economic Stabilization Board (ESB), "Official 'White Paper' Issued by the Japanese Government, July 4, 1947," p. 395, estimated 1.6 million wholly unemployed and 6.3 partially unemployed persons in April 1946. However, Takafusa Nakamura, *Postwar Japanese Economy,* p. 21, estimated 13.1 million jobless people: 7.6 million demobilized soldiers, 4 million unemployed, and 1.5 million repatriated civilians.

3. Andō, interviews with Okano Yasujirō of Mitsubishi Heavy Industries, p. 163, and Edo Hideo of Mitsui, pp. 144–145. Hosoya, pp. 17–27, has shown this inability to adjust to Occupation reform policies in detail for the 4 main zaibatsu holding companies. Noda Kazuo, *Sengo Keiei Shi,* pp. 19–22. For disruption and disorientation of the business community, see also Andō, interview with Ishikawa Ichirō of Nihon Sangyō Kyōgikai, especially p. 202. Ishikawa stressed the role of the purge, the economic deconcentration program, and the general uncertainty about Japan's economic future as inhibitors of business planning.

4. The passivity of business and government leaders has been characterized by some as "negative sabotage" because it included activities such as hoarding goods and evading reparations. For a sympathetic account of the plight of

Japanese businessmen and officials, Keizai Dantai Rengōkai, *Keidanren no Nijū-nen*, pp. 21–24; For less sympathetic ones, T.A. Bisson, *Prospects for Democracy in Japan*, pp. 113–117; Bisson, "Reparations and Reform in Japan"; Moore, pp. 27–30; Morley; Kazuo Kawai, *Japan's American Interlude*, pp. 139–140,; Burton Crane, *New York Times*, 3 April 1947, p. 3; and Hyoe Ouchi, *Financial and Monetary Situation in Post-War Japan*, pp. 17–19, 27. The Mutō Committee Interim Report on the Investigation of the Irregular Property Transactions appeared in *Official Gazette Extra*, Third Diet, House of Representatives, 29 November 1948, pp. 13–18. Its findings are summarized in SCAP, *Political Reorientation of Japan* I, 307–313.

5. *Keidanren no Nijū-nen*, pp. 21–24, 65; Horikoshi Taizō, ed., *Keizai Dantai Rengōkai Jū-nen Shi* I, 4–11; a translation of this document appears in Hosoya, pp. 27–32.

6. Hazama Hiroshi, *Nihon no Shiyōsha Dantai to Rōshi Kankei—Shakai Shi-teki Kenkyū*, pp. 228–235. Noda, pp. 242–246; Nihon Keieisha Dantai Renmei, *Nikkeiren Sanjū-nen Shi*, pp. 134–164.

7. Interview with Edo Hideo in Andō, pp. 145, 150, for Yoshida's role. Ouchi, *Financial and Monetary Situation in Post-War Japan*, p. 10, for Finance Ministry. Benjamin C. Duke, *Japan's Militant Teachers: A History of the Left-Wing Teachers' Movement*, p. 40, for Ministry of Education. See also Theodore Cohen, *Remaking Japan: The American Ocupation as New Deal*. Richard Finn kindly provided a copy of the unpublished manuscript version of this book.

8. *Basic Problems for Postwar Reconstruction of Japanese Economy, Translation of A Report of Ministry of Foreign Affairs' Special Survey Committee. September 1946*, pp. 43–44. For another contemporary analysis that reached this conclusion, see ESB, "Official 'White Paper,' " p. 363.

9. A Ministry of Labor survey in 1947 found that 88% of Japanese unions were enterprise unions. Ōkōchi and Matsuo I, 150.

10. The explanations for the phenomenon of the enterprise union have been discussed at great length in academic and popular literature, centering on a debate between those who emphasize a cultural orientation toward a personal, patriarchal-family-inspired model of industrial relations and those who stress the overriding need for job security among workers in the hungry postwar years. For a thoughtful recent analysis of enterprise unions, see Taishiro Shirai, "A Theory of Enterprise Unionism."

11. Fujiwara Akira, *Senryō to Minshū Undō*, parts 2–3.

12. The two federations did not include all Japanese labor. Many enterprise unions remained unaffiliated, while some set up a third, much smaller federation. Ōkōchi Kazuo, *Sengo Nihon no Rōdō Undō*, pp. 87–88; Miriam S. Farley, *Aspects of Japan's Labor Problems*, pp. 72–75. The full Japanese titles of the two federations are Nihon Rōdō Kumiai *Sōdōmei* and Zen Nihon *Sangyōbetsu* Rōdō Kumiai Kaigi.

13. SCAP. *Monthly Summation* 13 (October 1946), p. 167.

14. Ōhara Shakai Mondai Kenkyūjo, pp. 30–31; surrender speech text in *Nippon Times,* 15 August 1945.

15. Ōhara Shakai Mondai Kenkyūjo, pp. 30–31; Also Ōkōchi and Matsuo, *Sengo* I, 80 which lists the demand as ¥1,000 per miner.

16. The 1,086 non-Chinese POW miners all were repatriated in September 1945. Their numbers had dwindled from 10,203 in the previous month. Nezu, p. 622. The number of Chinese POW miners fell from a peak of 9,384 in July to 1,613 in September 1945. The regular SCAP bureaucracy in Hokkaido was more sympathetic to the miners than was the Eighth Army. Moore, p. 131.

17. Ōhara Shakai Mondai Keukyūjo, pp. 30–31.

18. SCAPIN-224, 1 November 1945.

19. Koreans greatly outnumbered other foreign miners, peaking at 133,644 in April 1945. They were concentrated in Hokkaido, but, since repatriation facilities were particularly poor—"in a state of paralysis"—this area was evacuated last. Nezu, p. 622, Nihon Tankō Rōdō Kumiai, pp. 47, 49, suggests that this delay was due to the desire of the officials to maintain production, since the proportion of foreign workers was highest in the Hokkaido mines, at 45% of the mine force.

20. At the end of 1945, 35.4% (141,860 persons) of all Japanese miners were in unions, while in Hokkaido 74.7%, or 66,135 miners were unionized. Ōkōchi and Matsuo, *Sengo* I, 98, 415. Over the first postwar months, 42 coal mines reported "uprisings" involving 90,000 people. Nezu, p. 622.

21. The full name of the federation was *Zen* Nihon *Tankō* Rōdō Kumiai Rengō. Zentan had almost 100,000 members by the end of 1946 and helped found the Sanbetsu inter-industry federation. The founding meeting is reported in SCAP, *Monthly Summation* 5 (February 1946), p. 192. For a schematic view of the complex changes in coal-miner union organizations over time, see Rōdō Sōgi Chōsakai ed., *Sekitan Sōgi,* p. 41.

22. Interview with Hara Shigeru, later a Tanrō official, in Kondō and Osanai, p. 148.

23. Rōdō Sōgi Chōsakai, ed., *Sekitan Sōgi,* pp. 45–46, 50.

24. Nishimura Takeo. "Jinmin Saiban no Shinsō," (15 April 1946), pp. 43–44, quoted in Moore, p. 132. A major issue in most of the early coal-mine disputes was hoarded food and clothes that mine managers had kept back from the workers in order to sell on the black market.

25. The miner put "carrying out of responsibility by managers" as the second most important goal, and wages third. Interview with Hara in Kondō and Osanai, pp. 147–148; Five of the union leaders were later sentenced to 3–5 months in jail for the people's-court incident, however. Rōdōshō Rōsei-kyoku, *Shiryō Rōdō Undō Shi, 1945–46,* pp. 47–58.

26. 27 August 1946 statement, quoted in Farley, p. 50.

27. Sumiya Mikio, "Mitsubishi Bibai Sōgi," in Chōsa Hōkoku, ed., Tokyo, Tokyo Daigaku Shakai Kagaku Kenkyūjo, 1971, *Sengo Shoki Rōdō Sōgi Chōsa,* 13: 15–32, as quoted in Moore, p. 60.

28. Moore, pp. 126–132, 154–156; Rōdō Sōgi Chōsakai, *Sekitan Sōgi,* pp. 65–69.

29. Quoted in Rōdōshō, 1945–46, p. 46.

30. Eiji Takemae, "GHQ Labor Policy during the Period of Democratization 1946–1948: the Second interview with Mr. Theodore Cohen," pp. 103, 117; Takemae, *Sengo Rōdō Kaikaku GHQ Rōdō Seisaku Shi,* pp. 87–88, for government and SCAP policies; Moore, Ch. 6 for implications of the union tactic.

31. Rōdō Sōgi Chōsakai, *Sekitan Sōgi,* p. 75. SCAP officials were certainly convinced by this argument. Theodore Cohen, *Remaking Japan,* pp. 219, 270, 320.

32. Moore, Ch. 5.

33. Beatrice G. Reubens, " 'Production Control' in Japan"; also Moore, p. 153, for this argument. When the electric-power workers threatened production control in March 1946, Hassōden went to the Ministry of Commerce and Industry for help. It was at this point that the Japanese government spoke out against production control. *Nihon Hassōden Kabushiki Gaisha Shi,* p. 290.

34. This paragraph is drawn from Keizai Dōyūkai, *Keizai Dōyūkai Jūgo-nen Shi,* pp. 12, 19–25. See also Hideichirō Nakamura, "Plotting a New Economic Course," for the explication of a March 1946 article that strongly influenced Keizai Dōyūkai.

35. Rōdōshō, pp. 393–402; Rōdō Sōgi Chōsakai, *Sekitan Sōgi,* pp. 101–107. Noda, p. 250.

36. Koji Taira, *Economic Development and the Labor Market in Japan,* p. 180. Andrew Gordon, *The Evolution of Labor Relations in Japan,* pp. 369–371, documents the transition from active to consultative joint councils in several large Tokyo-area firms.

37. Rōdōshō, pp. 111–116. The union engaged in production control after the company unilaterally rejected a contract that it had previously agreed to, an act that one of the management participants later criticized as "disruptive" *(rambō).* Interview with Hagiwara Kichitarō in Kondō and Osanai, pp. 90–94.

38. Maeda was one of the leading individuals in reestablishing management power nationally. He first organized the Hokkaido mine owners in December 1945 and helped develop the regional and industry-level organizations that merged into Nikkeiren in 1948. See 3-part interview with Maeda by Nakamura Takafusa and Itō Takashi.

39. Nikkeiren, "Keieiken Kakuhō ni Kan suru Ikensho" (Opinion on securing

management rights), 10 May 1948, reprinted in Ōkōchi Kazuo, ed., *Rōdō*, p. 102; SCAP, *Monthly Summation 33* (June 1948), p. 32, for government. Nakamura Hideichiro, pp. 17–20, for Keizai Dōyūkai opinion.

40. Rōdō Sōgi Chōsakai, *Densan Sōgi*, p. 39. Densan was formally established on 5 May 1947.

41. Rōdō Sōgi Chōsakai, *Densan Sōgi*, pp. 20, 36. Survey by Tokyo Daigaku Shakai Kenkyūjo, cited in Akita Nariyoshi, Arizumi Makoto, and Tosaka Ranko, "Denki Sangyō Rōdō Kumiai (Densan)," pp. 110, also pp. 60–74, 86–87, 106.

42. Note that this tactic highlights one of the positive aspects of the enterprise-union form for workers, since the office staff was part of the same bargaining unit as the production workers. Rōdōshō, pp. 26–27.

43. Reprinted in Ōkōchi, *Rōdō*, pp. 27–28.

44. These principles were to (1) protect the standard of living of union members and their families, (2) cooperate with management to democratize the electric-power industry, (3) adhere to the closed-shop principle, (4) establish a management-labor joint council in order to participate in management, (5) require prior consultation with the union before any reorganization concerning personnel, (6) pledge devotion by union officers to union affairs, (7) defend the right to strike, (8) work for automatic extension of these points for three months. Reprinted in Rōdō Sōgi Chōsakai, *Densan Sōgi*, p. 42.

45. Rōdōshō, p. 129; Tokyo Daigaku Shakai Kagaku Kenkyūjo, *Densan Jū-gatsu Sōgi (1946–nen)—Sengo Shoki Rōdō Sōgi Shiryō*, p. 11.

46. In 1947, wages had increased to 60% of coal production costs from about 30% in the 1930s. Mitsubishi Economic Research Institute, *Monthly Circular* 218: 20 (January 1948). Similarly, the personnel costs of 9 major electric-power companies had increased from 22.8% of total costs in 1944 to 42.9% in 1947. ESB, "Official 'White Paper,' " p. 369.

47. Naomichi Funahashi, "The Industrial Reward System: Wages and Benefits," p. 362.

48. Rōdō Sōgi Chōsaka, *Densan Sōgi*, pp. 65–68; Andrew Gordon, *The Evolution of Labor Relations in Japan*, pp. 351–355.

49. Tokyo Denryoku Shashi Henshu Iinkai, p. 183. In April 1947, the coal miners won a contract covering over 90% of coal workers, which included a sliding wage scale based on the cost of living. Farley, p. 166. Densan was a founding member of Sanbetsu, and its wage system was quickly adopted by the federation. SCAP, *Monthly Summation*, 11 (August 1946), p. 170; Akita, et al., p. 88.

50. Rōdō Sōgi Chōsakai, *Densan Sōgi*, p. 62.

51. Theodore Cohen, "Labor Democratization in Japan: The First Years," p. 169. Cohen was critical of this trend and considered the unions to have been excessively political. Both Nakayama Ichirō and Ōkōchi Kazuo argue that

the unions were *appropriately* politically active, given the politicization of all issues at the time. Rōdō Sōgi Chosakai, *Densan Sōgi,* Introduction and Part One. They further point out, as do Akita, et al., pp. 9, 87–88, that Densan generally stayed within the confines of issues related to the electric-power industry and at the time was considered to be an "economistic" rather than a particularly political union.

52. Rōdō Sōgi Chōsakai, *Densan Sōgi,* p. 70.
53. Nihon Hassōden Kabushiki Gaisha, pp. 289–290.
54. A movie script written by Densan in late 1946 on the union drive of that year also argued for a fundamental change in the organization of all industry. Farley, p. 115.
55. Densan Chūō Kyōdō Tōsō Iinkai, 7 October 1946 edition, Densan Yōkyū Kyūyo Minshuka An, quoted in Denki Jigyō Saihensei Shi Kenkōkai. *Denki Jigyō Saihensei Shi,* pp. 142–143. Also see Tokyo Daigaku Shakai Kagaku Kenkyūjo, pp. 16–25; Also Ōkōchi, *Rōdō,* pp. 27–28. As early as December 1945, the Hassōden union demanded the abolition of *amakudari,* the practice of reserving high management slots for retiring bureaucrats. Nihon Hassōden Kabushiki Gaisha, p. 287.
56. Akita, et al, p. 125.
57. *Denki Jigyō Saihensei Shi,* pp. 143–144; Densan Chūō Kyōdō Tōsō Iinkai, 7 October 1946 edition, Densan Yōkyū Kyūyo Minshuka An, quoted in Rōdō Sōgi Chōsakai, *Densan Sōgi,* pp. 70–72.
58. *Denki Jigyō Saihensei Shi,* pp. 144–145. Note that the participation of ordinary consumers as the third, swing group had been replaced by "outside experts."
59. See Andrew Gordon, *Evolution of Labor Relations in Japan,* pp. 351–355, for the tie to wartime proposals by government bureaucrats. The Densan wage system has also been criticized from a Marxist perspective as a key defeat in the struggle to tie wages to work rather than to seniority-based "need." See Eitaro Kishimoto, "Labour-Management Relations and the Trade Unions in Post-War Japan (1) - Revival and Reestablishment of the Labour-Management Relations Based on Seniority," *Kyoto University Economic Review* 38:1: 5–9 (April 1968). For Tokugawa peasants, see Stephen Vlastos, *Peasant Protests and Uprisings in Tokugawa Japan.*
60. Ernest J. Notar, "Japan's Wartime Labor Policy: A Search for Method," p. 318.

5. GOVERNMENT ECONOMIC PLANNING AND THE DEBATE OVER STATE CONTROL OF THE COAL MINES, 1945–1947

1. *Miyamoto Yuriko Senshū,* Tokyo. Shin Nihon Shuppansha, 1968, pp. 4, 10, translated and quoted in Susan Phillips, "Beyond Borders: Class Struggle

and Feminist Humanism in *Banshū heiya*," *Bulletin of Concerned Asian Scholars*, 19.1 (January–March 1987), p. 60.

2. Arisawa, ed., *Shōwa Keizai Shi*, pp. 14–15.

3. Ibid., pp. 39–47.

4. Arisawa Hiromi stated in a September 1984 interview that the coal miners were widely respected for keeping coal production levels up.

5. In October 1946, Yoshida called the strike wave "a criminal act of hostility" and branded the union leaders "avowed enemies of the people in scheming the downfall of our country." SCAP, *Monthly Summation* 13 (October 1946), pp. 37–38. His most flamboyant statement occurred in his 1947 New Years's Day State of the Nation address, when Yoshida castigated the unions in language redolent of prewar oppression as "lawless elements." John W. Dower, *Empire and Aftermath*, pp. 333–341.

6. Later, most of these men moved over to the Economic Stabilization Board when it was established in August 1946 and continued their activities from that agency. Tatsurō Uchino, *Japan's Postwar Economy*, p. 253.

7. Shigeru Yoshida, *The Yoshida Memoirs*, pp. 75–76, 79–80. See Dower, *Empire and Aftermath*, pp. 362–366, for Yoshida's choice of these thinkers and for his generally antipathetic attitude toward liberals and Marxists. Yoshida was equally daring in his choice of Wada Hiroo as Minister of Agriculture. Wada, a Socialist, was not a member of the Ministry of Foreign Affairs group, but shared many of their ideas. He harked back to an earlier era of economic planning, having worked for the wartime Cabinet Planning Board with Inaba Hidezō. For Yoshida's choice of Wada, see Masumi Junnosuke, *Postwar Politics in Japan, 1945–1955*, pp. 110–111, 120–121.

8. Ministry of Foreign Affairs, Special Survey Committee.

9. Ibid., p. 124.

10. Ibid., p. 60.

11. Ibid., p. 79.

12. Ibid., p. 40. Note that they identified three positive legacies of wartime and defeat: economic planning, development and diffusion of modern industrial techniques, and also freedom from the economic burden of maintaining armed forces, which have all been cited as important contributory factors to Japan's postwar economic success. See Nakamura Takafusa, *Postwar Japanese Economy*, pp. 14–20, for this argument.

13. Ministry of Foreign Affairs, Special Survey Committee, p. 6.

14. These three paragraphs are from ibid., pp. 58–59.

15. Ibid., p. 91.

16. Their ideas were very influential in Japan in 1946. For example, Keizai Dōyūkai used this Ministry of Foreign Affairs report as the text for its first general meeting in May. Keizai Dōyūkai, p. 21.

17. Edwards personally saw state control as the least attractive alternative to

zaibatsu control of the economy, according to Schonberger, "Zaibatsu Dissolution and the American Restoration of Japan," p. 17. The Draper Report of April 1948 was an important turning point in this, as in other areas of American economic policy. The report warned that "care must also be taken that breaking up of the Zaibatsu monopolies does not lead to the growth of governmental monopolies." "Report on the Economic Position and Prospects of Japan and Korea: Measures Required to Improve Them," 26 April 1948, NA, RG 331, Box 2312, Folder: (36) (end) "Johnson Report" or "Draper Report." Microfiche copy in Diet Library, Gendai Seiji Shishitsu, CAS (B) 00313.

18. Wakimura Yoshitarō recalled that his fellow commissioners at the Holding Company Liquidation Commission simply did not understand the reasoning behind U.S. anti-trust law, because it was so alien to them. See also Ishikawa Ichirō's argument that the United States could afford an anti-monopoly law because of its vast natural-resource base and high technological level, while Japan needed some monopoly industries. Both interviews in Andō, pp. 193–194, 208.

19. This is a major theme of Bisson, *Prospects for Democracy in Japan*.

20. Report on Minister of Finance Ishibashi's speech to the Diet of 25 July 1946, *Oriental Economist* 13. 195: 518–523 (10 August 1946), is the basis for this discussion.

21. It is probably no accident that Ishibashi's pro-growth and pro-business policy directly contravened SCAP reparations policy as articulated by U.S. Ambassador Pauley. Pauley had proposed that Japanese industry be cut back to provide for the needs of the Japanese people at the 1930–1934 standard of living, minus the industrial capacity that had gone into the war effort. This reparations plan was a significant deterrent to reconstruction in 1946. Ishibashi agreed with Pauley that the munitions plants were not being used for civilian purposes, but his theory implied that all Japan's productive capacity (converted to peacetime uses) was necessary to provide jobs until Japan had full employment. Thus, nothing was available for reparations.

22. This meeting probably took place in late February 1946. Ishibashi Tanzan, *Ishibashi Tanzan Zenshū* XV, 208.

23. *Oriental Economist* 13. 195: 518–523 (10 August 1946).

24. Ibid.; Sharon H. Nolte, *Liberalism in Modern Japan*, pp. 288, 292–293, for Ishibashi's postwar conservatism. One of the ways Ishibashi planned to assure full employment was to limit the ability of trade unions to agitate for higher wages. Martin Bronfenbrenner, "Four Positions on Japanese Finance," contrasts this to the "ESB line," articulated by people like Inaba Hidezō and Wada Hiroo, which emphasized "standard-of-living recovery." See also Bronfenbrenner's essay, "Economic History—Occupation-Period Economy (1945–1952)."

25. Martin Bronfenbrenner, "Inflation Theories of the SCAP Period," pp. 142–143.

26. The Japanese fiscal year runs from 1 April to the following 31 March. Arisawa Hiromi, *Senji-Sengo no Kōgyō Seisaku,* quoted in Nakamura Takafusa, "Sengo Tōseiki ni okeru Sekitan Kōgyō no Chikuseki Katei," p. 210.

27. On 5 November 1946, Yoshida, who did not want to strengthen the ESB, established a "Coal Committee" within the Foreign Ministry composed mainly of the economic planning group there to propose a solution to the "March Crisis." This body announced the goal of 30,037,000 tons of coal production in fiscal 1947. The Coal Committee members, however, *did* believe that the ESB was the most appropriate agency for national economic planning, so they did not develop into an alternative bureaucratic center. Arisawa, *Shōwa Keizai Shi* II, 56.

28. Arisawa is the preeminent economic historian of this period as well as a central participant in policymaking. He is also a mentor of such prominent economic historians as Nakamura Takafusa and Sakisaka Masao.

29. For initial SCAP reaction to the priority-production policy, see Economic and Scientific Section, SCAP, "Program for Economic Stabilization (B) (Summary)," 16 February 1947, reprinted in Ōkurashō, Zaisei Shishitsu, pp. 514–515.

30. Arisawa, *Shōwa Keizai Shi* II, 57.

31. Arisawa explained: "The relationship of the two basic materials sectors, coal and steel, is one of mutual deficiency and so they will mutually reinforce production of each other." Arisawa Hiromi, *Senji-Sengo no Kōgyō Seisaku,* quoted in Nakamura Takafusa, "Sengo Tōseiki," p. 210. For a slightly different version, which stressed SCAP's role in the choice of coal, see Keizai Kikakuchō, *Gendai Nihon Keizai no Tenkai: Keizai Kikakuchō-30-nen Shi,* pp. 405–406. Arisawa retold this story in an interview that I conducted in 1984.

32. Johnson, *MITI and the Japanese Miracle,* p. 182.

33. Matsuoka Tamao, *Sengo Kyūshū ni okeru Sekitan Sangyō Saihensei to Gōrika,* pp. 64–65.

34. ESB, "1948 White Paper," quoted in SCAP. GHQ. Statistics and Reports Section, *History of the Non-Military Activities of the Occupation of Japan,* Historical Monograph, #45, "Coal," p. 22.

35. Mitsubishi Economic Research Institute (MERI), *Monthly Circular,* nos. 216–217 (November–December 1947), pp. 20–21.

36. Jerome B. Cohen, *Japan's Economy in War and Reconstruction,* p. 162.

37. Nezu, p. 914.

38. The compromise of allowing general subsidies reflected the real pressure Japanese consumers put on the government to provide basic goods and services at an affordable price. This was one of many times the idea of ending the subsidies came up. Everyone agreed that they were bankrupting the treasury,

but repeatedly came to the same conclusion: Politically, the government could not afford to protect industry from inflation without also offering some effective price controls to ordinary households. Since the subsidies were concentrated in basic necessities, popular pressure to maintain them was very strong. Bronfenbrenner, "Four Positions on Japanese Finance," pp. 281–288. Keidanren, for example, issued a tortuous opinion on the subject which stated a desire to end subsidies but cautioned against any immediate action. Horikoshi II, 360.

39. S. Ikeda, "An Analysis of Post-war Government Subsidies," MERI, *Monthly Circular* no. 239 (October 1949), p. 11. Ikeda included government loans in this study. For comments on subsidies in 1940, see Allen, "Japanese Industry," pp. 733–734.

40. For example, labor costs in the coal industry were ¥6.49 per ton in the first half of 1943, or 34% of the total per-ton cost of ¥19.32. In the first half of 1946, this cost had shot up to ¥187.67 per ton. It had also increased as a percentage of total costs, to 50% of ¥314.53. "Analysis of Japanese Business Results," MERI, *Monthly Circular* nos. 226–227 (September–October 1948), p. 13.

41. In 1949, the United States instituted an economic austerity program in Japan. See Ch. 7. S. Ikeda, "An Analysis of Post-war Government Subsidies," p. 8. On 1940–1949 subsidies, see also Sonoda Minoru, *Sengo Sekitan Shi,* p. 6.

42. SCAP, Historical Monograph, #34, "Price and Distribution Stabilization: Non-Food Program," p. 54, and #45, "Coal," p. 64; Nakamura Takafusa, "Sengo Tōseiki," p. 226; Dick K. Nanto, "The United States' Role in the Postwar Economic Recovery of Japan," p. 267.

43. Nezu, p. 915. In July 1947, the consumer price was revised to ¥1,208.58 for general consumption and ¥600 for special industries, widening the gap between favored sectors and the rest of the economy. MERI, *Monthly Circular* nos. 216–217 (November–December 1947), pp. 20–21; The government had already resorted to a stratified price system for goods *sold to* the coal industry, which had paid low prices for lumber, steel, and concrete since October 1945. Sonoda, p. 2. Under Katayama this system was changed to a subsidy to certain industries—steel, gas, electric power, chemical fertilizer, cement, soda, shipping, manufactured salt, and private railways—to pay their coal bills. Nakamura Takafusa, "Sengo Tōseiki," p. 231.

44. Nakamura Takafusa, "Sengo Tōseiki," p. 226; MERI, *Monthly Circular* nos. 216–217 (November–December 1947), pp. 20–21; "Coal Mining: Japan's Economic Rehabilitation Problem No. 1," *Journal of Finance and Commerce* 1.8 (15 August 1948).

45. Kinoshita, p. 89, reports that, in 1947, production costs were ¥842 at Miike and ¥942 at Takashima per ton, but the Mitsui and Mitsubishi mines

were paid ¥1,201 and ¥1,444 respectively, for a per-ton excess profit of ¥359 and ¥502. In the electric-power industry, the subsidy was based on average costs as well, but, since the 10 state-supervised firms pooled their accounts in these years, it did not affect the profitability of the firms relative to each other.

46. Sekitan Kyōkai, *Sekitan Rōdō Nenkan* (Tokyo, 1947), p. 43, as quoted in Nakamura Takafusa, "Sengo Tōseiki," pp. 229–230. Emphasis in original.

47. The RFB opened its doors on 24 January 1947, but the functional start of the funding program had begun in August 1946 when the Industrial Bank of Japan began a reconstruction loan program. When the books of the Industrial Bank of Japan division were transferred to the RFB in January 1947, ¥2,866 million worth of loans had already been made to industry. On paper, the RFB was supposed to go beyond the priority-production program and stimulate reconstruction. It was designed to fund new projects, including the replacement of equipment that had been destroyed during the war. The RFB loans also differed from subsidies in that they went to individual firms, rather than industries. Also, they were technically loans rather than grants, although in reality over half of the RFB loans were never paid back, and the bank acted as a side-door subsidy program. *Oriental Economist* 15.308 (6 November 1948), p. 938; Nihon Kaihatsu Ginkō Jū-nen Shi Hensa Iinkai, ed., *Nihon Kaihatsu Ginkō Jū-nen Shi,* p. 488.

48. Nanto, pp. 210, 214. The figures in yen were ¥44.2 billion and ¥111.16 billion. The chart on his p. 237 shows the 1948 loans as 22.8% of all loans *to industry.*

49. Foreign Affairs Association, *Japan Yearbook: 1949–1952,* ([1952]) p. 295; Nanto, p. 241.

50. They were equally critical of the RFB's main beneficiary, the coal industry. On 31 March 1949, the Diet passed a law that authorized the issue of ¥10,794 million in national bonds to redeem the coal operators' debts at the RFB and to indemnify them for losses incurred between 6 July 1947 and 22 June 1948. A SCAP historian called this the "last outright grant" to the coal industry. SCAP, Historical Monograph, #45, "Coal," p. 69.

51. *Nihon Kaihatsu Ginkō Jū-nen Shi,* p. 473. The most important non-industrial RFB borrowers were the 10 government distribution corporations, which by law were financed only through the Japanese government. They accounted for about 20% of total RFB loans.

52. Nakamura Takafusa, "Sengo Tōseiki," p. 240.

53. Jerome B. Cohen, *Japan's Economy in War and Reconstruction,* pp. 459–460.

54. Koji Taira, "Unions, Ideologies, and Revolutions in Japanese Enterprise during the Occupation," p. 174.

55. Ibid., p. 181. The "socialist" measures were the priority-production policy

and the creation of the short-lived Economic Reconstruction Conferences, mentioned in the previous chapter.

56. See Yanase Tetsuya, *Sekitan Sangyō no Kōzōteki Kiki,* cited in Nakamura Taka-fusa, "Sengo Tōseiki," pp. 212–213.

57. "The RFB and its Operation," 31 January 1949, J.M. Dodge Manuscripts, p. 10, cited in Nanto, p. 236.

58. Yada, *Sengo Nihon no Sekitan Sangyō,* p. 72; Nakamura Takafusa, "Sengo Tōseiki," p. 225.

59. *Oriental Economist* 15.272 (28 February 1948), p. 159.

60. Nakamura Takafusa, "Sengo Tōseiki," p. 223.

61. The Ashida Cabinet fell in October 1948 and was replaced by a caretaker government, headed by Yoshida Shigeru. In January 1949, Yoshida's party did extremely well at the polls and became the first postwar administration with real political strength.

62. The plan was based on the Far Eastern Commission statement that the 1934–1936 standard of living was an appropriate goal for a peaceful Japan. Because of the 25% increase in population and the essentially static production of agriculture and fishing, the ESB planners calculated that mining and manu-facturing would have to increase to 125 percent of 1934–1936 production to support the population at the approved level. This increase was to be mainly in heavy rather than light industry. The ESB suggested changes that would make this goal possible in five years, by 1954. (The second draft changed the date to 1953.) This timetable meant that SCAP would have to both raise the permissible level of production in Japan and cancel the reparations program.

63. Arisawa and Inaba, pp. 22–23, for reprints of these Economic Rehabilitation Plans. For Yoshida's rejection of the ESB plan, see Nakamura Takafusa, "Keizai Keikaku no Seikaku to Igi," p. 1.

64. The proposals of the Socialist and Minshutō parties are reprinted in Ōkōchi, ed. *Shiryō Sengo 20-nen Shi, Rōdō* IV, 74–77, while the Communist and Kokumin Kyōdō Party plans can be found in Kikuike Toshio, *Rinji Sekitan Kōgyō Kanri Hō no Kenkyū,* Appendix, pp. 49–53. See also Unno Yukitaka, Kobayashi Hideo, and Shiba Hiroshi, eds., *Sengo Nihon Rōdō Undō Shi* II, 50–54.

65. Verbatim Minutes of the 14th Meeting of the Allied Council on Japan, 4 September 1946, and the 17th Meeting, 16 October 1946, pp. 7–15. Diet Library. Gendai Seiji Shi Shitsu. Microfiche number FEC (A) 422–446.

66. "Coal Mining: Japan's Economic Rehabilitation Problem Number 1," *Jour-nal of Finance and Commerce* 1.8:22–29 (15 August 1948); Nezu, pp. 782–808.

67. Commander C. Freile of ESS/Industry, 17th Meeting of the Allied Council on Japan, 16 October 1946.

68. *Nippon Times,* 24 September 1946, p. 2; See SCAPIN #1984, "Stabilization of the Coal Industry," 10 March 1949, in Ministry of Foreign Affairs of Japan. Special Records Division, *Documents Concerning the Allied Occupation and Control of Japan* IV, 87–88; Sherwood M. Fine, *Japan's Postwar Industrial Recovery,* p. 24.

69. Within the bureaucracy, the ESB and the Coal Bureau were the most favorably inclined toward state control, while Yoshida himself and the regular bureaus of the Ministry of Commerce and Industry (MCI) were least enthusiastic. The Coal Bureau was an external agency of the MCI. *Nippon Times,* 6 September 1946, p. 3. For Zen's statement, see *Nippon Times,* 8 September 1946, p. 1. For Hoshijima, see *Nippon Times,* 9 September 1946, p. 2, and 10 September 1946, p. 1; Nezu, p. 784; Sangyō Seisaku Shi Kenkyūjo, ed., *Sangyō Seisaku Shi Kenkyū Shiryō: Sengo ni okeru Sekitan Kōgyō Seisaku,* p. 23. This article is reprinted word for word in Tsūshō Sangyō Shō ed., *Shōkō Seisaku Shi, Kōgyō,* part 2, pp. 220–233.

70. *Nippon Times,* 27 September 1946, p. 2; Ishibashi Tanzan, *Ishibashi Tanzan Zenshū* XV, 210.

71. Nezu, p. 784; Arisawa and Inaba II 65; As the industry-wide analogue to labor-management councils, the operators also accepted this body as a preferable alternative to production control by the unions. Nihon Tankō Rōdō Kumiai, p. 115.

72. From Hayashi Yoshimi, "Katayama Naikaku to Tankō Kokka Kanri," p. 227.

73. Ibid., p. 227.

74. Nezu, p. 785.

75. Ibid., p. 119; Unno et al., II, 53.

76. Uchino, pp. 38–39.

77. In another example, on 14 April 1947, 10 public corporations *(kōdan)* were established as exclusive wholesalers of goods such as coal, petroleum, and fertilizer in order to control the distribution process. This aspect of the priority-production policy was not fully enforced until the Katayama Administration.

78. See, for example, Nezu and Nakamura Takafusa, "Sengo Tōseiki,", pp. 207–244; Johnson, *MITI and the Japanese Miracle;* Richard J. Samuels, "State Enterprise, State Strength, and Energy Policy in Transwar Japan."

79. This was actually Keidanren's precursor, Keidanren Taisaku Iinkai. Horikoshi II, 366. For examples of SCAP opinions, see "An Economic Program for Japan," Norbert A. Bogdan and Frank M. Tamagna to W.F. Marquat, Chief, ESS, 3 May 1946; "Inflation and its Threat to Occupation Objectives," T.A. Bisson to Chief, Government Section/SCAP, 23 October 1946; "Program for Economic Stabilization (B) (Summary)," SCAP/ESS, 16 February 1947, reprinted in Ōkurashō Zaisei Shishitsu XX, 499–505, 505–507, 514–515;

SCAPIN # 613, "Coal Production," 17 January 1946, reprinted in Ministry of Foreign Affairs, *Documents Concerning the Allied Occupation and Control of Japan* IV, 72; *New York Times,* 3 April 1947, p. 3. See also, Theodore Cohen, *Remaking Japan,* p. 262.

80. Uchino, p. 253.

81. The White Paper stressed the problems of production recovery, inflation, and overexpenditure by the government, by private enterprises, and by households. These were to be addressed by controlling wages and prices and channeling material resources into necessary production. Underproduction and inflation were the key problems it pinpointed. ESB, "Official 'White Paper' Issued by the Japanese Government, July 4, 1947," pp. 362–363. Partial Japanese text is in Arisawa and Inaba II, 5–8.

82. Interview with Okita Saburō in Keizai Kikakuchō, *Keizai Kikakuchō Nijū-nen Shōshi,* pp. 228–229.

83. Unno, et al. II, 52.

84. For SCAP, see Theodore Cohen, *Remaking Japan,* pp. 317–318, 321–323.

85. *Nihon Keizai Shinbun,* 2 August 1947, as quoted in Hayashi, p. 229; Sangyō Seisaku Shi Kenkyūjo, *Sangyō Seisaku Shi Kenkyū Shiryō,* p. 23. In fact, the original, 4-party position had included a rider that state control would be achieved through "abolishing bureaucratic controls," which suggests the basic ambivalence within the compromise. Nezu, pp. 785–786; Allan B. Cole, George O. Totten, and Cecil H. Uyehara, *Socialist Parties in Postwar Japan,* pp. 16–17, 151.

86. *Official Gazette Extra* 3 July 1947, First Diet, House of Representatives, p. 9, and *Official Gazette Extra* 5 July 1947, First Diet, House of Representatives, p. 10.

87. *Official Gazette Extra* 5 July 1947, First Diet, House of Representatives, p. 10.

88. Sangyō Seisaku Shi Kenkyūjo, ed., *Sangyō Seisaku Shi Kenkyū Shiryō,* p. 23. The following discussion is drawn from this source, pp. 23–35, and Nezu, pp. 786–794. Both sources contain the MCI draft in full.

89. Unno et al. II, 52.

90. The main features of the 15 August draft were as follows: (1) All mines were to be categorized as either general or designated mines. General mines would only be supervised by the state, while designated mines would be under stronger control. (2) In the case of the general mines, the government could change operations plans by ministerial order; in the case of designated mines, the government itself would make the plans. (3) The duties and responsibilities of the coal-mine controller in designated mines would be to conduct the affairs of the enterprise, but this must be in consultation with the employees. (4) In cases where the decisions of the joint production council in designated mines were not obeyed, the head of the Coal Bureau would

make final decisions. (5) The Coal Bureau Chief could request arbitration from the Labor Relations Board, along with a 30-day cooling-off period.

91. NA, RG 59, Department of State, OR Report 4695, "An Analysis of the Japanese Law providing for Temporary State Control of Coal Mining," 14 June 1948, p. 8.

92. The President of Hokutan Coal Company, Hagiwara Kichitarō, commented on this in regard to a discussion of his attempt, many years later, to get the title and extensive debts of his mines nationalized by the government. Interview with Hagiwara Kichitarō in Kondō and Osanai, pp. 88–110. See also Shinobu Seizaburō, *Sengo Nihon Seiji Shi* II, 641–645.

93. Nezu, p. 788.

94. Hayashi, pp. 229, 232.

95. Tanaka Jirō, Satō Isao, and Nomura Jirō, eds., "Tankō Kikkan Jiken," in *Sengo Seiji Saiban Shiroku* I, 335–336.

96. Kiso interview in Kondō and Osanai, pp. 110–113; Shinobu Seizaburō, *Sengo Nihon Seiji Shi* II 643–644, 662; See also Yoshimichi Ito, "Monetary Contribution in Japanese Politics," *Contemporary Japan* 17.4–6; 182–184 (April–June 1948). Tanaka won the appeal because his construction firm had built some housing for Kiso's mining company, and both men argued that the money was an advance payment for this service. Tanaka et al., p. 348.

97. This was also by far the largest single donation received by any of the parties. Yanaga, p. 80; Miki Yonosuke, "Zaisei—Seiki Kenkin no Uchimaku."

98. Nihon Keieisha Dantai Renmei, *Nikkeiren Sanjū-nen Shi,* pp. 146–147, 193–200.

99. Nihon Tankō Rōdō Kumiai, *Tanrō Jū-nen Shi,* pp. 167–168; Matsuoka, pp. 80–81. The two union proposals are reprinted in Ōkōchi, *Rōdō,* pp. 74–77.

100. Letter reprinted in SCAP, Historical Monograph, #45, "Coal," Appendix 9; See also Theodore Cohen, *Remaking Japan,* pp. 316, 322–323.

101. Mizutani speech to the Diet, 1 October 1947, reprinted in Mizutani Chōsaburō Den Kankōkai, ed., *Mizutani Chōsaburō Den,* pp. 206–207. Interview with Katayama in Andō, *Shōwa Keizai Shi e no Shōgen,* p. 268.

102. On 17 September, Major General Marquat, head of the Economic and Scientific Section of SCAP, told Ministers Wada and Mizutani that the official position of SCAP was that coal nationalization for the sake of raising production was an internal Japanese affair, but that he personally, speaking as a private American citizen, did not think that it was a good idea. "Sekitan Kokkan sono ta ni Kan suru Wada - Mizutani Ryōdaijin Fine-Marquat Daishō Kaiken Yōshi," 17 September 1947 in Keizai Kikakuchō Toshokan

Shokō. Keizai Antei Honbu Shiryō, as quoted in Hayashi, "Katayama Naikaku," p. 235.

103. NA, RG 59, Department of State OR Report 4695, "An Analysis of the Japanese Law providing for Temporary State Control of Coal Mining," 14 June 1948, p. 12.

104. Unno et al. II, 54.

6. U.S. AUSTERITY POLICY AND RATIONALIZATION THEORY

1. Phrase is from Under Secretary of State Dean Acheson's famous Delta Council speech, "The Requirements of Reconstruction," 8 May 1947, reprinted in Arthur M. Schlesinger, ed., *The Dynamics of World Power: A Documentary History of United States Foreign Policy, 1945–1973,* Vol. I, *Western Europe,* pp. 47–52. See also citations in Ch. 3.

2. Statement by Major General Frank R. McCoy at the Meeting of the Far Eastern Commission, 21 January 1948, reprinted in Ministry of Foreign Affairs, *Documents Concerning the Allied Occupation and Control of Japan* IV, 13–15; Government and Relief in Occupied Areas (GARIOA) funds were also extended from their original purpose of preventing disease and unrest to economic recovery. U.S. aid (GARIOA and EROA) for industrial materials during the Occupation came to $310.7 million plus an additional $95.14 million for petroleum products. All U.S. government aid to Japan during the Occupation totaled about $2 billion. Quote from ESS, "Program for a Self-supporting Japanese Economy" (Blue Book), November 1948, Ōkurashō, Zaisei Shishitsu, XX, 544–546; See also Nanto, pp. 31, 68, 109; William S. Borden, *The Pacific Alliance,* p. 75; Fine, *Japan's Postwar Industrial Recovery,* p. 33.

3. For example, contrast "An Economic Program for Japan," Norbert A. Bogdan and Frank M. Tamagna to W.F. Marquat, Chief, ESS/SCAP, 3 May 1946 to "Program for a Self-Supporting Japanese Economy," (Blue Book), ESS/SCAP, November 1948, reprinted in Ōkurashō, Zaisei Shishitsu XX, 499–505 and 544–546.

4. For evolution of Japanese policy, see Keizai Kikakochō, Sengo Keizai Shi Hensan Shitsu, *Sengo Keizai Shi (Keizai Antei Honbu),* pp. 81–86; Arisawa and Inaba, *Shiryō Sengo 20-nen Shi* II 22–23, for reprints of the first and second drafts of the Economic Rehabilitation Plan. Keidanren issued a statement on this plan on 23 September 1948 which was basically favorable. It warned the government not to make any long-term plans that a different political party would drastically change if it were to gain power and asked that highest priority be to make firms profitable. Arisawa and Inaba, *Shiryō Sengo 20-nen Shi* II 25. See also Bronfenbrenner, "Four Positions on Japanese Finance," pp. 286–287.

5. Keizai Kikakuchō, Sengo Keizai Shi Hensan Shitsu, p. 80; See also ESB, "White Paper of 1948," excerpted in *Contemporary Japan* 17.4–6:214–222. (April–June 1948).

6. The second draft of the ESB plan moved up the recovery timetable from 1954 to 1953 and placed greater emphasis on investment and production recovery and less on consumption recovery. The Japanese also would have been willing to reduce the national deficit by eliminating the cost of the Occupation, or the "termination-of-war" costs. These added up to 31% of the general budget in fiscal 1947, 23% in 1948, 14%, 16%, and 13% in the next three years. This point is made by Bronfenbrenner, "Inflation Theories of the SCAP Period," p. 148, and by Watanabe Takeshi, speech at the Japan Association for the Study of History of the Occupation, 29 September 1984. For an example of Japanese government reliance on foreign aid, see Keizai Kikakuchō, Sengo Keizai Shi Hensan Shitsu, p. 76. For business, see Keizai Dōyūkai, "Nihon Keizai Jiritsuka no Kenkyū—Bōei Kōzō to Chūshin to shite," 2 July 1948, in Takemae archives at Tokyo Keizai Daigaku.

7. "Report on the Economic Position and Prospects of Japan and Korea: Measures Required to Improve Them," 26 April 1948. Two other key documents in the development of the stabilization policy were the report of the June 1948 special mission, headed by Ralph Young of the Federal Reserve Board, and the SCAP November 1948 "Blue Book" on the Japanese economy, written by Sherwood Fine. The Blue Book also explicitly stated that the domestic standard of living in Japan had to be sacrificed to export competitiveness. See note 2.

8. Borden, especially pp. 5–9; Richard N. Gardner, *Sterling-Dollar Diplomacy*.

9. Fearey, pp. 137–138, 167–174. For example of British apprehension about renewed Japanese economic trade, see the comments of Mr. Graves of the British Embassy in Washington, D.C. of 28 May 1948, FRUS, 1948 VI, 792–793; Japanese exports to the United States also were blocked by protectionist tariffs. For example, when Japanese tuna exports increased at the end of the Occupation, west-coast fishermen prevailed upon Congress to raise the tariff on tuna from 12.5% to 45%. Jerome B. Cohen, "Economic Problems of Free Japan," p. 67.

10. The 3 reparations studies were: "Report on Japanese Reparations" (First Strike Report), by Special Committee on Japanese Reparations, War Department, 18 February 1947, reprinted in Ōkurashō, *Shōwa Zaisei Shi* XX, 464–471; Overseas Consultants, Inc., *Report on Industrial Reparations Survey of Japan to the United States of America,* New York, February 1948; "Report on the Economic Position and Prospects of Japan and Korea: Measures Required to Improve Them," 26 April 1948, NA, RG 331, Box 2312, Folder:(36) (end) "Johnston Report," Also known as the "Draper Report." Microfiche copy in Diet Library, Gendai Seiji Shi Shitsu, CAS (B) 00313. See Ōkurashō, *Shōwa*

Zaisei Shi: Shūsen kara kōwa made, Sōsetsu, Baishō-Shūsen Shori Vol I for the reparations issue in full.

11. See speech by Secretary of the Army Kenneth Royall for an early declaration of change on this policy. "United States Policy for Japan," reprinted in Ministry of Foreign Affairs. Special Records Division, *Documents Concerning the Allied Occupation and Control of Japan* IV, 4–10. DRB, "Concerning Findings of the Deconcentration Review Board in the case of the Nippon Soda Company," 11 September 1948, in Ōkurashō, *Shōwa Zaisei Shishitsu* XX, 405–407.

12. Edward J. Burger, "Japan's Newly Reorganized Power Industry is Patterned After Ours."

13. SCAP. General Headquarters. Statistics and Reports Section, Historical Monograph #25, "Deconcentration of Economic Power," p. 87.

14. "Statement by Chester W. Hepler, Chief of Labor Division, Economic and Scientific Section, GHQ, SCAP, Concerning the Three Principles of Wage," 11 December 1948 in Ministry of Foreign Affairs, Special Records Divison, *Documents Concerning the Allied Occupation and Control of Japan* IV, 181.

15. The Ministry of Foreign Affairs, *The Trade Union Movement in Postwar Japan*, p. 6; Nihon Keieisha Dantai Renmei, pp. 202–203.

16. The 9-point "Program to Achieve Economic Stabilization" of 18 December 1948 is reprinted in Fearey, pp. 220–222. The 9 points were (1) achieving a true balance in the consolidated budget, (2) strengthening the program of tax collection, (3) rigorously limiting credit extension, (4) establishing an effective program to achieve wage stability, (5) strengthening price-control programs, (6) improving foreign trade and foreign-exchange controls, (7) improving the allocation and rationing system, particualrly to the end of maximizing exports, (8) increasing production of all essential indigenous raw material and manufactured products, (9) improving the food-collection program.

17. Major General William Marquat, Chief of ESS, speech to the Labor-Management Conference on Economic Stabilization, 27 January 1949, reprinted in full in *Contemporary Japan* 18.1–3: 145–150, (January–March 1949).

18. Most contemporary critics argued that Dodge's budget-balancing measures were effective but that the price, in the form of economic depression, was too high. Recently, however, some scholars have argued that inflation was already slowing in Japan as a result of Japanese government measures in 1948, and, therefore, Dodge's tactics were unnecessary. Nakamura Takafusa and Dick K. Nanto both make the argument that the Japanese inflation rate was down to an acceptable 7–10% in late 1948 and Dodge lowered it to 0% at the cost of recession. Nakamura, *The Postwar Japanese Economy*, p. 39; Nanto, p. 290. Watanabe Takeshi commented on 29 September 1984 that

Dodge had told him that the yen was set purposely low as an export incentive, to allow Japan to become a high-efficiency exporter.

19. Nanto, pp. 168–174, gives the clearest explanation of the intricacies of the counterpart aid fund. The government was an unusually important source of capital in postwar Japan. Since the assets of private firms had not been revaluated on paper, they were very low compared to the inflation-swollen postwar costs of doing business. This distortion meant that few firms had collateral on which they could borrow. See also Joseph M. Dodge statement to the press on 7 March 1949, reprinted in _Contemporary Japan_ 18.1–3: 151, (January–March 1949). For a contemporary Japanese assessment of Dodge, see ESB, _Report on Current Economy: Japan's Economy Stabilization Program,_ p. 1.

20. This was the ESB estimate, including hidden unemployment. ESB, "Stabilization and Reconstruction," 9 March 1949, Dower Collection, pp. 5–8, 26–27; The Prime Minister's Office statistics give a lower figure but show that the total number of unemployed doubled from the monthly average 1948 figure of 190,000 persons to about 380,000 persons in 1949, and, by March 1950, had risen to 460,000 persons. Office of the Prime Minister, Bureau of Statistics, _Japan Statistical Year Book,_ pp. 784–785; See also Tsūshō Sangyō Shō, Shōkō Seisaku Shi Kankōkai, ed., _Sangyō Gōrika (sengo),_ pp. 10, 51.

21. Tsūshō Sangyō Shō, Shōkō Seisaku Shi Kankōkai, _Sangyō Gōrika,_ p. 51; See also Matsuoka, pp. 119–123.

22. ESB, "Japan's Economy Since Enforcement of Stabilization Program," (1949 White Paper), 9 November 1949, English translation from Dower Collection, p. 69.

23. For two contemporary American analyses that reached this conclusion, see Sherwood Fine, "Japan As SCAP Sees It," address to the San Francisco Chamber of Commerce 26 May 1949, Dower Collection. Also Jerome Cohen, _Japan's Economy in War and Reconstruction,_ pp. 503–504.

24. For example, Hyoe Ouchi, "Dodge Plan and the Japanese Economy."

25. Army Under Secretary Draper stated in 1950 that the stabilization program could not have been successful without the cooperation of Yoshida Shigeru and Hayato Ikeda. William H. Draper, Jr. "The Rising Sun of Japan," p. 7.

26. ESB, Economic Reconstruction Planning Committee, "Stabilization as We See It," 1 March 1949, pp. 9, 17–18. Dower Collection.

27. Noda 1, 465–466; Keizai Dōyūkai, pp. 42–47.

28. Kei Hoashi, "Japan's Economic Rehabilitation" _Contemporary Japan_ 18.10–12 (October–December 1949), p. 458.

29. The ESB also warned that the plan would be disproportionately harsh on small businesses. "Stabilization and Reconstruction," 9 March 1949, p. 27.

30. ESB, "Stabilization as We See It," pp. 3–5.

31. The ESB estimated that the 1949 standard of living was at only 59% of the prewar period (1934–1936), but SCAP argued that 80–85% was a more accurate figure. ESB, "Japan's Economy Since Enforcement of Stabilization Program," (1949 White Paper), 9 November 1949, pp. 115–116; Memo from Kenneth D. Morrow, ESS/Programs and Statistics Division Chief to Sherwood Fine, "ESB 'White Paper,' " November 1949, Dower Collection; Soong H. Kil, "The Dodge Line and the Japanese Conservative Party," pp. 110–116, 129.

32. ESB, "Stabilization as We See It," 1 March 1949, p. 9; Arisawa Hiromi, "Nihon Shihon Shugi no Unmei."

33. Nakayama Ichirō, "Nihon Keizai no Kao." For this debate, see also Tsuruta Toshimasa, *Sengo Nihon no Sangyō Seisaku,* pp. 24–30.

34. MITI. Enterprise Bureau, *Kigyō Gōrika no Shomondai,* 1952, pp. 23–25, quoted in Tsūshō Sangyō Shō, Shōkō Seisaku Shi Kankōkai, *Sangyō Gōrika,* p. 6.

35. ESB, "Japan's Economy Since Enforcement of Stabilization Program," p. 117.

36. Arisawa Hiromi, "Japan Prepares for Free Economy," *Contemporary Japan* 11.7–9 (July–September 1950), p. 423.

37. MITI. Enterprise Bureau proposal to the Cabinet, "Points Concerning Enforcement of Enterprise Rationalization Policy," 5 July 1949, reprinted in Tsūshō Sangyō Shō, Shōkō Seisaku Shi Kankōkai, *Sangyō Gōrika,* pp. 37–39.

38. Cabinet Decision, "Points Concerning Industrial Rationalization," reprinted in ibid., pp. 42–43.

39. ESB, "Japan's Economy Since Enforcement of Stabilization Program," pp. 109–110.

40. See speech by ESB Director of 4 April 1949, in *Contemporary Japan* 18.4–6: 259–267 (April–June 1949).

41. MITI's Enterprise Bureau, *Kigyō Gōrika no Shomondai,* 1952, pp. 23–25, quoted in Tsūshō Sangyō Shō, Shōkō Seisaku Shi Kankōkai, *Sangyō Gōrika,* p. 5.

42. Nikkeiren Special Committee on Rationalization, 12 April 1949, reprinted in Arisawa and Inaba II, 183.

43. 5 July 1949, MITI. Enterprise Bureau proposal to the Cabinet, "Points Concerning Enforcement of Enterprise Rationalization Policy," reprinted in Tsūshō Sangyō Shō, Shōkō Seisaku Shi Kankōkai, *Sangyō Gōrika,* pp. 37–39.

44. For 1949 attitudes, see ibid, p. 38. 1957 perspective in MITI, *Sangyō Gōrika Hakusho,* quoted in same, pp. 3–5.

45. Yung Ho Park, "The Governmental Advisory Commission System in Japan." The original members of the Industrial Rationalization Council were Ishikawa Ichirō (chair), Chairman of Keidanren; Ichimada Naoto, Director General of the Bank of Japan; Kawakita Teiichi, President of the Industrial Bank of Japan; Miki Takashi, President of Japan Iron and Steel Manufactur-

ing Co.; Moroi Kanichi, President of Chichibu Cement Co.; Hara Yasu-saburō, President of Nippon Kayaku Co.; Ōkano Yasujirō, President of Mitsubishi Heavy Industries; Komamura Suketada, President of Gōshō Co.; and Toyoda Masataka, President of the Central Bank for Commercial and Industrial Associations and Chair of the Japanese Federation of Smaller Enterprises.

46. This argument is made by Nakamura Seiji. Interview, 27 November 1984.

47. Nakamura Takafusa, *The Postwar Japanese Economy,* p. 15; Solomon B. Levine and Hisashi Kawada, *Human Resources in Japanese Industrial Development,* pp. 55–56, 173–174, 267–268.

48. Memo for Chief, ESS, "Increased Production by Improved Technology," 14 January 1949, and "Establishment of the first University extension at Waseda, [1949] for a course on efficiency engineering," no date, both NA, RG 331, Box 7421, File: General Correspondence 1949, ESS/ Scientific and Technical Division Acting Chief, Harry C. Kelly. Also Edgar McVoy of ESS/ Labor to H. Wohl, Assistant to Chief of ESS/Fair Trade Practices, Cover Letter to "Report of Meeting of (SCAP) Subcommittee on Industrial Management Improvement," 9 May 1950, concerning a conference for selected Japanese on better industrial management, Box 7421, File: Industrial Rationalization Councils; Also untitled memo, 9 November 1949 document in SCAP records is a request for funds to send 5 Japanese petroleum experts to study in the United States, Box 9248, File: Petroleum, 1948–49; SCAP, Historical Monographs, #41, "The Petroleum Industry," pp. 20–22 and #45, "Coal," pp. 31–34; See also POLAD (Sebald) to Secretary of State, 5 November 1949, "Effect of Industrial Rationalization Program on Medium and Small Industries," based on discussion with William Vaughn, M. Class, and Edward Welsh, all of ESS, in NA, RG 59, Department of State Main Decimal file, 1945–1949, Box 7144, File: 894.60/1 January 1948–1949; Allison memo to Dulles, 26 April 1950, FRUS, 1950, VI, 1182–1185.

49. See records of SCAP/NRS/Mining and Geology Division, especially Box 9248, File: Personnel—Japanese, Technical Visitor Program and Action and File: Personnel—Japanese Technical Visitor. There was even talk of exporting Japanese technical advisors to Southeast Asia. A 1949 State Department study estimated that Japan could send abroad about 1,330 experts in industry, mining, and metallurgy. The study found that, since Japan's mining techniques were advanced enough to sustain war against the West for five years, "these techniques could be turned advantageously to the peaceful development of mineral resources in areas less advanced technologically." However, the State Department did have concerns about the fact that the Southeast Asians "reportedly retain considerable antagonisms toward the Japanese." "Possibility of Technological Assistance from Japan to Underdeveloped Areas," 30 March 1949, NA, RG 59, Department of State, Office of Intelligence

Research, Report no. 4930PV. Also see Ambassador-at-Large Philip C. Jessup, Report of 3 April 1950, FRUS, 1950, VI, 68–79; See also NA, RG 331, Box 9247, File: Organization Studies—Government Agencies, Ben Page, Scientific Consultant to NRS/ Mining and Geology Division, Memo for Record on the formation of a Japanese committee to compile data in both English and Japanese on the geology and mineral resources of Korea, Manchuria, North China, China, and Formosa, 10 November 1950.

50. NA, RG 331, Box 9247, File: Industrial Management and Training, "Conference on a Program for Improvement of Industrial Management in Japan, held in Tokyo," 31 March 1950; See also Noda, pp. 618–621; Mary Walton, *The Deming Management Method,* pp. 10–16.

51. The phrase "technological sloth" is from Fine, *Japan's Postwar Industrial Recovery,* p. 4.

52. Andrew Gordon, *Evolution of Labor Relations in Japan,* pp. 388–389.

53. Takemae, *Sengo Rōdō Kaikaku: GHQ Rōdō Seisaku Shi,* pp. 340–386.

54. Kawai, p. 166; Duke, pp. 89–92; Interview with Kaku Saijirō in Andō, pp. 218, 221; See also Howard Schonberger, "American Labor's Cold War in Occupied Japan."

55. Nakayama Ichirō, in Rōdō Sōgi Chōsakai ed., *Densan Sōgi,* pp. 5, 10; Nihon Keieisha Dantai Renmei, pp. 202–207; Hideaki Okamoto, "Management and Their Organizations," pp. 202–204. See also Andrew Gordon, *Evolution of Labor Relations in Japan,* pp. 367–374.

7. *Austerity and Rationalization in Practice: The Energy Industries*

1. Uchino, p. 62.

2. "Coal Industry Rationalization," *Oriental Economist* 17.396: 780–783 (29 July 1950).

3. Labor efficiency in 1935 was 216 tons per year per miner. 1949 figure is for April through June only. ESB, "Japan's Economy Since Enforcement of Stabilization Program," 9 November 1949, p. 35, Dower Collection; G. C. Allen, *Japan's Economic Expansion,* p. 108; Foreign Capital Research Society, *Japanese Industry* 1950, p. 12 and 1951, p. 11; See also the Coal Rationalization Subcommittee of the Industrial Rationalization Committee report of July 1950, summarized in *Oriental Economist* 17.396: 780–783 (29 July 1950); Kinoshita, p. 97.

4. *Oriental Economist* 14.255 (18 October 1947), p. 839.

5. Interestingly, the total number of mines rose again during the Korean War boom to 882, before falling to 805 in 1954 and continuing down from there to 31 in 1983. Yada, *Sengo Nihon no Sekitan Sangyō,* p. 74; Shigen

Enerugī Chō, Chōkan Kanbō Sōmuka, ed., *Sōgō Enerugī Tōkei, 1984,* pp. 310–311.

6. Phrase is from Arisawa Hiromi in "Sengo Sangyō Seisaku no Naka no Keizai Gakusha"; Yada, *Sengo Nihon no Sekitan Sangyō,* p. 84; Yada, *Sekitan Gyōkai,* p. 69.

7. Nakamura Takafusa, "Sengo Tōseiki," p. 238; Arisawa, *Enerugī,* pp. 301, 297–301.

8. Kinoshita, p. 86; A Ministry of Labor survey in August 1949 found that Japanese employers failed to pay ¥704 million in wages due. Noda, *Sengo Keiei Shi,* p. 27 of appendix; See also Ōkōchi and Matsuo I, 318; SCAP. General Headquarters. Statistics and Reports Section, Historical Monograph, #45 "Coal," p. 17; Arisawa, *Enerugī,* p. 256.

9. Personal interview with Abe Yōichi, 3 October 1984; Interviews in Kondō and Osanai, with Hagiwara Kichitarō, p. 89; Kiso Shigeyoshi, pp. 110–122, Hara Shigeru, p. 150.

10. Zentan joined with the Sōdōmei union, Nihon Kōsan Rōdō Kumiai, and several other unions in a single national federation, Tankyō Rōdō Kumiai Zenkoku Kyōgikai, in January 1947. This split into Tanrō (Nihon Tankō Rōdō Kumiai Dōmei) and Zen Nihon Sekitan Sangyō Rōdō Kumiai in October 1947. These two unions merged in March 1949 but the new Tanrō split again in June, and the breakaway group named itself Nihon Kōsan Rōdō Kumiai. In October 1952, this group merged with a dissident Tanrō faction to become Zen Nihon Sekitan Kōgyō Rōdō Kumiai (Zen Tankō). Tanrō and Zen Tankō both survived into the 1960s.

11. Rōdō Sōgi Chōsakai, *Sengo Rōdō Sōgi Jittai Chōsa, Sekitan Sōgi* I, 41.

12. After the union went back on strike on 14 May, SCAP Labor Chief Chester Hepler told the government that the stike could not continue past 20 May. Later Robert Amis, of the same division, mediated between the union and the employers; Ibid., pp. 168–173; SCAP, Historical Monograph, #45 "Coal," p. 19.

13. Rōdō Sōgi, *Sekitan Sōgi,* p. 175.

14. Hara Shigeru in Kondō and Osanai, p. 152; Chōsakai, *Sekitan Sōgi,* p. 173. The coal miners were also the first to secede from a Communist-dominated general council of trade unions, Zenrōren, in March 1949. Daily Labor Press, ed., *The Labor Union Movement in Postwar Japan,* p. 49.

15. Speech by ESB Director of 4 April 1949, reprinted in *Contemporary Japan* 18.4–6: 259–267 (April–June 1949); ESB, "Japan's Economy Since Enforcement of Stabilization Program," (1949 White Paper), 9 November 1949, p. 105, English translation from Dower Collection; "Japan's Coal Industry Undergoes Transformation," *Journal of Finance and Commerce* 8.2: 9–10 (15 August 1949).

16. Horikoshi II, 373–377. The steel companies also planned to import Chi-

nese coal until November 1950. Arisawa, *Nihon Sangyō Hyaku-nen Shi,* p. 382.

17. The Americans also recognized the depth of these trade problems. They considered allowing trade between China and Japan until December 1951 because of a similarly gloomy assessment of Japan's survival without it. See Nancy Bernkopf Tucker, "American Policy Toward Sino-Japanese Trade in the Postwar Years: Politics and Prosperity"; Howard Schonberger, "John Foster Dulles and the China Question in the Making of the Japanese Peace Treaty"; Schonberger, "Peacemaking in Asia: The United States, Great Britain, and the Japanese Decision to Recognize Nationalist China, 1951–52"; Yoko Yasuhara, "Japan, Communist China, and Export Controls in Asia, 1948–52"; John W. Dower, "Yoshida Shigeru and the Scales of History"; Dower, *Empire and Aftermath,* pp. 400–414.

18. Ōkōchi and Matsuo I, pp. 318–319.

19. Arisawa, *Shōwa Keizai Shi,* II, 133; Arisawa, *Nihon Sangyō Hyaku-nen Shi,* p. 382. The Japanese were alarmed by the spring 1950 "Schuman Plan" to integrate European steel industries, since they knew they could not compete with a well-organized European export push. *Japan Economic Weekly* 6.139: 1–7 (8 June 1950).

20. Nihon Seitetsu Kabushiki Gaisha Shi Henshū linkai, ed., *Nihon Seitetsu Kabushiki Gaisha Shi, 1934–1950,* pp. 417–418.

21. Arisawa, *Nihon Sangyō Hyaku-nen Shi,* p. 382; Professor Funahashi Naomichi mentioned in an interview on 9 May 1984 that he had done an independent study of the steel industry in 1948 for the Ōhara Shakai Mondai Kenkyūjo, a private research institute, and came to the same conclusions. See also Muzaffer Erselcuk, "Iron and Steel Industry in Japan."

22. Interview with Ishii Kinnosuke, 9 August 1984. Confirmed in interview with Abe Yōichi, 3 October 1984. Yada argues that, until after the Suez crisis, the largest coal companies retained their prestige, not only because of their administrative power and tradition, but also because they continued to make profits. Interview, 15 May 1984.

23. Reprinted in Tsūshō Sangyō Shō, Seisaku Shi Kankōkai, *Shōkō Seisaku Shi, Sangyō Gōrika (sengo)* X 63–64.

24. The private banks presented the same problem as other private investors (whether Japanese or foreign) to the government planners. They did not want to use their funds for the projects that the government considered to be of highest priority. See "An Outline of Japanese Economy in 1949," *Fuji Bank Bulletin* 1.1 (April 1950), p. 21, which paints an extremely gloomy picture of the Japanese economy. See also Tsūshō Sangyō Shō, Seisaku Shi Kankōkai, *Sangyō Gōrika,* X, 48–49; Kil, pp. 214–215.

25. The Bank of Japan did this in a number of ways, including special financing of inventories, rediscounting foreign-trade bills, lowering the cost of loans

secured by debentures of the Industrial Bank of Japan, and expanding special financing allotments for medium and small enterprises. ESB, *Report on Current Economy,* pp. 6–7, 60.

26. Nanto, p. 291; ESB, *Report on Current Economy,* pp. 6, 13, 60; Thomas F. Adams and Hoshii Iwao, *A Financial History of the New Japan,* p. 55; Horikoshi II, 371–373.

27. ESB, *Report on Current Economy,* p. 13; George C. Allen, *A Short Economic History of Modern Japan,* pp. 186–192.

28. Martin Bronfenbrenner, "Inflation Theories of the SCAP Period," pp. 150–151.

29. SCAP, Historical Monograph, #45 "Coal," pp. 23–34; Robert Y. Grant, "Japanese Mining and Petroleum Industries: Programs under the Occupation"; NA, RG 331, Box 9248, Folder: Personnel, Japanese Technical Visitor.

30. SCAPIN #1984, "Stabilization of the Coal Industry," 10 March 1949, Ministry of Foreign Affairs, *Documents Concerning the Allied Occupation and Control of Japan* IV, 87–88; Sherwood Fine, *Japan's Postwar Industrial Recovery,* p. 24.

31. ESB, "Report: Designation of Enterprises and Standard for Elimination" 22 August 1947, reprinted in Ōkurashō, Zaisei Shishitsu, ed, *Shōwa Zaisei Shi: Shūsen kara Kōwa made,* XX, 367; Katayama letter to MacArthur, 4 September 1947, cited in SCAP, Historical Monograph, #25, "Deconcentration of Economic Power," p. 11.

32. Tokyo Denryoku Sha Shi Henshu Iinkai, pp. 202–203. Another group that submitted a reorganization plan was a federation of prefectural and municipal groups. This group wanted to return to the system used in the early 1930s, before the electric-power industry had been centralized, when many distribution installations had been operated by prefectures and cities. Basic Plan for Prefectural and Municipal Administration of the Electric Power Distribution Industry, reprinted in Denki Jigyō Saihensei Shi Kenkōkai, p. 157, and in *Tokyo Denryoku 30-nen Shi,* p. 204.

33. *Tokyo Denryoku 30-nen Shi,* p. 203.

34. Technical personnel overwhelmingly favored this type of plan throughout the electric-power industry. Usami Shōgo, *Denryoku Kai Sengoku Shi,* p. 19; Arisawa, *Nihon Sangyō Hyaku-nen Shi,* p. 376.

35. For the Hassōden proposal, see Nihon Hassōden Kabushiki Gaisha, "Saihensei Keikaku Sho," April 1948, at Chūō Denryoku Kenkyūkai Archives, or substantially reprinted in *Tokyo Denryoku 30-nen Shi,* pp. 193–197. Shindō's remarks in roundtable discussion in *Tōyō Keizai Shinpō* 2313: 10–14 (13 March 1948). Both Hassōden and the Haiden argued that their plan would be more attractive to foreign investors. Most businessmen favored Hassōden's argument that the stability of Treasury backing would prove more enticing than would private firms. Ōtani Ken, *Kōbō,* p. 132.

36. Matsunaga 1950 plan, text in *Denki Jigyō Saihensei Shi,* pp. 829–842. This was eventually what happened, but the technical difficulties surrounding this strategy were not resolved until 1958.

37. First quotation reprinted in Kurihara, p. 390. Second is from "Proposed Reorganization Plan of the Electricity Industry," April 1948, submitted by the 9 Haiden, p. 7, NA, RG 311, Fair Trade Practices Division, Box 8448, File: Restraint of Trade Study-POWER; The Haiden proposal, "Denki Jigyō Saihensei Keikaku An," April 1948, is at Denki Chūō Kenkyūkai and is substantially reprinted in *Tokyo Denryoku 30-nen Shi,* pp. 197–202.

38. Usami, p. 16. See Arisawa, *Enerugī,* p. 128, for details on subsidies.

39. Matsunaga Yasuzaemon, *Denryoku Saihensei no Omoide,* pp. 22–23; Ōtani, p. 129; Usami Shōzo interview, 8 August 1984.

40. Matsunaga, p. 10; Matsunaga interview in Andō, p. 376; Nagase Shūsen of Chūō Denryoku Kenkyūjo interview, 9 August 1984. See also Watanabe Takeshi, *Senryōka no Nihon Zaisei Oboegaki,* pp. 71–76, for discussion of the importance of electric-power company loans and the J.L. Kaufmann trip in 1947.

41. The Central Labor Relations Board had ordered that such a committee be established on 19 December 1947, probably in response to Densan charges that the managers were negotiating in bad faith. SCAP, *Monthly Summation* 31 (April 1948), pp. 210–211.

42. *Denki Jigyō Saihensei Shi,* pp. 314–327. The committee did discuss ways to attract foreign capital at length. Ōtani, p. 131.

43. This was partly because of a surprise ruling by the HCLC on 27 May 1949 that the 9 power-distribution companies could not be reorganized under the deconcentration law, although Hassōden could. HCLC, *Final Report on Zaibatsu Dissolution,* 10 July 1951, p. 61. The notes and papers of the HCLC are unavailable to researchers to date. HCLC chairman Noda Iwajirō later critically reviewed the decision to reorganize the electric-power industry, arguing that the reorganization order was "carelessly" applied to the electric-power industry and "was not in accord with the spirit of the economic deconcentration law." Interview in Andō, p. 138.

44. Burger had been to Japan on contract to the War Department in March 1947 to study the effects of the atomic-bomb explosion on the electric-supply system of Hiroshima. See R.M. Van Duzer, Jr., and E. J. Burger, "Japanese Appraisal of Atomic Bomb Damage to Hiroshima Utility System."

45. DRB memo to MacArthur, "The Board's Recommendations in the Matter of [Hassōden and the Haiden]" 17 June 1949, NA, RG 331, Box 8457, File: OM-7, Marquat. This is a revision of the 11 June 1949 memo that is reprinted in SCAP, Historical Monograph, #25, "Deconcentration of Economic Power," p. 113, and is substantively identical.

46. DRB, "Final Report of the Deconcentration Review Board," 15 July 1949,

in Ōkurashō, *Shōwa Zaisei Shi* XX, 419–423. Mr Burger's bias in favor of the American regulatory system and this hostility to government control seem to explain the DRB's relative harshness toward the electric-power industry. I have seen no evidence to support the common Japanese argument that the DRB was acting in conjunction with the international oil companies to control the Japanese energy sector. For this argument, see Seiji Keizai Kenkyūjo, *Nihon no Denryoku Sangyō,* pp. 4–7, 21–23; Ōtani, p. 135.

47. Kennedy had been president of a small electric-power company in Ohio before the war. A Japanese translation of this document is reprinted in *Tokyo Denryoku 30-nen Shi,* p. 210; An English draft version is summarized in Marquat memo to Almond, 17 January 1950, NA, RG 331, Box 6189, Folder: 10, 463: Power and Electricity, Data Concerning step-up in, etc.; See also Matsunaga, p. 38.

48. Matsunaga, pp. 19–20, 40; Ōtani, p. 138.

49. Marquat memo to Almond, 17 January 1950.

50. A. Suzuki, All Japan Electric Workers Union to Col M.E. Scott, Plans and Policy, G-4, "A re-appeal for further consideration of the problem of electric power industry reorganization," 22 July 1949, NA, RG 331, Box 404, File: 463, Fuel, etc; See also Akita, et al., pp. 137–138.

51. There seems to have been some infighting on labor issues in relation to electric power too. On 18 February 1950, the Chief of the Labor Division, Robert Amis, sent an acid memo to Marquat requesting that he muzzle the members of the Industry and Utilities and Fuel Divisions who were advising electric-power managers to reject a wage agreement that had been painfully hammered out with the Central Labor Relations Board. Memo from Robert T. Amis to Marquat, 18 February 1950, "Conciliation Award in Electric Power Industry," NA, RG 331, Box 6189, Folder: 10, 463: Power and Electricity, Data Concerning step-up in, etc.

52. Akita, et al., pp. 138–139; Horikoshi II, 414.

53. A study by Tokyo University's Shakai Keizai Kenkyūjo found that, in 1948, the union was evenly balanced between Communist and *mindō* members. Between 14 and 17% of active members and 39% of the standing committee members were Communists, while 13–19% of general and 36% of standing committee members were in the *mindō* group. Most of the rest were uncommitted or unknown. Reported in Rōdō Sōgi Chōsakai, *Densan Sōgi,* p. 85; Akita, et al., pp. 107–110.

54. Rōdō Sōgi Chōsakai, *Densan Sōgi,* pp. 30, 37.

55. The *mindō* proposal to end regional strikes is reprinted in ibid., pp. 87, 91–92; See also Akita, et al., pp. 107, 123, 125.

56. *Denki Jigyō Saihensei Shi; Tokyo Denryoku 30 -nen Shi,* p. 214.

57. Ōtani, pp. 143–145.

58. *Tokyo Denryoku 30-nen Shi,* p. 219; G.R. Roames, Chief, ESS/Utilities and

Fuels Division Memo to Marquat, "Report on Reorganization of Electric Power Industry," 7 February 1950, NA, RG 331, Box 6189, Folder: 10, 463: Power and Electricity, Data Concerning step-up in, etc.; Ōtani, pp. 158–159; Usami, p. 18.

59. G.R. Roames, "Report on Reorganization of Electric Power Industry"; SCAP, Historical Monograph, #46, "Expansion and Reorganization of the Electric Power and Gas Industries," pp. 29–42; Matsunaga, pp. 35–36; Matsunaga interview in Andō, p. 373; From this time, Matsunaga became an important political backer for Ikeda. Usami, pp. 22, 26; Ōtani, pp. 152–153.

60. Miki's plant was in Kyushu. Miki, who was an officer of both Nikkeiren and Keidanren at the time, spoke for heavy industry. Miki Takashi, testimony to Diet, April 1950, in Shin Keizaisha Editorial Board, ed., *Denki Jigyō Saihensei Kakukai no Iken*, Chūō Denryoku Kenkyūkai archives. Nissankyō also came out in favor of the Miki plan. Horikoshi II, 416. This was the dominant business opinion of the day according to interviews with Watanabe Ichiro, 8 August 1984, Nagase Seiji, 9 August 1984, Miyoshi Shuichi, 27 July 1984. See also *The Japan Economic Weekly* 6.154 (21 September 1950), which favored Matsunaga's plan and commented on persistent rumors that Hassōden bribed Diet members to buy their votes on this issue.

61. *Asahi Shinbun* editorial of 28 January 1950, *Mainichi Shinbun* editorial of 23 January 1950, and Nissankyō statement of March 1950, reprinted in Shin Keizaisha Editorial Board, ed. See also Matsunaga, pp. 23, 17, 37–38; Ōtani, pp. 149–158; Usami, p. 22.

62. T.O. Kennedy to Marquat, "Electric Power Industry in Japan," 2 June 1950, NA, RG 331, Box 6189, Folder: 10, 463: Power and Electricity, Data concerning step-up in, etc.

63. ESB, "Economic Self-Supporting Program of Japan," 20 January 1951, pp. 56–57. English version in Dower Collection.

64. SCAP, Historical Monograph, #41, "The Petroleum Industry," pp. 64–65.

65. "Report on Japanese Reparations" (First Strike Report), by Special Committee on Japanese Reparations, War Department, 18 February 1947, reprinted in Ōkurashō, *Shōwa Zaisei Shi* XX, 464–471; SCAPIN #1920/1, "Information of General Application Pertaining to SCAPIN 1920 . . . petroleum storage tank facilities," 9 July 1948.

66. Overseas Consultants, Inc., *Report on Industrial Reparations Survey of Japan to the United States of America*, p. 173–74.

67. Yaichi Sasaki, "Petroleum Refineries at a Crossroads," *Oriental Economist* 22.522 (April 1954), p. 194; *Oriental Economist* 19.506 (December 1952), p. 118; Peter R. Odell, *Oil and World Power: Background to the Oil Crisis*.

68. "Report on the Economic Position and Prospects of Japan and Korea: Measures Required to Improve Them," 26 April 1948.

69. Their assumption that the Japanese economy would be decentralized shows

that this report was still based on a structural analysis of Japanese aggression that was to fade from U.S. consciousness before long. ESS, "Industrial Disarmament and Economic Control of Japan," 22 January 1947, reprinted in Ōkurashō, *Shōwa Zaisei Shi* XX, 510–514.

70. "Memo of Conversation of 20 May 1949 concerning Petroleum Refineries in Japan," by Max Bishop, Chief of Division of Northeast Asian Affairs, Department of State, NA, RG 59, Dept. of State Decimal File, 1945–1949, Box 7118, file 894.6363/ 1/1/45–12/31/49; SCAP, Historical Monograph #41, "The Petroleum Industry," p. 64.

71. H. Noel, "The Petroleum Refineries of Japan," ESS/SCAP, Tokyo, 25 March 1949, pp. 1–2.

72. Ibid. p. 5.

73. "Transcript of Roundtable Discussion on American Policy Toward China Held in The Department of State, October 6–8 1949," *The Declassified Documents Quarterly Catalog* (1976) Vol. II, 316B, p. 48 of document. The most striking aspect of Kennan's remarks is their acceptance of the need to help Japan recreate an economic empire. The U.S. government restricted petroleum sales to the Peoples' Republic of China at about the same time. Yashuhara.

74. Petroleum Advisory Group, "Report on the Petroleum Advisory Group, November 1945 to June 1951," Tokyo: SCAP, 1951, pp. 7, 24; SCAPIN #2027, "Operation of Pacific Coast Refineries and Import of Crude Petroleum," 13 July 1949, reprinted in Ministry of Foreign Affairs, *Documents Concerning the Allied Occupation and Control of Japan* IV, 63–65.

75. MITI, *Japanese Mining Industry 1955*, p. 3.

76. "Japan's Oil Industry Reviving: Crude Oil Imports and Foreign Investment, Two Props," *Journal of Finance and Commerce* 3.8:26–27 (15 August 1950).

77. Petroleum extraction and marketing was one of the most concentrated industries in the world, dominated by 7 huge companies. Anthony Sampson, *The Seven Sisters and the World They Made;* Odell. See also *Oriental Economist* 19.506 (December 1952), p. 118; "Petroleum," *Oriental Economist* 16.317 (15 January 1949), pp. 35–36.

78. This discussion is drawn primarily fron Inokuchi, pp. 387–403.

79. "Petroleum Industry (2)," *Oriental Economist* 16.325 (12 March 1949), p. 234.

80. ESB, "Measures to be taken with respect to the introduction of Foreign Capital in Japan," 26 November 1947, exhibited a positive but cautious attitude and stated that "basic industries should be kept immune from . . . control by foreign capital." The ESB document, "Private Foreign Investment," 19 December 1949, was much more enthusiastic about investment from abroad. In two years, the attitude at the ESB had shifted markedly. Both Dower Collection. SCAP, *Monthly Summation* 34 (July 1948), pp. 31–32, 64–65;

Oriental Economist, 17.414: 1282 (2 December 1950); *Japan Economic Weekly,* 2.49: 1–4 (9 September 1948); 6.142: 10–11 (29 June 1950); Bank of Japan, *Postwar Japanese Economy: A Note To Foreign Investors.* The business organizations agreed that foreign capital was the best way to develop self-sufficiency. See Keizai Dōyūkai, "Nihon Keizai Jiritsuka no Kenkyū—Bōei Kōzō to Chūshin to shite," 2 July 1948, Takemae Archives at Tokyo Keizai Daigaku; Noda, p. 464; Keizai Dōyūkai, *Keizai Dōyūkai Jūgo-nen Shi,* p. 40. For Ashida's reliance on foreign capital, see Keizai Kikakuchō, Sengo Keizai Shi Hensan Shitsu, *Sengo Keizai Shi (Keizai Antei Honbu),* p. 76.

81. ESB, "Stabilization and Reconstruction," 9 March 1949, pp. 11–13; ESB. Economic Reconstruction Planning Committee, "Stabilization as We See It," 1 March 1949, pp. 17–18. Both in Dower Collection.

82. ESB, "Stabilization as We See It," p. 17.

83. *Japan Economic Weekly* 4.100: 1–6 (8 September 1949); 5.119: 1–6, (19 January 1950); 8.196: 1–10 (12 July 1951).

84. This foreign-exchange budget was used until 1964, when Japan was pressured to conform to IMF regulations. Robert S. Ozaki, *The Control of Imports and Foreign Capital in Japan,* pp. 10–12, 28. Both the Foreign Exchange and Foreign Trade Control Law and the Foreign Investment Law, as well as other related documents, are reprinted in this book.

85. The Foreign Exchange Law was amended in 1979 and the Foreign Investment Law was abolished at that time. Ozaki, p. 78; T. Kubota, "Induction of Private Foreign Capital in Japan after the War," Mitsubishi Economic Research Institute (MERI), *Monthly Circular* 264: 11–12 (November 1951).

86. Ozaki, p. 164. From 1961, these laws were modified to allow more foreign ownership, but, in the period under review, they remained in force as originally designed.

87. Leon Hollerman, "International Economic Controls in Occupied Japan"; J. V. Mladek and E. A. Wichin of the IMF staff, "Report on Exchange and Trade Controls in Japan," 18 November 1949, reprinted in part in Ōkurashō, *Shōwa Zaisei Shi* XX, 659–662. See Allen, *A Short Economic History of Modern Japan,* p. 185, for comments on uses of foreign-exchange controls to promote economic policy.

88. "Recent Developments of Foreign Investment Policies in Japan," by anonymous person from Mitsubishi Chemical Industries Ltd., MERI, *Monthly Circular* 234: 14–20 (May 1949).

89. The Cabinet Order concerning the Acquisition of Properties and/or Rights by Foreign Nationals of 15 March 1949 was the original legal basis for many of the petroleum contracts but it was superseded on 5 May 1950 by the Foreign Investment Law.

90. Ishizaki, pp. 205–206; Noguchi Teruo and Idemitsu Sazō in Kondō and Osanai, pp. 60, 38.

91. This meant that Kōa competed with Caltex (Japan) to sell oil products, and, in February 1951, Kōa decided to withdraw from retail sales, concentrate on refining, and market only through Caltex.
92. Interview with Noguchi Teruo in Kondō and Osanai, pp. 59–60.
93. Interview with Idemitsu Sazō in Kondō and Osanai, pp. 37–38.
94. *Journal of Finance and Commerce* 3.8 (15 August 1950); *Japan Economic Weekly* 5.126 (9 March 1950); 8.189 (24 March 1951); 8.196 (12 July 1951). The opposition from the Bank of Japan may have been due to the effect of the case on a related issue, borrowing by Japanese trading companies from foreign banks. The trading companies were eager to do so because interest rates were about 3% cheaper at the foreign banks. The Bank of Japan resisted this, arguing that it endangered its regulation of domestic finance and that it was a wasteful use of foreign exchange.

8. POST-AUSTERITY RATIONALIZATION: JAPAN IN THE WORLD ECONOMY

1. Michael Schaller, *The American Occupation of Japan: The Origins of the Cold War in Asia,* pp. 212–233. See also Borden, pp. 125–129; John W. Dower, *Empire and Aftermath,* pp. 373–400; Howard Schonberger, "The Japan Lobby in American Diplomacy, 1947–1952." For representative documents discussing this issue, see the following selections from *FRUS,* 11 March 1950, VI, 46–51; 16 March 1950, VI, 58–62; 3 April 1950, VI 68–79. Also see Tracy Voorhees's memo of 10 January 1950, "U.S. Economic Aid to Far Eastern Areas," enclosed in NSC 61 of 27 January 1950, available on microfilm, *Documents of the National Security Council, 1947–1977,* 1980.
2. Borden, p. 129. See also Voorhees's memo in preceding note.
3. Quotations are from NSC 48/5 of 17 May 1951, reprinted in *FRUS,* 1951, VI, 33–39. For this issue, see Dower, *Empire and Aftermath,* pp. 373–400.
4. Production levels surpassed the absolute prewar level in 1951 and 1952, but in per capita terms they were still low because of the population increase since the 1930s. Takafusa Nakamura, *The Postwar Japanese Economy,* pp. 41–42; *New York Times,* 3 January 1952, p. 81; Jerome Cohen, "Economic Problems of Free Japan," memorandum number 2 of the Center of International Studies, Princeton University, 22 September 1952, p. 18; Arisawa Hiromi, *Shōwa Keizai Shi* II, 110.
5. For Eisenhower opinion, see *FRUS,* 4 March 1954, 1952–54, XII, 392–397, and 1 December 1954, XII, 1002–1014. For petroleum, see *FRUS,* 18 January 1951, 1951, VI, 804–880; 30 January 1951, VI, 830–833; 16 February 1951, VI, 156–164. The ESB staff, in an official history, commented that they did not know precisely what the economic cooperation policy meant until Marquat returned from talks in Washington and issued a statement on 16 May 1951, although the term was used from January 1951.

Keizai Kikakuchō. Sengo Keizai Shi Hensan Shitsu, ed., *Sengo Keizai Shi (Keizai Antei Honbu Shi)*, p. 217.

6. See comments of Hara Akira in Thomas Berkman, ed. *The Occupation of Japan: The International Context*, especially pp. 190–191.

7. The objective of this document was economic self-sufficiency by the end of fiscal year 1953. This was defined as a program that "will enable not only balancing of international payments but also simultaneous improvement in living standard." ESB, "Economic Self-Supporting Program of Japan," 20 Janaury 1951. Dower Collection. A small portion of this 75-page document is reprinted in Ōkurashō. Zaisei Shishitsu, *Shōwa Zaisei Shi, Eibun Shiryō* XX, 551–552.

8. FRUS, 20 August 1952, 1952–54, XIV, 1314–1316; "Government thinks Japan Will Require American Aid Even After Peace Treaty," *The Japan Economic Weekly* 8.185: 8–9 (26 April 1951).

9. For concern about unemployment, see Nakayama Ichirō, "Unemployment in Japan," *Contemporary Japan* 21.7–9: 478–471 (July–September 1952); T. Yamabe, "The Recent Labour Situation in Japan," MERI, *Monthly Circular* 271: 8–13 (June 1952). For the Minister of Finance's gloomy assessment, see FRUS, 1952–54, XIV, 1267–1269. For Yoshida quotation, see Maeda Riichi, "Yoshida-san to Kankoku," (Yoshida and Korea), Kasekikai Kaihō 295, September 1970, as quoted in Dower, *Empire and Aftermath*, p. 316.

10. Saburō Ōkita, "Competitive Value of Japanese Export Goods," *Contemporary Japan* 20.4–6: 245–247 (April–June 1951). Ōkita was Chief of the Research Section of the ESB at the time.

11. *New York Times*, 3 January 1952, p. 75. Suzuki Gengo, then Financial Commissioner of Japan, commented recently that, in 1954, the Ministry of Finance decided against a yen devaluation, because Prime Minister Yoshida no longer had a firm hold on political power. Conference on the Occupation of Japan: The Impact of the Korean War, 16 October 1986, sponsored by the MacArthur Memorial Foundation, Norfolk, Virginia.

12. "Korean Ceasefire Move Upsets Japanese Businessmen," *Japan Economic Weekly* 8.185: 1–3 (5 July 1951); Saburō Ōkita, "Competitive Value of Japanese Export Goods," pp. 245–247.

13. ESB, "Basic Ideas Underlying Economic Self-support Program," 4 October 1950, Dower Collection, also in Ōkurashō, *Shōwa Zaisei Shi* XX, 549–551; ESB, "Economic Self-Supporting Program of Japan," 20 January 1951. The ESB self-sufficiency measures largely dovetail with the MITI report of the following month. "Report of the Industrial Rationalization Commission," February 1951, reprinted in Tsūshō Sangyō Shō, Shōkō Seisaku Shi Kankō-kai, *Shōkō Seisaku Shi, Sangyō Gōrika, (Sengo)* X, 65–74.

14. ESB, "Impact of Direct Procurement on our National Economy," March 1951 and ESB, "Impact of Direct Procurement on our National Economy,"

[May 1951], are two examples. Both Dower Collection. This request was denied by Marquat on 19 May 1951. See Ōkurashō, *Shōwa Zaisei Shi* XX, 569–572.

15. See preceding ESB citations; ESB, *Economic Survey of Japan, 1950–51,* August 1951, pp. 16–20; *FRUS,* 3 September 1951, 1951, VI, 1320–1323, for Dodge comments.

16. Friedman, pp. 73–78.

17. MITI, Enterprise Bureau, ed. "Waga Kuni Shuyō Sangyō no Jittai," quoted in Keizai Kikakuchō. Sengo Keizai Shi Hensanshitsu, ed., *Sengo Keizai Shi (Keizai Antei Honbu Shi),* p. 219; Tsūshō Sangyō Shō, Shōkō Seisaku Shi Kankōkai, *Sangyō Gōrika,* p. 55.

18. For Yoshida's and his advisors' attitude that "Japanese government economists are generally incompetent," see *FRUS,* 1951, VI, 810. See comments in Sangyō Seisaku Shi Kenkyūjo, ed., "Sengo Sangyō Seisaku ni Kan Suru Zadankai, [I]—Sōkatsu, Hokan (Keisha Seisan kara Jiyū Keizai no Tenkai e)," pp. 104–105, 112.

19. ESB, "Basic Ideas underlying Economic Self-Support Program," 4 October 1950; ESB, "Economic Self-Supporting Program of Japan," 20 January 1951; MITI Enterprise Bureau, ed. "Waga Kuni Shuyō Sangyō no Jittai," in Keizai Kikakuchō. Sengo Keizai Shi Hensanshitsu, *Sengo Keizai Shi (Keizai Antei Honbu Shi),* p. 219; Tsūshō Sangyō Shō, Shōkō Seisaku Shi Kankōkai, *Sangyō Gōrika,* pp. 65–74.

20. Discussion of Japanese Peace Treaty with Mr. Ikeda, 2 May 1950, *FRUS* 1950, VI, 1194–1198. See also *FRUS* 1951, VI, 1336–1339 and 1320–1323.

21. *FRUS,* 1951, VI, 1336–1339. *FRUS,* 1952–54, XIV, 1267–69; *FRUS,* 1952–54, XII, 551.

22. U.S. military spending in Japan increased again during the American-Vietnamese War. NSC 5429/2, "Review of U.S. Policy in the Far East," 20 August 1954, FRUS, 1952–54, VI, 769–776; NSC 6008/1, "U.S. Policy Toward Japan," 11 June 1960, in *Documents of the NSC, 1947–1977, Second Supplement;* Allen, *A Short Economic History of Modern Japan,* pp. 173–174.

23. Arisawa, *Shōwa Keizai Shi* II, 133–137; Arisawa, *Nihon Sangyō Hyaku-nen Shi,* p. 382. Kawasaki was generally criticized for building a plant that could operate only at full capacity and so would not be able to curtail operations during a depression. This was not considered appropriate behavior for a *private* company. (*"Nittetsu igai wa narubeku yaranai hō ga ii."*)

24. This law brought together a number of provisions that had been used earlier in single industries, such as accelerated depreciation (which was made more generous and expanded to apply to 30 industries), foreign-exchange allocations, and loans. The new law introduced subsidies for experimental opera-

tion of new technology and pledged state responsibility for improvements to road and rail lines, harbors, telecommunications, and water supply.

25. Arisawa, *Nihon Sangyō Hyaku-nen Shi,* p. 382. This Chiba plant embodied the new rationalization policy. The President of the company, Nishiyama Yatarō, had an unusual background in a technical field and incorporated many new energy-saving, resource-saving ideas. For example, all the factory equipment was highly pressurized to save operating costs.

26. Arisawa, *Enerugī,* pp. 298–310; Kinoshita; Matsuoka; Yada, *Sengo Nihon no Sekitan Sangyō,* Ch. 3; Sonoda, p. 24. See also Arisawa, *Shōwa Keizai Shi* II, 136–137. Sumiya Mikio, an expert on small mines, is the main non-industry dissenter from this position. Interview, 11 May 1984.

27. Arisawa, *Enerugī,* p. 311.

28. Ibid., pp. 298, 310.

29. The tension between large and small coal producers was expressed institutionally in March 1951 when all but the 18 largest coal companies walked out of the Japan Coal Mining Association, which from that time became exclusively a pressure group for those 18 companies. The other firms then set up the independent Japan Coal Mine Federation in May 1951. The resentments of the smaller firms, that the large ones controlled the price structure and influenced government policy to benefit only themselves, mirrored the complaints of the small coal operations in the 1930s. Kiso interview in Kondō and Osanai, pp. 118–120.

30. This included coal-industry spokesman Abe Yōichi. For a lengthy discussion of this issue, see Yada, *Sengo Nihon no Sekitan Sangyō,* Ch. 3. Also see Arisawa, *Enerugī,* p. 313.

31. Personal interview, 20 September 1984. "Sekkaku 30 sen man ton made kita kara . . ."

32. Wakao Fujita, "Labor Disputes," in Okochi, Karsh, and Levine, p. 354; Ōkōchi, *Sengo Nihon no Rōdō Undō,* p. 174.

33. Nihon Tankō Rōdō Kumiai, pp. 329–357; Rōdō Sōgi Chōsakai, *Sengo Rōdō Sōgi Jittai Chōsa, Sekitan Sōgi* I, 183–188; Interview with Kaku Saijirō in Andō, pp. 219–222, provides interesting insights into the Ministry of Labor position on the Red Purge.

34. The full title was Nihon Rōdō Kumiai Sōhyōgikai. Interview with Hara Shigeru in Kondō and Osanai, pp. 149–150.

35. July 1950 Sōhyō membership is given as 3.1 million in Daily Labor Press, p. 49.

36. The wage increase would have been considerable. The union asked for an increase from ¥550 to ¥1,060 per day for underground workers and from ¥365 to ¥560 for surface workers. In the end, they accepted a 10% wage increase. Japan, Labor Ministry, *Labor Yearbook for 1952,* p. 48; "Labor," *Oriental Economist* 21. 508 (February 1953), p. 94.

37. Sōhyō was also politically active in this period. It led the opposition to Japanese support for the Korean War and also lobbied against proposed legislation to restrict civil liberties.

38. Labor Ministry, *Labor Yearbook for 1953,* pp. 30–31; "Labor Disputes Still On," *Journal of Finance and Commerce* 5.12 (15 December 1952), p. 11. For popular attitudes, personal interviews with Arisawa Hiromi, 20 September 1984, and Funahashi Naomichi, 9 May 1984. "Labor," *Oriental Economist* 21. 508 (February 1953), p. 94.

39. This discussion draws on Nihon Tankō Rōdō Kumiai, pp. 400–420; "Labor Disputes Still On," *Journal of Finance and Commerce,* p. 10; Kazutoshi Kōshiro, "Development of Collective Bargaining in Postwar Japan," in Taishiro Shirai, ed., *Contemporary Industrial Relations in Japan,* pp. 222–225.

40. Sumiya Mikio, "Implications of Technological Change in Industrial Relations in Japan." See also Taishiro Shirai, "A Theory of Enterprise Unionism," in Shirai, *Contemporary Industrial Relations in Japan,* p. 139.

41. It led to an emphasis on seniority in wage decisions, since this criterion roughly approximated both skill (as managers wanted) and need (as unions wanted). As such, it was acceptable to both management and labor. It also meant a promise by employers of relative job security for permanent, full-time employees in return for union acceptance of a fairly narrow definition of employee, to exclude temporary and "part-time" workers.

42. Andrew Gordon, *Evolution of Labor Relations in Japan,* p. 383.

43. Rōdō Sōgi Chōsakai, *Sekitan Sōgi,* pp. 252–258.

44. Sonoda, p. 24. See also Arisawa, *Enerugī,* p. 298.

45. Hara Shigeru interview in Kondō and Osanai, p. 151.

46. Rōdō Sōgi Chōsakai, *Sekitan Sōgi,* pp. 256–258.

47. Benjamin Martin, "Japanese Mining Labor: The Miike Strike"; Rōdō Sōgi Chōsakai, *Sekitan Sōgi,* pp. 263–264. Funahashi Naomichi cites this strike as the decisive turning point for the coal industry. Interview, 9 May 1984.

48. The union was able to change the formula for calculating wage costs in 1956. From then, "price shift preparation funds," "additional investment reserve funds," etc, became the favorite places to disguise profits. Kinoshita, p. 103.

49. Sonoda, p. 36, Inaba Hidezō and Miyazaki Isamu, "Sekitan Kōgyō no Shōrai o Omou," p. 452.

50. Nihon Tankō Rōdō Kumiai, pp. 409–410.

51. Interview with Kiso Shigeyoshi in Kondō and Osanai, pp. 110–122.

52. Sonoda, p. 26–29; Nihon Kaihatsu Ginkō. Jū-nen Shi Hensa Iinkai, *Nihon Sangyō no Hatten to Kindaika,* p. 40.

53. Tsūshō Sangyō Shō, Shōkō Seisaku Shi Kankōkai, *Sangyō Gōrika,* pp. 65–75. This was the main document on rationalization from the Japanese government of this period; Note also ESB, "Economic Self-Supporting Program of Japan," 20 January 1951.

54. The Foreign Investment Council, which advised the Ministry of Finance, issued quarterly announcements of desired technology. This was virtual assurance of an import license for the listed items. The 26 March 1952 list concentrated on metal, machinery, mining, and chemical industries. Jerome Cohen, "Economic Problems of Free Japan," pp. 35–36; Ozaki, pp. 89–101. See also Terutomo Ozawa, *Japan's Technological Challenge to the West, 1950–1974: Motivation and Accomplishment,* pp. 20–21.

55. Japanese government memo on the Operation of Japan Development Bank, 6 August 1951, [probably by Ministry of Finance], Ōkurashō, *Shōwa Zaisei Shi* XX, 822–824. Originally, the JDB was not authorized to issue debentures because SCAP vetoed this, but, in 1952, the Japanese government amended the bank charter on this point. SCAP had wanted the JDB to lend only to other banks, rather than to industries, but gave in to the Japanese government, which wanted to use the loans to enforce its "key-industry" rationalization program. Kil, pp. 222, 227.

56. The average cost of mining coal at the 22 mines in 1952 was 35% higher, at ¥4,752 per ton. Sonoda, p. 28; Kinoshita, p. 100.

57. The affected coal mines saved ¥1.1 billion on taxes because of this measure alone. They saved a further ¥5 billion in 1952 on special retroactive reductions in interest rates for government loans. Kinoshita, p. 102.

9. ELECTRIC POWER: REORGANIZATION, RATIONALIZATION, AND EXPANSION

1. "Water Resources Development and Cement," *Commerce Japan* 5.3 (March 1954).

2. ESB, "Achievement of Economic Self-Sufficiency." June? 1950. Abridged version in Arisawa and Inaba, p. 147; For stringent restrictions on power consumption in 1951, see "Electric Power Shortage Affects Production," *Journal of Finance and Commerce* 4.11: 8–9 (15 November 1951).

3. "What of the Electricity Industry?" *Journal of Finance and Commerce* 3.8 (15 August 1950), p. 13; "Power Industry Checkmated," *Oriental Economist* 17.403: 978–979 (16 September 1950).

4. G. R. Roames, Utilities and Fuels to Kennedy, Director of Production and Utilities, "Prohibition against Electric Power Company Construction," 9 September 1950, NA, RG 331, Box 6189, Folder:11, "463: Power, Electric, Steam, Atomic"; Ōtani, p. 171.

5. Densan document of 12 July 1950, reprinted in Rōdō Sōgi Chōsakai, *Densan Sōgi,* pp. 94–99.

6. Akita, et al., pp. 144–145. After the Red Purge, the Kantō unit was left with only 60% of its workers, Kansai with 69.9%, Kyushu with 95.1%, and all the others with 98–99% of their members.

7. *Denki Jigyo Saihensei Shi,* p. 812.

8. T.O. Kennedy to Marquat, "Proposed action re reorganization and regulation of the Electric and Gas Utility industries," 10 March 1950, NA, RG 331, Box 6189, Folder:10, "463: Power and Electricity, Data concerning step-up in, etc."

9. MacArthur to Yoshida, 26 October 1950, MacArthur Memorial Archives, CinC-Personal File. I am grateful to Richard Finn for this document.

10. For Japanese arguments, see Matsunaga, p. 19; Usami, p. 23; also personal interview with Nagase Shūsen of Chūō Denryoku Kenkyūjo, 9 August 1984. For the intervention on behalf of Mitsubishi Electric, see Hosoya, pp. 196–197, 202. For the 1953 incident, see discussion of foreign loans below.

11. The only person I encountered who praised MacArthur's actions on this issue was Matsunaga's chronicler, Usami Shōgo, who remembered the General with "the highest esteem." Interview, 8 August 1984. For controversy, see Kurihara Tōyō, *Denryoku,* p. 390; Also personal interview with Watanabe Ichirō, 8 August 1984.

12. The rate structure had already been altered in 1949 in several significant ways that acted to encourage industrial power use. These were maintained after the industry reorganization. The first was that regional rates were substituted for a single national one. Second, seasonal rates were introduced. Third, previously consumers had been fined for using more electric power than contracted for, in order to limit total power use. This was changed to a system in which large-scale customers could use as much power as they wanted (unless government restrictions were in effect), but any power used beyond the allocated amount was charged at a higher rate. The rationale shifted from one based on scarcity to attempts to raise power sales revenue. Finally, the companies were allowed to retain a larger amount of profit than previously. Kurihara, pp. 472–473.

13. Note that government funds supplied an even higher percentage of construction costs. See Table 10. Electric power received the lion's share of government funds in the early 1950s, as high as 52.3% of all government capital to industry in 1954. Counterpart aid fund money to the industry totaled ¥63.1 billion between 1949 and 1952. Kurihara, pp. 466–469; *Nihon Kaihatsu Ginkō Jū-nen Shi,* pp. 495–497, 181.

14. From 1955, internal reserves were consistently a more important funding source than were private Japanese banks. The government also changed its JDB lending policy in 1955 from a blanket distribution of funds on the basis of the importance of the project alone to one based on the ability of the company to find alternative funding sources. Interview with Nagase Shūsen, 9 August 1984; Kurihara, pp. 469–474; *Nihon Kaihatsu Ginkō Jū-nen Shi,* pp. 177, 184.

15. This plan was devised by the new Minister of Trade and Industry, Ishibashi Tanzan, to limit the debt burden of basic industries. Ikeda Hayato had sug-

gested a similar plan earlier, but it had been withdrawn because private banks had opposed a provision that had given more power to the JDB. Ishibashi compromised with the banks on this point. "Gov't Is Taking Steps to Terminate Over-Borrowing by Foreign Trade, Coal-Electric Power Industries," *Journal of Finance and Commerce* 8.2: 5–7 (15 February 1955). See also Kozo Yamamura, *Economic Policy in Postwar Japan: Growth Versus Democracy*, pp. 49–51, 129–151.

16. "Controversy on World Bank Power Loan Talks," *Journal of Finance and Commerce* 6.10: 13–14 (15 October 1953); Ashiwara Shigeyoshi interview in Kondō and Osanai, p. 317; *FRUS, 1952–54*, XIV, 1267–1269, 1273, 1281–1286, 1328–1330.

17. Overseas Consultants, Inc., *Tadami River Power Investigation for the Public Utilities Commission of the Government of Japan*, May 1952, at Diet Library. The Japanese government later submitted a scaled-down request to the World Bank for a $120-million hydroelectric plan, but this was also rejected. *FRUS, 1952–54*, XIV, 1196, 1284–1285, 1368–1369, 1416–1428; See also *FRUS, 1951*, VI, 1466, and "World Bank Power Loan," *Journal of Finance and Commerce* 6.11: 7–8 (15 November 1953).

18. The Export-Import Bank continued to handle loans such as the $60-million cotton credit awarded to the Bank of Japan for cotton purchases in the United States in October. *New York Times*, 27 October 1953, p. 39. *FRUS, 1952–54*, XIV, 1416–1421; "World Bank Power Loan," pp. 7–8.

19. For example, the 3 companies had to get approval from the World Bank in 1958 before joining a power-sharing system with the other 4 power companies on Honshu. Ashiwara Shigeyoshi in Kondō and Osanai, p. 319.

20. "Controversy on World Bank Power Loan Talks," *Journal of Finance and Commerce* 6.10: 13–14 (15 October 1953); "Loan from World Bank Opposed," *Oriental Economist* 21.516: 480 (October 1953).

21. "World Bank Power Loan," pp. 7–8; Personal interview with Miyoshi Shuichi, 27 July 1984.

22. The International Bank for Reconstruction and Development, *The International Bank for Reconstruction and Development, 1946–1953*, pp. 9, 42, 49–50; W.A. Iliff, "The World Bank and Its Function"; Eugene R. Black, "International Bank for Reconstruction and Development."

23. The KLM loan of $7 million was for aircraft to be purchased in the United States. The International Bank for Reconstruction and Development, p. 7, 108, 126–128, 159; *FRUS, 1952–54*, XIV, 1427–1428.

24. *FRUS, 1952–54*, XIV, 1427–28.

25. Ashiwara interview in Kondō and Osanai, p. 318.

26. *Nihon Kaihatsu Ginkō Jū-nen Shi*, pp. 178, 184. See also *New York Times*, 16 October 1953, p. 36. Kurihara chart p. 468, for list of foreign capital loans from 1953 to 1961.

27. "Labor," column in *Oriental Economist* 20.506: 198 (December 1952), 21.507: 39 (January 1953), and 21.508: 94 (February 1953).

28. The percentage of labor costs to total costs steadily decreased over the next few years because of the weakness of the union and the more capital-intensive new technology. In 1952, labor was 29.3% of total costs; in 1953, 27.7%; in 1954, 26.7%; and in 1955, 24.4%. Electric Power Productivity Study Team, II, of Japan, under auspices of the International Cooperation Administration, "Brief Report on Electric Power Industry in Japan," pp. 30–33. Pamphlet in U.S. Department of State Library.

29. Rōdō Sōgi Chōsakai, *Densan Sōgi,* p. 47.

30. Nikkeiren sent several memoranda to the government on these issues. See "Request Concerning Action Against Anticipated Strike in the Public Utilities," of 9 October, and "Our Opinion on the Densan Strike" of 26 October, in Rōdō Sōgi Chōsakai, *Densan Sōgi,* p. 67; Akita, et al., p. 146.

31. Electric Power Productivity Study Team, pp. 32–33.

32. "Shiryō: Den Rōren no Chingin Yōkyū Hōshiki"; Satō Nakashi, "Denki Kigyō no Gijutsu Kakushin to Den Rōren."

33. Arisawa, *Nihon no Enerugī Mondai,* pp. 78–79.

34. Ibid., pp. 78–79, 96–97.

35. Takahashi Saburō, "The Electric Power Industry"; "Merry-Go-Round in Electric Power Industry," *Journal of Finance and Commerce* 5.10:12–13 (October 1952); *Commerce Japan* 3.3, March 1954, p. 22.

36. Several interviewees thought that that was a mistake: Watanabe Ichirō, 25 September 1984, Nagase Shūsen, 9 August 1984, Miyoshi Shuichi, 27 July 1984.

37. For nervousness, see interview with Hagiwara Kichitarō in Kondō and Osanai, pp. 99–102.

38. "Merry-Go-Round in Electric Power Industry," *Journal of Finance and Commerce,* 5.10: 12–21 (15 October 1952). See also "Japanese Electric Industry Floodlighted by Appointment of Washington Ambassadors," *Japan Economic Weekly* 10.240: 1–3 (May 1952).

39. The Trust Bank Group gave ¥10 million to the Liberals, but the power companies also gave ¥5 million to the Progressive Party. In 1955, the power companies topped the list of corporate contributors to the newly merged Liberal Democratic Party with a donation of ¥20 million. By this time, the coal operators had dropped to fourth place with a contribution of only ¥10 million. Yanaga Chitoshi, pp. 80–85. See also Miki.

40. While the private companies paid 5% to 7% for their loans in the 1950s, the EPDC paid only 1.63% in 1953 and then gradually more, up to 4.45% in 1960. This was an indirect form of aid to the electric-power companies, since it allowed the EPDC to sell its wholesale power to them at a lower rate. Kurihara, p. 470.

41. The equipment was supplied by Euclid, Bucyrus-Erie, Caterpillar, and other large firms over a 3-year period. Dengen Kaihatsu Kabushiki Kaisha (EPDC), *Information on the Projects for Loan from International Bank for Reconstruction and Development*, 30 July 1954, p. EPDC-3002.

42. *Information on the Projects for Loan from International Bank for Reconstruction and Development*, Ch. 12, pp. 2, 5.

43. Kurihara, p. 468.

44. *Information on the Projects for Loan from International Bank for Reconstruction and Development*, pp. 8–10, 8–12, 11–1. There was an earlier precedent for this type of arrangement. The U.S. government had loaned heavy equipment directly to the National Police Reserve in late 1952. FRUS, 1952–54, XIV, 1308–1311. See also FRUS, 1952–54, XIV, 1613–1614 for U.S. government training of Japanese technicians from defense-production industries.

45. The first report was distributed as the Denryoku Setsubi Kindaika Chōsa Iinkai, "Denryoku Setsubi Kindaika o Kosshi to suru Shin Denryoku Rokka-nen Keikaku no Gaiyō," 30 March 1930, in the Takemae Collection. An English translation of "The Fourth Recommendation for Modernization of Electric Power Industry in Japan," by Matsunaga, September 1958, is available at the Chūō Denryoku Kenkyūjo Archives. See also John D. Eyre, "Japan's Electric-Power Supply."

46. In fiscal 1952, the power companies used an average standard coal of 5,640 calories per ton with 19.62% efficiency, but this had changed to 5,448-calorie coal with 30.58% efficiency in fiscal 1959. Arisawa, *Enerugī*, p. 296.

47. In the late 1950s, the Japanese imposed tariffs on machine-tool imports, but this measure was also overwhelmed in 1964 by a set of tariff-liberalization measures. Friedman, pp. 74–83.

48. *Electrical Review*, 145 (19 August 1949): p. 347. For patterns of equipment purchases over time, see A.J. Surrey and J.H. Chesshire, *The World Market for Electric Power Equipment: Rationalization and Technical Change*.

49. *Nihon Kaihatsu Ginkō Jū-nen Shi*, p. 178; "Electric Machinery Industry Reinvigorated by Power Development Project," *Journal of Finance and Commerce* 6.4: 14–15 (15 April 1953) and "World Bank Power Loan," pp. 7–8, for debate over whether to use Japanese or foreign technology. Surrey and Chesshire argue that the electric-machinery makers later used the World Bank requirement that all contracts it funded be opened to international bidding to enter Third World markets.

50. Yanaga, p. 178; Rodney L. Huff, "Political Decision-making in the Japanese Civilian Atomic Energy Program," p. 3. For pre-surrender Japanese research into atomic power, see John W. Dower, "Science, Society, and the Japanese Atomic-Bomb Project During World War II."

51. Stanley Levey, "Nuclear Reactor Urged for Japan," *New York Times*, 22 September 1954, p. 14. Senator Estes Kefauver argued in an appended article

that building atomic power plants in Asia "would provide a vivid answer to the Soviet lie about our political motives and atomic development."

52. Horikoshi II, 442.

53. MITI, *Japanese Mining Industry, 1955*, p. 15. Matsunaga Yasuzaemon was the first to urge the coal-mine operators to look for uranium deposits in the early 1950s. Interview with Abe Yōichi, 3 October 1984.

54. The most famous of these was an "Atoms for Peace Exhibition" staged in Hibiya Park in November–December 1955, which Shōriki sponsored jointly with the U.S. Information Service. Yanaga, pp. 182–183, 192.

55. Ibid., p. 199. For a recent critique of the Forum and Japan's atomic-energy policy, see Yuki Tanaka, "Rationality and Irrationality in Japanese Industry: The Economics of Nuclear Power."

56. These Japanese industrial groups purchased nuclear technology from abroad. Mitsubishi signed with Westinghouse, Hitachi-Fuji and Mitsui with General Electric, and Sumitomo with the German Kraftwerke Union. Richard F. Kosobud, "Civilian Nuclear Energy and Weapons Proliferation: An Analysis of Japanese and U.S. Views."

57. Ashiwara Shigeyoshi in Morikawa Hidemasa, ed., *Sengo Sangyō Shi e no Shōgen: Kyōdaika no Jidai*, pp. 322–323. See also Surrey and Chesshire.

58. The United States handled uranium enrichment for Japan. Japan's Atomic Energy Commission first chose to import a British Calder-Hall reactor design in 1956, largely because it ran on natural rather than enriched uranium. However, a serious accident in Britain in 1958 involving another Calder-Hall reactor tarnished its safety record, and the Japanese government bought most of its subsequent atomic technology from Westinghouse and General Electric, which both used enriched uranium, light-water designs. This change of heart may have been influenced by the 9 power companies, which had already signed import contracts with the two American firms for commercial atomic power plants. "Development of Atomic Energy in Japan," *Fuji Bank Bulletin* 7.3: 39 (September 1956); Huff, pp. 67–70. In 1979, the EPDC imported the technology for a heavy-water reactor from Canada, partly to limit dependence on U.S. sources. The government and private firms have also put considerable resources into the development of independent Japanese technology, particularly in the 1980s.

10. COAL VERSUS OIL: THE 1950s

1. The Sofremines firm was hired after the Japanese government, the Japan Productivity Center, and the World Bank jointly solicited bids in October 1956 for an analysis of the Japanese coal industry. "Sofremines Report Concerning the Japanese Coal Mining Industry," September 1957, original English copy in Sekitan Kyōkai offices.

2. See Table 4, p. 76.

3. Sonoda, p. 33; Inaba and Miyazaki, p. 450.

4. Inaba and Miyazaki, p. 452.

5. The allocations for petroleum went from $144 million to $136.6 million for the 1954–1955 fiscal year. The oil industry had requested $170 million. "Gov't Set to Recontrol Heavy Oil To Save Foreign Currency," *Journal of Finance and Commerce* 7.6: 7 (15 June 1954). Allocated fuel-oil imports in 1954 were enough to supply only an estimated two-thirds of demand. *Oriental Economist* 22.524: 291 (June 1954); Nakamura Takafusa, *The Postwar Japanese Economy*, pp. 54–59.

6. Inaba and Miyazaki, p. 454.

7. Ozaki, pp. 26–27, Arisawa, *Nihon no Enerugī Mondai*, pp. 84–85.

8. Martha Caldwell, "Petroleum Politics in Japan: State and Industry in a Changing Policy Context," pp. 76, 88.

9. Idemitsu Sazō interview in Kondō and Osanai, p. 43. The *Nisshō Maru* was actually completed in late 1951, but SCAP requested that Idemitsu refrain from launching it until after the Occupation ended. Nihon Sekiyu Shi Henshū Shitsu, pp. 516, 530–531; Ezra Vogel, *Comeback*, pp. 46–49, for impact on the shipbuilding industry.

10. The government, which preferred to process oil in Japan, changed the foreign-exchange-allocations structure in 1955 to make imports of oil products more difficult. This was just about the same time that the tariff on products was raised to 6.5%. Arisawa, *Nihon no Enerugī Mondai*, p. 85.

11. Arisawa, *Nihon Sangyō Hyaku-nen Shi*, pp. 373–374; Arisawa, *Nihon no Enerugī Mondai*, p. 90, states that, from 1955, the refiners could import 50% more crude on the same allotment as in earlier years because they could handle lower quality grades.

12. Arisawa, *Nihon no Enerugī Mondai*, pp. 86–91. Another area of competition was over new refinery sites. This was particularly fierce over the rights to the ex-military refineries at Yokkaichi and Tokuyama. Arisawa, ed., *Nihon Sangyō Hyaku-nen Shi*, pp. 472–476. For a good English summary of this struggle, see Mark S. Brown, "The Emergence of Japanese Interests in the World Oil Market," pp. 34–36.

13. First quotation from Inaba and Miyazaki. Second from "Crisis in Coal Mining Industry," *Contemporary Japan*, 23:394(1953).

14. Under this law, 135 mines with a productivity of 4,160,000 tons were eligible for rationalization assistance. Arisawa, *Enerugī*, p. 313.

15. Interview with Yada Toshifumi, 9 April 1984.

16. Interview with Funahashi Naomichi, 9 May 1984; Nihon Sangyō Kōzō Kenkyūkai, *Nihon Sangyō Kōzō no Kadai* I, 541, 551–552.

17. This was the most controversial part of the package. Sonoda, p. 49.

18. The 1953 amendment to the Anti-Monopoly Law also relaxed restrictions on

stockholding, interlocking directorships, and mergers. It redefined key phrases in the law, such as "competition which is contrary to the public interest" and "unreasonable restraint of trade," to allow more restrictive behavior. Rationalization cartels were also allowed on a smaller scale in comparatively strong industries. For example, the iron-and-steel industry was allowed to import scrap iron at a predetermined price under the "rationalization cartel" provision in 1953. Kozo Yamamura, *Economic Policy in Postwar Japan*, pp. 54–61; Hosoya, pp. 235–236.

19. Horikoshi II, 395–397, 402–403.

20. The Coal Rationalization Law passed the Diet on 30 July 1955. It also included provisions for a government coal stockpile and for a labor-arbitration board to handle mine-labor disputes. A special new semi-governmental body, the Coal Mine Adjustment Corporation, was established to close inefficient mines. Arisawa, *Enerugī*, pp. 311–312; Sonoda, pp. 49–54; Nihon Kaihatsu Ginkō, *Nihon Sangyō no Hatten to Kindaika*, p. 40.

21. Aki Kōichi, "Japan's Energy Resources."

22. "Petrochemical Industry in Japan," *Fuji Bank Bulletin* 7.2:15 (June 1956); "Development of Petrochemical Industries in Japan," *Fuji Bank Bulletin* 9.2:22 (June 1958).

23. Tsūshō Sangyō Shō. Kanbō Chōsaka, *Enerugī Tōkeishū*, pp. 62–63.

24. Arisawa, *Enerugī*, p. 313; Sonoda, pp. 37, 60.

25. Arisawa, *Enerugī*, pp. 314–315.

26. Arisawa, *Nihon no Enerugī Mondai*, pp. 75–76.

27. Abe Yōichi claimed that the price of oil in Japan was consistently lower than in either the United States or Europe from 1955. Interview, 3 October 1984.

28. Miike coal supplied Miike Gōsei Company, where coal gas was made right on the premises and supplied to Tōatsu Ōmuta, the fertilizer firm. This was one of the first Japanese *kombinato*. Arisawa Hiromi, *Enerugī*, p. 295.

29. In 1950, the electric-power industry consumed only 9.8% of all coal used in Japan, but, by 1960, this had risen to 23.0%. Steel plants had also increased their share from 14.2% to 18.6%, but this figure included some imported coal. The only other consumer in this period to increase its percentage of total coal used was the ceramics industry, from 6.9% to 8.6%. Japan produced 38.5 million tons of coal in 1950 and 51.0 million tons in 1960. Prime Minister's Office, *Japan Statistical Yearbook*, 1961, pp. 135, 142. See also Arisawa, *Enerugī*, p. 294.

30. For example, see roundtable discussion with Hiromi Arisawa, Yoshitaro Wakimura (incorrectly rendered as Gitarō), and Ten-nichi Koichi, "Crisis in Coal Mining Industry," *Contemporary Japan* 23.4–6: 393–395 (April–June 1955).

31. Oil became the big issue, according to Hagiwara Kichitarō, from 1955. He said that the signals should have been clear from about 1950, but "we did

not feel it yet then." Interview with Hagiwara Kichitarō in Kondō and Os-anai, p. 89. See also article by the President of Furukawa Mining Company, Eiichi Shinkai, which argued that the coal industry deserved far more government funding that it had previously received. "Coal Industry Equipment Funds," *Oriental Economist* 23. 531: 23–26 (January 1955).

32. Keidanren tried to mediate between the coal and electric-power industries at that time, but was unable to satisfy both sides. Sonoda, p. 69.

33. Even less defensible was the attempt to reintroduce the brand-name system. In 1954, there were over 3,000 brand names of coal on the market, because the big coal companies were trying to do just this. Arisawa, *Enerugī*, pp. 304–305.

34. Tonedachi Masahisa, "Japan's Lagging Oil Development."

35. Yoshi Tsurumi, "Japan," in Raymond Vernon, ed., *The Oil Crisis*, p. 113–128. Both Martha Caldwell, pp. 85–87, and Mark Brown argue that considerable behind-the-scenes support of Yamashita existed within MITI. From 1965, the Japanese reevaluated their official policy and stepped up efforts to find oil overseas, but, by the time the Japanese companies were capable of overseas exploration, most of the oil fields of the world were already under the control of the majors, nationalized, or in technically inaccessible areas, e.g. undersea.

36. Arisawa, *Nihon Sangyō Hyaku-nen Shi*, p. 472.

37. Ibid., pp. 472–476; Arisawa, *Nihon no Enerugī Mondai*, p. 91.

38. Between 1951 and 1961, Japanese oil companies borrowed ¥500.7 billion from the international oil companies and ¥211 billion from foreign banks. Japanese affiliates of the international oil firms accounted for ¥309.9 billion of that, while unaffiliated firms secured ¥401.8 billion of which ¥260.7 billion was borrowed in 1961. MITI. Mining Bureau. Oil Division. "Sekiyu Sangyō no Genshō" 1962 ed. reprinted in Arisawa, *Nihon no Enerugī Mondai*, p. 92. *The Role of Foreign Governments in Energy Industry*, pp. 321–331. See also Inokuchi, *Sekiyu*, pp. 505–512.

39. *Nihon Sekiyu Shi*, p. 521. The United States military had, however, already committed itself to protecting 64 Japanese oil-refining and storage facilities in cooperation with the Japanese police force. See Report of the Headquarters, Far East Command, "Protection of Japanese Vital Installations in Event of Disaster" of November 1952, summarized in NSC Progress Report in the Implementation of NSC 29, "Security of Strategically Important Industrial Operations in Foreign Countries," of 8 June 1953 in *Documents of the NSC, 1947–1977*, Supplement 1, Reel 1, 1983.

40. Shibagaki Kazuo, "Hatan Shita Nihon no Shigen Seisaku."

41. He went on to argue that U.S. capital was also necessary to encourage Japanese development of Southeast Asia. "United States-Japan Economic Relation," *Contemporary Japan* 22. 1–3: 30–37 (January–March 1953).

42. This is my impression and is corroborated by Mark Brown, pp. 26, 32. Brown stresses the attempts of the Japanese government to develop an independent presence in the international oil industry more than I do.
43. Jerome Cohen, "Economic Problems of Free Japan," pp. 56–57.
44. Ozaki, pp. 127–130; Johnson, *MITI and the Japanese Miracle*, p. 204.
45. ESB, "Economic Self-Supporting Program of Japan," 20 January 1951, Dower Collection. This ambivalence is also reflected in official American assessments of Japanese attitudes toward private foreign investment in the early 1950s. See *FRUS*, 1952–54, XIV, 1516–1517, 1623–1627, 1656–1659, and 1682–1684.
46. A MITI study in June 1953 found that 53% of total foreign investment in Japan was concentrated in the oil-refining industry. Similarly, 55% of foreign loans were to that industry. This latter percentage dropped to 25% after the huge World Bank loan in September. Seiji Keizai Kenkyūjo, *Nihon ni okeru Gaikoku Shihon*, p. 161.
47. Huff, p. 103.
48. Sonoda, pp. 124–125.

11. PLANNING FOR AN ECONOMY BASED ON IMPORTED OIL

1. Arisawa, *Enerugī*, p. 294.
2. In fact, the government provided about 40% of fiscal 1960 construction costs in the coal industry by guaranteeing ¥2,140 million in interest-free loans. Sonoda, p. 71.
3. The law restricting the use of oil in heavy boilers was also extended until August 1963 on the Commission's recommendation. However, shortly afterward, the heavy-boiler law was "weakened to the extent that it is practically ineffectual," because of opposition by the electric-power companies. Tsuchiya Kiyoshi, "The Coal Industry," p. 481. The power companies were allowed to build plants technically incapable of burning coal for the first time in 1960. Ashiwara in Morikawa, pp. 321–322; Eyre, p. 549.
4. Tsūshō Sangyō Shō. Shōkō Seisaku Shi Kankōkai, ed., *Sangyō Gōrika (sengo)*; Johnson, *MITI and the Japanese Miracle*, pp. 252–254, for a description of the development of this policy.
5. Johnson, *MITI and the Japanese Miracle*, pp. 251–252; Ozaki, pp. 39–54.
6. Sonoda, pp. 79–80; Hans H. Baerwald, "Tensions in Japanese Politics: Coal and Korea," p. 183.
7. Samuels notes that this law was patterned directly on a 1932 law of the same name, which had very strong economic nationalist overtones. Richard J. Samuels, *The Business of the Japanese State*, pp. 198–199.
8. Caldwell, pp. 90–110.

9. Yada, *Sekitan Gyōkai*. For a later critique of this policy, see Shibagaki, p. 72.

10. The other major collieries agreed to supply coal to Miike's customers during the strike, as they generally did for each other during a big strike. Interview with Abe Yōichi, 3 October 1984; Martin.

11. Often Dōmei "raiders" charged union leaders with being insufficiently anti-Communist and used this as justification for starting a second union, a tactic developed during the Occupation but still in use in 1960. Tadashi Hanami, *Labor Relations in Japan Today*, p. 133; Alice H. Cook, *An Introduction to Japanese Trade Unionism*, pp. 98–99. See also Alice H. Cook, "Political Action & Trade Unions: A Case Study of the Coal Miners in Japan."

12. Benjamin Martin, p. 29.

13. Kitazawa Tsutomu, ed., *Ken Domon Shashinshu—Chikuhō no Kodomotachi*.

14. Merriman shows that the central Japanese government allocated resources to regions in a way that encouraged equity rather than maximized national economic growth between 1960 and 1970. David Merriman, "Government Investment, Economic Growth and Regional Equity in Japan."

15. Baerwald, p. 183. The Independent Minimum Wage Law of 1957, which provided a *voluntary* formula for establishing a minimum wage, was first used to regulate wages in the coal-mining industry in 1963. Cook, *Introduction to Japanese Trade Unionism*, p. 15.

16. Sonoda, pp. 76–78.

17. The President of Hokutan Coal Company stated that the 1961 long-term contracts with Fuji Steel and Tokyo Gas saved Hokutan from bankruptcy. Interview with Hagiwara Kichitarō in Kondō and Osanai, p. 94. See also Sonoda, pp. 89–96.

18. Ronald Dore, "Industrial Policy and how the Japanese do it."

19. For the Income-Doubling Plan, see Nakamura Takafusa, *The Postwar Japanese Economy*, pp. 83–89, and Uchino, pp. 109–116. Uchino notes that Nakayama Ichirō made important conceptual contributions to this plan.

20. Ironically, the success of the Income-Doubling Plan solved the problem of unemployed coal miners in a Draconian way. From the early 1960s, the younger miners were able to find other jobs in the expanding economy. They migrated to the cities and left the depressed coal regions. By 1964, a shortage of miners had become the most serious problem in the mines. If these conditions had existed just a few years earlier, probably Tanrō would have been more willing to accept rationalization measures. See Tsuchiya, "The Coal Industry," pp. 478–483, on this point.

21. Levine and Kawada stress the importance of the 1958 Vocational Training Act as a statement of government support for advanced worker training. Levine and Kawada, pp. 130–133.

22. *Basic Problems for Postwar Reconstruction of Japanese Economy*, p. 2.

Bibliography

Bibliography

INTERVIEWS

Abe Yōichi, 3 October and 5 October 1984. President, Mutsu-Kogawa Atomic Development Corporation, formerly Chairman, Nihon Sekitan Kyōkai.

Arisawa Hiromi, 13 September and 20 September 1984. Professor Emeritus, University of Tokyo.

Funahashi Naomichi, 16 March and 9 May 1984. Professor, Ōhara Shakai Mondai Kenkyūjo.

Ishii Kinnosuke, 9 August 1984. Professor, Obirin College.

Makino Fumio, 10 July 1984. Staff economist, Chūō Denryoku Kenkyūjo.

Miyoshi Shuichi, 27 July 1984. Professor, Sophia University, formerly *Asahi Shinbun* journalist.

Nagase Shūsen, 9 August 1984. Researcher, Chūō Denryoku Kenkyūjo.

Nakamura Seiji, 27 November 1984. Professor Emeritus, Seinan University.

Nakamura Takafusa, 5 September 1984. Professor, Tokyo University.

Obori Hiroshi, 2 October 1984. President, Kyōdō Oil Company, formerly at the Ministry of Commerce and Industry, on the staff of the Public Utilities Commission, at the Electric Power Development Company.

Sakisaka Masao, 26 March 1984. Chairman of the International Energy Forum, formerly at Economic Planning Agency.

Sumiya Mikio, 16 December 1983 and 11 May 1984. President, Japan Women's College, formerly Professor, Tokyo University.

Usami Shōgo, 8 August 1984. Retired journalist and close associate of Matsunaga Yasuzaemon.

Watanabe Ichirō, 8 August and 25 September 1984. President, DCC Corporation, formerly of Denki Chūō Kenkyūjo.

Yada Toshifumi, 9 April 1984, 15 May 1984, 16 August 1984. Professor, Sekitan Kenkyū Shiryō Sentā, Kyūshū University.

ARCHIVES

United States. National Archives.
Japan. Diet Library. Gendai Seiji Shishitsu.
Chūō Denryoku Kenkyūkai Archives.
Takemae Eiji Collection of Postwar Economic History at Tokyo Keizai Daigaku.
John W. Dower, Personal Collection.

JOURNALS

Commerce Japan
Contemporary Japan
Fuji Bank Bulletin
Japan Economic Weekly
Japan Quarterly
Foreign Capital Research Society, *Japanese Industry*.
Journal of Finance and Commerce
Mitsubishi Economic Research Institute, *Monthly Circular*
New York Times
Nippon Times
National Diet, *Official Gazette Extra*
Oriental Economist
Tōyō Keizai Shinpō

BOOKS AND ARTICLES

Ackerman, Edward. *Japan's Natural Resources and Their Relation to Japan's Economic Future.* Chicago, University of Chicago Press, 1953.
Adams, Thomas F. and Hoshii Iwao. *A Financial History of the New Japan.* Tokyo, Kodansha International, 1972.
Aki Kōichi. "Japan's Energy Resources," *Japan Quarterly* 3.3: 287–292 (July 1956).
Akita Nariyoshi, Arizumi Makoto, and Tosaka Ranko. "Denki Sangyō Rōdō Kumiai (Densan)" (The electric power industry workers' union—Densan). In Ōkōchi Kazuo, ed., *Nihon Rōdō Kumiai Ron* (A study of the Japanese labor union). Tokyo, Yuhikaku, 1953.
Allen, George C. "Japanese Industry: Its Organization and Development to 1937." In Elizabeth B. Schumpeter, ed., *The Industrialization of Japan and Manchukuo, 1930–1940: Population, Raw Materials and Industry.* New York, MacMillan, 1940.

————. *Japan's Economic Expansion.* London, Oxford University Press, 1965.

————. *A Short Economic History of Modern Japan.* Rev. ed. London, Allen and Unwin, 1972.

Allinson, Gary D. "Japan's Keidanren and its New Leadership," *Pacific Affairs* 60.3:385–407 (Fall 1987).

Anderson, Irvine H. *The Standard-Vacuum Oil Company and United States East Asian Policy, 1933–1941.* Princeton, Princeton University Press, 1975.

Andō Yoshio, ed. *Shōwa Keizai Shi e no Shōgen* (Testimony toward an economic history of the Shōwa period). Tokyo, Mainichi Shinbunsha, 1966. This work has also been issued with the variant title of *Shōwa Seiji Keizai Shi e no Shōgen* (Testimony toward a political and economic history of the Shōwa period).

Arisawa Hiromi, "Nihon Shihon Shugi no Unmei" (The destiny of Japanese capitalism), *The Hyōron,* February 1950, pp. 5–14.

————. *Nihon no Enerugī Mondai.* (Energy issues in Japan). Tokyo, Iwanami Shinsho, 1963.

————, ed. *Enerugī* (Energy). *Gendai Nihon Sangyō Kōza* (Lectures on modern Japanese industry), ed. Kawamura Taiji, Vol. III. Tokyo, Iwanami Shoten, 1960.

————. ed. *Nihon Sangyō Hyaku-nen Shi* (A century of Japanese industry). Tokyo, Nihon Keizai Shinbunsha, 1966.

————, ed. *Shōwa Keizai Shi* (Shōwa economic history). 2 vols. Tokyo, Nihon Keizai Shinbunsha, 1980.

———— and Inaba Hidezō, eds. *Keizai* (Economics). *Shiryō Sengo 20-nen Shi* (Documentary history of the postwar 20 years), Vol. II. Tokyo, Nihon Hyōronsha, 1966.

———— and Wakimura Yoshitarō interview. In "Sengo Sangyō Seisaku no Naka no Keizai Gakusha" (The economists in the midst of postwar industrial policymaking), *Ekonomisuto,* 24 August 1982, pp. 44–58.

Asada Sadao. "The Japanese Navy and the United States." In Dorothy Borg and Shumpei Okamoto, eds., *Pearl Harbor as History: Japanese-American Relations, 1931–1941.* New York, Columbia University Press, 1973.

Asahi Shinbunsha Keizaibu (Asahi Newspaper Economics Desk), ed. *Asahi Keizai Nenkan, 1955* (Asahi economic yearbook, 1955). Tokyo, 1955.

Ayusawa, Iwao. "Developments in Organized Labor, 1–3," *Contemporary Japan* 21.4–6: 231–235 (April–June 1952); 21.7–9: 410–424 (July–September 1952); 21.10–12: 541–554 (October–December 1952). Later republished as *Organized Labor in Japan.* Tokyo, Foreign Affairs Association, 1962.

Baerwald, Hans H. "Tensions in Japanese Politics: Coal and Korea," *Asian Survey* 3.4: 183–186 (April 1963).

Bank of Japan. *Postwar Japanese Economy: A Note to Foreign Investors.* Tokyo, 1949–1950.

Barnet, Richard. *The Lean Years.* New York, Simon and Schuster, 1980.

Barnhart, Michael A. *Japan Prepares for Total War: The Search for Economic Security.* Ithaca, Cornell University Press, 1987.

Bisson, T.A. *Japan's War Economy.* New York, Institute of Pacific Relations, 1945.

———. "Reparations and Reform in Japan," *Far Eastern Survey* 16.21: 241–247 (17 December 1947).

———. *Prospects for Democracy in Japan.* New York, Macmillan, 1949.

———. *Zaibatsu Dissolution in Japan.* Berkeley, University of California Press, 1954.

Black, Eugene R. "International Bank for Reconstruction and Development," *Canadian Banker,* Autumn 1952, pp. 23–31.

Borden, William S. *The Pacific Alliance: United States Foreign Economic Policy and Japanese Trade Recovery, 1947–1955.* Madison, University of Wisconsin Press, 1984.

Borg, Dorothy and Shumpei Okamoto, eds. *Pearl Harbor as History: Japanese-American Relations, 1931–1941.* New York, Columbia University Press, 1973.

Bronfenbrenner, Martin. "Four Positions on Japanese Finance," *Journal of Political Economy* 58.4: 281–288 (August 1950).

———. "Inflation Theories of the SCAP Period," *History of Political Economy* 7.2: 137–148 (1975).

———. "Economic History—Occupation-Period Economy (1945–1952)," *Encyclopedia of Japan.* Tokyo, Kodansha, 1983. II, 154–158.

Brown, Mark S. "The Emergence of Japanese Interests in the World Oil Market." Harvard University, Program on United States-Japan Relations, Occasional Paper #83-1, August 1983.

Buckley, Roger W. *Occupation Diplomacy: Britain, the United States, and Japan, 1945–1952.* London, Cambridge University Press, 1982.

Burger, Edward J. "Japan's Newly Reorganized Power Industry is Patterned After Ours," *Electrical World* 136:124–127 (8 October 1951).

Burkman, Thomas, ed. *The Occupation of Japan: The International Context.* Norfolk, MacArthur Memorial Foundation, 1984.

Caldwell, Martha. "Petroleum Politics in Japan: State and Industry in a Changing Policy Context." PhD dissertation, University of Wisconsin-Madison, 1981.

Cohen, Jerome B. *Japan's Economy in War and Reconstruction.* Minneapolis, University of Minnesota Press, 1949.

———. "Fiscal Policy in Japan," *Journal of Finance* 5.1: 110–125 (March 1950).

———. "Economic Problems of Free Japan." Memorandum number 2 of the Center of International Studies, Princeton University, 22 September 1952.

Cohen, Theodore. "Labor Democratization in Japan: The First Years." In Lawrence Redford, ed., *The Occupation of Japan: Economic Policy and Reform.* Norfolk, The MacArthur Memorial, 1980.

————. *Remaking Japan: The American Occupation as New Deal.* New York, The Free Press, 1987. [Posthumously edited by Herbert Passin.]

Cole, Allan B., George O. Totten, and Cecil H. Uyehara. *Socialist Parties in Postwar Japan.* New Haven, Yale University Press, 1966.

Cook, Alice H. *An Introduction to Japanese Trade Unionism.* Ithaca, Cornell University Press, 1966.

————. "Political Action & Trade Unions: A Case Study of the Coal Miners in Japan," *Monumenta Nipponica* 22. 1–2: 103–121 (1967).

Cook, Blanche Wiesen. *The Declassified Eisenhower: A Startling Reappraisal of the Eisenhower Presidency.* New York, Doubleday, 1981.

Daily Labor Press, ed. *The Labor Union Movement in Postwar Japan.* Tokyo, 1954.

The Declassified Documents Quarterly Catalog. Washington, D.C., Carrollton Press.

Denki Jigyō Saihensei Shi Kenkōkai. *Denki Jigyō Saihensei Shi* (The history of the electric-power industry reorganization). Tokyo, 1952.

Denryoku Shinpō (Electric-power news bulletin). "Denryoku Saihensei Jū-nen Kinen Tokushū Gō" (Special ten-year issue on reorganization of the electric-power industry) 7.77 (May 1961).

Documents of the National Security Council, 1947–1977, and *Second Supplement.* Frederick, University Publications of America, 1980, 1983.

Dore, Ronald. "Industrial Policy and how the Japanese do it," *Catalyst* 2.1 (Spring 1986).

————. *Flexible Rigidities.* Stanford, Stanford University Press, 1986.

Dower, John W. "Science, Society, and the Japanese Atomic-Bomb Project During World War II," *Bulletin of Concerned Asian Scholars* 10.2:41–54 (April–June 1978).

————. *Empire and Aftermath: Yoshida Shigeru and the Japanese Experience, 1878–1954.* Cambridge, Council on East Asian Studies, Harvard University, 1979.

————. "Yoshida Shigeru and the Scales of History." Paper presented at the Symposium on The Allied Occupation of Japan in World History at Hosei University, 30 November 1983, and published as "Yoshida Shigeru no Shiteki Ichi," in Sodei Rinjirō, ed., *Sekai Shi no Naka no Nihon Senryō.* Tokyo, Nihon Hyōronsha, 1985.

Draper, Jr., William H. "The Rising Sun of Japan," *Commercial and Financial Chronicle* 172:4958 (9 November 1950).

Duke, Benjamin C. *Japan's Militant Teachers: A History of the Left-Wing Teachers' Movement.* Honolulu, University Press of Hawaii, 1973.

Duus, Peter. "The Reaction of Japanese Big Business to a State-controlled Economy in the 1930s," *International Review of Economics and Business* 31.9: 819–832 (September 1984).

Economic Stabilization Board. *Economic Survey of Japan (1951–52).* [Tokyo] Economic Stabilization Board, July 1952.

————. "Official 'White Paper' Issued by the Japanese Government, July 4, 1947," *Contemporary Japan* 16.7–9: 362–402 (July–September 1947).

————. "White Paper of 1948," excerpted in *Contemporary Japan* 17.4–6: 214–222 (April–June 1948).

————. *Report on Current Economy: Japan's Economy Stabilization Program.* Tokyo, 1950.

Edwards, Catherine. "Allies in Conflict: The American Perspective." Paper presented at the Symposium on The Allied Occupation of Japan in World History at Hosei University, 1 December 1983, and published as "Tairitsu suru Rengōkoku—Amerika no Kanten" in Sodei Rinjirō, ed., *Sekai Shi no Naka no Nihon Senryō.* Tokyo, Nihon Hyōronsha, 1985.

Electric Power Productivity Study Team, II, of Japan under auspices of the International Cooperation Administration. "Brief Report on Electric Power Industry in Japan." December 1957.

Encyclopedia of Japan. Tokyo, Kodansha, 1983.

Erselcuk, Muzaffer. "Iron and Steel Industry in Japan," *Economic Geographer* 23: 105–129 (1947).

Eyre, John D. "Japan's Electric-Power Supply," *Geographical Review* 55.4: 546–562 (October 1965).

Farley, Miriam S. *Aspects of Japan's Labor Problems.* New York, John Day Press for Institute of Pacific Relations, 1950.

Fearey, Robert A. *The Occupation of Japan, Second Phase: 1948–50.* New York, MacMillan, 1950.

Feis, Herbert. *The Road to Pearl Harbor: The Coming of War Between the United States and Japan.* Princeton, Princeton University Press, 1950.

Fine, Sherwood M. "Japan's Postwar Industrial Recovery," *Contemporary Japan* 21.4–6: 165–216 (April–June, 1952). Reprinted as *Japan's Postwar Industrial Recovery.* New Dehli, Eastern Economist Pamphlet 13, 1953.

Foreign Affairs Association. *Japan Yearbook: 1949–1952.* Tokyo, [1952].

Friedman, David. *The Misunderstood Miracle: Industrial Development and Political Change in Japan.* Ithaca, Cornell University Press, 1988.

Frost, Peter. "Changing Gears: the Concept of 'Reverse Course' in Studies of the Occupation." Paper presented at the International Conference on The Occupation of Japan at Amherst College, 21 August 1980.

Fujiwara Akira. "The Role of the Japanese Army." In Dorothy Borg and Shumpei Okamoto, eds., *Pearl Harbor as History: Japanese-American Relations, 1931–1941.* New York, Columbia University Press, 1973.

————. *Senryō to Minshū Undō* (The Occupation and popular movements). In *Nihon Minshū no Rekishi* (Japanese people's history) Vol. X. Tokyo, Sanseidō, 1975.

Funahashi, Naomichi. "The Industrial Reward System: Wages and Benefits." In Okochi Kazuo, Bernard Karsh, and Solomon B. Levine, eds., *Workers and*

Employers in Japan: The Japanese Employment Relations System. Princeton and To-kyo, Princeton University Press and University of Tokyo Press, 1974.

Gale, Roger W. "Tokyo Electric Power Company: Its Role in Shaping Japan's Coal and LNG Policy." In Ronald A. Morse, ed., *The Politics of Japan's Energy Strategy: Resources-Diplomacy-Security.* Research Papers and Policy Studies 3, Institute of East Asian Studies, Berkeley, University of California Press, 1981.

Gardner, Richard N. *Sterling-Dollar Diplomacy: The Origins and the Prospects of Our International Economic Order.* New York, McGraw-Hill, 1969.

Gayn, Mark. *Japan Diary.* New York, William Sloane, 1948.

Gluck, Carol. "Entangling Illusions—Japanese and American Views of the Oc-cupation." In Warren Cohen, ed., *New Frontiers in American-East Asian Rela-tions.* New York, Columbia University Press, 1983.

Gordon, Andrew. "Labor Relations From War to Postwar." Unpublished paper prepared for the Association for Asian Studies, San Francisco, 25–27 March 1983.

————. *The Evolution of Labor Relations in Japan: Heavy Industry, 1853–1955.* Cambridge, Council on East Asian Studies, Harvard University, 1985.

Gordon, Richard L. *The Evolution of Energy Policy in Western Europe: The Reluctant Retreat from Coal.* New York, Praeger, 1970.

Grant, Robert Y. "Japanese Mining and Petroleum Industries: Programs under the Occupation," *Science* 112: 577–588 (17 November 1950).

Hadley, Eleanor, M. *Antitrust in Japan,* Princeton, Princeton University Press, 1970.

————. "Zaibatsu," and "Zaibatsu Dissolution," *Encyclopedia of Japan.* Tokyo, Kodansha, 1983. VIII, 361–366.

————. "The Economic Reforms of the Occupation from the Perspective of 1983." Presented at the Symposium on The Allied Occupation of Japan in World History at Hosei University, 30 November 1983, and published as "1983-nen kara Mita Senryōka no Keizai Kaisaku," in Sodei Rinjirō, ed., *Sekai Shi no Naka no Nihon Senryō.* Tokyo, Nihon Hyōronsha, 1985.

Halliday, Jon. *A Political History of Japanese Capitalism.* New York, Pantheon, 1975.

Hanami, Tadashi. *Labor Relations in Japan Today.* Tokyo, Kodansha Interna-tional, 1979.

Hane, Mikiso. *Peasants, Rebels, & Outcastes: The Underside of Modern Japan.* New York, Pantheon, 1982.

Harari, Ehud. *The Politics of Labor Legislation in Japan; National-International In-teraction.* Berkeley, University of California Press, 1973.

Hayashi Yoshimi. "Katayama Naikaku to Tankō Kokka Kanri" (The Katayama Cabinet and national management of the coal industry), *Kindai Nihon Kenkyū Nenpō* (Journal of modern Japanese studies), Vol. IV. Kindai Nihon Kenkyū-kai, 1982.

Hazama, Hiroshi. "Historical Changes in the Life Style of Industrial Workers." In Hugh Patrick, ed., *Japanese Industrialization and its Social Consequences*. Berkeley, University of California Press, 1976.

————. *Nihon no Shiyōsha Dantai to Rōshi Kankei—Shakai Shiteki Kenkyū* (Japanese management organizations and labor-management relations—Research in social history). Tokyo, Nihon Rōdō Kyōkai, 1981.

Hein, Laura E. "Energy and Economic Policy in Postwar Japan, 1945–1960." PhD dissertation, University of Wisconsin-Madison, 1986.

Hogan, Michael J. "American Marshall Planners and the Search for a European Neocapitalism," *American Historical Review* 90.1: 44–72 (February 1985).

————. *The Marshall Plan: America, Britain, and the reconstruction of Western Europe, 1947–1952*. Cambridge, Cambridge University Press, 1987.

Holding Company Liquidation Commission. *Laws, Rules and Regulations Concerning the Reconstruction and Democratization of Japanese Economy*. Tokyo, Kaiguchi Publishing Company, 1949.

————. *Final Report on Zaibatsu Dissolution*. 10 July 1951.

Hollerman, Leon. "International Economic Control in Occupied Japan," *Journal of Asian Studies* 38.4: 707–719 (August 1979).

————. "Interventionism and Foreign Trade: Statistics in Occupied Japan." In Leon Hollerman, ed., *Japan and the United States: Economic and Political Adversaries*. Boulder, Westview Press, 1980.

Horikoshi Taizō, ed. *Keizai Dantai Rengōkai Jū-nen Shi* (Ten-year history of the Federation of Economic Organizations). 2 vols. Tokyo, Keizai Dantai Rengōkai, 1962.

Hosoya, Masahiro. "Selected Aspects of the Zaibatsu Dissolution in Occupied Japan, 1945–1952." PhD dissertation, Yale University. 1982.

Huff, Rodney L. "Political Decision-making in the Japanese Civilian Atomic Energy Program." PhD dissertation, George Washington University, 1973.

Ienaga, Saburō. *The Pacific War, World War II and the Japanese*. New York, Pantheon, 1978, (Japanese ed. 1968).

Iliff, W.A. "The World Bank and Its Function," *United States Investor* 64: 1323–1332 (20 June 1953).

Inaba Hidezō and Miyazaki Isamu. "Sekitan Kōgyō no Shōrai o Omou" (Considerations on the future of the coal-mining industry), *Sekitan Hyōron* (Coal review), August 1954, pp. 450–458.

Inokuchi Tōsuke. *Sekiyu* (Oil). *Gendai Nihon Sangyō Hattatsu Shi* (A history of the development of modern Japanese industry), Vol. II. Tokyo, Gendai Nihon Sangyō Hattatsu Shi Kenkyūkai, 1963.

International Bank for Reconstruction and Development. *The International Bank for Reconstruction and Development, 1946–1953*. Baltimore, Johns Hopkins Press, 1954.

Ishibashi Tanzan. *Tanzan Kaisō*. (Tanzan's recollections) [1951]. Reprinted in

Ishibashi Tanzan Zenshū Iinkai, ed., *Ishibashi Tanzan Zenshū*. (The collected works of Ishibashi Tanzan), Vol. XV. Tokyo: Tōyō Keizai Shinpōsha, 1972.

Ishizaki Juro. *Sekiyu Nikki, Senchū-Sengo*. (Oil diary, wartime and postwar). Tokyo, Nihon Keizai Shinbunsha, 1979.

Itō Mitsuharu. "Munitions Unlimited: The Controlled Economy," *The Japan Interpreter* 7: 353–363 (Summer–Autumn 1972).

Ito Yoshimichi. "Monetary Contribution in Japanese Politics," *Contemporary Japan* 17.4–6: 182–184 (April–June 1948).

Iwao Yasuzumi, ed. *Nihon no Enerugī Mondai* (Energy issues in Japan). Tokyo, Jiji Tsūshinsha, 1974.

Japan Coal Association, ed. *International Coal Conference, October 1963*. Tokyo, 1963.

Japanese National Committee of the World Petroleum Congress. *The Petroleum Industry in Japan*. Tokyo, 1959.

Johnson, Chalmers. "The Reemployment of Retired Government Bureaucrats in Japanese Big Business," *Asian Survey* 14:9531–9565 (1974).

——————. *MITI and the Japanese Miracle: The Growth of Industrial Policy, 1925–1975*. Stanford, Stanford University Press, 1982.

Kahn, Herman. *The Emerging Japanese Superstate: Challenge and Response*. Englewood Cliffs, Prentice-Hall, 1970.

Kawai, Kazuo. *Japan's American Interlude*. Chicago, University of Chicago Press, 1960.

Keizai Dantei Rengōkai. *Keidanren no Nijū-nen*. (Twenty years of the Federation of Economic Organizations). Tokyo, 1969.

Keizai Dōyūkai. *Keizai Dōyūkai Jūgo-nen Shi*. (A fifteen-year history of the Japan Committee for Economic Development). Tokyo, 1962.

Keizai Kikakuchō (Economic Planning Agency). *Keizai Kikakuchō Niju-nen Shōshi* (A short twenty-year history of the Economic Planning Agency). Tokyo, Ōkurashō Insatsukyoku, 1966.

——————. *Gendai Nihon Keizai no Tenkai: Keizai Kikakuchō 30-nen Shi* (The development of the modern Japanese Economy: The thirty years of the Economic Planning Agency). Tokyo, Ōkurashō Insatsukyoku, 1976.

——————, Sengo Keizai Shi Hensan Shitsu. *Sengo Keizai Shi (Keizai Antei Honbu)* (Postwar economic history—The Economic Stabilization Board). Tokyo, Ōkurashō Insatsukyoku, 1964.

Kikuike Toshio. *Rinji Sekitan Kōgyō Kanri Hō no Kenkyū* (Studies on the temporary state control of coal mines law). Fukuoka, Kyūshū Daigaku Sangyō Rōdō Kenkyūjo, 1953.

Kil, Soong H. "The Dodge Line and the Japanese Conservative Party." PhD dissertation, University of Michigan, 1977.

Kinoshita Etsuji. *Nihon no Sekitan Kōgyō* (Japan's coal-mining industry). Tokyo, Nihon Hyōron Shinsha, 1957.

Kitazawa Tsutomu, ed. *Ken Domon Shashinshu—Chikuhō no Kodomotachi* (The collected photography of Ken Domon—The children of Chikuhō). Fukuoka, Chikuhō Shoshukukan, 1960.

Kondō Kanichi and Osanai Hiroshi, eds. *Sengo Sangyō Shi e no Shōgen: Enerugī Kakumei-Bōei Seisan no Kiseki* (Testimony toward a postwar industrial history: The energy revolution and the center of defense production). Tokyo, Mainichi Shinbunsha, 1978.

Kosai Yutaka. *The Era of High-Speed Growth: Notes on the Postwar Japanese Economy.* Tokyo, University of Tokyo Press, 1986. (Japanese ed. 1981).

Kōshiro, Kazutoshi. "Development of Collective Bargaining in Postwar Japan." In Taishiro Shirai, ed. *Contemporary Industrial Relations in Japan.* Madison, University of Wisconsin Press, 1983.

Kosobud, Richard F. "Civilian Nuclear Energy and Weapons Proliferation: An Analysis of Japanese and U.S. Views." Unpublished working paper of the Chicago Council on Foreign Relations, [1980].

Kubota, Akira. *Higher Civil Servants in Postwar Japan.* Princeton, Princeton University Press, 1969.

Kurihara Tōyō. *Denryoku* (Electric power). *Gendai Nihon Sangyō Hattatsu Shi* (A history of the development of modern Japanese industry), Vol. III. Tokyo, Gendai Nihon Sangyō Hattatsu Shi Kenkyūkai, 1963.

Levine, Solomon B. *Industrial Relations in Postwar Japan.* Urbana, University of Illinois Press, 1958.

———. "Labor," in *Encyclopedia of Japan.* Tokyo, Kodansha, 1983. IV, 343–349.

——— and Hisashi Kawada. *Human Resources in Japanese Industrial Development.* Princeton, Princeton University Press, 1980.

Lockwood, W.W. *The Economic Development of Japan: Growth and Structural Change.* Rev. ed. Princeton, Princeton University Press, 1968.

Magaziner, Ira C. and Thomas M. Hout. *Japanese Industrial Policy.* Berkeley, Institute of International Studies, University of California, 1981.

Maier, Charles. "The Politics of Productivity: Foundations of American International Economic Policy after World War II." In Peter Katzenstein, ed., *Between Power and Plenty.* Madison, University of Wisconsin Press. 1978. pp. 23–49. This article also appeared in *International Organization* 31: 607–633 (Autumn 1977).

Maki, John M., tr. and ed. *Japan's Commission on the Constitution: The Final Report.* Seattle, University of Washington Press, 1980.

Martin, Benjamin. "Japanese Mining Labor: The Miike Strike," *Far Eastern Survey* 30:26–30 (February 1961).

Martin, Edwin M. *The Allied Occupation of Japan.* New York, Institute of Pacific Relations, 1948.

Masumi, Junnosuke. *Postwar Politics in Japan, 1945–1955.* Berkeley, Institute of East Asian Studies, University of California Press, 1985.

Matsunaga Yasuzaemon. *Denryoku Saihensei no Omoide* (Recollections of the reorganization of electric power). Tokyo, Denryoku Shinbunsha, 1976.

Matsuoka Tamao. *Sengo Kyūshū ni okeru Sekitan Sangyō Saihensei to Gōrika* (The reorganization and rationalization of the postwar coal industry in Kyūshū). Tokyo, Nihon Gakujutsu Shinkōkai, 1954.

Mayo, Marlene. "American Economic Planning For Occupied Japan: The Issue of *Zaibatsu* Dissolution, 1942–1945." In Lawrence Redford, ed., *The Occupation of Japan: Economic Policy and Reform.* Norfolk, The MacArthur Memorial, 1980.

McCormick, Thomas J. "Drift or Mastery? A Corporatist Synthesis for American Diplomatic History," *Reviews in American History* 10.4: 318–330 (December 1982).

McNelly, Theodore. "The Renunciation of War in the Japanese Constitution," *Political Science Quarterly* 77.3: 350–378 (September 1962).

Merriman, David. "Government Investment, Economic Growth and Regional Equity in Japan." Harvard University, Program on United States-Japan Relations, Occasional Paper, July 1987.

Miki Yonosuke. "Zaisei- Seiki Kenkin no Uchimaku" (The inside story on political contributions from big business), *Chūō Kōron* 78. 6102–6112 (June 1963).

Minami, Ryōshin. *Power Revolution in the Industrialization of Japan: 1885–1940.* Tokyo, Kinokuniya, 1987.

Ministry of Foreign Affairs, Special Survey Committee. *Basic Problems for Postwar Reconstruction of Japanese Economy.* Translation of A Report of Ministry of Foreign Affairs' Special Survey Committee, September 1946. Rev. ed. Tokyo, The Japan Economic Research Center, July 1977.

———. Special Records Division. *Documents Concerning the Allied Occupation and Control of Japan.* 6 vols. Tokyo, Tōyō Keizai Shinpōsha, 1949.

———. *The Trade Union Movement in Postwar Japan.* Tokyo, 1965.

Ministry of International Trade and Industry. *Japanese Mining Industry, 1955.* Tokyo, 1956.

Ministry of Labor. *Labor Yearbook.* Tokyo, annual.

Mizutani Chōsaburō Den (Biography of Mizutani Chōsaburō). Kyoto, Mizutani Chōsaburō Den Kankōkai, 1963.

Moore, Joe B. *Japanese Workers and the Struggle for Power, 1945–1947.* Madison, University of Wisconsin Press, 1983.

Morikawa Hidemasa, ed. *Sengo Sangyō Shi e no Shōgen: Kyōdaika no Jidai* (Testimony toward a postwar industrial history: The era of bigness). Tokyo, Iwanami Shoten, 1977.

Morley, James. "The First Seven Weeks," *The Japan Interpreter* 6.2: 151–164 (Summer 1970).

Morse, Ronald A., ed. *The Politics of Japan's Energy Strategy: Resources-Diplomacy-Security*. Research Papers and Policy Studies, Vol. III. Berkeley, Institute of East Asian Studies, University of California Press, 1981.

Murakami, Yasusuke. "Toward a Socioinstitutional Explanation of Japan's Economic Performance." In Kozo Yamamura, ed. *Policy and Trade Issues of the Japanese Economy: American and Japanese Perspectives*. Seattle, University of Washington Press, 1982.

Muramatsu, Michio and Ellis S. Krauss. "Bureaucrats and Politicians in Policy-making; The Case of Japan," *The American Political Science Review* 78.1: 126–146 (March 1984).

———. "The Conservative Policy Line and the Development of Patterned Pluralism." In Kozo Yamamura and Yasukichi Yasuba, eds. *The Political Economy of Japan*, Vol. I: *The Domestic Transformation*. Stanford, Stanford University Press, 1987.

Nakamura Hideichiro. "Plotting a New Economic Course," *Japan Echo*, Special Issue, "Economy in Transition" 6: 11–20 (1979).

Nakamura Masanori, *Nihon no Rekishi—Rōdōsha to Nōmin* (History of Japan—laborers and farmers). *Nihon no Rekishi* (History of Japan), Vol. XXIX. Tokyo, Shogakkan, 1976.

Nakamura Seiji. "Sengo no Enerugī Seisaku" (Postwar energy policy). In Iwao Yasuzumi, ed., *Nihon no Enerugī Mondai* (Japan's energy problems). Tokyo, Jiji Tsūshinsha, 1974.

Nakamura Takafusa. "Sengo Tōseiki ni okeru Sekitan Kōgyō no Chikuseki Katei" (The capital-accumulating process of the coal industry in Japan, 1945–1949), *Shakai Kagaku Kiyō,* Tokyo Daigaku Kyōiku Yōgakubu 6:207–244 (1956).

———. "Keizai Keikaku no Seikaku to Igi" (The character and significance of economic planning in Japan), *Sengo 20-nen no Keizai Seisaku* (The annual of the Japan Economic Policy Association, 1968). Keisō Publishing.

———. *The Postwar Japanese Economy: Its Development and Structure*. Tokyo, University of Tokyo Press, 1981. (Japanese ed. 1980).

———. *Economic Growth in Prewar Japan*. New Haven, Yale University Press, 1983. (Japanese ed. 1971).

——— and Itō Takashi. 3-part interview with Maeda Hajime. *Ekonomisuto,* 7 July, pp. 76–83; 14 July, pp. 82–91; and 21 July 1970, pp. 76–82.

Nakayama Ichirō. "Nihon Keizai no Kao" (The face of the Japanese economy), *The Hyōron,* December 1949, pp. 1–9.

Nanto, Dick K. The United States' Role in the Postwar Economic Recovery of Japan. PhD dissertation, Harvard University, December 1976.

Nezu Tomoyoshi. *Sekitan Kokka Tōsei Shi* (History of state control of the coal industry). Tokyo, Nihon Keizai Kenkyūjo, 1958.

Nihon Chōki Shinyō Ginkō, Sangyō Kenkyūkai (Japan Long-Term Credit Bank, Industrial Research Association). *Jūyō Sangyō Sengo 25-nen Shi* (Twenty-five-year postwar history of important industries). Tokyo, Sangyō to Keizai, 1972.

Nihon Hassōden Kabushiki Gaisha, ed. *Nihon Hassōden Kabushiki Gaisha Shi* (History of the Japan Electric-Power Generating Company). Tokyo, 1954.

Nihon Kaihatsu Ginkō, Jū-nen Shi Hensa Iinkai (Japan Development Bank), (The ten-year history project), ed. *Nihon Kaihatsu Ginkō Jū-nen Shi* (Ten-year history of the Japan Development Bank). Tokyo, 1963.

――――. *Nihon Sangyō no Hatten to Kindaika* (The development and modernization of Japanese industry). Tokyo, 1963.

Nihon Keieisha Dantai Renmei. *Nikkeiren Sanjū-nen Shi* (Thirty-year history of the Japan Federation of Employers' Associations). Tokyo, 1981.

Nihon Rōdō Kyōkai, ed. *Gōrika to Rōdō Kumiai* (Rationalization and labor unions). Tokyo, 1962.

Nihon Sangyō Kōzō Kenkyūkai. *Nihon Sangyō Kōzō no Kadai* (Japanese industrial structure). 2 vols. Tokyo, 1955.

Nihon Seitetsu Kabushiki Gaisha Shi Henshū Iinkai, ed. *Nihon Seitetsu Kabushiki Gaisha Shi, 1934–1950* (History of the Japan Steel Company, 1934–1950). Tokyo, 1959.

Nihon Sekiyu Shi Henshū Shitsu. *Nihon Sekiyu Shi,* (History of Japan Oil Company). Tokyo, Nihon Sekiyu Kabushiki Gaisha, 1968.

Nihon Tankō Rōdō Kumiai, ed. *Tanrō Jū-nen Shi* (Ten-year history of Tanrō). Tokyo, Rōdō Junpōsha, 1964.

Noda Kazuo. *Sengo Keiei Shi* (Postwar management history). *Nihon Keiei Shi* (Japan management history), Vol. I. Tokyo, Nihon Seisansei Honbu, 1965.

Nolte, Sharon H. *Liberalism in Modern Japan: Ishibashi Tanzan and His Teachers, 1905–1960*. Berkeley, University of California Press, 1987.

Notar, Ernest J. "Japan's Wartime Labor Policy: A Search for Method," *Journal of Asian Studies* 44.2: 311–328 (February 1985).

Odell, Peter R. *Oil and World Power: Background to the Oil Crisis*. Rev. ed. London, Penguin Books, 1980.

Office of the Prime Minister, Bureau of Statistics. *Japan Statistical Yearbook*. Tokyo, Japan Statistical Association, annual.

Ōhara Shakai Mondai Kenkyūjo. *Taiheiyō Sensōka no Rōdō Undō* (The labor movement during the Pacific War). Special volume in *Nihon Rōdō Nenkan* series. Tokyo, Rōdō Junpōsha, 1965.

Okamoto, Hideaki. "Management and their Organizations." In Okochi Kazuo, Bernard Karsh, and Solomon B. Levine, eds., *Workers and Employers in Japan: The Japanese Employment Relations System*. Princeton and Tokyo, Princeton University Press and University of Tokyo Press, 1974.

Ōkōchi Kazuo. *Sengo Nihon no Rōdō Undō* (The postwar labor movement). Tokyo, Iwanami Shinsho, 1955.

———, ed. *Nihon Rōdō Kumiai Ron* (A study of the Japanese labor union). Tokyo, Yuhikaku, 1953.

———, ed. *Rōdō* (Labor). *Shiryō Sengo 20-nen Shi* (Documentary history of the postwar 20 years), Vol. IV. Tokyo, Nihon Hyōronsha, 1966.

———, Bernard Karsh, and Solomon B. Levine, eds., *Workers and Employers in Japan: The Japanese Employment Relations System*. Princeton and Tokyo, Princeton University Press and University of Tokyo Press, 1974.

——— and Matsuo Hiroshi. *Nihon Rōdō Kumiai Monogatari* (The story of Japan's labor-union history). *Sengo* (Postwar). 2 vols. Tokyo, Chikuma Shobō, 1969.

Ōkurashō, Zaisei Shishitsu (Ministry of Finance, Financial History Group), ed. *Eibun Shiryō* (English-language documents). Vol. XX in *Shōwa Zaisei Shi: Shūsen kara Kōwa made* (Shōwa financial history: From the end of the war to the peace treaty). Tokyo, Tōyō Keizai Shinpōsha, 1983.

———. *Sōsetsu, Baishō Shūsen Shori* (General introduction, reparations and termination of war measures), Vol. I. In *Shōwa Zaisei Shi: Shūsen kara Kōwa made* (Shōwa financial history: From the end of the war to the peace treaty). Tokyo, Tōyō Keizai Shinpōsha, 1984.

Oppler, Alfred C. *Legal Reform in Occupied Japan: A Participant Looks Back*. Princeton, Princeton University Press, 1976.

Ōsawa Etsuji. *Denryoku Jigyōkai* (The electric-power industry). Tokyo, Kyōikusha, 1975.

Oshima, Harry T. "Reinterpreting Japan's Postwar Growth," *Economic Development and Cultural Change* 31.1: 1–43 (October 1982).

Ōtani Ken. *Kōbō—Denryoku Minei-Bunkatsu no Kattō* (Destiny—The complicated story of the privatization and division of the electric-power industry). Tokyo, Shiramomo Shobō, 1984.

Ouchi, Hyoe. *Financial and Monetary Situation in Post-War Japan*. Tokyo, Japan Institute of Pacific Studies, 1948.

———. "Dodge Plan and the Japanese Economy," *Contemporary Japan* 18.4–6 233–236 (April–June 1949). Translated from *The Hyōron*, June 1949.

Overseas Consultants, Inc. *Report on Industrial Reparations Survey of Japan to the United States of America*. New York, February 1948.

———. *Tadami River Power Investigation for the Public Utilities Commission of the Government of Japan*. May 1952.

Overseas Electrical Industry Survey Institute, Inc. *Japan's Electric Power Industry 1963*. Tokyo, 1963.

Ozaki, Robert S. *The Control of Imports and Foreign Capital in Japan*. New York, Praeger, 1972.

Ozawa, Terutomo. *Japan's Technological Challenge to the West, 1950–1974: Motivation and Accomplishment*. Cambridge, MIT Press, 1974.

Park, Yung Ho. "The Governmental Advisory Commission System in Japan," *Journal of Comparative Administration* 3.4: 435–467 (February 1972).

Pascale, Richard and Thomas P. Rohlen. "The Mazda Turnaround," *Journal of Japanese Studies* 9.2: 219–263 (1983).

Patrick, Hugh and Henry Rosovsky, eds., *Asia's New Giant: How the Japanese Economy Works*. Washington, D.C., The Brookings Institution, 1976.

Pempel, T.J. "Japanese Foreign Economic Policy: The Domestic Basis for International Behavior." In Peter J. Katzenstein, ed., *Between Power and Plenty*. Madison, University of Wisconsin Press, 1978. This article also appeared in *International Organization* 31: 723–773 (Autumn 1977).

———. *Policy and Politics in Japan: Creative Conservatism*. Philadelphia, Temple University Press, 1982.

Petroleum Advisory Group. *Report of the Petroleum Advisory Group, November 1945 to June 1951*. Tokyo, Supreme Command for the Allied Powers, 1951.

Phillips, Susan. "Beyond Borders: Class Struggle and Feminist Humanism in *Banshū Heiya*," *Bulletin of Concerned Asian Scholars* 19.1: 56–65 (January–March 1987).

Redford, Lawrence, ed. *The Occupation of Japan: Economic Policy and Reform*. Norfolk, The MacArthur Memorial, 1980.

Reubens, Beatrice G. " 'Production Control' in Japan." *Far Eastern Survey* 15.22: 344–347 (6 November 1946).

Rice, Richard. "Economic Mobilization in Wartime Japan: Business, Bureaucracy, and Military in Conflict," *Journal of Asian Studies* 38: 689–706 (August 1979).

Rōdō Sōgi Chōsakai (Labor Dispute Research Association), ed. *Sengo Rōdō Sōgi Jittai Chōsa* (Factual research on postwar labor disputes), Vol. I, ed. Arisawa Hiromi. *Sekitan Sōgi* (Coal disputes). Tokyo, Chūō Kōronsha, 1957.

———. Vol. II ed. Nakayama Ichirō. *Densan Sōgi* (Japan electric-power industry workers' union struggles) Tokyo, Chūō Kōronsha, 1957.

Rōdōshō, Rōseikyoku (Ministry of Labor, Labor Policy Bureau). *Shiryō Rōdō Undō Shi, 1945–46* (Documentary history of the labor movement, 1945–46). Tokyo, Rōmu Gyōsei Kenkyūsho, 1951.

The Role of Foreign Governments in Energy Industry. Office of International Affairs, Department of Energy, Washington, D.C., Government Printing Office, October 1977.

Sampson, Anthony. *The Seven Sisters and the World They Made*. Toronto, Hodder and Stoughton, 1975.

Samuels, Richard J. "State Enterprise, State Strength, and Energy Policy in Transwar Japan." MIT Working Paper EL 83-010, March 1983.

———. "The Industrial Destructuring of the Japanese Aluminum Industry," *Pacific Affairs* 56.3: 495–509 (Fall 1983).

————. *The Business of the Japanese State: Energy Markets in Comparative and Historical Perspective.* Ithaca, Cornell University Press, 1987.

Sangyō Seisaku Shi Kenkyūjō, ed. *Sengo Sangyō Seisaku ni Kan Suru Zadankai, {1}—Sōkatsu, Hokan (Keisha Seisan Kara Jiyū Keizai no Tenkai e)* (First symposium on postwar industrial policy—Synthesis and commentary: The shift from priority production to a free economy). Tokyo, 20 March 1975.

————. [Maeda Yasuyuki]. *Sangyō Seisaku Shi Kenkyū Shiryō: Sengo ni okeru Sekitan Kōgyō Seisaku* (Documents on the history of industrial policy: Postwar policy toward the coal mines). Tokyo, Tsūshō Sangyō Chōsakai Toranomon Bunshitsu, 1977.

Satō Nakashi. "Denki Kigyō no Gijutsu Kakushin to Den Rōren" (The technological revolution in the electricity industry and Den Rōren). In Nihon Rōdō Kyōkai, ed. *Gōrika to Rōdō Kumiai* (Rationalization and labor unions). Tokyo, Nihon Rōdō Kyōkai, 1962.

Schaller, Michael. *The American Occupation of Japan: The Origins of the Cold War in Asia.* New York, Oxford University Press, 1985.

Schlesinger, Arthur M., ed. *The Dynamics of World Power: A Documentary History of United States Foreign Policy, 1945–1973.* 6 vols. New York, Chelsea House Publishers, 1973.

Schonberger, Howard. "Zaibatsu Dissolution and the American Restoration of Japan," *Bulletin of Concerned Asian Scholars* 5.2: 16–31 (September 1973).

————. "The Japan Lobby in American Diplomacy, 1947–1952." *Pacific Historical Review* 46.3: 327–359 (August 1977).

————. "American Labor's Cold War in Occupied Japan," *Diplomatic History* 3.3: 249–272 (Summer 1979).

————. "John Foster Dulles and the China Question in the Making of the Japanese Peace Treaty," In Thomas Burkman, ed. *The Occupation of Japan: The International Context.* Norfolk, The MacArthur Memorial Foundation, 1984.

————. "Peacemaking in Asia: The United States, Great Britain, and the Japanese Decision to Recognize Nationalist China, 1951–52," *Diplomatic History* 10.1: 59–74 (Winter 1986).

Schumpeter, Elizabeth B. "Japan, Korea and Manchukuo, 1936–1940." In Schumpeter, ed. *The Industrialization of Japan and Manchukuo, 1930–1940: Population, Raw Materials, and Industry.* New York, MacMillan, 1940, pp. 403–408.

————. ed. *The Industrialization of Japan and Manchukuo, 1930–1940: Population, Raw Materials, and Industry.* New York, MacMillan, 1940.

Seiji Keizai Kenkyūjo. *Nihon ni Okeru Gaikoku Shihon* (Foreign capital in Japan). Tokyo, Tōyō Keizai Shinpōsha, 1955.

————. *Nihon no Denryoku Sangyō* (The Japanese electric-power industry). Tokyo, Tōyō Keizai Shinpōsha, 1959.

————. [Itagaki Setsuo]. *Nihon no Sekiyu Sangyō* (The Japanese oil industry). Tokyo, Tōyō Keizai Shinpōsha, 1959.

Senshi Sōsho. Kaigun Gunsenbi—Shōwa Jūroku-nen Jūichi-gatsu made (General war history: Naval war preparations—to November 1941). [Suekui Naomasa, comp.] Tokyo, Asagumo Shinbunsha, 1969.

Shibagaki Kazuo. "Hatan Shita Nihon no Shigen Seisaku" (Japan's ruined resource policy), *Ekonomisuto*, 8 January 1974.

Shigen Enerugī Chō, Chōkan Kanbō Sōmuka, ed. (Agency of Natural Resources and Energy, General Secretariat). *Sōgō Enerugī Tōkei, 1984* (Comprehensive energy statistics, 1984). Tokyo, Tsūshō Sangyō Kenkyūsha, 1984.

Shin Keizaisha Editorial Board, ed. *Denki Jigyō Saihensei Kakukai no Iken* (Opinion from various circles on reorganization of the electric power industry). Tokyo, 1951.

Shinobu Seizaburō. *Sengo Nihon Seiji Shi, 1945–1952* (A Political History of Postwar Japan, 1945–1952). 4 volumes. Tokyo, Keisō Shobō, 1967.

Shirai, Taishiro. "A Theory of Enterprise Unionism." In Taishiro Shirai, ed. *Contemporary Industrial Relations in Japan*. Madison, University of Wisconsin Press, 1983.

————, ed. *Contemporary Industrial Relations in Japan*. Madison, University of Wisconsin Press, 1983.

"Shiryō: Den Rōren no Chingin Yōkyū Hōshiki" (Reference materials: Den Rōren's wage-demand formula). *Nihon Rōdō Kyōkai Zasshi* 16: 79–81 (July 1960).

Sodei Rinjirō. "A Question of Paternity." In Harry Wray and Hilary Conroy, eds. *Japan Examined: Perspectives on Modern Japanese History*. Honolulu, University of Hawaii Press, 1983.

————, ed., *Sekai Shi no Naka no Nihon Senryō* (The occupation of Japan in world history). Tokyo, Nihon Hyōronsha, 1985.

Sofremines Company. "Sofremines Report Concerning the Japanese Coal Mining Industry," September 1957.

Solomon, Albert H. "Revision of the Japanese Mining Law under the Occupation," *Washington Law Review*, special issue, 1977.

Sonoda Minoru. *Sengo Sekitan Shi* (Postwar history of coal). Fukuoka, Sekine Sokuritsu 20 Shūnen Kinenkai, 1970.

Stockwin, J.A.A. *Japan: Divided Politics in a Growth Economy*. New York, Norton, 1975.

Sumiya, Mikio. "Implications of Technological Change in Industrial Relations in Japan," *British Journal of Industrial Relations* 3.2: 210–218 (July 1965).

————. "The Development of Japanese Labour Relations," *Developing Economies* 4: 499–515 (1966).

Supreme Commander for the Allied Powers. *Political Reorientation of Japan: September 1945–September 1948*. (1949). 2 vols. Reprinted Westport, Greenwood Press, 1970.

————. *Summations of the Non-Military Activities in Japan.* nos. 1–35, monthly. September/October 1945–August 1948.

————. General Headquarters. Statistics and Reports Section. *History of the Non-Military Activities of the Occupation of Japan.* Tokyo, SCAP, 1951–1952, Historical Monograph Series:
#24. "Elimination of Zaibatsu Control"
#25. "Deconcentration of Economic Power"
#34. "Price and Distribution Stabilization: Non-Food Program"
#41. "The Petroleum Industry"
#45. "Coal"
#46. "Expansion and Reorganization of the Electric Power and Gas Industries"

Surrey, A.J. and J.H. Chesshire. *The World Market for Electric Power Equipment: Rationalization and Technical Change.* Sussex, Science Policy Research Unit, University of Sussex, 1972.

Taira, Koji. *Economic Development and the Labor Market in Japan.* New York, Columbia University Press, 1970.

————. "Unions, Ideologies, and Revolutions in Japanese Enterprise During the Occupation." In Lawrence Redford, ed., *The Occupation of Japan: Economic Policy and Reform.* Norfolk, The MacArthur Memorial, 1980.

Takahashi Makoto. "The Development of Wartime Economic Controls," *Developing Economies* 5.4: 648–665 (1967).

Takahashi, Saburō. "The Electric Power Industry," *Japan Quarterly* 6.2: 240–250 (April 1959).

Takemae, Eiji. "GHQ Labor Policy during the Period of Democratization, 1946–1948: the Second Interview with Mr. Theodore Cohen," *The Journal of the Tokyo Keizai University,* no. 122 (1981).

————. *Sengo Rōdō Kaikaku: GHQ Rōdō Seisaku Shi* (The postwar labor reforms: The history of GHQ labor policy). Tokyo, Tokyo Daigaku Shuppankai, 1982.

Tanaka Jirō, Satō Isao, and Nomura Jirō, eds. *Sengo Seiji Saiban Shiroku* (Historical records of postwar political trials), Vol. I. Tokyo, Daiichi Hōki, 1981.

Tanaka, Yuki. "Rationality and Irrationality in Japanese Industry: The Economics of Nuclear Power," Unpublished paper of the Centre for Asian Studies, University of Adelaide, July 1988.

Terkel, Studs. *"The Good War" An Oral History of World War Two.* New York, Pantheon, 1984.

Textor, Robert B. *Failure in Japan with Keystones for a Positive Policy.* (1951). Westport, Greenwood Press, 1972.

Thayer, Nathaniel. *How the Conservatives Rule Japan.* Princeton, Princeton University Press, 1969.

Tokyo Daigaku Shakai Kagaku Kenkyūjo, ed. *Densan Jū-gatsu Sōgi (1946-nen):*

Sengo Shoki Rōdō Sōgi Shiryō (Densan's october strike [1946]: Research materials on early postwar labor struggles). Tokyo, 1979.

Tokyo Denryoku Shashi Henshu Iinkai. *Tokyo Denryoku 30-nen Shi* (Thirty-year history of the Tokyo Electric-Power Company). Tokyo, Tokyo Denryoku Kabushiki Gaisha, 1983.

Tonedachi, Masahisa. "Japan's Lagging Oil Development," *Japan Quarterly* 29.1: 97–104 (January–March 1982).

Totten, George O. *The Social Democratic Movement in Prewar Japan.* New Haven, Yale University Press, 1966.

Tsuchiya Kiyoshi. "The Coal Industry," *Japan Quarterly* 9.4: 478–483 (October 1962).

Tsurumi, Yoshi. "Japan," *Daedalus,* Fall 1975, pp. 113–127. Reprinted in Raymond Vernon, ed. *The Oil Crisis.* New York, Norton, 1976.

Tsuruta Toshimasa. *Sengo Nihon no Sangyō Seisaku* (The industrial policy of postwar Japan). Tokyo, Nihon Keizai Shinbunsha, 1982.

Tsūshō Sangyō Shō, Kanbō Chōsaka (MITI, Research Division). *Enerugī Tōkeishu* (Compilation of energy statistics). Tokyo, 1962. Later versions of this annual handbook are by Shigen Enerugī Chō, Chōkan Kanbō Sōmuka and titaled *Sōgō Enerugi Tōkei* (Comprehensive Energy Statistics). (Agency of Natural Resources and Energy, Director General's Secretariat).

Tsūshō Sangyō Shō, Shōkō Seisaku Shi Kankōkai (Ministry of International Trade and Industry, Commission on the History of Trade and Industry Policy), ed. *Sangyō Gōrika (sengo)* (Postwar industrial rationalization). Vol. X in *Shōkō Seisaku Shi* (History of trade and industry policy). Tokyo, 1972.

———. *Kōgyō* (Mining industry, part 2). Vol XXIII in *Shōkō Seisaku Shi* (History of trade and industry policy). Tokyo, 1980.

Tucker, Nancy Bernkopf. "American Policy Toward Sino-Japanese Trade in the Postwar Years: Politics and Prosperity," *Diplomatic History* 8.3: 183–208 (Summer 1984).

Uchino, Tatsurō. *Japan's Postwar Economy: An Insider's View of Its History and Its Future.* Tokyo, Kodansha International, 1983. (Japanese ed. 1978).

United States, Department of State. *Foreign Relations of the United States.* 1946–1954.

Unno Yukitaka, Kobayashi Hideo, and Shiba Hiroshi, eds. *Sengo Nihon Rōdō Undō Shi* (History of the postwar Japanese labor movement). 2 vols. Tokyo, Sanichi Shobō, 1962.

Usami Shōgo. *Denryoku Kai Sengoku Shi—Kunizukuri ni Kaketa Otokotachi* (At war in the world of electric power: The men whose ventures built a country). Tokyo, Daiyamondosha, 1984.

Van Duzer, Jr., R.M. and E.J. Burger. "Japanese Appraisal of Atomic Bomb

Damage to Hiroshima Utility System," *Electrical World* 128:98–103 (8 November 1947).

Vernon, Raymond, ed. *The Oil Crisis.* New York, W.W. Norton, 1976.

Vlastos, Stephen. *Peasant Protests and Uprisings in Tokugawa Japan.* Berkeley, University of California Press, 1986.

Vogel, Ezra. *Comeback—Case by Case: Building the Resurgence of American Business.* New York, Simon and Schuster, 1985.

Walton, Mary. *The Deming Management Method.* New York, Dodd, Mead, & Co., 1986.

Ward, Robert E. and Frank Joseph Shulman, eds. *The Allied Occupation of Japan, 1945–1952: An Annotated Bibliography of Western Language Materials.* Chicago, American Library Association, 1974.

Watanabe Takeshi. *Senryōka no Nihon Zaisei Oboegaki* (Notes on Japanese finance during the Occupation). Tokyo, Nihon Keizai Shinbunsha, 1966.

Watanabe Yōzō. "Sekiyu Sangyō to Sengo Keizai Hō Taisei (The oil industry and the structure of postwar economic laws)." In Tokyo Daigaku Shakai Kagaku Kenkyūjo, ed., *Kaikakugo no Nihon Keizai* (The Japanese economy after the reforms), Vol. VIII. In *Sengo Kaikaku* (Postwar reforms). Tokyo, Tokyo Daigaku Shuppankai, 1975.

Wheeler, Jimmy W., Merit E. Janow, and Thomas Pepper. *Japanese Industrial Development Policies in the 1980's: Implications for U.S. Trade and Investment.* Hudson Institute Report for the U.S. Department of State, Croton-on-Hudson, October 1982.

Wilkins, Mira. "The Role of U.S. Business." In Dorothy Borg and Shumpei Okamoto, eds., *Pearl Harbor as History: Japanese-American Relations, 1931–1941.* New York, Columbia University Press, 1973.

Williams, Justin, Sr. *Japan's Political Revolution under MacArthur: A Participant's Account.* Athens, University of Georgia Press, 1979.

Wray, Harry and Hilary Conroy, eds. *Japan Examined: Perspectives on Modern Japanese History.* Honolulu, University of Hawaii Press, 1983.

Yada Toshifumi. *Sengo Nihon no Sekitan Sangyō* (The postwar Japanese coal industry). Tokyo, Shinhyōron, 1975.

———. *Sekitan Gyōkai* (The coal industry). Tokyo, Kyōikusha Shinsho, Sangyōkai Shirisu 45, 1977.

Yamamura, Kozo. *Economic Policy in Postwar Japan: Growth Versus Democracy.* Berkeley, University of California Press, 1967.

———. "Japan's Deus ex Machina: Western Technology in the 1920s," *Journal of Japanese Studies* 12.1: 65–94 (Winter 1986).

———, ed. *Policy and Trade Issues of the Japanese Economy: American and Japanese Perspectives.* Seattle, University of Washington Press, 1982.

Yanaga, Chitoshi. *Big Business in Japanese Politics.* New Haven, Yale University Press, 1968.

Yasuhara, Yoko. "Japan, Communist China, and Export Controls in Asia, 1948–52," *Diplomatic History* 10.1: 75–90 (Winter 1986).

Yoshida Shigeru. *The Yoshida Memoirs, The Story of Japan in Crisis.* (1961). Westport, Greenwood Press, 1973.

Index

412 *Index*

Harvard East Asian Monographs

STUDIES IN THE MODERNIZATION OF THE REPUBLIC OF KOREA: 1945–1975

125. Katherine F. Bruner, John K. Fairbank, and Richard T. Smith, *Entering China's Service: Robert Hart's Journals, 1854–1863*

126. Bob Tadashi Wakabayashi, *Anti-Foreignism and Western Learning in Early Modern Japan: The* New Theses *of 1825*

127. Atsuko Hirai, *Individualism and Socialism: The Life and Thought of Kawai Eijirō (1891–1944)*

128. Ellen Widmer, *The Margins of Utopia:* Shui-hu hou-chuan *and the Literature of Ming Loyalism*

129. R. Kent Guy, *The Emperor's Four Treasuries: Scholars and the State in the Late Ch'ien-lung Era*

130. Peter C. Perdue, *Exhausting the Earth: State and Peasant in Hunan, 1500–1850*

131. Susan Chan Egan, *A Latterday Confucian: Reminiscences of William Hung (1893–1980)*

132. James T. C. Liu, *China Turning Inward: Intellectual-Political Changes in the Early Twelfth Century*

133. Paul A. Cohen, *Between Tradition and Modernity: Wang T'ao and Reform in Late Ch'ing China*

134. Kate Wildman Nakai, *Shogunal Politics: Arai Hakuseki and the Premises of Tokugawa Rule*

135. Hans Ulrich Vogel, *Chinese Central Monetary Policy and Yunnan Copper Mining in the Early Qing (1644–1800)*

136. Jon L. Saari, *Legacies of Childhood: Growing Up Chinese in a Time of Crisis, 1890–1920*

137. Susan Downing Videen, *Tales of Heichū*

138. Heinz Morioka and Miyoko Sasaki, *Rakugo: The Popular Narrative Art of Japan*

139. Joshua A. Fogel, *Nakai Ushikichi in China: The Mourning of Spirit*

140. Alexander Barton Woodside, *Vietnam and the Chinese Model: A Comparative Study of Vietnamese and Chinese Government in the First Half of the Nineteenth Century*

141. George Elison, *Deus Destroyed: The Image of Christianity in Early Modern Japan*

142. William D. Wray, ed., *Managing Industrial Enterprise: Cases from Japan's Prewar Experience*

143. T'ung-tsu Ch'ü, *Local Government in China under the Ch'ing*

144. Marie Anchordoguy, *Computers Inc.: Japan's Challenge to IBM*

145. Barbara Molony, *Technology and Investment: The Prewar Japanese Chemical Industry*

146. Mary Elizabeth Berry, *Hideyoshi*

147. Laura E. Hein, *Fueling Growth: The Energy Revolution and Economic Policy in Postwar Japan*

148. Wen-hsin Yeh, *The Alienated Academy: Culture and Politics in Republican China, 1919–1937*